Y0-ABE-700

Education

04/05

Thirty-First Edition

EDITOR

Fred Schultz

University of Akron (Retired)

Fred Schultz, former professor of education at the University of Akron, attended Indiana University to earn a B.S. in social science education in 1962, an M.S. in the history and philosophy of education in 1966, and a Ph.D. in the history and philosophy of education and American studies in 1969. His B.A. in Spanish was conferred from the University of Akron in May 1985. He is actively involved in researching the development and history of American education with a primary focus on the history of ideas and social philosophy of education. He also likes to study languages.

McGraw-Hill/Dushkin

530 Old Whitfield Street, Guilford, Connecticut 06437

Visit us on the Internet
http://www.dushkin.com

Credits

1. **How Others See Us and How We See Ourselves**
   Unit photo—© 2004 by Sweet By & By/Cindy Brown.
2. **Rethinking and Changing the Educative Effort**
   Unit photo—© 2004 by PhotoDisc, Inc.
3. **Striving for Excellence: The Drive for Quality**
   Unit photo— © 2004 by Sweet By & By/Cindy Brown.
4. **Morality and Values in Education**
   Unit photo—© 2004 by Cleo Freelance Photography.
5. **Managing Life in Classrooms**
   Unit photo—© 2004 by Cleo Freelance Photography.
6. **Cultural Diversity and Schooling**
   Unit photo—© 2004 by PhotoDisc, Inc.
7. **Serving Special Needs and Concerns**
   Unit photo—© 2004 by Cleo Freelance Photography.
8. **The Profession of Teaching Today**
   Unit photo—© 2004 by PhotoDisc, Inc.
9. **A Look to the Future**
   Unit photo—© 2004 by Cleo Freelance Photography.

Copyright

Cataloging in Publication Data
Main entry under title: Annual Editions: Education. 2004/2005.
1. Education—Periodicals. I. Schultz, Fred, comp. II. Title: Education.
ISBN 0–07–286138–X   658'.05   ISSN 0272–5010

Thirty-First Edition

Cover image © 2004 PhotoDisc, Inc.
Printed in the United States of America   1234567890BAHBAH54   Printed on Recycled Paper

Editors/Advisory Board

Members of the Advisory Board are instrumental in the final selection of articles for each edition of ANNUAL EDITIONS. Their review of articles for content, level, currentness, and appropriateness provides critical direction to the editor and staff. We think that you will find their careful consideration well reflected in this volume.

To the Reader

In publishing ANNUAL EDITIONS we recognize the enormous role played by the magazines, newspapers, and journals of the public press in providing current, first-rate educational information in a broad spectrum of interest areas. Many of these articles are appropriate for students, researchers, and professionals seeking accurate, current material to help bridge the gap between principles and theories and the real world. These articles, however, become more useful for study when those of lasting value are carefully collected, organized, indexed, and reproduced in a low-cost format, which provides easy and permanent access when the material is needed. That is the role played by ANNUAL EDITIONS.

Here we are in the early twenty-first century in the 2004/2005 school year, and the challenges we confront are as important as ever. The dialogue currently developing as to what educational policy alternatives are best for our present and future is of great interest to all of us. This year's edition attempts to reflect perspectives on which policy alternatives are best for educators and their students.

Issues regarding the purposes of education as well as the appropriate methods of educating have been debated throughout all generations of literate human culture. This is because the meaning of the word "educated" shifts within ideological realms of thought and cultural belief systems. There will always be debates over the purposes and the ends of "education" as it is understood in any time or place. This is because each generation must continuously reconstruct the definition of "education" based upon its understanding of "justice," "fairness," and "equity" in human relations, and each generation must locate and position their understanding of social and personal reality.

In the twenty-first century, educators are presented with many new challenges caused by many forces at work in human society. We must decide what knowledge is of most worth and what basic skills and information each child, of whatever heritage, needs to know. We must face this question once and for all. It is no longer a choice; it is a duty if we are disciplined persons interested in the well-being of our children and adolescents. We have before us a great qualitative challenge, our response to which will determine the fate of future generations of our society.

The technological breakthroughs now developing in the information sciences will have an amazing impact on how people learn. The rates of change in how we learn and how we obtain information is already increasing at a very rapid pace that will assuredly continue.

The public conversation on the purposes and future directions of education is lively as ever. Alternative visions and voices regarding the broad social aims of schools and the preparation of teachers continue to be presented. *Annual Editions: Education 04/05* attempts to reflect current mainstream as well as alternative visions as to what education ought to be. Equity issues regarding what constitutes equal treatment of students in the schools continue to be addressed. This year's edition contains articles on teacher preparation, staff development ideas for teachers already in the schools, and other issues of concern to both the general public and the teaching profession. The debate over whether all public monies for education should go to the public schools or whether these funds should follow the student into either public or private schools has again intensified.

Communities are deeply interested in local school politics and school funding issues. There continues to be healthy dialogue about and competition for the support of the various "publics" involved in public schooling. The articles reflect spirited critique of our public schools. There are competing, and very differing, school reform agendas being discussed. All of this occurs as the United States continues to experience fundamentally important demographic shifts in its cultural makeup.

Compromise continues to be the order of the day. The many interest groups within the educational field reflect a broad spectrum of viewpoints ranging from various behaviorist and cognitive developmental perspectives to humanistic, postmodernist, and critical theoretical ones.

In assembling this volume, we make every effort to stay in touch with movements in educational studies and with the social forces at work in schools. Members of the advisory board contribute valuable insights, and the production and editorial staffs at the publisher, McGraw-Hill/Dushkin, coordinate our efforts. Through this process we collect a wide range of articles on a variety of topics relevant to education in North America.

The readings in *Annual Editions: Education 04/05* explore the social and academic goals of education, the current conditions of the nation's educational systems, the teaching profession, and the future of American education. In addition, these selections address the issues of change and the moral and ethical foundations of schooling. As always, we would like you to help us improve this volume. Please rate the material in this edition on the postage-paid *article rating form* provided at the back of this book and send it to us. We care about what you think. Give us the public feedback that we need.

Fred Schultz
Editor

Contents

UNIT 1
How Others See Us and How We See Ourselves

Six articles examine today's most significant educational issues and current public opinion about U.S. schools.

Unit Overview   xviii

The concepts in bold italics are developed in the article. For further expansion, please refer to the Topic Guide and the Index.

UNIT 2
Rethinking and Changing the Educative Effort

Seven articles discuss the many aspects of school reform and the reality at work in today's educational system.

The concepts in bold italics are developed in the article. For further expansion, please refer to the Topic Guide and the Index.

UNIT 3
Striving for Excellence: The Drive for Quality

Five selections examine the debate over achieving excellence in education by addressing issues relating to questions of how best to teach and the quality of American schooling today.

UNIT 4
Morality and Values in Education

Five articles examine the role of American schools in exploring humanistic and character education and in teaching morality and social values.

The concepts in bold italics are developed in the article. For further expansion, please refer to the Topic Guide and the Index.

UNIT 5
Managing Life in Classrooms

Five selections consider the importance of building effective teacher-student and student-student relationships in the classroom, with emphasis on bullying, playgrounds, and classroom management.

The concepts in bold italics are developed in the article. For further expansion, please refer to the Topic Guide and the Index.

UNIT 6
Cultural Diversity and Schooling

Six articles discuss issues relating to fairness and justice for students from all cultural backgrounds and how curricula should respond to cultural pluralistic student populations.

The concepts in bold italics are developed in the article. For further expansion, please refer to the Topic Guide and the Index.

UNIT 7
Serving Special Needs and Concerns

Five articles examine some of the important aspects of education, which include students' right to privacy, bridging reading gaps, and teaching behavior in suburban high schools.

The concepts in bold italics are developed in the article. For further expansion, please refer to the Topic Guide and the Index.

UNIT 8
The Profession of Teaching Today

Four articles assess the current state of teaching in U.S. schools and how well today's teachers approach subject matter learning.

UNIT 9
A Look to the Future

Three articles look at old and new forms of schooling that break from traditional concepts of education in America and point the way toward the possible future of American education.

The concepts in bold italics are developed in the article. For further expansion, please refer to the Topic Guide and the Index.

The concepts in bold italics are developed in the article. For further expansion, please refer to the Topic Guide and the Index.

Topic Guide

This topic guide suggests how the selections in this book relate to the subjects covered in your course. You may want to use the topics listed on these pages to search the Web more easily.

On the following pages a number of Web sites have been gathered specifically for this book. They are arranged to reflect the units of this *Annual Edition.* You can link to these sites by going to the DUSHKIN ONLINE support site at *http://www.dushkin.com/online/.*

ALL THE ARTICLES THAT RELATE TO EACH TOPIC ARE LISTED BELOW THE BOLD-FACED TERM.

Accreditation of teacher education
43. Preparing Teachers for Public Schools: Just More Cannon Fodder?

Behavioral policies
3. The 'Re-Engineered' Child
24. A Profile of Bullying
25. Bullying—Not Just a Kid Thing
26. A Positive Learning Environment Approach to Middle School Instruction
27. The Rewards and Restrictions of Recess
28. Home Front

Bullying
24. A Profile of Bullying
25. Bullying—Not Just a Kid Thing

Change and education
7. Reinventing America's Schools
8. There Is Another Way: A Different Approach to Education Reform
9. Kudzu, Rabbits, and School Reform
10. Four-Day School Week?
11. School Choice—Really
12. Sweeten the Pot for Middle America
13. Last Holdout Against Educational Freedom
17. April Foolishness: The 20th Anniversary of A Nation at Risk
45. An Emerging Culture
46. The Future of Education: Student Options

Children's literature
36. Bridging the Summer Reading Gap
37. A Fresh Look at Series Books

Classroom management
3. The 'Re-Engineered' Child
24. A Profile of Bullying
25. Bullying—Not Just a Kid Thing
26. A Positive Learning Environment Approach to Middle School Instruction
27. The Rewards and Restrictions of Recess
28. Home Front

Critical thinking
18. "Of Course It's True; I Saw It On The Internet!" Critical Thinking in the Internet Era

Cultural diversity and schooling
29. Education Is Critical to Closing the Socioeconomic Gap
30. "He May Mean Good, But He Do So Doggone Poor!"
31. Twelve Ways to Have Students Analyze Culture
32. Language Differences or Learning Difficulties
33. The Evils of Public Schools
34. Can Every Child Learn?

Culture and education
29. Education Is Critical to Closing the Socioeconomic Gap
30. "He May Mean Good, But He Do So Doggone Poor!"
31. Twelve Ways to Have Students Analyze Culture
32. Language Differences or Learning Difficulties

Demographics
1. When I Was Young

Discipline
3. The 'Re-Engineered' Child
24. A Profile of Bullying
25. Bullying—Not Just a Kid Thing
26. A Positive Learning Environment Approach to Middle School Instruction
27. The Rewards and Restrictions of Recess
28. Home Front
45. An Emerging Culture

Excellence in education
7. Reinventing America's Schools
9. Kudzu, Rabbits, and School Reform
14. Classroom Crisis: It's About Time
15. Needed: Homework Clubs for Young Adolescents Who Struggle With Learning
16. A Nation Deceived
17. April Foolishness: The 20th Anniversary of A Nation at Risk
18. "Of Course It's True; I Saw It On The Internet!" Critical Thinking in the Internet Era

Future of education
1. When I Was Young
44. Dreams of a Livable Future
45. An Emerging Culture
46. The Future of Education: Student Options

Gallup Poll
6. The 35th Annual Phi Delta Kappan/Gallup Poll of the Public Attitudes Toward the Public Schools

Going to college
4. College Isn't for Everyone
5. More Families Hide Assets to Qualify for Financial Aid

Health issues
2. Is America Raising Unhealthy Kids? Yes, But Teachers Can Do Something About It

Homework
15. Needed: Homework Clubs for Young Adolescents Who Struggle With Learning

How others see us
1. When I Was Young
2. Is America Raising Unhealthy Kids? Yes, But Teachers Can Do Something About It
3. The 'Re-Engineered' Child
4. College Isn't for Everyone
5. More Families Hide Assets to Qualify for Financial Aid
6. The 35th Annual Phi Delta Kappan/Gallup Poll of the Public Attitudes Toward the Public Schools

World Wide Web Sites

The following World Wide Web sites have been carefully researched and selected to support the articles found in this reader. The easiest way to access these selected sites is to go to our DUSHKIN ONLINE support site at *http://www.dushkin.com/online/*.

AE: Education 04/05

The following sites were available at the time of publication. Visit our Web site—we update DUSHKIN ONLINE regularly to reflect any changes.

General Sources

Education Week on the Web
http://www.edweek.org

At this *Education Week* home page, you will be able to open its archives, read special reports on education, keep up on current events in education, look at job opportunities, and access articles relevant to educators today.

Educational Resources Information Center
http://www.eric.ed.gov

This invaluable site provides links to all ERIC sites: clearinghouses, support components, and publishers of ERIC materials. You can search the ERIC database, find out what is new, and ask questions about ERIC.

Internet Resources for Education
http://web.hamline.edu/personal/kfmeyer/cla_education.html#hamline

This site, which aims for "educational collaboration," takes you to Internet links that examine virtual classrooms, trends, policy, and infrastructure development. It leads to information about school reform, multiculturalism, technology in education, and much more.

National Education Association
http://www.nea.org

Something about virtually every education-related topic can be accessed via this site of the 2.3-million-strong National Education Association.

National Parent Information Network/ERIC
http://npin.org

This is a clearinghouse of information on elementary and early childhood education as well as urban education. Browse through its links for information for parents and for people who work with parents.

U.S. Department of Education
http://www.ed.gov

Explore this government site for examination of institutional aspects of multicultural education. National goals, projects, grants, and other educational programs are listed here as well as many links to teacher services and resources.

UNIT 1: How Others See Us and How We See Ourselves

Charter Schools
http://www.edexcellence.net/topics/charters.html

Open this site for news about charter schools. It provides information about charter school research and issues, links to the U.S. Charter Schools Web site, and Best on the Web charter school sites.

Pathways to School Improvement
http://www.ncrel.org/sdrs/pathwayg.htm

This site of the North Central Regional Educational Laboratory leads to discussions and links about education, including the current state of education, reform issues, and goals and standards. Technology, professional development, and integrated services are a few of the subjects also discussed.

UNIT 2: Rethinking and Changing the Educative Effort

The Center for Innovation in Education
http://www.center.edu

The Center for Innovation in Education, self-described as a "not-for-profit, nonpartisan research organization" focuses on K–12 education reform strategies. Click on its links for information about and varying perspectives on school privatization and other reform initiatives.

Colorado Department of Education
http://www.cde.state.co.us/index_home.htm

This site's links will lead you to information about education-reform efforts, technology in education initiatives, and many documents of interest to educators, parents, and students.

National Council for Accreditation of Teacher Education
http://www.ncate.org

The NCATE is the professional accrediting organization for schools, colleges, and departments of education in the United States. Accessing this page will lead to information about teacher and school standards, state relations, and developmental projects.

Phi Delta Kappa International
http://www.pdkintl.org

This important organization publishes articles about all facets of education—from school vouchers and charter schools to "new dimensions" in learning.

UNIT 3: Striving for Excellence: The Drive for Quality

Awesome Library for Teachers
http://www.awesomelibrary.org

Open this page for links and access to teacher information on everything from educational assessment to general child development topics.

Education World
http://www.education-world.com

Education World provides a database of literally thousands of sites that can be searched by grade level, plus education news, lesson plans, and professional-development resources.

EdWeb/Andy Carvin
http://edwebproject.org

The purpose of EdWeb is to explore the worlds of educational reform and information technology. Access educational resources around the world, learn about trends in education policy and

www.dushkin.com/online/

information infrastructure development, examine success stories of computers in the classroom, and much more.

Kathy Schrock's Guide for Educators
http://www.discoveryschool.com/schrockguide/

This is a classified list of sites on the Internet found to be useful for enhancing curriculum and teacher professional growth. It is updated daily.

Teacher's Guide to the U.S. Department of Education
http://www.ed.gov/pubs/TeachersGuide/

Government goals, projects, grants, and other educational programs are listed here as well as many links to teacher services and resources.

UNIT 4: Morality and Values in Education

Association for Moral Education
http://www.amenetwork.org/

AME is dedicated to fostering communication, cooperation, training, curriculum development, and research that links moral theory with educational practices. From here it is possible to connect to several sites on ethics, character building, and moral development.

Child Welfare League of America
http://www.cwla.org

The CWLA is the United States' oldest and largest organization devoted entirely to the well-being of vulnerable children and their families. This site provides links to information about issues related to morality and values in education.

Ethics Updates/Lawrence Hinman
http://ethics.acusd.edu

This site provides both simple concept definition and complex analysis of ethics, original treatises, and sophisticated search engine capability. Subject matter covers the gamut from ethical theory to applied ethical venues. There are many opportunities for user input.

The National Academy for Child Development
http://www.nacd.org

This international organization is dedicated to helping children and adults reach their full potential. Its home page presents links to various programs, research, and resources into such topics as ADD.

UNIT 5: Managing Life in Classrooms

Classroom Connect
http://www.classroom.com

This is a major Web site for K–12 teachers and students, with links to schools, teachers, and resources online. It includes discussion of the use of technology in the classroom.

Global SchoolNet Foundation
http://www.gsn.org

Access this site for multicultural educational information. The site includes news for teachers, students, and parents, as well as chat rooms, links to educational resources, programs, and contests and competitions.

Teacher Talk Forum
http://education.indiana.edu/cas/tt/tthmpg.html

Visit this site for access to a variety of articles discussing life in the classroom. Clicking on the various links will lead you to electronic lesson plans covering a variety of topic areas from Indiana University's Center for Adolescent Studies.

UNIT 6: Cultural Diversity and Schooling

American Scientist
http://www.amsci.org/amsci/amsci.html

Investigate this site to access a variety of articles and to explore issues and concepts related to race and gender.

American Studies Web
http://www.georgetown.edu/crossroads/asw/

This eclectic site provides links to a wealth of resources on the Internet related to American studies, from gender studies to race and ethnicity. It is of great help when doing research in demography and population studies.

Multicultural Publishing and Education Council
http://www.mpec.org

This is the home page of the MPEC, a networking and support organization for independent publishers, authors, educators, and librarians fostering authentic multicultural books and materials. It has excellent links to a vast array of resources related to multicultural education.

National Institute on the Education of At-Risk Students
http://www.ed.gov/offices/OERI/At-Risk/

The At-Risk Institute supports research and development activities designed to improve the education of students at risk of educational failure due to limited English proficiency, race, geographic location, or economic disadvantage.

Prospects: The Congressionally Mandated Study of Educational Growth and Opportunity
http://www.ed.gov/pubs/Prospects/index.html

This report analyzes cross-sectional data on language-minority and LEP students in the United States and outlines what actions are needed to improve their educational performance. Family and economic situations are addressed. Information on related reports and sites is provided.

UNIT 7: Serving Special Needs and Concerns

Constructivism: From Philosophy to Practice
http://www.stemnet.nf.ca/~elmurphy/emurphy/cle.html

Here is a thorough description of the history, philosophy, and practice of constructivism, including quotations from Socrates and others, epistemology, learning theory, characteristics, and a checklist.

National Association for Gifted Children
http://www.nagc.org/home00.htm

NAGC, a national nonprofit organization for gifted children, is dedicated to developing their high potential.

National Information Center for Children and Youth With Disabilities (NICHCY)
http://www.nichcy.org/index.html

NICHCY provides information and makes referrals in areas related to specific disabilities, early intervention, special education and related services, individualized education programs, and much more. The site also connects to a listing of Parent's Guides to resources for children and youth with disabilities.

UNIT 8: The Profession of Teaching Today

Canada's SchoolNet Staff Room
http://www.schoolnet.ca/home/e/

Here is a resource and link site for anyone involved in education, including special-needs educators, teachers, parents, volunteers, and administrators.

www.dushkin.com/online/

Teachers Helping Teachers
http://www.pacificnet.net/~mandel/

This site provides basic teaching tips, new teaching methodology ideas, and forums for teachers to share their experiences. Download software and participate in chat sessions. It features educational resources on the Web, and new ones are added each week.

The Teachers' Network
http://www.teachers.net

Bulletin boards, classroom projects, online forums, and Web mentors are featured on this site, as well as the book *Teachers' Guide to Cyberspace* and an online, 4-week course on how to use the Internet.

Teaching with Electronic Technology
http://www.wam.umd.edu/~mlhall/teaching.html

Michael Hall's Web site leads to many resources of value to those contemplating the future of education, particularly regarding the role of technology in the classroom and beyond.

UNIT 9: A Look to the Future

Goals 2000: A Progress Report
http://www.ed.gov/pubs/goals/progrpt/index.html

Open this site to survey a progress report by the U.S. Department of Education on the Goals 2000 reform initiative. It provides a sense of what goals educators are reaching for as they look toward the future.

Mighty Media
http://www.mightymedia.com

The mission of this privately funded consortium is to empower youth, teachers, and organizations through the use of interactive communications technology. The site provides links to teacher talk forums, educator resources, networks for students, and more.

Online Internet Institute
http://www.oii.org

A collaborative project among Internet-using educators, proponents of systemic reform, content-area experts, and teachers who desire professional growth, this site provides a learning environment for integrating the Internet into educators' individual teaching styles.

We highly recommend that you review our Web site for expanded information and our other product lines. We are continually updating and adding links to our Web site in order to offer you the most usable and useful information that will support and expand the value of your Annual Editions. You can reach us at: *http://www.dushkin.com/annualeditions/*.

UNIT 1
How Others See Us and How We See Ourselves

Unit Selections

1. **When I Was Young**, John Fetto
2. **Is America Raising Unhealthy Kids?** Denise Willi
3. **The 'Re-Engineered' Child**, Andrea Petersen
4. **College Isn't for Everyone**, W. J. Reeves
5. **More Families Hide Assets to Qualify for Financial Aid**, Michelle Higgins
6. **The 35th Annual Phi Delta Kappan/Gallup Poll of the Public Attitudes Toward the Public Schools**, Lowell C. Rose and Alec M. Gallup

Key Points to Consider

- Describe the change in American population statistics between 1950 and the present. How have these changes affected education?

- What can teachers do about the unhealthy dietary practices of children and adolescents?

- How can we most accurately assess public perceptions of the educational system?

- What is the fundamental effect of public opinion on national public policy regarding educational development?

 **Links: www.dushkin.com/online/**
These sites are annotated in the World Wide Web pages.

Charter Schools
http://www.edexcellence.net/topics/charters.html
Pathways to School Improvement
http://www.ncrel.org/sdrs/pathwayg.htm

There are many ways in which children and youth are educated. One of the causes as well as one of the results is that the social, racial, and cultural landscape in the United States is becoming more and more diverse and multifaceted. How youth respond to current issues is a reflection of their perceptions as to how older citizens respond to social reality. How to improve the quality of educational services remains a concern of the general public. Public perceptions of the nation's efforts in the education of its youth are of great importance to those who work with children and youth. We must be attentive to the peoples' concerns; we cannot ignore them.

How the people served by a nation's schools perceive the quality of the education they received is of great interest, because public perceptions can translate into either increased or decreased levels of support for a nation's educational system. Achieving a public consensus as to what the aims or purposes of education ought to be can be difficult. Americans debate what the purposes of education should be in every generation. Many different sorts of schools exist at both the elementary and the secondary levels. Many different forms of "charter" schools are attracting the interest of parents; some of these charter schools are within public school systems and some are private ones. Parents wish to have choices as to the types of schools their children attend.

Schools need to be places where students and teachers feel safe, places that provide hope and that instill confidence in the prospect for a happier and better future for all. The safety of students and teachers in schools is a matter of concern to many persons due to tragic events in the recent past. Schools also need to be places where students can dream and hope and work to inform themselves in the process of building their futures. Schools need to help students learn to be inquiring persons.

There are several major policy issues regarding the content and form of schooling that are being debated. We are anticipating greater ranges of choice in the types and forms of schooling that will become available to our children and youth. The United States has great interest in policy issues related to increased accountability to the public for what goes on in schools. Also, we are possibly the most culturally pluralistic nation in the world, and we are becoming even more diverse.

We may be approaching a historic moment in our national history regarding the public funding of education and the options parents might be given for the education of their children. Some of these options and the lines of reasoning for them are explored in this volume. Financial as well as qualitative options are being debated. Scholars in many fields of study as well as journalists and legislators are asking how we can make our nation's schools more effective as well as how we might optimize parents' sense of control over how their children are to be educated.

Young people "read" certain adult behaviors well; they see it as hypocrisy when the adult community wants certain standards and values to be taught in schools but rewards other, often opposite, behaviors in society. Dialogue regarding what it means to speak of "literacy" in democratic communities continues. Our students read much from our daily activities and our many information sources, and they form their own shrewd analyses of

what social values actually do prevail in society. How to help young people develop their intellectual potential and become perceptive students of and participants in democratic traditions are major public concerns.

There is serious business yet to be attended to by the social service and educational agencies that try to serve youth. People are impatient to see some fundamental efforts made to meet the basic educational needs of young people. The problems are the greatest in major cities and in more isolated rural areas. Public perceptions of the schools are affected by high levels of economic deprivation among large sectors of the population and by the economic pressures that our interdependent world economy produces as a result of international competition for the world's markets.

Studies conducted in the past few years, particularly the Carnegie Corporation's studies of adolescents in the United States, document the plight of millions of young persons. Some authors point out that although there was much talk about educational change in the 1990s, those changes were only marginal and cosmetic at best. States responded by demanding more course work and tougher exit standards from schools. With still more than 25 percent of schoolchildren in the United States living at or below the poverty level, and almost a third of them in more economically and socially vulnerable nontraditional family settings, the overall social situation for many young people continues to be difficult. The public wants more effective responses to public needs.

So, in the face of major demographic shifts and of the persistence of many long-term social problems, the public watches how schools respond to new as well as old challenges. In recent years, these challenges have aggravated rather than allayed much public concern about the efficacy of public schooling. Various political, cultural, corporate, and philanthropic interests continue to articulate alternative educational agendas. At the same time the incumbents in the system respond with their own educational agendas, which reflect their views from the inside.

READER REQUEST: YOUR QUESTIONS ANSWERED

WHEN I WAS YOUNG...

Not only are Americans going to school in record numbers, they're also staying in school longer.

BY JOHN FETTO

To the Editors of *American Demographics*:

Politicians continue to attack our K–12 system of public education, proffering some vague notion that if we could just have teachers and schools as good as those we had when we were growing up, everything would be better. I argue that things weren't better 40 or 50 years ago. In fact, I believe they were worse. However, I'm unable to locate comparable education statistics from the 1950s or 1960s that could be measured against today's figures. Are statistics regarding high school completion, college attendance, teen drug usage, teen pregnancy and the like available for such a comparison?
Rick DeGraw
Maricopa Community Colleges
Tempe, Ariz.

Dear Rick:

There are actually quite a few surveys, dating as far back as the mid-1800s, that continually collect data on school-age children and education. Of course, there are certain aspects of the lives of young Americans, including their use of alcohol and drugs, for which continuous data collection has only recently begun.

Some of the oldest studies on education can be found in the annually published *Digest of Education Statistics,* from the National Center for Education Statistics (NCES). According to the latest edition of the digest, released in February 2002, there were 46.5 million students enrolled in the nation's public and private elementary and secondary schools as of the 1998–1999 school year (the latest complete year for which data is available), or 91 percent of those between the ages of 5 and 17—the highest percent of any year on record. A half century earlier (1949–1950), the number of enrolled pupils was just 25.1 million, or 83 percent of all young people. The data reveals that

NEW KIDS, SAME OLD PROBLEMS

In Gallup polls sponsored by Phi Beta Kappa that have been conducted every year since 1970, Americans continue to cite "lack of discipline" and "lack of financial support" as major problems facing the nation's public schools. In more recent years, concerns about overcrowding and school violence have cropped up, while concerns over racial segregation have gone by the wayside.

ITEMS MOST FREQUENTLY CITED BY THE GENERAL PUBLIC AS A MAJOR PROBLEM FACING PUBLIC SCHOOLS:

	1970	1985	2002
Lack of discipline	18%	25%	17%
Lack of financial support	17%	9%	23%
Fighting/violence/gangs	—	—	9%
Use of drugs	11%	18%	13%
Large schools/overcrowding	—	5%	17%
Getting good teachers	12%	10%	8%
Integration/segregation/racial discrimination	17%	4%	—

—Not identified as a major problem

Source: Gallup/Phi Beta Kappa

the student-to-teacher ratio today is markedly lower than it was "back then." In 1949, there were 26.1 students per instructional staff member (which, in addition to teachers, includes principals, supervisors, librarians, etc.); by the fall of 1998, there were 12.6 students per staff member.

Statistics from the U.S. Census Bureau show that Americans are not just going to school in record numbers, they're also staying there longer. In 1940, barely a quarter of Americans age 25 and older (18 million adults) had completed high school. By 1960, 41 percent of the population (41 million adults) had at least a high school diploma. Today, 84 percent of all adults age 25 and older (147 million individuals) have completed secondary school, and many of them have gone on to college: The percentage of Americans with a four-year college degree is now 26 percent, up from just 5 percent in 1940.

YOU EARNED IT

The percent of Americans with a college diploma has increased dramatically during the past half century, especially among black men and women.

PERCENT OF ADULTS AGE 25+ WHO HAVE COMPLETED 4 YEARS OF COLLEGE OR MORE:

	1950	1962*	1970	1980	1990	2000
All adults	6%	9%	11%	17%	21%	26%
Whites	NA	10%	12%	18%	22%	28%
Men	NA	12%	15%	22%	25%	31%
Women	NA	7%	9%	14%	19%	26%
Blacks	2%	4%	5%	8%	11%	17%
Men	2%	4%	5%	8%	12%	16%
Women	2%	4%	4%	8%	11%	17%
Hispanics	NA	NA	NA	8%	9%	11%
Men	NA	NA	NA	10%	10%	11%
Women	NA	NA	NA	6%	9%	11%

*Detailed data for 1960 is not available; data from 1962 has been used instead.
NA: Data not available.

Source: U.S. Census Bureau

As educational attainment rises, so do employers' demands from the work force. In 1973, for example, only 28 percent of prime-age workers (defined as those between the ages of 30 and 59) had attended a postsecondary institution, according to a report published by the U.S. Department of Education. By 2000, 59 percent of prime-age workers said they had continued their education after completing high school. Money is also drawing more Americans to get a college degree. In 2000, men and women with a bachelor's degree earned 79 percent more each year than their peers who had just a high school diploma.

Women these days are freer to continue their education without having to care for a baby. According to the National Center for Health Statistics, there were just 45.9 births per 1,000 women ages 15 to 19 in 2001, the lowest number ever recorded. In fact, the teen birth rate has been falling fairly consistently since the height of the Baby Boom years in 1957, when there was a record 96.3 births for every 1,000 teenage girls.

Drug use, however, has not seen a similar decline. According to a study on drug use of high school seniors, conducted each year since 1975 by the University of Michigan, 55 percent of students in the class of 1975 had tried at least one illicit drug. By 2002, 53 percent of students had tried drugs—hardly a significant reduction. Drug use is actually higher among high school seniors today than it was during the late '80s and early '90s.

Another problem that has captured the attention of parents and educators more recently is school violence. While hard numbers on the topic can be found dating back only to the early '90s, it appears that the situation is already improving. According to "Indicators of School Crime and Safety," a report published by the NCES and the Bureau of Justice Statistics, the number of nonfatal crimes against students ages 12 through 18, occurring either at school or on the way to or from school, fell to 1.9 million in 2000 (the latest year for which data is available) from a high of 3.8 million reported in 1994. That's a 50 percent reduction.

Although you didn't ask about suicide information specifically, you might find it sobering that the rate which young people (ages 15 to 24) take their own lives has risen significantly over the years. In 1950, the NCES reported that there were 4.5 suicides for every 100,000 individuals ages 15 to 24; in 2000, there were 10.4 suicides. Among certain subgroups, the rate is even higher. For white males between 15 and 24 years of age, for instance, the suicide rate today is 18.2, up from 6.6 in 1950. That's something to think about when celebrating advances in other areas.

HOW TO REACH US:

John Fetto
Fax: (212) 716-8472
E-mail: jfetto@mediacentral.com
Address: 261 Madison Avenue, 9th floor, New York, NY 10016

From *American Demographics*, April 2003, pp. 8-9. © 2003 by PRIMEDIA Business Magazines & Media Inc.

SPECIAL REPORT: KIDS' HEALTH

IS AMERICA RAISING Unhealthy KIDS?

YES, BUT TEACHERS CAN DO SOMETHING ABOUT IT

Children across the U.S. are failing to make the grade when it comes to fitness and nutrition.
Some experts say kids' lack of exercise, and the excess of junk food in their diets,
may negatively affect their academic performance....

By Denise Willi

Couch Potato Crisis

Diabetes, obesity, little physical exercise...
the news is bleak for the health of America's children

Nine million American children aged 6 to 19 are over-weight. That is triple the number of 20 years ago, according to the Centers for Disease Control and Prevention. Between video games, computers, and TV, children have become more sedentary than ever before. One study found that 33 percent of children watched three hours or more of television daily. Much of that time involves kids watching about 10,000 commercials for junk food a year, according to researchers at Yale University. Throw in the fact that only two percent of American kids eat the recommended daily requirements for all five major food groups, and it's no wonder that we're in danger of raising a generation of super-sized youth.

"The kids aren't the problem, it's what we're modeling for them that's the problem," says Dr. Mary Story, a professor of Public Health Nutrition at the University of Minnesota. "Americans are eating more on the run. They're serving less fruits and vegetables at home and eating more at fast food restaurants. They're having fewer family meals and eating more convenience foods."

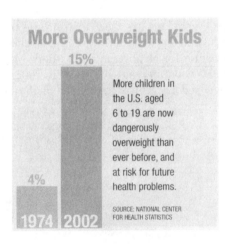

More Overweight Kids

15%

More children in the U.S. aged 6 to 19 are now dangerously overweight than ever before, and at risk for future health problems.

SOURCE: NATIONAL CENTER FOR HEALTH STATISTICS

4%

1974 2002

Schools are also playing a role in the health and fitness crisis facing children. Many have installed vending and soda machines to help close their budget gaps. While school lunches are generally healthier than before, many children head straight for the calorie-laden food items or snack machines. The problem is

4

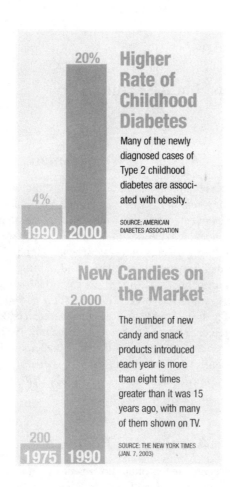

Higher Rate of Childhood Diabetes

Many of the newly diagnosed cases of Type 2 childhood diabetes are associated with obesity.

SOURCE: AMERICAN DIABETES ASSOCIATION

20%
4%
1990 2000

New Candies on the Market

The number of new candy and snack products introduced each year is more than eight times greater than it was 15 years ago, with many of them shown on TV.

SOURCE: THE NEW YORK TIMES (JAN. 7, 2003)

2,000
200
1975 1990

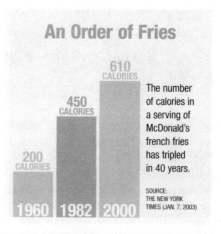

An Order of Fries

The number of calories in a serving of McDonald's french fries has tripled in 40 years.

SOURCE: THE NEW YORK TIMES (JAN. 7, 2003)

610 CALORIES
450 CALORIES
200 CALORIES
1960 1982 2000

6.5 HOURS/DAY OF TV
Kids are spending a record amount of time with TV & video games.

SOURCE: NIELSEN MEDIA RESEARCH

academics, but social skills, emotional skills, and health and fitness as well."

Studies show that children who are less active and eat poorly underachieve in the classroom. "Cutting recess time will not get the kind of academic results schools might be hoping for," says Dr. Vincent Ferrandino, Executive Director of the National Association of Elementary School Principals. "In fact, the opposite may occur."

Calling rising childhood obesity rates a "silent epidemic," former U.S. Surgeon General David Satcher chaired the Healthy Schools Summit in Washington, D.C., last fall, which focused on improving kids' health and educational performance. More than 500 educators, doctors, and nutritionists met to help develop statewide plans to address the issue through legislation and curricula to enhance nutrition, and fitness education.

exacerbated by schools increasingly cutting back on physical education and recess time in favor of academics.

"Everywhere in the nation, we're feeling the pressure of testing, testing, testing," says Beverly Samek, director of School Coordinated Health Programs for District 60 in Boulder, Colorado. "We've lost the connection to the whole child and what they need to be a successful person—not just

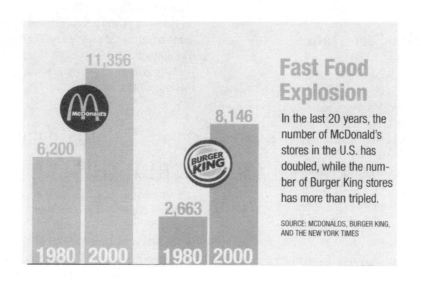

Fast Food Explosion

In the last 20 years, the number of McDonald's stores in the U.S. has doubled, while the number of Burger King stores has more than tripled.

SOURCE: MCDONALDS, BURGER KING, AND THE NEW YORK TIMES

11,356
6,200
1980 2000

8,146
2,663
1980 2000

Up & At 'em

Teachers share activities to build kids' bodies & minds

Darla Perry knows an active body means an active mind. So when her third-grade students have been sitting in their chairs too long, Perry gives their bodies—and their brains—a boost. She weaves 10 minutes of movement into her curriculum. When they're done, her students feel recharged and refreshed. Here are some creative ways other teachers are incorporating physical activity and nutrition into the classroom day. They all help to improve kids' exercise and healthy eating habits.

1 Ready, Set, Spell!

This game uses movement to stimulate the brain and motivates students to remember their spelling words. To do this activity, you'll need clipboards, crayons, and room for your students to walk briskly. First, create a worksheet for each child. Down the side of the worksheets write the names of six to ten colors. Have the children line up at a start line. Each child should have crayons that represent the colors listed on the worksheet. Place the clipboards with the worksheets about 15 to 25 yards away. Then, call out a color, announce a spelling word from that week's vocabulary list, and say "Go!" Have students walk briskly to their clipboards, spell the word on the correct space on their worksheets in the color you have called out, and return to the start line. Repeat this activity, each time with a different color and vocabulary word, until students have completed their worksheets. When students are finished, have them grab their clipboards and head back to the start!

—*Carol Goodrow, Grade Two, Parker Memorial School, Tolland, CT*

2 Quick-Feet Math

Running and/or brisk walking lends itself to an unlimited number of lessons that reinforce math concepts. Whether you run or walk as a class, tell students to set a goal at the beginning of the year of how many miles or laps around the schoolyard they will complete each week. Have students keep a calendar to record their laps or miles as they try to reach that goal. Then have them use those calendars to add their total laps, convert the laps to miles, get the class total for the week, and average their daily, weekly, and monthly totals. You can even use brisk walking or running to teach the metric system, converting meters into miles.

—*Peter Saccone, Grade Five, Meridian Elementary School, El Cajon, CA*

3 Healthy-Body Salad

This lesson is a great way to teach young children about how healthy eating benefits the heart and mind. You can do it to celebrate a great week of student work, or as the culmination of a thematic unit about My Amazing Heart/Body. Tell students you will have a "heart-friendly party" with healthy foods that are fun to prepare and tasty to eat. Ask each child to bring in a healthy ingredient to make a salad—such as green-leaf lettuce (rather than iceberg, which has low nutritional value), carrots, black olives, low-fat cheese, or fat-free dressing. As each child adds his or her ingredient into a large bowl, describe how the ingredient is a heart-smart food. Then toss the salad and enjoy! For added fun, serve angel food cake with fresh strawberries.

—*Cammie Breedlove, Grade One, Grove Hill Elementary, Grove Hill, AL*

4 Animated Food Chain

When students incorporate movement into a unit about the food chain, they're more likely to remember what they've learned. To help them, have students choose a plant that is a producer—either a fruit or vegetable—that they will act out during an imaginary growing period. Tell students not to reveal their choice and remain silent. Then have them make their bodies as low to the ground as they can, as if they were simulating the shape of a plant that has yet to grow. Tell students they will grow based on the sound and rhythms of a hand drum. Then play the drum very softly when they are seedlings in the ground, medium loud when they are half way to maturation, and very loud when they are fully mature and ready to be harvested. Walk around and gently tap each student to signal that they can reveal what plant they have grown into. You might also ask students to tell what they know about the plant or describe its nutritional value.

—*Patty Aronofsky, Grade Four, Beulah Heights Elementary, Pueblo, CO*

5 Heart-Thumping Science

This cross-curricular lesson will show students the benefits of being physically active by teaching them what a healthy heart rate should be. As part of a science respiratory system unit, have students create a three-column chart with the following headings: date, pulse at rest, pulse after activity. Teach students how to find their pulse on their wrists or necks. Have them count their pulse rates for 15 seconds and multiply that number by four to get a pulse rate per minute. Set aside 15 minutes a day for the following: First, have each student record his or her pulse at rest on the chart. Then have kids do a vigorous activity indoors or out—a fast walk, jog, or jumping jacks—for five minutes. After five minutes call "time," and count down 4, 3, 2, 1. Have students record their pulse after the activity. At the end of two weeks, have students use their data to find mean, median, mode, and range of resting versus active pulse. Use the statistics to build double-line graphs with both pulses. Then have students write an essay or paragraph comparing and contrasting the two and telling what they learned.

—*Suzanne Bechina, Grade Five, Ben Franklin Elementary School, Pueblo, CO*

6 Roundabout Writing

This active, story-writing lesson helps build students' cardiovascular strength while getting their creative juices flowing. First, tell students to take out paper and pencil and to stand at their desks. Give them a topic to write about (e.g., You've just landed on an unexplored planet. Describe life on that planet). Then give students two minutes to start their stories. After two minutes, call "time" and tell students to walk briskly around the perimeter of the classroom and find another paper to stop at without sitting down. Give students four minutes to read what's on the paper and add to it. After four minutes, call time. Repeat the process three more times. Students must stop when time is called, even if it's mid-sentence. The next student can pick up from that exact spot. Tell students to go back to their own paper, read what others wrote, and then add their own ending to the story. Then have students share their stories with the class.

—*Julie Fischer, Grade Six, Spann Elementary School, Pueblo, CO*

7 The Great Plot Race

This lively activity helps students hone sequencing skills for the major events of a story. First, prepare a list of the main events of a story the class is reading. Using a 36- or 48-point font, type one event per page. Print out the events and laminate them as cards. Collate the cards into sets of four or more, then mix up each set so the cards are not in sequential order. Put each set into a folder. Then divide the class into groups of four, giving each member a number from one to four. Designate sections of the classroom wall as "hanging" areas, where students will tape or tack the events in order. Give each group a folder with a set of cards containing the event cards. At the sound of a starting whistle, the group arranges the events in sequential order. As soon as the group has all of the events in order, Runner 1 hangs the first event in that team's area of the room. When Runner 1 returns and is seated, Runner 2 hangs the second event. Continue until all the events are hung.

—*Susan Van Zile, Grade Six, Eagle View Middle School, Mechanicsburg, PA*

Visit **www.scholastic.com/instructor** for a full and rich array of kids' books on health, nutrition, and exercise.

Denise Willi is a freelance writer based in Sleepy Hollow, New York. She has written and edited for *The Washington Post* and *Reader's Digest*.

The 'Re-Engineered' Child

*Schools Target Mean Looks, Name-Calling, Even Playing Alone;
Some Worry It Goes Too Far*

By Andrea Petersen

ON A RECENT morning at Candor Elementary School in rural New York, 12 first-graders sit cross-legged on the floor and sing:

"I'm a little boy with glasses, the one they call a geek. A little girl who never smiles 'cuz I've got braces on my teeth."

The sing-along is part of a new program to turn Candor Elementary into a "Ridicule Free Zone." It is just one example of a nationwide campaign with a rather ambitious goal: make childhood nicer.

Spurred partly by new research showing the lasting effects of teasing, a mix of educators and mental-health counselors—as well as new laws in many states—are accelerating efforts to eradicate typical childhood behavior such as gossiping and even giving dirty looks. They are tinkering with cliques, trying to turn loners into joiners and launching assaults on whispering and garden-variety nastiness.

Fifteeen states have laws requiring schools to put "antibullying" policies into place. As a result, darting another kid a mean look is considered bullying in Connecticut.

In some Louisiana schools, playing alone at recess can land a child in a counselor's office. At Leary Elementary School in Warminster, Pa., teachers set up tomboys on playdates with other girls. The school also has "peace tables" where kids confront their recess nemesis.

Some schools are adopting rules that force children to play with everyone, even kids they don't get along with. Known as "You Can't Say You Can't Play" policies, they essentially forbid a child to say "no" if a kid asks to go out and play. The idea is to prevent feelings of rejection.

These policies are designed to dismantle the Darwinian order of the classroom, creating a schoolyard utopia where no shy child sits alone at the lunch table and no kid with glasses ever gets called "four eyes." But some people are starting to worry

that such practices could produce kids who lack the skills to deal with the slings and arrows of the rest of life. After all, isn't seventh grade supposed to be miserable?

The American Civil Liberties Union recently weighed in against one program. Last year, it challenged a school policy in East Providence, R.I., that defined bullying as including teasing, "harmful gossip" and exclusion. The ACLU claimed the rule could squelch individuality and expression. The policy went into effect in November.

Sometimes the kids themselves revolt against compulsory niceness: At Leary Elementary, teacher Debbie Walker told her second graders to use "I" statements when verbally tussling with other kids. (OK: "I feel bad when you swipe my book." Not OK: "You're a thief.") But the students found ways to adhere to the letter of the rule—while unequivocally violating its spirit. "Kids would say stuff like, 'I… hate you,'" Ms. Walker says. So she changed the rule. Now the children have to start their sentences with the words "I feel."

Even advocates wonder if all this will make kids less resilient when they inevitably encounter disappointment later in life. "We worry about the future," says Gloria Wetzel, principal at Leary Elementary. "Are we making them too soft?"

At Candor Elementary, students air disagreements and work to come up with solutions at weekly class meetings that can resemble grown-up group therapy. Sometimes they turn into interventions: During a recent meeting of Denise Ahart's third-grade class, kids confronted a class bully who had been tripping and pushing classmates. He "had a cycle he couldn't break," says one eight-year-old girl. In the ensuing discussion, he tells his classmates that he was lonely and hoped that "playing around" would get him attention. It seems to have worked: Everyone agrees that the problem is mostly resolved.

OK—Or Not OK?

What should parents worry about in the behavior crackdown? We asked two psychiatrists, Henry J. Gault in Deerfield, Ill., and James C. MacIntyre of Albany Medical College in New York:

- **Shooting another child a dirty look**
  Should You Worry: No. Eye rolling is the dirty look du jour among kids and while it can be annoying to adults, it's benign.

- **Being in a clique**
  Should You Worry: No. Having a few loyal pals is good for a child's self esteem. Signs of trouble: If the clique excludes other kids, or if one child dictates how others dress or act.

- **Being a tomboy**
  Should You Worry: Probably not. But things could get tougher later: "The social acceptability of being a tomboy fades at adolescence," says Dr. Gault. Possible fallout: teasing.

- **Your child only has a handful of friends**
  Should You Worry: Probably not. This is actually more a problem for Type-A parents—the ex-football stars and homecoming queens—than their progeny. "It can be painful to see their child labeled as not a popular kid," says Dr. MacIntyre.

- **Gossiping**
  Should You Worry: Probably. It's a common form of bullying among girls and it can get vicious. A typical tactic—these days as early as fifth grade—is to spread rumors that another girl is a "slut."

Ticking Time Bomb

The heightened sensitivity gained steam in 1999 after shootings at Columbine High School and four other schools. A year later, a U.S. Secret Service study concluded that the perpetrators in most school shootings were actually the victims of bullying.

Other new research has cast playground bullying as a much more serious social ill than previously thought. Children who are the objects of mild teasing are more likely to suffer from depression in adulthood. Kids identified as elementary-school bullies are six times as likely as nonbullies to be convicted of a crime by age 24.

The growth in the number of school psychologists in some states also means there are more professionals around to intervene. In California, for example, the number of school psychologists jumped almost 20% in the past six years to 4,063 psychologists, up from 3,388 in 1997.

The American Medical Association has issued its own call to arms in a 2001 report that encourages members to use pediatric visits to identify bullies and victims.

As a result, that little kid on the sidelines now looks like a depressed adult in the making, or even a ticking time bomb. In Louisiana, Laura Harper of the local American Federation of Teachers office holds nine-day workshops for recess monitors, cafeteria workers and bus drivers. She teaches them to act when they see kids playing by themselves. "It is not normal to have a child that doesn't want to join in activities," says Ms. Harper. "If the antisocial behavior doesn't stop, we need to get that child to a counselor. They can become suicidal."

A host of national bullying prevention programs have cropped up and are helping schools fulfill the new state laws. In the "Don't Laugh at Me" program—instituted by a New York-based nonprofit, Operation Respect—kids are taught to trade put downs for "put ups."

Kids Policing Each Other

The Anti-Defamation League's "Names Can Really Hurt Us" program gets kids to talk about times they have been bullied. The Southern Poverty Law Center's year-old "Mix It Up at Lunch" day effort encourages students to spend a lunch period sitting with kids who aren't in their clique.

A cornerstone of the new movement is enlisting kids to police each other for teasing and nastiness, sort of a junior version of the neighborhood-watch program. At St. Thomas More school in Spokane, Wash., students can fill out a "Request for Assistance" report when they see another child pushing, gossiping or "ostracizing." If a child is caught bullying a third time, the class determines a punishment that can include Saturday detention or eating lunch alone for a week.

"No one wants to get a third offense. They are afraid other kids are going to really stick it to them," says Principal Douglas P. Banks, adding that the two-year-old policy has cut down on teasing and bullying incidences at the Catholic school.

The middle school in Urbana, Ohio, launched a policy whereby second-time teasing offenders have to write "reflection" papers (which their parents must sign). The kids must answer the questions: "How did my victim feel when I did what I did? And, "What do I plan to do to change my behavior."

Peer mediation programs, where fellow students broker a solution between two "disputants," are also popular. Patterson Elementary School in Lakewood, Colo., launched such a program four years ago, after the shooting at its neighbor Columbine High School. Kids agree not to call each other names or interrupt as they consider solutions to typical recess arguments.

Schools are also starting support groups in the hopes of creating happier kids. At White River Elementary in Noblesville, Ind., 150 students are in groups with names like self-esteem, grief and anger management. In the anger-management group, kids are taught deep breathing and to "take excess energy and go ride your bike or do jumping jacks rather than hauling off and hitting your brother or sister," says Julie Schalburg, the counselor.

'It Must Be Pretty Bad'

At Candor Elementary, school counselor Barbara Provus stages mock conversations and writes scripts for kids who have a tough time talking to other children. One fourth grader carries Ms. Provus's scripts on index cards in his pockets.

Some parents are surprised at how hands-on educators have become. When Ann Smith's fifth-grader, Whitney, came home recently and said she had been sent to the principal's office, Mrs. Smith thought "it must be pretty bad." It turned out that Whitney, a student at Patterson Elementary in Colorado, was simply stuck in a classic preteen friendship triangle: two quarreling friends wanted her to choose between them. "It didn't seem like that huge of a deal," she says, though Mrs. Smith says she was thankful for the help.

And it is unclear whether children who have this kind of intervention are actually nicer when they hit high school. "I couldn't say I would recognize which kids have gone through a program of antiharassment or no bullying," says Rodger S. Cilley, dean of students at Gonzaga Prepatory School in Spokane, Wash. Gonzaga Prep gets students from about 40 middle schools, including St. Thomas More, the school with the "Request for Assistance" forms. "I know some of the Thomas More kids; I wouldn't say they were any more sensitive than the other kids here."

Meanwhile, a few kids worry that the language they have learned in tolerance programs might actually mark them for trouble. In Warminster, Leary Elementary is the only elementary school with a comprehensive peer-mediation program out of six schools that feed into the middle school. Leary's sixth-graders face the next school year with trepidation. "They'll probably just think you're talking gibberish," says 10-year-old Stephen Schmidt. "They are going to be three times my size, so they'll probably just beat me up anyway."

COLLEGE ISN'T FOR EVERYONE

"… Going to college is an utter waste of time for those students who have emerged from high school neither literate nor numerate, with cultural focuses revolving around hip-hop and body piercing and with zero interest in changing their behavior."

BY W. J. REEVES

APPROXIMATELY 15,000,000 Americans are enrolled in college, although about half of them probably *shouldn't be!*

During the junior year of high school, students and, to a greater extent, their parents start to fret about getting the teenager into a college. Most of these students are unable to be admitted to first-rate schools like Williams College or the Ivy League institutions, but they and their parents believe that a college education, from any school, is necessary to succeed in the 21st century. However, Edward E. Gordon reports in an article entitled "Creating Tomorrow's Work Force" (*The Futurist*, August, 2000) that 70% of the workers in the coming decades will not need a four-year college degree, but, rather, an associate degree from a community college or some type of technical certificate. Thus, moms and dads, who foot the bill, delude themselves that going to any four-year college

will make their sons and daughters literate, analytical, culturally aware, technologically advanced, and therefore employable.

In America today, there exists a goal that the majority of the nation's youth should go to college and that access should be the byword for higher education. On the surface, this sounds like a great idea; in reality, it is not.

Access in its most-extreme form —open admissions—was instituted at The City University of New York during the turmoil of the 1960s. Any student who had graduated from high school, with no regard given to grade point average (GPA) and/or the SAT scores, was allowed into one of the CUNY schools. Today, while that policy is officially off the books, many of its aspects remain. CUNY is not alone in its attitude toward access. In every state, midrange colleges exist by some form of easy access, for access=numbers, and low numbers= cess=numbers, and low numbers=

low funding, and really low numbers=no college. Connected with access is *retention*, which means that, once inside the college, the students are more or less guaranteed graduation.

An examination of the relationship among access and retention and preparation for the 21st-century workplace is illuminating:

Being there. It is hard to be a productive worker if one appears occasionally, yet token appearances, sometimes just cameos, are tolerated in college. Jennifer Jacobson in "Rookies in the Classroom" (*The Chronicle: Career Network*, July 18, 2002) details a professor's experience with attendance: "Some of them have amazingly intricate excuses, such as one student who explained that his parent's credit card had been canceled and by the time he'd driven home to get a new card, the bookstore had sold out the texts he'd needed." In the meantime, the student had simply not come to class. One solution to this problem is to use "click-and-brick courses" (classes which combine online and in-class instruction), for being absent online is not possible.

On time. With regard to punctuality, Jacobson's article also tells of a fledgling professor's encounter with a student who arrived late for class with the excuse that she'd been "caught in a traffic jam after visiting a sick grandmother." After she lamented "What was I to do?," the young professor learned after class from another student that the reason for lateness was a lie and that the person being visited was the late-to-class student's "out-of-town boyfriend."

After four years, the bad habits of not being on time and attending sporadically have become second nature. Such habits are unlikely to make for a very productive worker.

Cultural awareness. Most liberal arts colleges tout the virtues of a well-rounded education. Becoming aware of a culture usually involves reading. In my Core Literature class that covers Western and non-Western works, the major problem is the refusal to read the assigned texts.

Teaching can be a lonely profession when the only person in the classroom who has read all of *The Scarlet Letter* is the professor. In their handbooks, many moderately difficult-to-enter colleges state certain requirements, but many students spend most of their time trying to get around the requirement of reading. Their methods include shortcuts (*Cliff Notes*) and cheating (buying a paper online about an assigned work of literature). Such evasions of becoming learned are not the hallmark of the well-rounded.

Becoming culturally aware involves change, and change is frightening. Faced with a dilemma in a play, poem, or novel, many students become angry if pressed to offer a point of view. Expansion of vistas is not on their agenda. They want me to provide some notes, which they, or someone, will copy or record, and they expect me to produce a test, which, when graded, will produce a range of grades from A to B+. An article in *The Chronicle* (July 12, 2002), "Reports of Grade Inflation May Be

Inflated," by Catherine E. Shoichet, states that "one-third of college students receive grades of C or below" and offers this number as evidence to attack the concept of grade inflation. This is skewed reasoning, for those students receiving C's in reality deserve F's, and the C is given to keep them in the college. Further, of what value is a degree with a C average from a mediocre college?

The end result is that students emerge from college with a diploma which the Victorian sage Matthew Arnold would characterize as "The Grand Thing without the Grand Meaning"—*i.e.,* merely a piece of paper.

Literacy. One would expect that, at the very least, colleges would not graduate students whose writing would be generously regarded as poor. One would be wrong.

Learning to write is supposed to be taken seriously. Sean Cavanagh, in an article entitled "Overhauled SAT Could Shake up School Curriculum" (*Education Week*, July 10, 2002), announces that the SATs will now include a writing test. Such a requirement sounds rigorous, but appearances are deceiving.

At one time, I scored the essay section of the GMAT, the required test for entrance into graduate schools of business where one would acquire an MBA. The test-takers were college graduates from every state and from countries around the world. Fully two-thirds of the essays I scored would not have passed my freshman composition class, yet I was expected to give a score of 4 (Passing) to such writing and, apparently, the graduate schools of business accepted such students. Access again had reared its ugly head. No graduate students=no graduate school.

Diversity. Since diversity is desired, many English-as-a-second-language (ESL) students are admitted to colleges. Once there, they must take an English composition class. In my experience, the majority of these students speak English only when compelled to. They sit in my classes, all together, in self-imposed segregation, speaking in their native language.

Outside the class, at home, and everywhere in their existence, they converse in a language other than English. These students need to spend several years in an adult edu-

cation program focused on the basics of the English language before applying to an institution of higher learning. Some of these ESL students work quite hard, but lack a basic understanding of the language. There is pressure put on professors to pass on to the world of work college graduates whose grasp of the English language is, to be kind, "shaky."

This is not to say that the ESL students are worse than the homegrown functional illiterates whose command of their own language is less than commanding. During the 1960s, I taught seventh-grade English in an inner-city junior high school. Now, I offer lessons on syntax and diction which I created for that junior high class to my present college classes, and I encounter failure in excess of 50%. Failing more than half of my class at the end of the semester would be asking for a public flogging. A recent case at Temple University, reported by Robin Wilson in her article, "The Teaching Equation Didn't Add Up" (*The Chronicle*, March 29, 2002), involved a tenured professor of mathematics who was fired for being an "extremely harsh grader" who was "rude" to his students. Another professor at the university remarked that "he noticed that if somebody flunks a lot of people then the administration doesn't like that, and I do what I think will not put me out on the street without a job." Translation? The inmates are running the asylum.

The anti-grammar league. At some point during the last century, it was determined by certain educators that providing an understanding of grammar was not necessary to the teaching of composition. In fact, those professors who do to this very day teach grammar are regarded as dinosaurs. One would be hard-pressed to find any articles advocating instruction in grammar in the two major journals about writing, *College English* and *College Composition*.

A colleague of mine told me last year about a set of papers he had saved from his graduate class, written by individuals who were studying to be teachers of English. A reading of these essays exposed errors in verb tense, subject-verb agreement, pronoun usage, run-ons, and fragments, all of which produce incoherence in an essay. Yet, constructing lessons to deal directly with grammar is frowned upon. In my class, the students and I address these errors with grammar exercises as I await the summons from Big Brother to stop such ancient rituals.

Who teaches whom? To capture the attitude of colleges toward the importance of composition, one need only examine the latest survey of academic salaries. In "Law Professors Again Get Top Pay" (*The Chronicle of Higher Education*, Aug. 12, 2002), Sharon Walsh, quoting from a survey conducted by the College and University Professional Association for Human Resources, states that the lowest salaries in the academic world are paid to professors of English composition. Low salaries reveal a low regard for literacy.

An extended scrutiny reveals another problem with the teaching of composition. When parents dip deeply into their savings to pay tuition bills, they expect their offspring to be taught by real professors. Their expectations will not be met.

Who are the composition teachers? Many of them are adjunct lecturers—*i.e.*, graduate students with no teaching experience whatsoever —and the college pays them a salary slightly lower than a pittance, provides no health benefits, and stuffs staff rooms with as many as 15 adjuncts who meet there with students to discuss corrected essays. During the last 10 years at my school, I've seen the number of adjuncts rise to its present-day level of over 50% in English composition classes. If literacy were considered truly important, one would expect a college to put on its front line the best and brightest faculty (and pay them properly), rather than allow those students that are new to college and in desperate need of composition instruction to be taught by an individual who is marginal to the school.

Parents are not getting much bang for their buck. Their children learn no soft skills and do not become literate or culturally aware. The other values supposedly gained from a traditional, four-year liberal arts education—that such graduates will bring to the marketplace creativity and initiative—are negated by many of my students who are passive and

expect me to make the work easy for them. They arrive in class with no questions—and at times with no books—and only grudgingly answer my questions. It would be illuminating for a parent to be a fly on the wall in my classroom and to observe his or her child's performance.

Solutions

What can be done? A college administrator could have the courage to let the word go forth that the college has admission standards and that access does not guarantee graduation. One of the state schools in New Jersey—The College of New Jersey, formerly Trenton State University—did exactly that, transforming itself from a college where admittance was rather easy into a tree institution of higher learning with high admission standards. An initial dip in enrollment occurred, but today the college is listed as one of the top bargains for a quality education in the country.

I would not count on the above scenario sweeping the country. Most administrators keep their ships of education afloat by scrounging for the few dollars that come their way from full-time equivalent students. FTEs are generated by easy access and retention.

A more-practical solution is for parents to find a cheap apartment some distance from the family home, deposit their son or daughter in it, along with the considerable clutter accumulated during a brief lifetime, and secure enrollment in a community college. The teachers at a community college earn a living by teaching. Therefore, the students are more likely to be taught by a full-time, professional teacher.

In addition, community colleges offer training in the technical fields where there are jobs. In the county in New Jersey where I live, students can obtain an associate degree in radiography and get a job. It has been estimated that 1,000,000 workers in the technical fields will be needed in the coming decades. How many job offers will come the way of a graduate of a moderately difficult-to-enter, four-year college with a 2.75 GPA in English, women's studies, or history?

Possibly the best course of action during senior year is to participate in one of the job cooperative programs that link high schools to the world of work. One such initiative at Allentown High School in central New Jersey is entitled the Senior Practicum. It is a for-credit class in which a student explores an interest in the workplace. The program's mission is to create an opportunity for high school seniors to learn to function as responsible, contributing adults. Serving as a rite of passage, it "provides a bridge from the traditional school structure to the self-directed, self-initiated world of adults." Participation in jobs ranging from work in retail sales to positions in a pain management clinic, the local police department, law offices, and architectural firms, students learn what is expected of them by the worth of work. After graduation, some of these students gain employment in the very business where they interned and find out that the employer will pay for their further education. However, the major benefit of such school-to-work programs is the personal growth as teenagers shed their childish ways and take a major step toward becoming adults.

Higher education is very expensive, taxing the resources of the already overtaxed, middle-class family. In addition to the cost, the college years are a moment in time that will never return. Again and again, in my night classes, I encounter adults, now burdened with kids and dead-end jobs, who, 10 years ago, wasted their time in college with adolescent behavior. Now, they tell me, "You know, Prof, if I had just listened to you back then, but I.... " I smile and nod and tune them out by repeating to myself the old saw: "If 'ifs' and 'buts' were ginger and nuts, what a Merry Christmas we'd all have."

The 19th-century novelist, and twice Prime Minister, Benjamin Disraeli wrote a book entitled *The Two Nations* which exposed the class gap in Victorian England. In 21st-century America, there is an education gap. Students with brains who have worked hard in high school can go to the top of the academic food chain and attend an Ivy League school, Stanford University, MIT, or Amherst College. Those students will lead this century. Others can receive a technical education at a local community college that will allow them to earn a good living. In his book, *Success Without a College Degree*, John T. Murphy reports that 75% of the American populace does not have a college degree, which means that those possessed of other than academic skills can find a way to succeed financially.

Then, there is the great, gray middle. Going to a midrange college is of value only for those students who wish to become educated and accept the fact that attendance, punctuality, and hard work are parts of the process. However, going to a college is an utter waste of time for those students who have emerged from high school neither literate nor numerate, with cultural focuses revolving around hip-hop and body piercing and with zero interest in changing their behavior. Parents should investigate one of the above solutions or invest their hard-earned dollars elsewhere while their offspring find employment in the world of the minimum wage.

W. J. Reeves *is professor of English, Brooklyn College of The City University of New York.*

More Families Hide Assets to Qualify For Financial Aid

By Michelle Higgins

DIANNE WRIGHT IS planning on sending her daughter to a top-notch college that costs around $30,000 a year. So what's she doing with the trust she set up to pay for her daughter's education? Spending it as fast as she can.

Facing rising tuitions and smaller portfolios, parents this year are going through even more contortions than usual to qualify their kids for financial-aid grants. Some pour money into annuities because they don't have to report them in financial-aid applications. Others, like Ms. Wright, spend down trusts before college rolls around. The basic aim is to make themselves look needier so they get more aid from either schools or the government.

The pressures on parents are worse than ever this year. Sixteen states have jacked up costs at public four-year colleges and universities by more than 10%, according to the National Center for Public Policy and Higher Education. At the same time, 17 states have decreased their total investment in student aid.

How much money can you have and still qualify for financial-aid grants? Once a family earns about $100,000 a year and has about $100,000 in assets, it is generally ineligible for need-based aid at most schools.

But the aid game has spawned a corps of financial planners who specialize in moving money so it doesn't count against you in financial-aid applications. One popular tactic: moving money from a child's account into a parent's account. Colleges expect students to contribute a higher percentage of their assets than a parent, so that can lower what a family is asked to contribute. Another approach: paying down your mortgage. Some financial-aid formulas don't count home equity, which creates an incentive for families to put more of their money into the house.

While such practices are legal, schools frown upon them. "We're asking about resources. And if they don't tell us about them, they are not being candid," says Jim Belvin, director of financial aid at Duke University. "If families are qualifying for aid that they don't really need, someone who really needed that money may not get it."

College-planning specialists see it differently. "It's a lot like how you approach the tax system," says Stephanie Hancock, one such planner. "You need to be familiar with the code."

While there are no hard numbers on how many well-heeled people actually use such tactics to get more financial aid, nearly everyone involved in the process says more of it is going on these days.

A new group, the National Institute of College Planners, was formed in April 2002, and it now offers a certification course in college financial strategies. Already 109 people have graduated, and 110 more are on their way. When American Express Financial Advisors began offering college-planning seminars to parent-teacher groups last fall, they expected about 1,000 requests for seminars in the first year. Instead, they got double that number in just the first four months.

John Hall of Los Angeles sought the help of Ms. Hancock last fall after hearing her give a seminar at his stepdaughter's school. Mr. Hall is a pharmacist who makes a six-figure income. His stepdaughter recently inherited enough money to cover at least one year of college. Ms. Hancock's recommendation: Invest the money in a fixed annuity, since most schools don't ask about them. That is partly because schools consider annuities a retirement vehicle, and they typically don't count retirement money when awarding aid.

Playing Hide and Seek with Financial Aid

To up their chances for financial aid, parents are positioning their money so they look more needy. Below are some commonly used strategies that are legal but generally frowned upon by colleges.

- **Minimize income.** Up to 47% of parental income is considered eligible to pay for school. So parents defer bonuses to keep their income low. Others sell losing stock positions to reduce their income, though only $3,000 of net losses can be taken each year.
- **Spend the kid's savings.** The more assets the student has, the less aid he or she is likely to get. Families can legally spend custodial accounts on anything that benefits their child's education, including private high-school tuition, an SAT prep course or a computer.
- **Keep savings in the parents' name.** A savings account in a parent's name instead of the child's can up their chances for getting aid.
- **Quit the summer job.** Student income is assessed at an even higher rate than parents' so it often pays to keep the kid out of work the year before aid is needed.
- **Pick your assets.** The cash value of life insurance, deferred annuities and personal property such as coin collections usually don't have to be reported on financial-aid applications.

There are essentially three different financial-aid formulas to determine how much aid you get: federal, used by all schools; "institutional," which is used by roughly 325 mostly private colleges; and a new "consensus approach" being used for the first time this year by 29 elite colleges.

The federal formula determines how much aid you get from the U.S. government. The other two formulas calculate how much aid you get from the colleges themselves. Many students at private colleges get aid from both sources.

The federal formula is the most basic. Students are expected to kick in about 35% of their assets each year, while parents—depending on their income and other factors—are expected to contribute between 2.6% and 5.6%. Home equity isn't counted when adding up assets.

The institutional formula used by most private colleges probes more deeply into your finances. Here, students are expected to contribute only 25% of assets and parents between 3% and 5%. But this model does count home equity and, depending on the school, may even examine what kind of car you drive.

The consensus approach looks at parent and student assets together and expects families to contribute only around 5% of them. These colleges generally won't consider home equity of more than 2.4 times the family income. The idea is to avoid penalizing a family that has a middle-class income but lives in a house that has shot up in value over the years.

Financial planners recommend a few basic strategies to maximize your chances to qualify for financial aid.

• Keep assets out of the student's name: Many parents set up college-savings plans such as Uniform Gift to Minor Accounts to save for school. But since they are considered a student's asset, most colleges expect up to 35% of the money in these accounts to be used each year for tuition. Since the money in the accounts is considered an irrevocable gift to the student, you can't simply take the money back. But you can spend it before college rolls around on educational-related costs like a new computer or private high-school tuition.

• Be careful with 529 plans: In just the past few years there has been an explosion in these tax-advantaged college-savings plans. If they're in your name or the student's name, the college will consider them when doling out aid. But parents can hide these assets by making the account owner someone like a grandparent, says Bruce Harrington, director of 529 plans at MFS Investment Management, a mutual-fund provider.

• Lower your income: Aid formulas expect parents to contribute from 22% to 47% of income. Parents sometimes defer bonuses to lower their income and get more aid. For the same reason, people are advised to postpone selling stocks or real estate in which they've realized a capital gain. Student income is assessed at an even higher rate than parents', so some students simply stop working just before they apply for financial aid.

• Use your house: The federal formula doesn't look at home equity, so paying down your mortgage is a way of hiding wealth. However, home equity is counted in the institutional formula used by most private schools. The result: Parents take out a home-equity loan, which makes them poorer under the formula, and use the proceeds to pay off credit-card bills, which aren't counted in financial-aid calculations.

• Don't Remarry: Both the institutional formula and the new consensus approach probe the financial status of stepparents. So more divorced parents put off getting remarried until after their kid gets a diploma. Herm Davis, an independent financial-aid counselor in Rockville, Md., says he has about 70 clients right now who are putting off getting remarried for this reason. "People are starting to take paying for college a little more seriously," he says.

From *Wall Street Journal*, March 12, 2003, pp. D1, D8, by Michelle Higgins. © 2003 by Dow Jones & Company, Inc. Reproduced with permission of Dow Jones & Company, Inc.

The 35th Annual
PHI DELTA KAPPA/GALLUP POLL
Of the Public's Attitudes Toward the Public Schools

BY LOWELL C. ROSE AND ALEC M. GALLUP

TAKE SCHOOLS that have strong public support from the communities they serve. Impose on those schools a major federal mandate that attempts to reach worthy goals using strategies that lack public approval, and you have the ingredients for a failed system. Recognizing the importance of the No Child Left Behind (NCLB) Act and the extent to which it involves the federal government in decisions affecting schools at the K–12 level, those who plan this annual poll decided to focus this year's edition on NCLB. To the surprise of this report's authors, the findings point to the situation described in the first two sentences. While the public sees improved student achievement as an important goal, it rejects the strategies used in NCLB. What is reported in the following pages should be cause for reflection and concern on the part of those who believe that success for every child is vital. We hope that this year's poll leads to a lively debate focused on strategies that will advance that goal.

Executive Summary

The 35th Annual Phi Delta Kappa/Gallup Poll of the Public's Attitudes Toward the Public Schools comes at a time when relationships at the federal, state, and local levels with regard to K–12 education are increasingly complex, change is the mantra of the day, and money is short in almost every state. Attention is currently directed at efforts to improve student achievement, with special emphasis on those minorities and other groups that have traditionally been less successful in gaining the quality of education needed for future success. These differences in school success have come to be known as the "achievement gap," a gap that virtually everyone agrees must be closed. How this is to be done and the relative roles of the parties involved are, however, matters involving uncertainty and controversy. This poll, the 35th in this series, addresses those issues.

The poll focuses on NCLB, the extension of the Elementary and Secondary Education Act, which became law in January 2002. Some questions deal directly with NCLB, while others address strategies associated with the act's implementation. Since NCLB's intention is to improve the public schools, a number of traditional poll questions—those dealing with grading the public schools, vouchers, problems the public schools face, the nature of the achievement gap, the challenge of getting and keeping good teachers, and the merits of the current emphasis on standardized testing—all fit nicely into the poll's focus. Taken as a whole, the results offer significant and timely information about the public's view of the state of our schools and current improvement efforts.

We begin this report with seven overarching conclusions. In each case, we refer by number to the tables in which data supporting the conclusion can be found. We then offer additional findings, followed by a comprehensive set of tables. Readers are invited to judge the appropriateness of the conclusions and to make their own interpretations of the data and what they tell us about the public's view of the public schools.

The authors believe the data support the following general conclusions:

1. The public has high regard for the public schools, wants needed improvement to come through those schools, and has little interest in seeking alternatives. The number assigning an A or a B to schools in their community is 48%, with an additional 31% assigning the grade of C. The number of A's and B's rises to 55% for public school parents and to 68% for parents asked to grade the public school their oldest child attends. The number believing that reform should come through the existing public schools is 73%, up from 69% in 2002, while the number of those seeking an alternative is down to 25%. (See Tables 1 through 4.)

2. The public sees itself as uninformed on the No Child Left Behind (NCLB) Act, with 69% saying they lack the information needed to say whether their impression of the act is favorable or unfavorable. Forty percent say they know very little about the NCLB, with an additional 36% saying they know nothing at all about the act. Somewhat surprisingly, public school parents consider themselves just as uninformed as others. (See Tables 5 and 6.)

3. Responses to questions related to strategies associated with NCLB suggest that greater familiarity with the law is unlikely to lead to greater public support.

- A total of 83% of respondents believe decisions regarding what is taught in the public schools should be made at the state level (22%) or by the local school board (61%). NCLB involves major federal intervention. (See Table 7.)
- Eighty-four percent believe the job a school is doing should be measured on the basis of improvement shown by students. NCLB requires that a specified percentage of students—in the school as a whole and in each subgroup—must pass a state test, and improvement is not a factor. (See Table 8.)
- Sixty-six percent believe a single test *cannot* provide a fair picture of whether a school is in need of improvement. NCLB bases this judgment on a state test administered annually in grades 3 through 8. (See Table 9.)
- Only 15% believe testing on English and math alone can produce a fair picture of whether or not a school is in need of improvement. Eighty-three percent believe it cannot. Under NCLB, whether a school is in need of improvement is determined solely by the percentage of students whose test scores meet the goal in English and math. (See Table 10.)
- Only 26% believe it is possible to accurately judge a student's proficiency in English and math on the basis of a single test. Seventy-two percent believe it is not possible. NCLB uses a state test given annually to determine student proficiency in English and math and then judges the school according to the percentage meeting the standard. (See Table 11.)
- Eighty percent are concerned either a great deal or a fair amount that relying only on testing in English and math to judge a school will mean less emphasis on art, music, history, and other subjects. NCLB relies only on English and math scores to judge a school. (See Table 12.)
- When offered two options for dealing with a school in need of improvement, 74% of respondents select making additional efforts to help students achieve in their present school, while 25% choose offering students the opportunity to transfer to a school not in need of improvement. NCLB does not rule out efforts to help students in their current school, but it mandates that the choice of a transfer be offered. (See Table 13.)

- Sixty-seven percent believe special education students should not be required to meet the same standards as other students. NCLB requires that the percentage of special education students showing proficiency must be the same as the percentage required for the total school and for all subgroups. (See Table 14.)
- Sixty-six percent believe the emphasis of NCLB on standardized testing will encourage teachers to teach to the tests, and 60% believe this would be a bad thing. NCLB mandates testing in grades 3 through 8 and in at least one high school grade. (See Tables 15 and 16.)

4. The public is concerned about getting and keeping good teachers, thinks teacher salaries are too low, and is willing to see higher salaries paid to teachers teaching in more challenging situations. Sixty-one percent say schools in their communities have trouble getting good teachers, and 66% say they have trouble keeping good teachers. Fifty-nine percent say teacher salaries are too low, and 65% believe higher salaries should be paid as an incentive for teaching in schools determined to be in need of improvement. (See Tables 19 through 22.)

5. The public continues to believe that closing the achievement gap between white students and black and Hispanic students is important but blames the gap on factors unrelated to the quality of schooling. Ninety percent believe closing the gap is either very important or somewhat important. The number attributing the gap to the quality of schooling dropped from 29% a year ago to 16% in 2003. In identifying factors that are either very important or somewhat important in creating the gap, 97% point to home life and upbringing; 97%, to the amount of parent involvement; 95%, to student interest or the lack thereof; and 94%, to community environment. (See Tables 23, 24, and 26.)

6. The public is not convinced that narrowing the achievement gap requires spending more money on low-achieving students. While divided on this matter, the public leans in the direction of spending the same dollars on each student. When asked whether the dollars spent on each student should be the same or should vary on the basis of student needs, 52% said the same, while 45% said the dollars spent should vary. And 58% of Americans believe that it is possible to narrow the achievement gap without spending more money on low-achieving students. (See Tables 25 and 38.)

7. A majority of respondents are opposed to vouchers and would oppose having their state adopt them, despite the 2002 U.S. Supreme Court decision stating that voucher plans do not violate the U.S. Constitution. The number of Americans in favor of allowing private school attendance at public expense fell to 38% this year, compared to 46% a year ago. The number opposed climbed from 52% to 60%. When reminded of the Supreme Court decision permitting such plans, 56% expressed opposition to having legislation enacted in their state that would permit private school attendance at public expense. (See Tables 28 and 29.)

Additional Findings and Conclusions

• Respondents regard funding as the biggest problem schools in their communities must face. Twenty-five percent mentioned funding, followed by 16% who mentioned discipline and 14% who mentioned overcrowded schools. (See Table 35.)

• The public is divided on whether parents in the community would have enough information to choose another school for their children to attend, as NCLB allows if their current school is identified as needing improvement. (See Table 17.)

• A slight majority of parents, 52%, would want a child of theirs who was failing in school to be tutored in his or her own school, not by an outside tutor as NCLB provides. (See Table 18.)

• Adequate Yearly Progress (AYP) is the standard used by NCLB to determine whether a school is in need of improvement. It is based on the percentage of students showing proficiency in English and math. Questions in the poll designed to measure the public's expectations regarding the annual determination of AYP that NCLB requires the state to make for each school provide interesting information but shed little light on such expectations. The collective responses to the two questions would, however, seem to call into question NCLB's goal of having every student demonstrate proficiency by 2013-14. (See Tables 36 and 37.)

• The public is evenly divided regarding the extent to which providing vouchers would improve achievement in schools in the community, with 48% of respondents saying achievement would improve and 48% saying it would get worse. Fifty-four percent believe achievement would improve for students using vouchers to go to private schools, and 59% believe achievement for students staying in the public schools would remain the same. (See Tables 30 through 32.)

• Given a full-tuition voucher, 62% of respondents would choose a private school for their child, while 35% would choose a public school. The choices change if the value of the voucher drops to half the cost of tuition, with 47% choosing a public school. (See Tables 33 and 34.)

• The public identifies factors unrelated to schooling as the causes of the achievement gap in which Asian students generally outperform their white peers. There is, in fact, little difference between the factors the public believes to be responsible for this "reverse gap" and those it believes to be responsible for the gap between whites and other minorities. (See Table 27.)

• The public attributes the failure of some students to learn to factors related to life outside the school and to lack of student interest, along with the school-related factors of lack of discipline and the quality of teaching. (See Table 39.)

• The public has little interest in the four-day school week as a means of cutting costs. (See Table 40.)

• And finally, respondents believe that the public will view schools that do not make AYP as "schools in need of improvement" and not as "failing schools." This is an interesting question that has been given added importance by the United States Department of Education. After routinely describing schools not making AYP as "failing schools" in the days immediately after the passage of NCLB, the department is currently stressing that such schools should be regarded simply as "schools in need of improvement." It will be interesting to see how the final arbiters, the media, deal with this issue. (See Table 41.)

Attitudes Regarding the Public Schools

Grading the Public Schools

The data regarding the grading of the public schools are summarized in Tables 1–3. Table 1 provides the grades for the schools in the community, Table 2 gives the grades for the nation's schools, and Table 3 reports parents' grades for the school their oldest child attends. The data show what they have shown every year, and the trend data displayed for every second year, starting in 1983, confirm the consistency of the public's grades. The public gives the schools high marks, and the grades improve the closer people are to the schools. That 68% of the parents give the public school their oldest child attends an A or a B is a truly remarkable approval rating for any institution. Moreover, the grades have remained remarkably steady through the years. In an interesting bit of data not in the tables, 30% of nonwhites, 18% below the total, give the community schools an A or a B. It seems reasonable to infer that this difference grows out of the achievement gap between whites and nonwhites.

TABLE 1. Students are often given the grades of A, B, C, D, and FAIL to denote the quality of their work. Suppose the public schools themselves, in your community, were graded in the same way. What grade would you give the public schools here—A, B, C, D, or FAIL?

	National Totals		No Children In School		Public School Parents	
	'03 %	'02 %	'03 %	'02 %	'03 %	'02 %
A & B	48	47	45	44	55	58
A	11	10	8	9	17	16
B	37	37	37	35	38	42
C	31	34	30	35	31	30
D	10	10	10	10	10	8
FAIL	5	3	7	3	3	3
Don't Know	6	6	8	8	1	1

Trend Data: Grades for Community Schools (National Totals)

	2003 %	2001 %	1999 %	1997 %	1995 %	1993 %	1991 %	1989 %	1987 %	1985 %	1983 %
A & B	48	51	49	46	41	47	42	43	43	43	31
A	11	11	11	10	8	10	10	8	12	9	6
B	37	40	38	36	33	37	32	35	31	34	25
C	31	30	31	32	37	31	33	33	30	30	32
D	10	8	9	11	12	11	10	11	9	10	13
FAIL	5	5	5	6	5	4	5	4	4	4	7
Don't know	6	6	6	5	5	7	10	9	14	13	17

TABLE 2. How about the public schools in the nation as a whole? What grade would you give the public schools nationally—A, B, C, D, or FAIL?

	National Totals		No Children In School		Public School Parents	
	'03 %	'02 %	'03 %	'02 %	'03 %	'02 %
A & B	26	24	26	25	26	20
A	2	2	1	1	5	2
B	24	22	25	24	21	18
C	52	47	52	46	49	51
D	12	13	11	13	13	11
FAIL	3	3	4	3	2	3
Don't know	7	13	7	13	10	15

TABLE 3. Using the A, B, C, D, FAIL scale again, what grade would you give the school your oldest child attends?

	Public School Parents	
	'03 %	'02 %
A & B	68	71
A	29	27
B	39	44
C	20	20
D	8	6
FAIL	4	2
Don't know	*	1

*Less than one-half of 1%.

Focus of School Improvement

This question was added in 1997 in an attempt to gauge public support for reform efforts originating outside the public schools. The responses consistently indicate that the public sees the existing public school system as the vehicle within which change should occur. The percentage of those expressing that opinion this year is up from last year and is the highest in five years.

TABLE 4. In order to improve public education in America, some people think the focus should be on reforming the existing public school system. Others believe the focus should be on finding an alternative to the existing public school system. Which approach do you think is preferable—reforming the existing public school system or finding an alternative to the existing public school system?

	National Totals					No Children In School					Public School Parents				
	'03 %	'02 %	'01 %	'00 %	'99 %	'03 %	'02 %	'01 %	'00 %	'99 %	'03 %	'02 %	'01 %	'00 %	'99 %
Reforming existing system	73	69	72	59	71	73	69	73	59	73	73	69	73	60	68
Finding alternative system	25	27	24	34	27	24	26	23	34	24	25	27	25	34	30
Don't know	2	4	4	7	2	3	5	4	7	3	2	4	2	6	2

No Child Left Behind Act

The Information People Have About NCLB

The summary at the beginning of this report indicated that people know very little about the NCLB Act, an extension of the Elementary and Secondary Education Act first passed in 1965. That conclusion is based on the two tables that follow. Table 5 shows that only 24% of the respondents said they know a great deal or a fair amount about NCLB. This contrasts with the 76% who said they know very little or nothing at all about it. A second question, presented in Table 6, asked whether the respondents' opinion of NCLB is favorable or unfavorable. Sixty-nine percent said that they did not know enough to say. As Table 5 shows, public school parents, the group most directly affected, felt themselves to be no more knowledgeable than any other group.

TABLE 5. Now, here are a few questions about the No Child Left Behind Act. How much, if anything, would you say you know about the No Child Left Behind Act—the federal education bill that was passed by Congress in 2001—a great deal, a fair amount, very little, or nothing at all?

	National Totals %	No Children In School %	Public School Parents %
A great deal plus a fair amount	24	25	22
A great deal	6	5	7
A fair amount	18	20	15
Very little	40	37	44
Nothing at all	36	38	34
Don't know	*	*	*

*Less than one-half of 1%.

TABLE 6. From what you know or have heard or read about the No Child Left Behind Act, do you have a very favorable, somewhat favorable, somewhat unfavorable, or very unfavorable opinion of the act—or don't you know enough about it to say?

	National Totals %	No Children In School %	Public School Parents %
Very favorable plus somewhat favorable	18	17	20
Very favorable	5	4	7
Somewhat favorable	13	13	13
Somewhat unfavorable	7	7	6
Very unfavorable	6	6	6
Don't know enough to say	69	69	68
Don't know	*	1	*

*Less than one-half of 1%.

The Strategies Used in NCLB

The public shows little support for the strategies that are an integral part of NCLB as it is being implemented. The tables in this section provide the documentation for the nine statements in the opening summary.

Statement 1. The public believes decisions regarding what is taught in the public schools should be made at the local level.

TABLE 7. In your opinion, who should have the greatest influence in deciding what is taught in the public schools here—the federal government, the state government, or the local school board?

	National Totals %	No Children In School %	Public School Parents %
Federal government	15	15	18
State government	22	22	21
Local school board	61	61	59
Don't know	2	2	2

Statement 2. The public believes the job a school is doing should be measured on the basis of improvement shown by students.

TABLE 8. Under the NCLB Act, a school's performance is evaluated annually based on the performance of its students. In your opinion, which is the better way to judge the job a public school is doing?

	National Totals %	No Children In School %	Public School Parents %
Whether students meet a fixed standard	14	15	13
Whether students show reasonable improvement from where they started	84	84	86
Don't know	2	1	1

Statement 3. The public believes a single test cannot provide a fair picture of whether a school is in need of improvement.

TABLE 9. According to the NCLB Act, determining whether a public school is or is not in need of improvement will be based on the performance of its students on a single statewide test. In your opinion, will a single test provide a fair picture of whether or not a school needs improvement?

	National Totals %	No Children In School %	Public School Parents %
Yes, will provide a fair picture	32	32	31
No, will not provide a fair picture	66	67	66
Don't know	2	1	3

Statement 4. The public believes a test based on English and math alone cannot produce a fair picture of whether or not a school is in need of improvement.

TABLE 10. According to the NCLB Act, the statewide tests of students' performance will be devoted to English and math only. Do you think a test covering only English and math would provide a fair picture of whether a school in your community is or is not in need of improvement, or should the test be based on other subjects also?

	National Totals %	No Children In School %	Public School Parents %
Test covering only English and math would provide a fair picure of whether a school is in need of improvement	15	14	18
Test should be based on other subjects also	83	84	81
Don't know	2	2	1

Statement 5. The public does not believe it is possible to accurately judge a student's proficiency in English and math on the basis of a single test.

TABLE 11. In your opinion, is it possible or not possible to accurately judge a student's proficiency in English and math on the basis of a single test?

	National Totals %	No Children In School %	Public School Parents %
Yes, possible	26	27	22
No, not possible	72	71	77
Don't know	2	2	1

Statement 6. The public is concerned that relying on testing in English and math only to judge a school will mean less emphasis on art, music, history, and other subjects.

TABLE 12. How much, if at all, are you concerned that relying on testing for English and math only to judge a school's performance will mean less emphasis on art, music, history, and other subjects? Would you say you are concerned a great deal, a fair amount, not much, or not at all?

	National Totals %	No Children In School %	Public School Parents %
A great deal plus a fair amount	80	80	82
A great deal	40	38	45
A fair amount	40	42	37
Not much	14	13	15
Not at all	6	7	3
Don't know	*	*	*

*Less than one-half of 1%.

Statement 7. The public believes that making additional efforts to help students achieve in a school judged to be in need of improvement is preferable to allowing students to transfer to a school not in need of improvement.

TABLE 13. Assume you had a child attending a school identified as in need of improvement by the NCLB Act. Which would you prefer, to transfer your child to a school identified as NOT in need of improvement or to have additional efforts made in your child's present school to help him or her achieve?

	National Totals %	No Children In School %	Public School Parents %
To transfer child to school identified as not in need of improvement	25	24	25
To have additional efforts made in child's present school	74	75	74
Don't know	1	1	1

Statement 8. The public does not believe special education students should be required to meet the same standards as other students.

TABLE 14. In your opinion, should students enrolled in special education be required to meet the same standards as all other students in the school?

	National Totals %	No Children In School %	Public School Parents %
Yes, should	31	31	31
No, should not	67	66	68
Don't know	2	3	1

Statement 9. The public believes the emphasis of NCLB on standardized testing will encourage teachers to teach to the tests and regards that as a bad thing. (Two tables address this statement.)

TABLE 15. In your opinion, will the current emphasis on standardized tests encourage teachers to "teach to the tests," that is, concentrate on teaching their students to pass the tests rather than teaching the subject, or don't you think it will have this effect?

	National Totals %	No Children In School %	Public School Parents %
Will encourage teaching to the tests	66	64	68
Will not have this effect	30	32	27
Don't know	4	4	5

TABLE 16. If the current emphasis on results is encouraging teachers to "teach to the tests," do you think this will be a good thing or a bad thing?

	National Totals %	No Children In School %	Public School Parents %
Good thing	39	38	40
Bad thing	60	61	58
Don't know	1	1	2

Other Questions Directly Related to NCLB

Two other questions in this poll related directly to NCLB are reported in Tables 17 and 18. The first sought to determine whether parents in the community would have the information needed to select a school not in need of improvement if given that choice. Public opinion is evenly divided. The second question involves an NCLB strategy in which parents with a child in a school in need of improvement can choose to have their child tutored by an outside provider selected from a list of providers approved by the state. This choice is limited to students who qualify under Title I's poverty standards. Fifty-two percent of the respondents say they would prefer to have the tutoring provided by teachers in the child's school.

TABLE 17. The NCLB Act allows parents of a child in a public school identified as in need of improvement to select another school in the same school district that is identified as NOT in need of improvement. Just your impression, would parents in your community have enough information about the local schools to be able to select a school that is not in need of improvement?

	National Totals %	No Children In School %	Public School Parents %
Yes, have enough information	47	46	48
No, do not have enough	49	49	50
Don't know	4	5	2

TABLE 18. Now, let's assume that your child was failing in his or her school. Which kind of tutoring would you prefer—tutoring provided by teachers in your child's school or tutoring provided by an outside agency that you would select from a state-approved list?

	National Totals %	No Children In School %	Public School Parents %
Tutoring provided by teachers in child's school	52	52	54
Tutoring provided by outside agency	45	46	42
Don't know	3	2	4

The Importance of Good Teaching

Getting and Keeping Good Teachers

NCLB requires that every classroom be staffed by a highly qualified teacher by the beginning of the 2005–06 school year. A highly qualified teacher is defined as a fully certified teacher, licensed in the subject area in which he or she is teaching.

The poll did not ask the public's opinion regarding this requirement and whether it could be met; however, it did ask a number of questions designed to determine the extent to which getting and keeping good teachers is a problem. The public believes that getting good teachers and keeping them are both problems for local schools. Nonwhites are even stronger in these beliefs, with 75% saying it is hard to get good teachers and 87% saying the same for keeping them. Looking back, we find that these same two questions were asked in the first poll in this series, in 1969, with 52% saying they felt local schools had a hard time getting good teachers and 48% saying they had a hard time keeping them.

TABLE 19. Do you think your local public school system has a hard time GETTING good teachers?

	National Totals %	No Children In School %	Public School Parents %
Yes, has hard time	61	60	62
No, does not	37	36	38
Don't know	2	4	*

*Less than one-half of 1%.

TABLE 20. Do you think your local public school system has a hard time KEEPING good teachers?

	National Totals %	No Children In School %	Public School Parents %
Yes, has hard time	66	65	68
No, does not	31	32	31
Don't know	3	3	1

Salaries Paid to Teachers

Salary is an obvious factor in attracting people to a particular job. Fifty-nine percent of respondents to this year's poll believe that the salaries paid teachers are too low. The trend data in Table 21 indicate that this is an area where public opinion has changed over the years. Thirty-three percent believed salaries were too low in 1969, and this figure changed little through 1985. However, the percentage then climbed to 50% by 1990 and has increased nine points since that time. This is almost certainly a reflection of the growing belief that high-quality teaching is the key to student achievement. This conclusion is reinforced by the data in Table 22, which show that 65% of respondents say that teachers should be paid even higher salaries for agreeing to teach in a school designated as in need of improvement.

TABLE 21. Do you think salaries for teachers in this community are too high, too low, or just about right?

	National Totals %	No Children In School %	Public School Parents %
Too high	6	6	6
Too low	59	58	60
Just about right	33	34	32
Don't know	2	2	2

Trend Data: Teacher Salaries, 1969 to 2003 (National Totals)

	'03 %	'90 %	'85 %	'84 %	'83 %	'81 %	'69 %
Too high	6	5	6	7	8	10	2
Too low	59	50	33	37	35	29	33
Just about right	33	31	43	41	31	41	43
Don't know	2	14	18	15	26	20	22

TABLE 22. In your opinion, should teachers be paid higher salaries as an incentive to teach in schools which have been identified as in need of improvement or not?

	National Totals %	No Children In School %	Public School Parents %
Yes, should	65	64	67
No, should not	33	34	32
Don't know	2	2	1

The Achievement Gap

Closing the Achievement Gap

Previous polls have made it clear that the public understands that there is a gap between the achievement of white students and that of Hispanic and black students.

This poll sought to probe further by exploring both the closing of the gap and the factors that the public believes cause it to exist. Tables 23–25 deal with the importance of closing the gap and the extent to which the public sees funding as a factor in achieving that goal. The public has been clear and consistent regarding the importance of closing the gap since this question was first asked in 2001. This year, 71% of respondents say that it is very important to close the gap, and an additional 19% say it is somewhat important. This response is uniform across all demographic groups. The responses in Table 24 indicate that the public continues to attribute the gap to factors other than schooling. Eighty percent indicate that this is the case, while only 16% cite the quality of schooling. Nonwhites differ somewhat, with 33% designating the quality of schooling as related to the achievement gap. This response has also been consistent over the three years, although the 16% this year is actually down 13 points from a year ago. The data in Table 25 indicate that the public believes the gap can be narrowed without spending more money to help low-achieving students. Fifty-eight percent indicate that this is the case, while 39% say additional funding for these students is essential.

TABLE 23. There is a recognized academic achievement gap between white students and black and Hispanic students, with white students consistently outperforming black and Hispanic students. How important do you think it is to close this gap—very important, somewhat important, not too important, or not important at all?

	National Totals			No Children In School			Public School Parents		
	'03 %	'02 %	'01 %	'03 %	'02 %	'01 %	'03 %	'02 %	'01 %
Very plus somewhat important	90	94	88	91	93	89	88	96	87
Very important	71	80	66	70	80	66	73	80	67
Somewhat important	19	14	22	21	13	23	15	16	20
Not too important	5	2	5	5	2	5	4	2	5
Not important at all	4	3	5	3	4	4	7	1	6
Don't know	1	1	2	1	1	2	1	1	2

TABLE 24. In your opinion, is the achievement gap between white students and black and Hispanic students mostly related to the quality of schooling received or mostly related to other factors?

	National Totals			No Children In School			Public School Parents		
	'03 %	'02 %	'01 %	'03 %	'02 %	'01 %	'03 %	'02 %	'01 %
Mostly related to quality of schooling	16	29	21	15	31	20	18	22	22
Mostly related to other factors	80	66	73	80	64	72	80	75	74
Don't know	4	5	6	5	5	8	2	3	4

TABLE 25. Do you think it is possible or not possible to narrow the achievement gap between white students and black and Hispanic students without spending more money than is currently being spent to help low-achieving students?

	National Totals %	No Children In School %	Public School Parents %
Yes, possible	58	56	62
No, not possible	39	41	36
Don't know	3	3	2

Factors Contributing to the Achievement Gap

The 2002 poll sought to find the factors that people think contribute to the achievement gap. Five factors were identified, and these were used in this year's poll to determine the importance assigned to each factor. The responses appear in Table 26. Table 27 uses the same factors but applies them to the achievement gap that exists between white students and Asian students, a gap in which the Asians come out ahead. With percentages ranging from 94% to 97%, the public identifies factors relating to parent involvement, home life, student interest, and community environment as very or somewhat important in explaining the gap between white students and black and Hispanic students. Regarding the reverse gap involving Asians and whites, the public places the same four factors at the top, with percentages ranging from 82% to 97%. Amount of family income is at the bottom in both cases. This is somewhat surprising given the demonstrated link between family income and test scores.

TABLE 26. In your opinion, how important do you think each of the following factors is in contributing to the achievement gap between white children and black and Hispanic children—very important, somewhat important, not very important, or not at all important?

	Very Plus Somewhat Important %	Very Important %	Somewhat Important %	Not Very Important %	Not at All Important %	Don't Know %
Amount of parent involvment	97	90	7	2	1	*
Home life and upbringing	97	87	10	2	1	*
Interest on the part of the student	95	80	15	3	1	1
Community environment	94	66	28	4	1	1
Racial bias	71	42	29	17	9	3
Amount of family income	66	26	40	23	10	1

*Less than one-half of 1%.

TABLE 27. There is also a recognized academic achievement gap between Asian students and white students, with Asian students consistently outperforming white students. How important do you think each of the following factors is in explaining this gap—very important, somewhat important, not too important, or not important at all?

	Very Plus Somewhat Important %	Very Important %	Somewhat Important %	Not Very Important %	Not at All Important %	Don't Know %
Amount of parent involvment	95	83	12	2	2	1
Home life and upbringing	93	80	13	4	2	1
Interest on the part of the student	97	85	12	2	1	*
Community environment	82	49	33	13	4	1
Racial bias	57	30	27	24	17	2
Amount of family income	52	17	35	33	14	1

*Less than one-half of 1%.

Choice, Public and Private

Choosing a Private School to Attend at Public Expense

This year's poll included two questions dealing with the public's view of using public funds to finance attendance at private schools. The first is the trend question that has been asked in each year since 1995. A quick review of the trend line will show that support was reasonably stable in the late 1990s and has moved up and down since 2000 (Table 28). This year, support drops by eight points from last year, to 38%. The difference between the two political parties is evident here, with 48% of Republicans and 31% of Democrats in favor. The second question (Table 29) was asked specifically with regard to the Supreme Court decision last year that opened the door to the passage of voucher programs at the state level. Fifty-six percent of respondents indicate they would oppose this option in their state. Once again, the parties differ, with 53% of Republicans in favor, versus 31% of Democrats.

TABLE 28. Do you favor or oppose allowing students and parents to choose a private school to attend at public expense?

National Totals

	'03 %	'02 %	'01 %	'00 %	'99 %	'98 %	'97 %	'96 %
Favor	38	46	34	39	41	44	44	36
Oppose	60	52	62	56	55	50	52	61
Don't know	2	2	4	5	4	6	4	3

TABLE 29. Last year's Supreme Court decision says that the U.S. Constitution does not prevent a state from offering vouchers that parents can use to send their students to private schools at public expense. Do you favor or oppose your state making such vouchers available?

	National Totals %	No Children In School %	Public School Parents %
Favor	42	39	46
Oppose	56	60	52
Don't know	2	1	2

The Effect of Vouchers on Achievement

Those who propose vouchers argue that they would produce improved student achievement for the schools to which students move and for the public schools. The theory regarding the latter is that public schools would fear the loss of students and would take steps to improve. Table 30 reports results of a question designed to measure the public's view of the overall impact of vouchers on schools in the community. The public is divided on the question, with 48% saying achievement would improve and an equal percentage saying it would get worse. Republicans are significantly more likely than Democrats to say that overall achievement would improve, by a margin of 55% to 41%. Tables 31 and 32 deal with the effect on those who move to private schools and those who stay in the public schools. Fifty-four percent believe achievement would improve for those going to private schools, as compared to 26% who believe achievement would improve for those remaining in public schools. The 54% is down 11 points since 1997, while the 26% figure is an increase of nine points. Republicans are significantly more likely than Democrats to say that the achievement of those who move to private schools would improve (65% to 46%).

TABLE 30. In your opinion, would vouchers that allow parents to choose private schools improve student achievement in your community, overall, or not?

	National Totals %	No Children In School %	Public School Parents %
Improve	48	47	47
Would not improve	48	48	50
Don't know	4	5	3

TABLE 31. How about the students who used the vouchers to move to private schools. Do you think their academic achievement would improve, get worse, or remain the same?

	National Totals		No Children In School		Public School Parents	
	'03 %	'97 %	'03 %	'97 %	'03 %	'97 %
Improve	54	65	52	68	56	58
Get worse	4	4	4	4	4	4
Remain the same	37	28	40	25	35	35
Don't know	5	3	4	3	5	3

TABLE 32. How about the students who remain in the public schools. Do you think their academic achievement would improve, get worse, or remain the same?

	National Totals		No Children In School		Public School Parents	
	'03 %	'97 %	'03 %	'97 %	'03 %	'97 %
Improve	26	17	24	16	29	19
Get worse	12	11	13	11	10	11
Remain the same	59	70	60	70	57	68
Don't know	3	2	3	3	4	2

Choices the Public Might Make

Two final questions related to vouchers sought to determine the choices parents might make if given full-tuition vouchers to the school of their choice or half-tuition vouchers. The data in Table 33 indicate that, with full tuition available, 38% of respondents would choose a church-related private school, and 24% would choose a private school with no church affiliation. These percentages change significantly if the voucher covers only half the tuition, with 47% choosing to remain in the public schools (Table 34). It is interesting that, on the full-voucher question, 45% of Democrats would select a public school, as compared to 28% of Republicans.

TABLE 33. Suppose you had a school-age child and were given a voucher covering full tuition that would permit you to send that child to any public, private, or church-related school of your choice. Which kind of school do you think you would choose?

	National Totals %	No Children In School %	Public School Parents %
A public school	35	35	39
A church-related private school	38	37	38
A non-church-related private school	24	25	21
Don't know	3	3	2

TABLE 34. What if the voucher covered only half of the tuition, which do you think you would choose?

	National Totals %	No Children In School %	Public School Parents %
A public school	47	45	55
A church-related private school	34	34	29
A non-church-related private school	17	19	15
Don't know	2	2	1

Problems Facing the Public Schools

The one question that has been asked in each of the 35 polls conducted since 1969 deals with the problems

schools in the community face. It is a unique question in that it is often the only one for which those polled generate their own responses. This being the case, the percentage of mentions for any single problem is relatively low. Discipline was at the top of the list for 16 of the first 17 polls in this series. Drugs moved to the top of the list in 1986 and remained there for six years. Finance tied for the top in 2001 and took that position for itself in 2002. It solidifies that position this year with mentions by 25% of the respondents. Discipline is second with mentions by 16%, and overcrowded schools is third at 14%. No other problem attracts double-digit support. The once-dominant problem of drugs attracts only 9% of mentions, and fighting/violence/gangs is near the bottom with just 4%.

TABLE 35. What do you think are the biggest problems that the public schools of your community must deal with?

	National Totals			No Children In School			Public School Parents		
	'03 %	'02 %	'01 %	'03 %	'02 %	'01 %	'03 %	'02 %	'01 %
Lack of financial support/ funding/money	25	23	15	26	23	15	24	23	17
Lack of discipline, more control	16	17	15	17	18	17	13	13	10
Overcrowded schools	14	17	10	12	14	7	16	23	15
Use of drugs/dope	9	13	9	10	14	9	7	11	10
Difficulty getting good teachers/quality teachers	5	8	6	5	8	6	5	8	6
Standards/quality/basics	4	*	*	5	*	*	2	*	*
Fighting/violence/gangs	4	9	10	3	9	11	5	9	9
Low pay for teachers	4	*	*	4	*	*	3	*	*

*Less than one-half of 1%.

Public Expectations

Two questions were asked in this year's poll in an effort to gain some indication of the public's expectations regarding both school and student performance. Table 36 reports the opinion of respondents with regard to the number of schools not performing at an acceptable level in their state. Thirty-one percent place this number between 50% and 60%, and another 19% place it between 40% and 50%. These percentages seem high, given the grades the public assigns the schools. However, this question dealt with schools in the state, while the grading of the schools is based on those in the community. Table 37 reports the public's estimates regarding the percentage of students who would demonstrate proficiency on an English and math test based on high standards. Sixty-seven percent place the number above 60%. This question was focused on schools in the community, and that may well account for results that appear more positive.

TABLE 36. Forgetting the NCLB requirements for a moment, in your opinion, what percentage of the students in your state would you say are not performing at an acceptable level?

	National Totals %	No Children In School %	Public School Parents %
50% to 60%	31	28	35
40% to 50%	19	20	18
30% to 40%	21	20	21
20% to 30%	12	11	13
Below 20%	10	11	8
Don't know	7	10	5

TABLE 37. Just your best guess, what percentage of students in a public school in your community would you expect to pass an English and math test, assuming it was based on high standards?

	National Totals %	No Children In School %	Public School Parents %
Above 80%	20	20	21
Above 70%	26	26	25
Above 60%	21	20	22
Above 50%	17	18	14
Below 50%	15	14	18
Don't know	1	2	*

*Less than one-half of 1%.

Miscellaneous Questions

There are always a few questions that do not seem to fit into any category. Tables 38–41 report on such questions. The first deals with the funding of the public schools. For many years, equity was the goal in school funding, and that meant providing the same number of dollars for each student regardless of where he or she lived or family income levels. That concept is now challenged by the idea of adequacy, which means providing varying amounts of dollars based on a student's educational needs. Fifty-two percent of respondents say the dollars should be the same, while 45% would vary them (Table 38). The second question explores reasons why some students do not learn. The results are similar to those explaining the achievement gap, with lack of home and parental support and lack of student interest at the top. However, two factors related to schooling come into play, with 84% believing lack of discipline contributes either a great deal or a fair amount and 81% saying the same for the quality of teaching (Table 39). The third question asks about the four-day school week as a means of reacting to the funding shortage. Seventy-four percent of respondents reject this alternative (Table 40). Finally, a question was asked about how schools that do not meet NCLB standards will be described. Sixty-five percent of respondents say such schools will be described as "in

need of improvement," while 32% say they will be described as "failing" (Table 41).

TABLE 38. In your opinion, which is the better way for your state to fund the public schools—provide equal dollars per student or vary the number of dollars to meet each student's educational needs?

	National Totals %	No Children In School %	Public School Parents %
Provide equal dollars per student	52	53	50
Vary the number of dollars	45	44	49
Don't know	3	3	1

TABLE 39. I am going to read a list of reasons that have been suggested as to why students fail to learn. As I read each reason, would you tell me how much you think it contributes to learning failures in the public schools in your community—a great deal, a fair amount, not very much, or not at all?

	Great Deal Plus Fair Amount %	Great Deal %	Fair Amount %	Not Very Much %	Not at All %	Don't Know %
Lack of home or parental support	93	74	19	5	1	1
Lack of interest by the students themselves	90	60	30	8	1	1
Lack of discipline in the schools	84	60	24	10	5	1
Lack of good teaching	81	47	34	13	6	*
Lack of funding	78	45	33	14	7	1
Lack of community emphasis on education	78	43	35	15	6	1

*Less than one-half of 1%.

TABLE 40. As a means of saving money, some states are considering a four-day week consisting of longer school days. Would you favor or oppose such a plan in the public schools in your community?

	National Totals %	No Children In School %	Public School Parents %
Favor	25	24	27
Oppose	74	74	72
Don't know	1	2	1

TABLE 41. In your opinion, which one of the following descriptions do you feel will be usually applied to schools that do not meet the standards of the NCLB Act?

	National Totals %	No Children In School %	Public School Parents %
The school is in need of improvement	65	68	61
The school is failing	32	29	37
Don't know	3	3	2

Closing Statement

This poll reports public opinion on issues that are of major importance to decisions made every day regarding the public schools. The poll's authors believe that the findings accurately reflect the opinions expressed by those responding to the poll. The format is, however, carefully structured to allow the reader to make his or her own judgment on that question. It should be remembered that opinion does not necessarily reflect fact. Opinion is a snapshot of public attitudes at a particular point in time. While the matter may be open to question, the authors do not believe that public opinion should drive the policy and administrative decisions that govern the operation of the public schools. They do, however, recognize that those who ignore public opinion do so at their own peril. The wise course, when public support is missing, is to take time to build the support that will be essential to ultimate success.

Research Procedure

The Sample. The sample used in this survey embraced a total of 1,011 adults (18 years of age and older). A description of the sample and methodology can be found at the end of this report.

Time of Interviewing. The fieldwork for this study was conducted during the period of 28 May to 18 June 2003.

Due allowance must be made for statistical variation, especially in the case of findings for groups consisting of relatively few respondents.

The findings of this report apply only to the U.S. as a whole and not to individual communities. Local surveys, using the same questions, can be conducted to determine how local areas compare with the national norm.

Sampling Tolerances

In interpreting survey results, it should be borne in mind that all sample surveys are subject to sampling error, i.e., the extent to which the results may differ from what would be obtained if the whole population surveyed had been interviewed. The size of such sampling error depends largely on the number of interviews. For details and tables showing the confidence intervals for the data cited in this poll, please visit the Phi Delta Kappa website at http://www.pdkintl.org/kappan/kpoll0209 sample.htm.

Design Of The Sample

For the 2003 survey the Gallup Organization used its standard national telephone sample, i.e., an unclustered, directory-assisted, random-digit telephone sample, based on a proportionate stratified sampling design.

The random-digit aspect of the sample was used to avoid "listing" bias. Numerous studies have shown that households with unlisted telephone numbers are differ-

ent in important ways from listed households. "Unlistedness" is due to household mobility or to customer requests to prevent publication of the telephone number.

To avoid this source of bias, a random-digit procedure designed to provide representation of both listed and unlisted (including not-yet-listed) numbers was used.

Telephone numbers for the continental United States were stratified into four regions of the country and, within each region, further stratified into three size-of-community strata.

Only working banks of telephone numbers were selected. Eliminating non-working banks from the sample increased the likelihood that any sample telephone number would be associated with a residence.

The sample of telephone numbers produced by the described method is representative of all telephone households within the continental United States.

Within each contacted household, an interview was sought with the household member who had the most recent birthday. This frequently used method of respondent selection provides an excellent approximation of statistical randomness in that it gives all members of the household an opportunity to be selected.

Up to three calls were made to each selected telephone number to complete an interview. The time of day and the day of the week for callbacks were varied so as to maximize the chances of finding a respondent at home. All interviews were conducted on weekends or weekday evenings in order to contact potential respondents among the working population.

The final sample was weighted so that the distribution of the sample matched current estimates derived from the U.S. Census Bureau's Current Population Survey (CPS) for the adult population living in telephone households in the continental U.S.

Composition of the Sample

Adults	%	Education	
No children in school	65	Total college	58
Public school parents	32	College graduate	24
Nonpublic school parents	3	College incomplete	34
		Total high school	42
		High school graduate	33
		High school incomplete	9
Gender	**%**	**Income**	
Men	47	$50,000 and over	39
Women	53	$40,000–$49,000	12
		$30,000–$39,000	13
		$20,000–$29,000	13
		Under $20,000	17
		Undesignated	6
Race			
White	83		
Nonwhite	15		
Black	11		
Undesignated	1	**Region**	
		East	23
		Midwest	24
		South	31
		West	22
Age			
18–29 years	20		
30–49 years	41		
50 and over	38		
Undesignated	1	**Community Size**	
		Urban	25
		Suburban	51
		Rural	24

POLICY IMPLICATIONS
Of the 35th Annual Phi Delta Kappa/Gallup Poll

These four pages highlight the poll findings that have particularly strong implications for those making decisions regarding the public schools.

Grading the Public Schools

Findings and Implications: *The public has high regard for the public schools, wants needed improvement to come through those schools, and has little interest in seeking alternatives. Given this understanding, the quickest and best way to improve student achievement is to focus efforts on the existing public schools.*

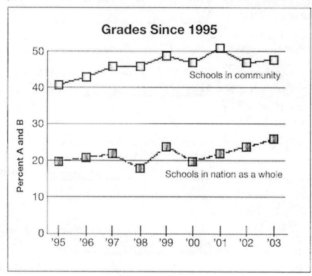

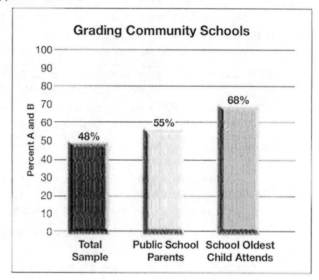

To improve schools in America:

Reform the existing public school system	73%
Find an alternative to the existing public school system	25%

No Child Left Behind (NCLB)

Findings and Implications: *The public sees itself as uninformed on NCLB, with more than two-thirds saying they lack the information to decide whether their view is favorable or unfavorable. The public will formulate its opinion of NCLB as it becomes more familiar with the law itself and with the results it produces. The impact on schools in the local community will be a key factor.*

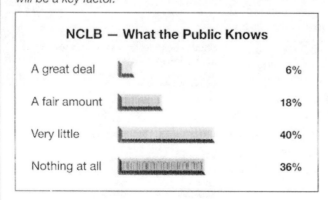

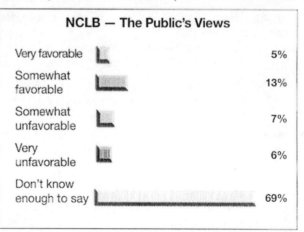

No Child Left Behind — A Look Ahead

Findings and Implications: *Responses to questions related to strategies associated with NCLB suggest that greater familiarity with the law is unlikely to lead to greater public support. The public will be even more resistant if there is a discrepancy between the government's judgment and the community's perception of the local schools.*

NCLB strategy: Have the federal government directly involved in determining the curricular emphasis, the testing program, and other means of assessment at the state and local levels.

Public view: Asked which level of government should exercise the greatest influence on what should be taught in the local schools, the public selects the local school board.

Greatest influence on local schools

Federal government: 15%

State government: 22%

Local school board: 61%

NCLB strategy: Judge a school by whether a fixed percentage of the overall student group and of each subgroup passes a standardized test.

Public view: Eighty-four percent say a school should be judged by the improvement shown by students, measured from the point at which they start.

Schools should be judged on improvement

84%

NCLB strategy: Determine whether a school is in need of improvement using a single standardized test given annually.

Public view: Sixty-six percent believe a single test will not provide a fair picture of whether a school needs improvement.

Single test does not show a fair picture

66%

NCLB strategy: Base the determination as to whether a school is in need of improvement on standardized testing in English and math only.

Public view: Eighty-three percent say the determination as to whether a school is in need of improvement should include other subjects in addition to English and math.

Include other subjects in addition to math and English

83%

NCLB strategy: Judge each student's proficiency in English and math using a single test given annually.

Public view: Seventy-two percent say it is not possible to judge a student's proficiency in English and math based on the results of a single test.

Proficiency can't be judged by a single test

72%

NCLB strategy: Judge a school's performance based on test results in English and math.

Public view: Forty percent say they are concerned a great deal that judging a school's performance on English and math only will mean less emphasis on art, music, history, and other subjects. Forty percent say they have a fair amount of concern, bringing the total expressing concern to 80%.

Concerned about lack of emphasis on other subjects

Great deal (40%) Fair amount (40%)

80%

NCLB strategy: Offer parents in a school designated as in need of improvement the option of transferring their student to a school not in need of improvement.

Public view: Given the option of transferring a student out of the school or having additional efforts made to help the student in the present school, 74% say that, if they had a student in a school in need of improvement, they would opt for additional efforts to help the student in the school.

Prefer additional efforts to help students in the current school

74%

NCLB strategy: Judge the performance of special education students using the same fixed percentage of students passing as is required for all other students and groups.

Public view: Sixty-seven percent say special education students should not have to meet the same standard that is used for all other students.

Should be different standards for special education students

67%

NCLB strategy: Base the judgment of a school's performance on standardized test results.

Public view: Sixty-six percent say the emphasis on standardized tests will encourage teachers to teach to the test. Sixty percent say this will be a bad thing.

Encourages "teaching to the test"

66%

"Teaching to the test" is a bad thing

60%

Teachers and Teacher Salaries

Findings and Implications: *The public is concerned about getting and keeping good teachers, thinks teacher salaries are too low, and supports paying higher salaries to teachers who are teaching in more challenging situations. Programs carefully tailored to meet these concerns are likely to enjoy public support.*

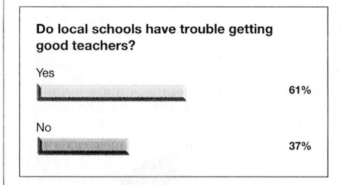

Do local schools have trouble getting good teachers?

Yes — 61%

No — 37%

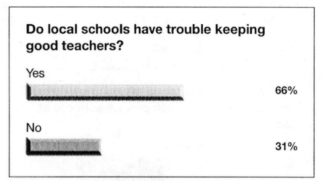

Do local schools have trouble keeping good teachers?

Yes — 66%

No — 31%

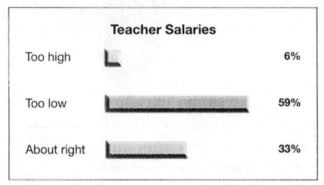

Teacher Salaries

Too high — 6%

Too low — 59%

About right — 33%

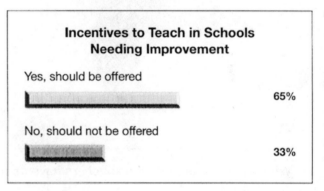

Incentives to Teach in Schools Needing Improvement

Yes, should be offered — 65%

No, should not be offered — 33%

The Achievement Gap

Findings and Implications: *The public believes closing the achievement gap is important, does not attribute the gap to the quality of schooling received, and believes it can be narrowed without additional funding. Given the public's preference for seeing improvement come through the existing public schools, the findings suggest strongly that closing the gap should be a collective effort involving the public schools and all those responsible for child rearing and development.*

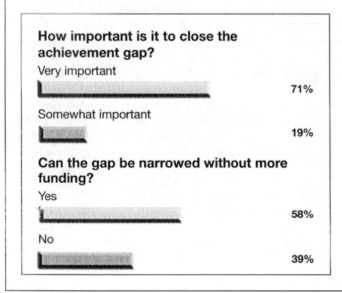

How important is it to close the achievement gap?

Very important — 71%

Somewhat important — 19%

Can the gap be narrowed without more funding?

Yes — 58%

No — 39%

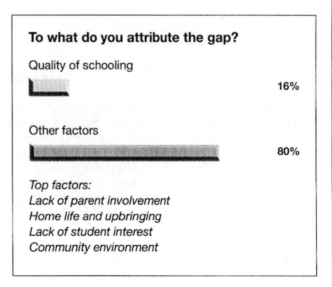

To what do you attribute the gap?

Quality of schooling — 16%

Other factors — 80%

Top factors:
Lack of parent involvement
Home life and upbringing
Lack of student interest
Community environment

Choice — Public and Private

Findings and Implications: *A majority of respondents are opposed to vouchers, would oppose having their state adopt vouchers despite the 2002 U.S. Supreme Court decision stating that voucher plans do not violate the U.S. Constitution, and offer mixed views on whether vouchers would improve student achievement in the community. Nothing in the poll results indicates that support for vouchers is increasing or that the level of support received any boost from the Supreme Court decision. Given the way support for vouchers has gone up and down in this poll in the last few years, it would be a mistake to make too much of the fact that support for permitting students and parents to choose private schools to attend at public expense dropped by 8% in this poll.*

Do you favor or oppose allowing students and parents to choose private schools at public expense?

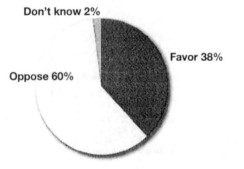

Don't know 2%
Favor 38%
Oppose 60%

Do you favor or oppose the voucher program the Supreme Court says is permissible under the U.S. Constitution?

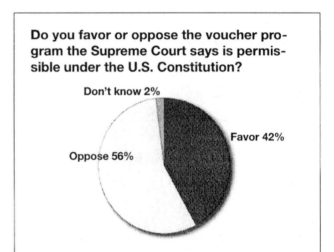

Don't know 2%
Favor 42%
Oppose 56%

What effect would offering vouchers have on student achievement in the community?

	Community Overall %
Improve	48
Not Improve	48

	Those Moving To Private Schools %	Those Staying In Public Schools %
Improve	54	26
Get worse	4	12
Stay the same	37	59

Concluding Statement

These are times of opportunity and challenge for the public schools. The opportunity springs from the growing awareness both inside and outside the education community of the importance of having each student move through the school experience and into adulthood armed with a high-quality education. The challenge lies in the lack of agreement on the best means for reaching that goal. Given these conditions, policy makers would do well to listen closely to what the public believes and what it is likely to support.

The poll results reported herein leave no doubt that the public wants improvement to come through the existing public school system. It is also clear that the public wants the emphasis to be on identifying those schools and students in need of improvement and then providing the help and assistance needed. NCLB offers real promise, with its focus on the need for every student to succeed in school, on the disaggregation of student test scores, and on accountability for results. The public has, however, identified the problems with NCLB. Those desiring to see NCLB's bright promise realized would be wise to hear and heed the public's message.

Conducting Your Own Poll

The Phi Delta Kappa Center for Professional Development and Services makes available PACE (Polling Attitudes of the Community on Education) materials to enable nonspecialists to conduct scientific polls of attitude and opinion on education. The PACE manual provides detailed information on constructing questionnaires, sampling, interviewing, and analyzing data. It also includes updated census figures and new material on conducting a telephone survey. The price is $60. For information about using PACE materials, write or phone Marcia Kazmierzak at Phi Delta Kappa International, P.O. Box 789, Bloomington, IN 47402-0789. Ph. 800/766-1156.

How To Order The Poll

The minimum order for reprints of the published version of the Phi Delta Kappa/Gallup education poll is 25 copies for $15. (Institutional purchase orders, cash, or MasterCard or VISA number required.) Additional copies are 50 cents each. This price includes postage for delivery (at the library rate). Where possible, enclose a check or money order. Address your order to Phi Delta Kappa International, P.O. Box 789, Bloomington, IN 47402-0789. Ph. 800/766-1156. If faster delivery is desired, phone the Shipping Department at the number listed below. Persons who wish to order the 309-page document that is the basis of this report should contact Phi Delta Kappa International, P.O. Box 789, Bloomington, IN 47402-0789. Ph. 800/766-1156. The price is $95, postage included.

UNIT 2

Rethinking and Changing the Educative Effort

Unit Selections

Key Points to Consider

- What are some issues in the debate regarding educational reform?

- Should the focus of educational reform be on changing the ways educators are prepared, on the changing needs of students, or on both of these concerns? Defend your answer.

- Compare American concepts about alternative schooling and the uses of public funds to the views of other countries on school choice issues.

 **Links: www.dushkin.com/online/**
These sites are annotated in the World Wide Web pages.

The Center for Innovation in Education
http://www.center.edu

Colorado Department of Education
http://www.cde.state.co.us/index_home.htm

National Council for Accreditation of Teacher Education
http://www.ncate.org

Phi Delta Kappa International
http://www.pdkintl.org

The dialogue regarding how to rethink and restructure the priorities of educational services is continuing; this is not surprising. There has been a similar dialogue in every generation of American history. Some of the debate centers on whether change and reform in education today should focus on restructuring how teachers are prepared or on research into the changing conditions of the lives of many American youth today and how to help them better meet the challenges in their lives.

The articles in this unit reflect a wide range of opinion about these concerns. Several new and exciting ideas are being proposed as to how we might reconceive the idea of *school* to encompass much more variety in school learning communities as well as to meet a broader range of the academic and social needs of today's youth.

American educators could have a much better sense of their own past as a profession, and the public could better understand the history of public education. In the United States, a fundamental cycle of similar ideas and practices reappears in school curricula every so many years. The decades of the 1970s and 1980s witnessed the rise of "behavioral objectives" and "management by objectives," and the 1990s brought us "outcome-based education" and "benchmarking" in educational discourse within the public school system's leadership. These are related behavioral concepts focusing on measurable ways to pinpoint and evaluate the results of educational efforts. Why do we seem to "reinvent the wheel" of educational thought and practice every so many decades? This is an important question worth addressing. Many of our ideas about change and reform in educational practice have been wrongheaded. There is a focus on more qualitative, as opposed to empirical, means of assessing the outcomes of our educative efforts; yet many state departments of education still insist on objective assessments and verifications of students' mastery of academic skills. How does this affect the development of imaginative teaching in schools? All of us in the education system are concerned, and many of us believe that there really are some new and generative ideas to help students learn basic intellectual skills and content.

Our current realities in the field of education reflect differing conceptions of how schooling ought to change. It is difficult to generalize regarding school quality across decades because of several factors; high schools, for instance, were more selective in 1900, when only 7 percent of American youths graduated from them. Today we encourage as many students as possible to graduate. The social purposes of schooling have been broadened; now we want all youths to complete some form of higher education.

We have to consider the social and ideological differences among those representing opposing school reform agendas for change. The differences over how and in what directions change is to occur in our educational systems rest on which educational values are to prevail. These values form the bases for differing conceptions of the purposes of schooling. Thus the differing agendas for change in American education have to be positioned within the context of the different ideological value systems that underpin each alternative agenda for change.

There are several currently contending (and frequently conceptually conflicting) strategies for restructuring life in schools as well as options open to parents in choosing the schools that they want their children to attend. On the one hand, we have to find ways to empower students and teachers to improve the quality of academic life in classrooms. On the other hand, there appear to be powerful forces contending over whether control of educational services should be even more centralized or more decentralized (site-based). Those who favor greater parental and teacher control of schools support greater decentralized site management and community control conceptions of school governance. Yet the ratio of teachers to nonteaching personnel (administrators, counselors, school psychologists, and others) continues to decline as public school system bureaucracies become more and more "top heavy."

In this unit, we consider the efforts to reconceive, redefine, and reconstruct existing patterns of curriculum and instruction at the elementary and secondary levels of schooling and compare them with the efforts to reconceive existing conflicting patterns of teacher education. A broad spectrum of dialogue is developing in North America, the British Commonwealth, Russia, Central Eurasia, and other areas of the world about the redirecting of learning opportunities for all citizens.

Prospective teachers here are being encouraged to question their own individual educational experiences as part of this process. We must acknowledge that our values affect our ideas about curriculum content and the purpose of educating others. This is perceived as vitally important in the developing dialogue over liberating all students' capacities to function as independent inquirers. The dramatic economic and demographic changes in our society necessitate a fundamental reconceptualization of how schools ought to respond to the many social contexts in which they are located. This effort to reassess and reconceive the education of persons is a vital part of broader reform efforts in society as well as a dynamic dialectic in its own right. How can schools, for instance, better reflect the varied communities of interest that they serve? What must they do to become better perceived as just and equitable places in which all young people can seek to achieve learning and self-fulfillment?

Each of the essays in this unit relates to the tension involved in reconceiving how educational development should proceed in response to all the dramatic social and economic changes in society today.

SCHOOL REFORM THAT WORKS

Reinventing America's Schools

Mr. Wagner presents evidence that the theory that high-stakes testing will improve performance is fatally flawed. To create better accountability systems, he argues that we need policy makers who truly understand the realities of schools and can work more collaboratively with educators. He also cites some important lessons from another country, where education systems have been reinvented through such a collaborative process.

BY TONY WAGNER

SINCE THE PASSAGE of the No Child Left Behind (NCLB) Act and now that many new state tests have been put in place, a great deal—and nothing at all—has changed in the universe of public education. What has changed is the frequency of standardized testing in schools and the consequences for educators and students of not performing well on these tests. What has not changed is the daily reality of teaching and learning for the overwhelming majority of students in America. To better understand how these two realities coexist side by side, let's visit two representative school districts—Boston and a "good suburban" school district in New York State.

In Massachusetts today, passing the new state test is now a requirement for earning a high school diploma—as it is, or soon will be, in most states. No longer can a district simply grant a student a diploma for showing up, going to class, and earning passing grades. In order to graduate, all students must pass the same standardized exam, which is given in 10th grade. Those who don't pass the first time will have several opportunities to take the test again.

But what is the students' reality? For the purposes of this article, I would like to leave aside serious questions about both the value and validity of the test itself and focus on the immediate consequences of this new policy. The Massachusetts Comprehensive Assessment System (MCAS) test has been severely criticized on a number of grounds by Anne Wheelock, Walter Haney, and other researchers. FairTest and the Massachusetts Coalition for Authentic Reform in Education have also put forward proposals for better assessment systems (see http://www.fairtest.org/).

Four years ago, about 4,900 ninth-graders began their high school careers in the Boston public schools. Today, as I write, there are approximately 3,400 12th-graders. Nearly one-third—1,500 students—have dropped out of the class in three years.

Among those who remain, 1,648 students—almost half the group that hopes to graduate this spring—have not passed the MCAS test despite having taken it numerous times. Unless something changes suddenly, only about one-third of the students who started out together four years ago will cross the stage in their caps and gowns. The statistics are similar in most urban American school districts.

Isn't this just an urban problem? Not at all. Let me take you to a "good" suburban district in New York State, one that has long been considered a "lighthouse" district known for its innovative practices. When I recently began consulting in this district, I asked what the dropout rate was. No one knew for sure, but everyone thought it was very low. So we began to look at the data together.

We discovered that only eight out of 10 students who start out in ninth grade end up with a diploma four years later—even after accounting for transfers. But a problem looms that is more serious still. Right now in New York State, all districts are allowed to grant two different kinds of high school diplomas: a so-called local diploma and a Regents diploma, which requires that students pass state exams and take a much more academically rigorous course of study. Beginning with the class of 2005, all students will be required to pass Regents Examinations and meet more rigorous standards in order to receive a high school diploma. There will be no more local diplomas. In this "good" suburban district, of the students who graduated last year, only about 60% received a Regents diploma. The rest got a local diploma, which will not be an option under the new state requirements.

So the real scorecard for this district looks like this at the moment: of the 500 or so ninth-graders who started out together, 100 will have dropped out before graduation. Of the remaining 400, only 240 will receive a Regents diploma. In other words, more than half the students who start out in ninth grade do not meet the state standards for a high school diploma that are to become effective in just two years. To the great credit of the leadership in this district, as I write, this new challenge is being widely discussed among teachers, parents, and community members, and, with strong support from the local corporate community, solutions are being sought. No longer is the district resting on its reputation. There are stirrings of a deep urgency for change.

Let me give you one glimpse of another—and more frightening—juxtaposition of new and old reality. I was recently asked to lead a retreat for a large group of Midwestern suburban public school superintendents. During the meals and in between the sessions, there was much discussion of what one superintendent called the "Sovietization" of American public education. These superintendents, like virtually all others with whom I've spoken in the last year, were deeply concerned about the implications of NCLB, passed more than a year ago with strong bipartisan support. That law requires that all schools improve student achievement (as measured on annual standardized tests in grades 1 through 8) by at least 5% every year—or suffer serious penalties. Many superintendents are concerned that the law will encourage districts to set their initial "benchmarks" very low, so that they can easily show progress—a trick many factories and communes used in the Soviet Union in order to meet production quotas. Many also doubt that the law is enforceable or that it will result in improved student learning. Nevertheless, it's the new reality for these superintendents, and they know it.

Now let me describe what has not changed for them. I showed the group of superintendents an excerpt of a tape featuring an English teacher in a suburban district teaching a 10th-grade class. The teacher reviewed the moral "problem" faced by the protagonist in a short story that the students had read. He talked about an imaginary problem that a boy might face if he wanted to ask a girl out on a date but had no money—a topic that caused some amusement and much nervous laughter—and then he asked students to begin to write a story of their own with a central problem, compose just the first paragraph, and then pass it on to the next author, who would write another paragraph and pass it on, and so on until the story was completed. In other words, the students were to undertake a group writing project.

I asked the superintendents to discuss whether they thought this was effective teaching and what their criteria were for judging. The overwhelming majority said that it was effective because they observed that students were engaged. The students appeared to be paying attention, and there were no discipline problems.

True enough. But there wasn't much thinking going on, either. The students were asked factual-recall questions only and then given a writing assignment that was more suited to an elementary school class, in my opinion. They were not asked for their interpretations of the story. They were not asked to discuss a real moral dilemma in their lives and compare it with the one in the story. And they were not asked to write an essay in which they would have to analyze a theme or an idea and provide supporting evidence. In other words, there was no intellectual rigor

to the engagement; students were not being asked to use their minds for anything more than factual recall. Nor did the superintendents comment on the often demeaning manner in which this teacher interacted with the women and minority students in the class.

In order to graduate from high school, these 10th-graders must now pass state tests. They should also have the skills required to succeed in college, to vote intelligently, to serve on juries, and to add value to the knowledge economy—all tasks that will require much more rigorous teaching if students are to be adequately prepared. Sadly, the overwhelming majority of superintendents did not see the gap between what these students were being taught and what they, as soon-to-be adults, must know and be able to do.

But their responses were hardly unique. My colleagues at the Harvard Graduate School of Education and I have shown this videotape to numerous audiences of education leaders in the last several years with the same result. In fact, when I've asked groups to grade the lesson, the average is a B+. But even more stunning is the range of grades that groups of educators in the same room—often from the same district—give the lesson: from an A to a D.

In summary, the new reality is that, in the last few years, with the increased emphasis on accountability and more and more high-stakes testing, the consequences of poor performance on standardized tests for students and for educators have grown steadily more serious. The policy theory—what some might call the theory of change—behind this new reality is that, if you raise the bar with tough new tests and raise the stakes for failure, performance will improve. But the theory is fatally flawed. It does not take into account the fundamental fact that, while we have a few examples of good individual schools, we do not know what a school system looks like in which all students master intellectual competencies at a high level. One simply doesn't exist anywhere in this country. Nor does the theory of change take into account the fact that we do not even have agreement on what good teaching looks like! Teaching is still considered an "art," performed in the privacy of one's classroom by people who prefer to think of themselves as self-employed. The number of school districts in this country that have effective teacher and principal supervision (not evaluation) programs in place can probably be counted on one hand.

Sadder still is the fact that the failure of this new accountability system is not likely to be blamed on the policy makers who passed the new laws. No, it is the victims—teachers, students, and their families—who will be held accountable. Ultimately, what is most likely to be "proved" a failure is the entire concept of public education. I do not believe that the intention of policy makers is to cripple or destroy public education. But I do think that most of the people—Democrats and Republicans alike—who pass these new laws know little or nothing about the daily reality of schools. I also believe that they do not have any idea how to create a very different kind of education and accountability system. It is this lack of informed, imaginative thinking and policy making that led me to write my most recent book, *Making the Grade: Reinventing America's Schools*, and to offer proposals for very different school, district, state, and national accountability systems.

Most of the people who pass the laws know little about the daily reality of schools.

But it took a trip to Denmark to confirm my hunches about what's possible and what works—and to give me a sense of hope for the future of public education. In the spring of 2001, I had the opportunity to accompany a small group of educators on a study tour of the Danish education system, sponsored by Marc Tucker and Judy Codding of the National Center on Education and the Economy. It is beyond the scope of this article to recount all that I learned on this trip, but let me describe a few highlights, from which we might learn. (Readers who want more in-depth information on the Danish education system should see the reports Marc Tucker and his colleagues have written at http://www.ncee.org/.)

Ten years ago, education reform in Denmark did not begin with new laws mandating more testing, as it did in the U.S. It began, instead, with a national conversation about values, about what it meant to be an educated citizen, as Denmark approached the 21st century. These discussions were promoted by the Danish Ministry of Education and took place throughout the country. The result is that today even elementary teachers know what skills students need to master for a knowledge economy and to be contributing citizens in a thriving democracy. The Danes decided that both education goals were of equal importance, as they began working to create much more rigorous education standards for all students.

Next, the ministry developed various incentives and policies that encouraged the creation of many different kinds of secondary schools and colleges, all of them rigorous, but which allowed students to develop mastery in different ways—some through conventional academic preparation, others in more of a technical or trade school environment. It is important to note, though, that these different kinds of schools were all considered "college prep," and a correspondingly diverse array of what we would call community colleges has been developed in parallel. The result: all Danish students graduate from high school "college ready," and almost all go on for some kind of post secondary education. In Denmark, there are many ways of becoming well educated, and there are carefully constructed safety nets for even the most educationally challenged and unmotivated students. There are almost no school dropouts in Denmark, despite the fact that the system is now educating an increasingly diverse population.

Meanwhile, the Danish tradition of small schools in which teachers spend as much as eight years with the same group of students continues to be the norm. Danes have long understood the importance of relationships in motivating students to want

to achieve and of a more "personalized" approach to teaching and learning—ideas that I explore at length in *Making the Grade*.

The Danes have also long understood that computer-scored tests "dumb down" the curriculum because computers cannot assess the most important intellectual competencies, such as critical thinking and problem-solving ability. So the kinds of standardized tests that have become the daily reality in virtually all U.S. public schools do not exist in Denmark. Instead, the Danes have created a comprehensive national system of oral and written examinations at both the elementary and secondary levels. Even more significant, these exams are developed, administered, and scored by educators—usually from a neighboring school or district. The results are used to continuously improve the curriculum and to guide teachers' professional development.

In short, the Danish system works. Nearly all students are educated to high standards and motivated as learners. Educators are esteemed, and morale seems excellent. The Danes are justifiably proud of what they've accomplished. Can the system be imported "as is" into the U.S.? Of course not. But perhaps one of the most significant lessons I learned on my trip was the importance of having leaders and policy makers who truly understand—and are committed to—public education. I was told that nearly two-thirds of the Danish Parliament consists of individuals who are or have been educators. Perhaps this explains how and why the Danes have moved so far ahead internationally in creating an education system that meets the demands of the 21st century.

While it may be a well-intentioned attempt at ensuring greater accountability and educational equality, thus far the high-stakes testing approach to change appears to be increasing our rates of failure and dropping out. Thus it works to widen the gap between education's haves and have-nots. At a deeper level, this reform strategy leaves unanswered the fundamental question of what good lessons look like that teach all students to use their minds well as citizens, workers, and lifelong learners. Nor does it answer the questions of what school systems must do to ensure that all educators master the new skills needed to teach such lessons and to motivate students to *want* to learn. Rather than waste so much time arguing over the merits of more testing, policy makers, business and community leaders, and educators must learn to work together in new ways to "reinvent" the American education system so that all students can find both challenge and joy in learning. The Danes may have a few lessons to teach us.

TONY WAGNER is co-director of the Change Leadership Group at the Harvard Graduate School of Education, Cambridge, Mass. His most recent book, Making the Grade: Reinventing America's Schools, *has just been released in paperback by RoutledgeFalmer. This article was adapted from the introduction to the new edition. He can be reached through his website at http://www.newvillageschools.org/. ©2003, Tony Wagner.*

From *Phi Delta Kappan*, May 2003, pp. 665-668. © 2003 by Tony Wagner.

SCHOOL REFORM THAT WORKS

There Is Another Way:
A Different Approach to Education Reform

Education reform is a long-term project, Mr. Levin and Mr. Wiens argue, and the Manitoba Education Agenda for Student Success will not meet the immediate political need to demonstrate "bold action." However, by focusing on teaching and learning, respecting all participants, building capacity, and making use of research, it just might achieve the goals we want for all our children.

BY BEN LEVIN AND JOHN WIENS

For THE LAST 20 years, governments across North America and around the world have been concerned with improving the outcomes of schooling. The pressure to make changes in schools is fueled by national and international test comparisons and driven by the belief that economic competitiveness rests increasingly on people's skills and knowledge.

The specifics of education reform vary from setting to setting, shaped by particularities of history, culture, political structures, demography, and other factors. Nonetheless, some common elements are evident across the English-speaking industrialized countries.[1] The main strategies have included:

- greater specification of curriculum standards and outcomes, with more focus on reading, writing, mathematics, science, and technology;
- more assessment of student outcomes and public reporting of the results on a school-by-school basis;
- greater opportunity for parents and students to choose the school the student attends;
- more pressure on teachers through measures that control their work, limit their pay, test their competence, and so on;
- altered finance structures to reward schools that are able to increase academic results or attract more students or both; and

- within these policy frames, greater decentralization of managerial responsibility to individual schools.

Kappan readers will be familiar with many examples. In the U.S., reforms in Chicago, Kentucky, North Carolina, Texas, and California have been the subject of much discussion, but every state has had some kind of major reform program, and some states have had several different reform programs over the last 10 years. Countries such as England and New Zealand as well as some of the Australian states have gone through some dramatic changes. In Canada, reforms have been particularly extensive in provinces such as Ontario and Alberta.

All this reform has produced a great deal of upheaval and much controversy. Many speeches have been made, much improvement has been promised, lots of money has been spent, and many educators have felt disheartened. The results in terms of increased student achievement have been generally disappointing. In reviewing five large-scale change efforts, Ken Leithwood, Doris Jantzi, and Blair Mascall concluded: "Most large-scale reforms have not produced gains [in student achievement], however.... Furthermore, where data were available on other types of student-related outcomes across the five cases, results were negative. None of the... cases of large-scale reform demonstrated evidence of increasing graduation rates, college attendance, or student retention."[2]

Why have the results of so many reforms been so disappointing? The answer is no great mystery. Reforms have not worked because they have not focused on the things that we know can affect student performance in schools.[3] To put it bluntly, improved student outcomes result from appropriate changes in classroom and school practices that are widely accepted and implemented by teachers, seen as meaningful by students, and supported by parents and communities.

We have in recent years been learning more and more about each of the elements of this definition. There is growing—though far from complete—agreement on approaches to teaching that are more and less effective. In areas such as reading, writing, mathematics, science, and citizenship we have increasing evidence on the kinds of instructional practices that are most likely to improve students' skills and commitment.

We also understand more about how to create real changes in teaching and learning practices in classrooms.[4] There is clear evidence about the importance of supporting teachers as they learn to use new practices. We understand the need to give students more information about educational purposes and a greater voice in shaping their own learning. And as knowledge about the powerful impact of families on learning has grown, we have learned more about how to bring parents and communities into the educational process more actively.

Reforms have not worked because they have not focused on the things that we know can affect student performance in schools.

Education policy based on research would focus on changing classroom practice, supporting validated curriculum and teaching models with extensive staff development, accepting the importance of local context, building strong relationships with families and communities, and building school capacity to improve. Very few of the large-scale reforms in the 1980s and 1990s were primarily organized around these purposes. Instead, many of them gave primary attention to questions of governance or market mechanisms or finance or testing. The results were predictable. If our focus is not on things that matter to student achievement, we should not expect improvements in student outcomes.

Moreover, effective reform should not be founded solely on economic concerns. Since the long period of strong economic growth in North America in the 1990s, which occurred in spite of allegations that schools were failing, attention has turned to the need to build and maintain social cohesion and the importance of citizenship and public participation.[5] Students and parents see these goals as vitally important. Moreover, economic and

social goals can be complementary. As Sue Berryman puts it:

> For the first time in our history, the education needed to function effectively in labor markets in both high- and low-skill jobs looks similar to that needed to participate effectively as citizens, to work through moral dilemmas, or to make intelligent purchases of often complex goods and services.... The educative challenge common to these disparate activities is to prepare individuals for thoughtful choice and judgment.[6]

Under the right circumstances it is possible to shape an education policy agenda that is consistent with our best current knowledge. That, we submit, is what has been happening for the last three years in the province of Manitoba, Canada. In the remainder of this article, we will describe the origins and substance of the Manitoba Education Agenda for Student Success, an alternative approach to education reform.

MANITOBA

Manitoba is a province of about one million people in the center of Canada. Although the population is primarily urban (with about two-thirds living in the capital city of Winnipeg), there are also many small communities spread over the province's 250,000 square miles, including many isolated ones in the north.

Manitoba has a diverse population. It has the highest proportion of Aboriginal people in Canada, at more than 12%, as well as immigrant populations from many parts of the world. There is also an important Francophone community. The Canadian constitution recognizes rights of Francophones and Aboriginal people, including some specific educational rights.

As is the case across Canada, the provincial department of education plays a substantial leadership role in education. Provinces define the curricula that all schools must follow. They also set the school calendar, provide a considerable amount of professional development, and set the regulatory framework for public schooling.

In 1999 Manitoba had 54 school districts, most of which enrolled fewer than 2,500 students. The province provided just over 60% of total funding, with the rest coming from local property taxes. Inequalities in spending from district to district are small by U.S. standards.

ORIGINS OF THE MANITOBA EDUCATION AGENDA

Manitoba had a Progressive Conservative government, generally seen to be market-friendly, from 1988 until 1999. In 1994 the government introduced an education reform program titled "New Directions," which identified a number of priority areas. Among the main changes made in education during the Conservative government's time in office were:

- new curricula in many subject areas, with increased focus on literacy and mathematics;
- the introduction of Reading Recovery into elementary schools;
- an increase in provincial testing, coupled with school-by-school publication of results (though for reasons of cost, the comprehensive provincial testing program promised in New Directions was never fully implemented);
- an expansion of distance education;
- changes in teacher education, including a five-year minimum preparation for new teachers and extended practica for student teachers; and
- the requirement that all schools have parent advisory councils with limited participation of teachers in these councils.

A number of these policies were positive and well regarded by educators and others. For example, many of the new curricula were of very high quality, a number of curriculum support documents for teachers proved to be very useful, and many schools found Reading Recovery very valuable. The government also provided support for the Manitoba School Improvement Program (www.msip. ca), a foundation-initiated organization that promotes secondary school improvement projects in the province.

However, these positive aspects were greatly overshadowed by a climate of negativity about schools. Educators believed that schools and teachers were being criticized unfairly and being blamed for problems not of their making. Concern also arose over cuts in funding to public schools coupled with substantial increases in public funding for private schools. During most of the 1990s, funding for public schools was either frozen or reduced, such that by a 1999, per-pupil spending was substantially less than it had been in 1992. Capital funding was also cut sharply, so that buildings began to deteriorate. To help school boards manage these budget reductions, the provincial government allowed them to require teachers to take up to eight days off without pay and then legislated limitations on the scope of collective bargaining. By the end of the decade, Manitoba school boards and educators felt unappreciated and victimized.

In September of 1999 Manitoba voters replaced the Progressive Conservative government with a New Democratic Party government. Although the new government made only a few policy commitments for education during the election, it was intent on rebuilding the public school system and renewing public confidence in the public schools.

A few moves were made very quickly after the election. For example, the government prohibited the Youth News Network (roughly equivalent to Channel One in the U.S.) from operating in Manitoba schools. In its first legislative session it restored collective bargaining rights of teachers that had been removed by the previous gov-

ernment. It began work to fulfill a promise to end the provincial standards test in grade 3 and to replace it with a beginning-of-year teacher-led assessment of third-grade students' skills in key areas of reading and mathematics. The minister and the department also began a series of meetings with the main stakeholder groups in education in the province, including not only teachers, school boards, and superintendents but also students and the Manitoba Association of Parent Councils. Several collective meetings were held to discuss common priorities. In addition, the government committed to increasing funding for schools at the rate of economic growth, and it has met that commitment in each of its first four years in office.

At the same time, work began on developing an overall education plan that would focus on a small number of priorities that had strong support from educators, the public, and research. Six such priorities were announced by the minister of education, Drew Caldwell, in June 2000 as the Manitoba Education Agenda:

- improving outcomes, especially for less successful learners;
- strengthening links among families, schools, and communities;
- strengthening school planning and reporting;
- improving professional learning opportunities for educators;
- strengthening pathways between secondary education, postsecondary education, and work; and
- linking policy and practice to research and evidence.

In developing these priorities, the government was particularly concerned with trying to defuse the acrimony and bitterness that had developed and with building a climate of trust and common effort among educational partners. For this to happen, the government's education priorities would have to be seen to be truly focused on the needs of students.

The six priorities were therefore chosen based on the following criteria:

- there was substantial research evidence to suggest that they could lead to improvements in student outcomes;
- they built on or complemented work that was already being done in Manitoba schools, as well as complementing other provincial policy initiatives in areas such as early childhood and poverty;
- they were ambitious in scope yet also achievable by schools given the realities of resources and of other demands on the system; and
- they were respectful of and would foster collaboration among educational partners both within and across school districts.

In other words, instead of having a top-down plan that was resented by people in schools, the intention was to develop an agenda that would be widely seen as positive, useful, and manageable and that many people could commit to.

During the 2000–01 school year, the department organized an extensive series of consultations on the agenda. Regional meetings were held across the province. School districts in the region were invited to send to the meetings a team that included students, parents, teachers, administrators, school board members, and other community representatives. At each meeting there was discussion of the provincial agenda as well as local concerns and initiatives related to the agenda. An important part of the process was conveying the message that the priorities did not just belong to the provincial government but should be shared by all partners. Hundreds of people participated in this process. The involvement of students and parents was particularly important, as evidenced at one meeting when a ninth-grade student from a rural school explained to a table of attentive adults what changes he felt were needed in education in the province and how they could be brought about!

The regional meetings culminated in a provincial conference on a beautiful Saturday in May of 2001. More than 250 people came together to talk about the agenda. About half of those present had also been at one of the regional meetings, while the other half included not only educators but also a wide variety of people who shared an interest in education and represented business, labor, community groups, schools of education, universities, and colleges.

This whole set of discussions made it clear that there was a great deal of agreement among all the parties on the basic elements of the agenda. Educators, students, parents, and others all liked the six priorities. Of course there were many different views on specific actions that should be taken, on the appropriate roles of various parties, and so on, but the basic content and approach of the agenda were widely supported. This process gave the government confidence to move forward.

THE ACTION PLAN

During the following year, work continued on turning the six priorities into specific action proposals with clear time lines. More than two dozen specific actions have been developed, all of which are linked to the six priorities and meet the criteria of being evidence-based and manageable.

A few examples of the specific actions that are now being developed may help readers see the kinds of directions the Manitoba Education Agenda for Student Success is supporting. (More information on the agenda is available at www.edu.gov.mb.ca/ks4/agenda.)

- In the fall of 2002, the province produced its first annual report on student achievement. This report uses a variety of indicators, not just test scores, and provides only aggregate provincial data. Indicators include marks in various subjects, retention in grade, high school completion, participation in postsecondary education, and so on. The indicators themselves were developed in consultation with various stakeholders. Individual school and district results are not reported.

- At the same time, the department is supporting school and district planning that is linked to locally developed indicators and includes local reporting to the community. Every school and district will be expected to provide a report to parents and the public based on indicators that are locally chosen. While progress must be linked to good data on how well schools are doing, Manitoba is not insisting that this process be standardized, and schools and districts may use a variety of meaningful outcome measures. The department is also increasing professional development for schools and districts in the areas of school planning, data analysis, and outcome evaluation.

- The department is developing parent-friendly materials on curriculum outcomes and expectations so that parents and the public can have a clear sense of what is expected from students at various grade levels. These materials are being posted on the provincial website but will also be made available to parents in print.

- Building on work already being done in many schools, Manitoba is moving toward portfolios linked to critical learning, employment, and citizenship skills for all high school students. Students and parents will be able and encouraged to think about their high school program in relation to lifetime skills as well as immediate curriculum requirements.

- The department is supporting greater parent and family involvement in schools by providing more professional development for parents and educators on effective involvement practices. The department is also developing a handbook for parents and schools on effective dispute resolution with an emphasis on having disputes resolved respectfully at the local level.

- Strengthening professional development for educators is a key need. Steps in this area include providing online learning materials for teachers, building online learning communities of educators with common interests, and focusing professional development on a limited set of high-priority issues rather than diluting it across a wide range of issues.

- To build links between schools and higher education, students are now able to take college and university courses and use them for high school as well as postsecondary credit (an idea borrowed from Minnesota). This system will allow schools to provide a wider range of programs. For example, small rural schools can use existing college distance-education courses as options for students in specialized areas where enrollment does not permit offering the course locally.

- Providing more information on current research to schools and the public is another important task. The department of education website is being linked to websites of well-known and credible research organizations. The department has also begun preparing summaries of research in priority areas for broad distribution in print and electronically to the public as well as educators. Public awareness of research will foster the development of sound public policy.

BARRIERS AND OBSTACLES

As reasonable and positive as this agenda seems to many people around the province, it has not been without its difficulties. Three of these challenges are especially important in helping us understand why education reform agendas of this kind are not more common.

The first and most important issue is that slow and steady reform programs do not generally meet political needs. In saying this we are not blaming politicians any more than we blame educators for the shortcomings of schools. Politicians are, by and large, rational actors responding to the dynamics of the system they inhabit. Those dynamics are not well understood by most people, which is one reason there is so much cynicism about politics.[7]

Education reform is a long-term project that can only be judged retrospectively.

One requirement of the political process is for governments to demonstrate that they are taking bold action to address what are perceived to be pressing social problems.[8] That is, after all, why we elect governments, so we should not be surprised when this is what they do. Strategies such as the Manitoba Education Agenda for Student Success do not suggest that there can be straightforward and immediate solutions to important problems, which is what voters often seem to want. The agenda does not have the simplicity of large-scale student or teacher testing or stiffer graduation requirements with their promised immediate results. It cannot easily be expressed in 25 words or less. It does not lead to controversy, so it has not generated very much media interest.

Education reform is a long-term project that can only be judged retrospectively. Supporting a multi-year reform

agenda requires a degree of commitment that transcends immediate political purposes, which is undoubtedly one reason the approach is not more common. Advocates of education reform face an important paradox. Reforms need to be high-profile to attract political attention and public interest. Yet the higher the profile, the harder it is to generate the required success and the more likely it is that a new government or chief executive will want to reverse direction. Moreover, grand promises that cannot be met, such as the U.S. goals for education set in 1990 or Canada's 1989 commitment to end child poverty, serve only to increase cynicism about the government's intentions. While our ultimate aims should be very ambitious, our more immediate targets must be seen to be achievable. A modest and focused agenda with somewhat less political visibility increases the chances that the priorities can be achieved and also that the plan can survive a change in government.

As the Manitoba agenda was developed, a second barrier presented itself—skepticism within the education system about the intentions of the government and the bona fides of the agenda. After years of being assailed by criticism of their work and bombarded with policies and requirements that were seen as unwise, impossible to implement, or both, many educators had a hard time believing that there could be a reform agenda that was truly collaborative, respectful of teachers, research based, and focused on education. There has been considerable suspicion about the government's intentions and a strong feeling that at some point we will return to the top-down demands that people have been used to. Worry has also been expressed about a sudden shift in direction in the event that a future election brings a change in the governing party.

These concerns reinforce the importance of seeing reform as a process of building skill and commitment among all educational partners. As schools, districts, parents, faculties of education, and others see the priorities in the agenda as consistent with their own ideas and initiatives, the goals should become so embedded in policy and practice that they will not readily be subject to reversal through political fiat. The more that education strategy focuses on long-term issues that support good teaching and learning practices, the more likely it is to be lasting and powerful.

Third, we are realizing that knowing what we want to do does not mean that we know how to do it. For example, the first priority in the Agenda is "improving outcomes, especially for less successful learners." While everyone agrees that reducing inequities in achievement is vitally important, we are not at all sure how best to make progress toward this goal. Is it more important to focus on early literacy, or would it be better to devote resources to preschool family literacy activities? Should we intensify instruction and instructional supports in key academic areas, or do we first need to help students feel secure and comfortable in the school? How much emphasis should be given to improving primary-grade skills versus trying to prevent or re-attract high school dropouts?

Even once these decisions are made, we do not necessarily know how to implement them. If we have learned anything from research on educational change, it is how difficult it is to implement changes in teaching and learning practices on a widespread and sustained basis.[9] How do we help hundreds or thousands of teachers to change their practices to be more effective? How do we build effective parent involvement practices? We know something about these questions, but we are far from having the answers.

This reality means that an approach to education reform has to expect and accept mistakes, failures, and shortcomings. Not everything will work satisfactorily. For example, when the department of education implemented the new formative grade-3 assessment in the fall of 2000, it soon became apparent that the assessment was requiring too much time on the part of teachers. Teachers rightly expressed the view that the policy was not sustainable in its original form. The department of education met with teacher leaders, surveyed teachers and parents, held focus groups, made revisions, discussed the proposed revisions with its partners, and made further changes. As a result, the 2001 round of the assessment proceeded with very few concerns, although there is still work to do so that it becomes an integrated part of teachers' ongoing instruction, as opposed to an externally mandated requirement that is unrelated to day-to-day teaching practice. A willingness to assess actions and make changes as required is an essential part of any realistic program of reform.

CONCLUSION

It is easy to write a glowing report on this or any other education reform plan at the outset. Every education reform program begins with promise of great things to come. As already noted, very few deliver on that promise.

Manitoba is attempting a different approach to reform. Focusing on teaching and learning, respecting all partners, building capacity, and basing our approach on the best available research and evidence will, we believe, provide a better way to achieve the goals we all want for our children.

Notes

1. For a fuller analysis of these issues, see Benjamin Levin, *Reforming Education: From Origins to Outcomes* (London: RoutledgeFalmer, 2001).
2. Ken Leithwood, Doris Jantzi, and Blair Mascall, "A Framework for Research on Large-Scale Reform," paper presented at the annual meeting of the American Educational Research Association, New Orleans, April 2002.
3. David Hopkins and Benjamin Levin, "Government Policy and School Improvement," *School Leadership and Management,* February 2000, pp. 15–30.
4. David Hopkins, *School Improvement for Real* (London: RoutledgeFalmer, 2001).
5. Joseph Heath, *The Efficient Society* (Toronto: Viking Press, 2001).
6. Sue Berryman, "Learning for the Workplace," in Linda Darling-Hammond, ed., *Review of Research in Education,* vol. 19 (Washington, D.C.: American Educational Research Association, 1992), p. 345.
7. A fuller discussion of the dynamics that drive governments can be found in Benjamin Levin, "Governments and School Improvement," *International Electronic Journal for Leadership in Learning,* 26 May 2001, www.ucalgary.ca/ ~iejll/volume5/levin.html.
8. Among the best discussions of these dynamics are Murray Edelman, *Constructing the Political Spectacle* (Chicago: University of Chicago Press, 1988); and Deborah Stone, *Policy Paradox* (New York: Norton, 1997).
9. Michael Fullan, *The New Meaning of Educational Change,* 3rd ed. (New York: Teachers College Press, 2001).

BEN LEVIN was deputy minister for education for the government of Manitoba from the fall of 1999 until the fall of 2002, when he returned to his position as professor of educational administration at the University of Manitoba, Winnipeg. JOHN WIENS was superintendent of the Seven Oaks School Division in Winnipeg until July of 2001, when he became dean of the Faculty of Education at the University of Manitoba.

From *Phi Delta Kappan,* May 2003, pp. 658-664. © 2003 by Phi Delta Kappa International, Inc. Reprinted by permission.

KUDZU, RABBITS, AND SCHOOL REFORM

We, the people, appear to understand that the linchpin of each American's necessary apprenticeship in democracy is a qualified, caring, competent classroom teacher, Mr. Goodlad points out. The role of Presidents and governors is to cheer us on, not to mislead us with the mythology of school reform.

BY JOHN I. GOODLAD

RECENTLY, colleagues and I were more than a little startled by a letter to the editor of one of our local newspapers. It had been wryly captioned "Civil Spirit," and it read as follows:

> Our son recently finished 90 hours of community service. The crime to fit this punishment? He just happens to be a graduating senior.
>
> We believe community service is a wonderful way for drunk drivers, juvenile delinquents—any member of society who has cost the community pain, money, etc.—to pay back a little of what they owe. Is it appropriate for productive, high-achieving high school students to be required to do more "punishment" than the average teenage burglar? In our opinion, *any* teenager who stays out of trouble is contributing to their community.

Presumably, the couple writing this letter assumed that they had performed their civic duty by bringing a high-achieving student into the world. Their son, in turn, had taken care of his community responsibilities through academic achievement.

I am reminded of a quite different letter to a newspaper editor reporting the behavior of an aging woman at an open meeting of a state's budget committee. Exasperated by the repeated cuts in allocations for schools, she stood up and spoke out in protest. The committee's chairman interrupted her.

> "You are a schoolteacher, I assume."
> "No, I am not," she replied.
> "Then you must have a daughter or son who is."
> "No, I do not."

> "Surely, grandchildren in school?"
> "I have no children," she replied, "but I have to live with everyone else's children."

THE HARD AND TOUGH AND THE SOFT AND TENDER

These two letters illustrate a long-standing tension regarding the purposes of our schools. At the turn of the 19th century into the 20th, William James referred to the "hard and tough" and the "soft and tender" as the warp and woof in the fabric of American social and political ideology. He saw the need for balancing the two. But they have tended to be out of balance, with one rising and the other falling in cycles of two to three decades, with schooling following several years behind.

The rhetoric of school purpose has been relatively stable, however. The dozen or so goals that surface again and again in commissioned reports and district guidelines for schools have consistently embraced personal, social, vocational, and academic attributes. In 1987 Mortimer Adler wove the rhetorical fabric this way: "Preparation for duties of citizenship is one of three objectives for any sound system of public schooling in our society. Preparation for earning a living is another, and the third is preparation for discharging everyone's moral obligation to lead a good life and make as much of one's self as possible."[1] Poll after poll and study after study have revealed that we want all three.

Nonetheless, reform era after reform era—each politically driven—puts policy and practice out of balance. Adults with quite ordinary academic records invent the past in exhorting schools to be hard and tough, as schools supposedly were for them. "Educating the whole child" is frequently viewed as the dangerous notion of woolly-headed progressive educators. Indeed, it is not so much the substance of reform cycles but more the side effects that do harm. Whether soft and tender or hard and tough, school reforms fade and die, frequently from their own excesses. But their side effects live on as "eduviruses" that add cost to the system and create roadblocks to the serious redesign and sustained improvement we need.

THE SCHOOL REFORM ENTERPRISE

More than in most European countries, U.S. education policy has tied schooling directly to the nation's economic health. In addition, we have lagged behind most developed nations in ensuring that young people receive the human services that ready them for school and buttress their educational experiences once they are enrolled. The landmark report of the National Commission on Excellence in Education, *A Nation at Risk,* employed military language and metaphor in tying the schools to our declining competitiveness in the global economy.[2] Had the charges been well founded, our schools would have been declared triumphant when the economy soared in the 1990s. But there was not a word of tribute. Instead, the current hard-and-tough era of school reform has overrun local schools like kudzu, threatening to squeeze out all else.

School reform has taken on social, political, and economic capital in its own right. Candidates Bush and Gore cloaked their Presidential campaigns in it. I shudder each time another elected state chief executive declares herself or himself to be an "education governor." President Reagan was monumentally bored with the prospect of a report from his National Commission on Excellence in Education—at least until his handlers convinced him of the political mileage to be gained from promoting school reform. Since then, the rituals have served politicians admirably. The trick is to keep alive and well the message that our schools are failing. Even though most parents rate their local schools quite high, particularly at the elementary level, they are told that there are bad schools out there and that the ills of those schools are contagious. We pay careful attention to these messages, and perhaps we don't notice that it is school reform that spreads these infections.

Should we relax, then, in the belief that our schools are just fine and need no change? Of course not. Is the need for improvement only in our urban centers, frequently cited as overwhelmed by viruses? Of course not, even though the needs in our cities are great, and the challenges daunting.

No, the harsh reality is that, should school reform outrun its political usefulness and victory be declared, our schools would no more be engines propelling the nation's economy than they were in 1983. Worse, they would be less connected to their long-standing social, personal, and intellectual purposes, even if the test scores were demonstrably improved beyond the rhetorical expectations of school reform, which is unlikely.

The trouble is that the school reform enterprise has been prescribing the wrong medicines for quite some time. It has ignored the broad purposes of schooling in a democratic society, ignored the huge body of research that would be eagerly examined if the field of interest were something other than schooling, and ignored the implications for school policy and practice of the relevant knowledge accumulating in such fields as anthropology, linguistics, psychology, sociology, and more. Some serious historical and philosophical inquiry might well have given weight to the opinions of political leaders. Moreover, the marginalized advice of critics was coming not just from self-serving "educationists," as charged, but from some of our most thoughtful analysts, scholars, and respected public figures. Of course, school reform has stirred one sector of the economy—particularly the testing industry and that growing panoply of companies seeking profit from the public's investment in schooling.

With the health needs of our schools scarcely examined, the choice of medicines could only reflect ill-informed opinion. The random coupling of ends and means leads to unintended, unexamined consequences. In the realm of human health, these are called side effects and are so labeled. In school reform, the side effects go unheralded and become viruses in the education system. When the next era of school reform comes around, the targets of blame are once more the students, their teachers, teacher educators, and the schools—the perennial victims of what Rona Wilensky refers to as the mythology of school reform.[3] Those who should be held accountable are by then out to lunch.

STANDARDS AND TESTING

The hard and tough has had a long run in schooling this time around. In the 1990s, it appeared that the usual excesses would be self-correcting. The idea of academic standards in subject matter, methods of inquiry, and even pedagogy surfaced and was advanced by such scholarly bodies as the National Academy of Sciences. National commissions did excellent work in developing standards in the major subjects of school curricula. "Standards" became the key word in promoting the cause of school reform nationwide. There were soon sets of national, state, and local district standards competing for attention, with accompanying tension over which should triumph.

The warnings of critics were quickly confirmed, however, when issues of what student attainment to measure and how to measure it arose right on schedule. The central issue had to do, of course, with aligning standards, tests, and classroom teaching. Who can be held accountable when the tests are prepared to measure the standards but teachers do not teach to the standards because they are ill prepared or because they disagree with them, and the test items are thus selected from content unfamiliar to the students?

This is familiar school reform terrain, visited and revisited in various forms and to little avail throughout the 20th century. A few decades ago, many states sought to harness teacher competencies to student proficiencies. Or was it teacher proficiencies to student competencies? Then pressure was brought to bear on higher education to prepare teachers in the required competencies. Or was it proficiencies? It was a costly undertaking in time and dollars, and it was extremely repugnant to people educated to be thoughtful decision makers. For several years after the whole enterprise collapsed, some state departments went on collecting data regarding institutional compliance. Were school reform not almost completely ahistorical, we might have something to show for each new era of reform, beginning with a critical appraisal of boondoggles about to be repeated. Since education is intended, in part, to keep us from repeating our mistakes, the conduct of education should be exemplary in avoiding repeated failures.

There is nothing wrong with standards. They guide and drive the whole of individual and collective behavior. And tests of many kinds provide useful feedback. Self-imposed standards and tests drive most of us, for better or for worse. Both guided my daily teaching and assessment of 34 pupils spread over eight grades in the one-room school for which I was steward many years ago. The results of standardized tests received months after their administration in my classroom would have helped me not at all. In planning each day's schedule, I had to know how well each child was reading, spelling, and figuring. And so it was for many subsequent years of teaching children, youths, and adults. And so it is with teachers generally They need and want help, of course, but they deeply resent both totalitarian intrusion into decisions for which they will be held responsible and the side effects that invariably accompany such reform mandates.

There is plenty in the standards and testing elements of the current school reform era that warrants careful scrutiny. The necessary analyses abound, and they are rich in thoughtful recommendations. Were the school reform enterprise not so isolated from and suspicious of the robust scholarly inquiry that now exists and the lessons to be learned from it, there could be useful residue from which constructive school change might be built.

However, it is characteristic of school reforms—whether of the soft and tender or hard and tough variety—not to fade gracefully away but to expire from their own excesses, leaving little residue. The problem with the present, long-lasting era lies not in its leaving too little residue, but too much. This baggage is made up partly of dangerous assumptions and partly of damage to specific human beings, to teaching as a career, to our educational institutions, and to the high level of intelligence the infrastructure of our democracy requires.

BETTER TEACHERS, BETTER SCHOOLS?

Now that the narrative of economic utility is driving our schools, the influence of the business community on school reform should come as no surprise. Not just high school or college graduation rates but grades and test scores rank high in the se-

lection of workers in many sectors of the marketplace. When high test scores fail to deliver the desired qualities, employers beat the drum for tougher standards and tests. What these employers do not understand is that high test scores predict high test scores, but not much else: not problem-solving skills, not good work habits, not honesty, not dependability, not loyalty, and not the dispositions and virtues embedded in our expectations for schooling.

Research on cognition reveals that the transfer of learning from one domain of human behavior to another is low. Each domain must be taught directly. The challenge to educators is illustrated by the fact that even students doing well in school-based mathematics commonly fail to recognize the same operations in daily life outside of school. Of course, there is little assurance that teachers, especially in elementary schools, will have had more than skimpy preparation in either the necessary mathematics or pedagogy. Nonetheless, serious attention to the education of educators ranked low in school reform eras throughout the 20th century.

Over the past year, I have been asking members of groups to which I speak to select from four items the one they believe to have *most* promise for improving our schools. Three of the four are politically popular:

- standards and tests mandated by all states;
- a qualified, competent teacher in every classroom;
- nonpromotion and grade repetition for all students who fail to reach grade-level standards on the tests; and
- schools of choice for all parents.

From an audience of about a thousand people at the 2001 National School Boards Association conference, one person chose the first. *All* the rest chose the second, which usually is the unanimous choice, whatever the group.

As part of a comprehensive study of teacher education in the United States, conducted in the late 1980s,[4] a colleague found no mention of teacher education in commissioned reports on school improvement and no mention of schools in commissioned reports on the improvement of teacher education between 1892 and 1986.[5] The National Commission on Teaching and America's Future connected the relationship between good teachers and good schools in its 1996 report and detailed the steps we must take in order to have competent, caring, and qualified teachers in every classroom by 2006. The media and the school reform industry yawned. School reform has a life of its own. It has little to do with what our schools are for or what most people want in the way of improving them.

Yet we find raising the scores on mandated tests, ending "social promotion," offering vouchers, and creating charter schools on the front burners of politically driven school reform. None of these—or even more promising alternatives—will go anywhere without competent, caring, qualified teachers. Laura Bush's presumably well-intentioned appeal to retiring military personnel to consider a second career in teaching only obscures the critical issues. If teaching our young in schools became a lifelong professional career—adequately rewarded and supported, with decision-making authority commensurate with responsibility—teacher shortages would fade away. The Flexner Report of 1910 propelled medical education from an apprenticeship model to a professional model, driven by scientific inquiry. But the process took several decades.[6] We could do the same for teacher education, teaching, and the schools if it were not for our beguilement with the mythology of school reform.

KUDZU, RABBITS, AND EDUVIRUSES

The ongoing debate over school policy and practice has narrowed almost exclusively to how to make standards and testing better. As I said above, there could be some positive residue. But this should not and must not continue to take our attention away from the baggage that almost invariably accompanies school reform—a rather nasty concept—and is passed along from reform era to reform era. It is not what is currently central to the debate in education but what is largely ignored that will ultimately bite back.

In 1876 the kudzu vine was introduced into the United States to shade the porches of southern mansions. In the 1940s it was widely planted to control erosion. Capable of growing luxuriously up to one foot per day, kudzu kills forests by entirely covering trees and shrubs. Today, it covers between two and four million acres in the southern U.S. and costs an estimated $50 million yearly in lost farm and timber production. Its initial appeal and use have long been forgotten.

At about the same time—and also to satisfy the desires of the privileged—wild rabbits were introduced into Australia. In 1859 Thomas Austin brought 24 rabbits from England and released them on his property in southern Victoria. Expected to expand in number and provide a hunting mecca for Austin and his guests, the rabbits quickly outran both these expectations and the exterminating capabilities of the hunters. During the seventh year following their importation, the successful shooting of over 14,000 scarcely dented the wild rabbit population. More than a century later, the introduction of rabbit calicivirus disease—intended to reduce the rabbit population—created a plague so deadly that it is now the target of one of the world's biggest biological control programs. Currently, the Australian government reports that, all told, rabbits cost the nation's agricultural industries hundreds of millions of dollars each year in loss of crops and land degradation.

The direct and indirect costs of the "eduvirus" school reform disease are much more difficult to calculate. As with the introduction of kudzu and rabbits, the explanations offered for proposed school reforms are virtuous: "It's all for the children." When *A Nation at Risk* sounded the alarm bell for school improvement, a variety of innovative initiatives, largely supported by private philanthropy, sprang into existence in most parts of the country. As with cottage industries, which schools largely are, those who plowed the fields and ground the wheat were doing what they believed in, and they were held responsible for that work. They put their careers on the line. As experienced educators, they understood the terrain and the dangers of introducing kudzu and wild rabbits into it. Limited resources and the

deep structures of schooling had the dual effect of restraining both progress (unfortunately) and foolishness (fortunately). Such conditions are unfavorable to the incubation and spread of eduviruses.

But then "McSchool" took over, and test scores became the bottom line. With some school districts, notably in Texas, tying administrators' salary adjustments to test scores, pressures on teachers and students to produce quickly followed. After the initial round of testing in Houston, outsourcing the schooling of some low achievers to a private firm bumped up scores the next time around in the schools from which they had departed. This and other maneuvers of dubious virtue and little educational value raised scores and attracted attention, but the curricular and pedagogical changes supposedly responsible remain obscure.

The speed with which school reform eduviruses have spread has far outpaced that of the side effects of introducing kudzu into the southern United States and rabbits into Australia. Rod Paige, then superintendent of the Houston schools, soon had a bully pulpit as secretary of education from which to tout a model of reform that aligned nicely with the education plank in President Bush's school reform platform: "Leave no child behind."

Meanwhile, far to the northwest of Houston, the teachers of a one-school rural district turned down the pro bono offer of a biologist-turned-science-educator to help the children understand the front-burner environmental issues of their community. They did not see how this would help raise test scores. On Long Island, hundreds of parents, many attracted initially to the long-standing high reputation of Scarsdale's schools, anticipated the arrival of the eduvirus. With school district support, they agreed to keep their children out of school on test day. Testing, they said, was destroying what had made their schools good.

IT'S ALL FOR THE CHILDREN

We readily identify with instances such as these even as we fail to connect with aggregated data. We read about the need for millions of new teachers over the next few years, and old proposals for getting more teachers more quickly are resurfacing. Yet career teachers and administrators in droves are taking early retirement or new jobs, and about one-third of new teachers leave during their first three years. Most states are putting pressure on colleges and universities to graduate their students, including future teachers, in four years. They also put pressure on schools to get the test scores up. But the overloaded preparation programs of primary teachers average just a course and a half in the teaching of reading, very little preparation in mathematics, and just one course in teaching math. But up with the test scores and leave no child behind.

Late in his Presidency, Bill Clinton took to the bully pulpit in advocating the abolition of so-called social promotion. The Bush Administration picked up the baton, and conservative school reformers blamed the practice on the soft-headed products of that liberal scheme, professional teacher education. Actually, the idea is a very hard-headed economic one. In the late

1890s, Charles William Eliot, president of Harvard University, and William Rainey Harper, president of the University of Chicago, expressed concern over the negative impact of nonpromotion on the educational and personal well-being of high school students, many of whom dropped out of school when they failed a grade. Their words affected practice not at all. But a study by Leonard Ayers in the next decade brought down the order to ease up on grade retention practices in many districts. Flunking large numbers of children in elementary schools increased the number of years they would have to spend in school and so increased the costs of their schooling. "It's all for the children" is often the language of school reform—but very little of it really is.

Several decades passed before educational research supported the concerns of Eliot and Harper regarding the negative effects of nonpromotion on the personal and social adjustment of children. While this research showed that children who struggled and were promoted to the next grade fared a little better, even in the academic domain, than comparable children who were retained, it also showed that slow progress takes its toll, whatever the grade placement. Children know when they are not doing well, and they are troubled by it. They don't need to be punished again by being branded failures. Subsequently, educators (when school reformers were not telling them what they had to do) figured out some ways to motivate, challenge, and assist even the slowest learners. But no reform era made their ideas politically correct. Today's conventional wisdom has it that the innovations of these educators were tried and found wanting. So much for innovation.

Arguments for children's well-being, no matter how well grounded, rarely win the day in eras of school reform. The current testing crusade has now become politically correct. Counterarguments commonly received the "you're against change" response. The data on the low correlation between test scores and honesty, civility, and civic, responsibility are brushed aside. The impact of failure on children's psyches is declared an illusion. There is scant debate over what to do or how to do it. The charge to school principals and teachers is to just do it.

But the spread of the eduviruses is slowly arousing concern. School board members, educators, and parents are more and more listening to the speeches and reading the writing of thoughtful critics. Once again, the expectations created by the rhetoric of reform have not been fulfilled. And, once again, it will be awareness of the economic implications that will accelerate the demise of still another failed school reform era.

To date, the counter movement has primarily addressed problems with "how" testing is used, not the shortcomings of testing as a vehicle for school improvement. The expressed concern of educators has been primarily with the narrow focus of the tests, the accompanying impact on teaching and the curriculum, and the high-stakes accountability attached to administrator, teacher, and student performance. At the time of this writing, five major education organizations are joining in an effort to provide guidelines for companies and organizations seeking to develop tests for the Bush plan to test all pupils yearly in grades 3 through 8.

What these organizations seek are assessments that are appropriate to a broad range of students, the results of which will

help teachers teach. Such a noble effort is more likely to slow, rather than accelerate, the testing frenzy. Indeed, should their intent be heeded, they might even derail the testing express altogether. Already the major lessons being learned in the current reform era is that enormous costs are associated with developing, printing, administering, scoring, and aggregating the results of even the present, much-less-sophisticated tests for millions of children. What the five groups are calling for—and what many others regard as desirable as well—would cost many times more, so long as the assumption prevails that determining school quality requires testing all or almost all students.

Once it becomes clear to states and local school districts that valid and useful testing, mandated on a broad scale, will not only cut into their own budgets but will also consume much of the 7% contributed to public schooling by the federal government, the well-meant proposals of these organizations will be dead on arrival. And several new boards will be nailed into the coffin being readied for the corpse of still another failed school reform effort. The most vocal leaders of that failed reform, if they are still around, will be first in line with their shovels as the casket disappears into the ground. Ironically, the cause of death will have been economic reality, not educational reasoning and moral principles.

WHAT OUR SCHOOLS ARE FOR

The most dismayingly scary characteristic of the current school reform era is the preoccupation with simplistic prescription devoid of diagnosis and purpose. Whether or not he actually said so, Alexander Hamilton considered the people, collectively, to be "a great beast." Thomas Jefferson wrote about the incompatibility of ignorance and freedom and viewed education as the route to civilizing the beast. Roughly half a century later, reflecting on his long visit to America, Alexis de Tocqueville wrote that "there is nothing more arduous than the apprenticeship of liberty." Writing in 1997, political scientist Benjamin Barber claimed, "There is only one road to democracy: education. And in democracy where freedom comes first—educators and politicians alike take notice—the first priority of education must be the apprenticeship of liberty. Tie every educational reform to this principle, and not only education but democracy itself will flourish."[7]

Is not an apprenticeship in democracy the primary mission of schooling? Given that this apprenticeship is arduous, dare we assume that our schools and the cacophony of "teaching" that occurs outside schools are providing it? I think not. Such is clearly not the intent of the education young people now receive during the time they are not in school. And the function of schools today appears to be more to sort the young for their place in society than to educate them for productive, responsible, satisfying participation in it.

No political leader has emerged to champion the relationships between education and democracy and the role of our schools in it. The Presidential debates preceding the elections of 1992, 1996, and 2000 exemplify the void. What stands out instead are empty homilies: all children ready for school, all children can learn, leave no child behind, post the Ten Commandments on classroom walls, and so on.

Perhaps the cataclysmic events of last September 11 will provide the needed wake-up call. Understandably, as Kevin Sack pointed out in the *New York Times* shortly after that day, school colors nationwide quickly changed to red, white, and blue. But will the schools be directed to provide the educational apprenticeship necessary to eradicate the misunderstandings that set people against people worldwide?

It appears that the writers of the Constitution were incredibly prescient. Even though the need for an educated citizenry is implicit, there is no mention of a federal responsibility for schooling. Still, Hamilton's beast did a pretty good job of democratizing itself, even as immigrants from all over the world added to its size and diversity. Observers came from far and wide to view the great American experiment of a democracy committed to schooling for all.

The American people have looked to their schools not only for the teaching of reading, writing, and figuring but also for the civilizing of their offspring. They have said over and over that they want it all from their schools: the development of personal, social, vocational, and academic attributes. The woman who protested the budget cuts, with whose story I began this article, had it right: we must live with all our children. It takes a nation to ensure the necessary apprenticeship in democracy for all of us. And we, the people, appear to understand that the linchpin of this apprenticeship is a qualified, caring, competent teacher in every classroom. The role of Presidents and governors is to cheer us on, not to mislead us with the mythology of school reform.

NOTES

1. Mortimer J. Adler, *We Hold These Truths* (New York: Macmillan, 1987), p. 20.
2. National Commission on Excellence in Education, *A Nation at Risk* (Washington, D.C.: U.S. Government Printing Office, 1983).
3. Rona Wilensky, "Wrong, Wrong, Wrong." *Education Week,* 9 May 2001, pp. 48, 32.
4. John I. Goodlad, *Teachers for Our Nation's Schools* (San Francisco: Jossey-Bass, 1990).
5. Zhixin Su, "Teacher Education Reform in the United States, 1890–1986," Center for Educational Renewal, Occasional Paper No. 3, College of Education, University of Washington, Seattle, 1986.
6. Abraham Flexner, *Medical Education in the United States and Canada* (New York: Carnegie Foundation for the Advancement of Teaching, 1910).
7. Benjamin R. Barber, "Public Schooling: Education for Democracy," in John I. Goodlad and Timothy J. McMannon, eds., *The Public Purpose of Education and Schooling* (San Francisco: Jossey-Bass, 1997), p. 31.

JOHN I. GOODLAD is professor emeritus at the University of Washington and president of the Institute for Educational Inquiry, Seattle.

Four-day School Week?

Policymakers have been eyeing the four-day school week as a way to cut education costs. There have been mixed results where the schedule has been adopted.

By Greta Durr

With promises of a 20 percent reduction in overhead and transportation costs, the four-day school week is growing more attractive to legislators seeking to cut education costs—especially in energy, transportation and classified personnel salaries. But while some states are looking at the four-day school week as a way to save money or as a creative option for rural areas, others have found it impractical.

The four-day week offers the same amount of class time in fewer days. Mostly these plans have been used by rural school districts and the savings are not always dramatic. There are other factors, however, that influence whether they are successful.

Custer School District in rural South Dakota adopted the four-day-a-week calendar in 1995 to reduce its annual budget by approximately $70,000. The savings weren't as much as estimated, but a school survey found that the switch boosted morale, reduced absenteeism, decreased the need for substitute teachers, and led to a boom in participation in extracurricular activities. The survey also indicated that teachers were covering more academic content than they had under the traditional five-day calendar.

But the idea didn't work in Utah where a modified school week pilot program ended a year early because the schools involved reported only moderate or no actual savings, as well as scheduling complications. Some districts in the pilot went to four-and-a-half-day weeks after two years, which cut into savings on transportation and heat.

The legislation allowing the program required that extracurricular activities like school sports, dances, plays and speech meets be scheduled on Thursday nights, Fridays or Saturdays so students would not have to travel on a regular school day.

"Most schools opted out," says Steve Laing, state school superintendent. "There are still a couple of schools that would like to do it, but not because they're planning on any savings." Laing explained that, for these schools, the benefits of the modified week (better morale, decreased absenteeism, reduced need for substitutes) meant more to the communities than the money they saved.

Oregon has two laws that deal with shortened school schedules and both have come into play as districts struggle to survive the worst budget deficit in 20 years. After Oregonians defeated a measure in January that would have increased income taxes for three years to prevent $310 million in cuts to schools and other programs, schools are looking at the four-day school week, as well as cutting five to 24 days from the school year.

"At least 16 districts are on the four-day week to cut costs," says Margaret Peterson of the state Board of Education, "and they would still meet compulsory education requirements. But other districts are looking at cutting days from the school year, which is allowed in Oregon during severe budget difficulties. Some of them will be allowed to drop below the number of hours required by state law."

Oregon's rural Morrow County School District 1 adopted the four-day school week offered through a state policy option to lower expenses 10 years ago. The district currently is saving an estimated $250,000 in a $14 million budget, mostly from salaries of classified employees, such as cooks, bus drivers and teacher's aides.

In some states, laws have to change in order to change school calendars. When a small Michigan district considered a four-day week, officials found they couldn't do it because teacher labor contracts and retirement requirements are set by the state in terms of days, not hours.

Representative Stephen Adamini penned a bill to make the changes from specifications in days to required hours. Approximately nine districts have contacted him about making the switch.

Student transportation costs really take a toll on sparsely populated districts in vast, rural areas, Adamini says. "Small districts are hanging by their fingernails looking for savings," he says. "Local schools should have this as an option."

Montana was still debating a four-day week when this issue of the magazine went to press. The bill's sponsor, Senator Sam Kitzenberg, a high school English teacher, wants to give districts more flexibility with scheduling and funding, despite the potential impact on local jobs. "We're looking for a lifeboat for Montana schools in case of cutbacks," he says. "We don't want it forced, we want it as an option."

Yet Representative Carol Juneau is worried about classified employees. "If we go to the four-day week, many cooks, bus drivers and custodians would lose wages. In our community, many of our local people work those jobs," she says.

Ten states have some school districts operating on a four-day week: Arizona, Colorado, Kansas, Louisiana, Michigan, New Mexico, Oregon, South Dakota, Wisconsin and Wyoming. States with legislation allowing the four-day school week include Arkansas, California, Minnesota and Illinois. Bills are pending in Michigan, Montana, Ohio and Virginia.

Greta Durr tracks education policy at NCSL.

Flashback

School Choice—Really

Back when our great-grandparents were children, trudging barefooted through blizzards to one-room schoolhouses warmed by the patriotic heat of Parson Weems and *McGuffey Eclectic Readers*, school "choice" meant just that: Parents had the *choice* of whether or not to send their young 'uns to the education factory. They lost that choice—but maybe everything that dies someday comes back.

Massachusetts was the first state to enact a compulsory schooling law, in 1852; by 1918 every state in the land of the free had abolished what had once seemed a basic freedom. The compellers blamed feckless American parents for bringing coercion upon themselves. As B. G. Northrop, secretary of the Connecticut State Board of Education, said in 1872: "To bring up children in ignorance *is* a crime and should be treated as such."

Compulsory education went fist in velvet glove with child-labor laws. The mines, mills, and farms in which young people labored were being emptied of children, as enlightened, usually childless progressives made war on the rights of rural and working parents to raise their children as they saw fit.

Parental resistance to compulsion was fierce. Coercive education was said to be "monarchical," "un-American," "un-Constitutional," and "inimical to the spirit of free democratic institutions." In 1848, the *North American Review* remarked of a typical parent in this original choice movement: "To compel him to educate his children would have been an invasion of his rights as a free-born Rhode Islander, which would not be endured."

From the start, compulsory education relied on military metaphors and brute threats. Educationist Calvin Stowe told the Ohio legislature in 1836, "A man has no more right to endanger the state by throwing upon it a family of ignorant and vicious children than he has to give admission to the spies of an invading army." One nineteenth-century zealot extolled the state's "right of eminent domain" over the minds of children. All in all, kid, you're just another brick in the wall.

What the anarchic American system needed was the lash of Prussian discipline, or so Americans were told. Martin Luther's 1524 letter to German rulers was widely quoted: "The civil authorities are under obligation to compel the people to send their children to school." Those authorities eventually obliged, when in 1717 Friedrich Wilhelm decreed that "parents are required on pain of heavy punishment" to place their children in state-run schools. A vast surveillance network of truant officers, police, and collaborating clergy saw to it that *Mutter und Vater* did their parental duty.

A 1914 U.S. Bureau of Education propaganda campaign aimed at the six Southern states lacking compulsory-education statutes praised the ruthless Teutons: "The successful enforcement of compulsory education has long been an enviable feature of the German school system."

Compulsion was the wave of the future, warned the agents of the Bureau of Education. Arguments for parental choice were "specious, superficial, and obsolete," declared the iron-fisted William H. Hand. The abolition of choice was "both modern and democratic." And so schooling became yet another basic function of the family expropriated by the state.

Except for the Amish, most Americans went supine before the statutes. Compulsory education gradually became one of those long-settled matters, like the existence of the income tax. The odd dissenter was written off as quaint or demented—until the 1960s and '70s, when a wave of New Leftish critics of Big Education, led by Paul Goodman and John Holt, took the paddle to what Goodman called "compulsory miseducation."

What the early progressives had found admirable—the regimented Prussian pedigree of forced schooling—the New Leftists found repellent. As Judson Jerome argued, "Compulsory education, like compulsory love, is a contradiction in terms. Where there is compulsion, a person... learns to be docile or rebellious; he learns to sit still for long hours without thinking; he learns to fear or hate or be sickeningly dependent upon authority figures.... If schools remain, the first business of the day should be to establish clearly and unequivocally that anyone is free to leave."

Ivan Illich, among the most prominent of the radical critics of schooling, called for a new amendment to the Constitution: "The state shall make no law with respect to the establishment of education." Illich died several months ago. His amendment, a mere 38 states shy of ratification, is an adorably truant orphan just waiting to be adopted.

—Bill Kauffman

Sweeten the Pot For Middle America

To make school vouchers truly popular, make sure there's something in them for suburbanites

By Frederick Hess

The Republican gains of November have prompted renewed calls for action on school vouchers and choice in education. In the past, supporters fretted that the Bush administration had abandoned school vouchers too readily in the face of fierce Democratic opposition in 2001 and that pro-voucher governors were not committed enough in the face of resistant legislatures.

The political calculus has clearly changed. In Washington, D.C., voucher supporter Judd Gregg of New Hampshire is the new chair of the Senate committee overseeing education. In Colorado, Texas, New Hampshire, and South Carolina, Republican gains have produced new enthusiasm among school choice proponents.

Meanwhile, voucher enthusiasts have gone on the legal offensive following the Supreme Court's June 2002 *Zelman v. Harris* decision, which ruled that religious schools could Constitutionally be included in voucher programs. In states like Massachusetts, Maine, and Vermont, they are challenging state constitutional strictures that prevent state monies from supporting religious schools, on the grounds that these violate First Amendment protections for the exercise of faith. Should voucher supporters win these battles, the field will be wide open for voucher programs.

Nonetheless, voucher proponents could be inadvertently steering themselves off a cliff. Proponents of school choice today find themselves in much the same position that the social-

engineering Left inhabited after LBJ's sweep a generation ago. Their ideas are ascendant, they stand on the side of social justice, they hale strong allies and spokespersons, and are winning prominent legal battles. Yet amidst the fruits of victory, something is missing: full approval from the mass of the American middle class.

Like the architects of LBJ's Great Society, voucherites express puzzlement as to why many suburbanites don't share their enthusiasm for school choice. Increasingly, I find myself in education-reform meetings where voucher advocates end up quietly berating white suburban families for showing insufficient regard for the education of disadvantaged urban children. Conservative school choice proponents nod along as compelling advocates for the urban underclass—like Howard Fuller, Robert Aguirre, and Floyd Flake—voice frustration that suburban whites have not fully embraced choice as a way to free minority children from failed urban schools.

That's no way to win a policy fight. Thirty years ago, the Great Society's champions berated and nagged middle-class America smack into the arms of the opposition. Enthralled by their own virtue and the elegance of their domestic policy prescriptions, Great Society liberals forgot about simple democratic notions like self-interest, concern about unintended consequences, and the public's natural risk aversion. They tried to guilt-trip the public into supporting their bold reforms. But showing the caution and good sense typical of a democratic majority, voters eventually opted for Republicans and moderate Democrats who were less likely to belittle their reservations.

Conservative advocates for school vouchers risk repeating this mistake. The dominant wings of the voucher movement are free-marketers on the one hand, and urban minorities tired of waiting for public school improvement on the other. The result has been a sometimes awkward marriage that has permitted conservatives to claim the potent language of civil rights, and tempted Republicans into believing they could make political inroads with black and Latino voters.

What these advocates have overlooked is the resistance to vouchers and other choice plans among suburban homeowners. While vouchers routinely win the support of 70 percent or more of urban populations, support levels are barely half that in the suburbs, even in favorably worded polls. This resistance has made voucher proponents increasingly frustrated. Are suburbanites just too naive and timid to see the problems with today's inefficient school monopolies? Or do they not care about issues of equity and equal opportunity?

It's time for choice proponents to recognize that suburban resistance to school choice is entirely rational, based largely on self-interest, and unlikely to go away. Otherwise the political clumsiness of voucherites could eventually create an unfortunate suburban backlash against school choice—in much the same way that ramrodding the Great Society programs through did in the late 1970s.

Imagine a hard-working couple, the Grays, who own four season tickets on the 40-yard line for the local pro football team. They invested lots of money and sweat in obtaining the seats, and now use them to share a special experience with their two children. The Grays value these hard-won tickets highly.

Now imagine that the Grays show up one Sunday to find that the stadium has adopted a first-come, first-served seating pattern. What do you predict their reaction is likely to be? Will they smile and say, "Oh, then that's all right!" after the stadium management explains, slowly and in few words, that the old system had produced inequitable results for the poor? Seems unlikely, doesn't it?

A great deal of American family life is now driven by the quality of the public schools in the district where a family happens to live. Parents who have sacrificed to purchase an expensive, heavily taxed home in a better school district have often done so largely because it confers a ticket to the local classrooms for their children. From their perspective, school choice proponents are suggesting that their tickets be torn up.

School choice has many merits and would, in the long run, make America's educational system much more competitive and impressive. But it's important to recognize that choice-based reform has severe distributional consequences. Those who own homes in districts with good schools risk losing tens or even hundreds of thousands of dollars in home equity (as Duke University economist Thomas Nechyba has illustrated). These parents worry they may no longer be able to assure their children access to the educational services they've already purchased. They may find that local schools no longer get the first

crack at quality teachers, or provide as uniformly desirable a peer group.

These are not small concerns. One can be troubled by the inequities of our existing system without pulling the rug out from under suburban families who have worked hard to get their children into decent schools. It is a simple reality that these families are unlikely to look benignly upon measures that might undercut the educational security they have struggled to achieve. This is why cities with troubled public school sytems like Cleveland, Milwaukee, Philadelphia, Dayton, and Washington, D.C. have embraced choice or charter schooling, while suburban communities with more successful schools have remained skeptical.

Let's stipulate that homeowners in good suburban districts will often start out with reservations about school reforms that hand all parents fully paid vouchers, negating the sacrifices they made to get their own children into functional schools. Like it or not, this sprawling bloc of educated and influential voters will prove pivotal to the fate of choice-based reforms. Even copious amounts of morally superior nagging won't change their minds.

What are the implications for voucher proponents? Quite simply, the concerns of these suburbanites need to be addressed, rather than dismissed. Specifically, efforts must be made to provide suburban parents with incentives, compensations, or limits on possible ill effects of publicly funded school choice. This can help ameliorate fear and opposition.

Fix our education system without pulling the rug out from under suburban parents who worked hard to get their children into decent schools.

One approach would be to convince suburban voters that even their "better" schools are much worse than they think, and that the system-wide benefits from choice will create a rising tide that lifts all schools. There is much evidence that suburban public schools, while not dysfunctional, could be much more effective and could benefit from competition. But such an effort will have to confront public skepticism. It risks being undercut if overly rosy instant benefits are promised and not delivered.

A second approach would be to compromise to mitigate possible negative side effects of choice plans. A favorite strategy so far has been to limit the area affected by school choice to urban districts, so as to immunize suburban voters from the change. The Milwaukee and Cleveland voucher programs stipulate that city students can only use their vouchers to attend suburban schools if the suburban districts approve (which they rarely do). Establishment of charter schools has also been limited in suburban communities. Reformers have used gradual changes and half measures, like choice among existing public schools only, to acclimate parents to the idea that the longstanding link between where you live and the schools your children attend is gradually dissolving. Of course, this limits the speed and effectiveness of choice-based reform.

A third approach has barely been considered. This would involve appealing to the reasoned self-interest of suburban parents by sweetening the potential of choice for their families. School choice laws might explicitly encourage new schools to provide options hitherto unavailable even to suburban parents—like alternative daily school schedules or annual calendars, or advanced courses that are currently not available or oversubscribed.

A more radical appeal to self-interest might involve using financial compensation to mitigate, or even undo, perceived negative effects of school choice. Homeowners who feel that the state has constricted their property rights through publicly funded school choice might be offered a tax deduction for the amount of assessed value a home loses in the aftermath of choice-based reform. Permitting homeowners to write this deduction off against current income over a period of time would temper their concerns. This would be analogous to authorities compensating the Grays for nullifying their stadium tickets.

For school choice supporters, self-righteous indignation is not the ticket to winning popular support. Heading down that path will eliminate any chance of broad political victory. Whether educational choice succeeds is ultimately in the hands of America's suburban middle class, so it is that group which advocates must now address—with respect, reason, and rational incentives.

Frederick Hess is an AEI scholar specializing in education reform.

Last Holdout Against Educational Freedom

Every modern nation except the U.S. allows school choice. Here's how our allies make it work.

By Charles Glenn and Jan de Groof

Over the last decade, we conducted a major study of how school systems operate in leading industrialized nations. We found that in every one of the two dozen countries we surveyed (which ranged from Canada, Britain, and Germany to Greece, Russia, and New Zealand), private citizens and religious organizations may operate non-governmental schools. Each country likewise permits parents to meet mandatory schooling requirements by sending their children to these private or religious schools.

The freedom to send one's children to non-government schools is well established in international law and educational practice, in the written constitutions of most free countries, and in the social norms of virtually every nation with universal schooling. Moreover, public funding is provided in virtually every country we surveyed to allow parents to send their children to whatever school they choose.

A right to public funding in support of school choice has emerged as the international standard, largely in response to popular demand. The United States is one of the few advanced countries that still mostly blocks public funding for non-government schools. This is a result of adamant opposition from teacher unions, as well as vestigial provisions in many state constitutions (written amidst nineteenth-century anxiety about Catholic immigrants) that block tax monies from going to religious schools.

The barriers to educational choice in the U.S. are clearly weakening, however. Opinion polls now find strong popular support for "a system giving parents government-funded vouchers to pay for tuition at the public, private, or religious school of their choice." This support is particularly strong (77 percent in favor, 14 percent opposed) among low-income parents in inner cities whose children attend public schools. Despite the strong opposition in certain elite circles, voucher funding for religious schools also enjoys strong support from the public (79 percent to 11 percent). This holds true for Dem-

ocrats (74 percent to 15 percent in favor) as well as Republicans (83 percent to 10 percent), and even for those who report they have no religious affiliation (76 percent to 17 percent).

While in most Western countries there is now great interest in measures that promote autonomy and diversity among schools, every government takes pains to provide a framework of regulation and accountability within which this educational freedom is exercised. The extent of this oversight varies a great deal from country to country. The limited autonomy of schools in France is in marked contrast to the wide autonomy that subsidized schools enjoy in Denmark.

But the last decade has been marked by a growing concern in many countries for effective systems of accountability. Willingness on the part of policymakers to allow both public and subsidized private schools to function more autonomously has usually been accompanied by a heightened demand for measurable academic results. In the U.S., researcher Terry Moe has found that though most Americans support public funding for the schools that parents choose, 88 percent are in favor of teacher certification requirements, 80 percent support curriculum requirements, 83 percent favor financial reporting and auditing requirements, and 86 percent want standardized student testing in order to hold schools accountable.

So what most citizens in the West want is something like a regulated free market for educational services. Citizens of prosperous modern nations believe it reasonable for parents to make choices about the schooling of their own children. The government should not block taxpayer money from following the students; it should limit itself to a regulating role, as it does in other markets.

In debates about extending educational freedom to lower-income families through publicly funded school choice, a litany of well-worn objections is repeatedly thrown down. It is alleged that government support for parental choice will:

- undermine society by teaching strange or dangerous doctrines
- create unequal access and benefit the "advantaged"
- lead unsophisticated parents to choose inferior schools
- weaken government-operated schools via harsh competition
- threaten the status and rights of teachers.

In addition, some *supporters* of private schools worry that they could lose their distinctive character and effectiveness if they begin to rely on public funding.

The results of our study, however, suggest that each of these problems can be avoided by careful design. Everything depends on how parental choice of schools is organized. Because school choice is the norm nearly everywhere except in the U.S., there are many real-life examples of how parental choice can be structured to avoid potential problems. Let's look at how some of our neighbors have avoided the theoretical pitfalls outlined above.

Teaching strange and dangerous doctrines?

This is the original argument for a government monopoly on schooling. The claim is that all children in a society need to be taught the same set of values and loyalties else separate hostile camps will grow up within a nation. This warning has been endlessly repeated, in Europe and the U.S., over the last two centuries. Yet it has never been validated by experience. Despite millions of youngsters educated in Catholic and other private schools in the countries we studied, levels of mutual suspicion and religious conflict have dropped steadily.

It is true that some parents might choose schools that teach beliefs regarded with distaste by other parts of the public. But in a free society this does not mean that these parents should be denied the right to have these beliefs taught to their children, or that the state is entitled to impose some alternate belief on children.

Most people would agree that there are certain messages from which children should be shielded at school, or notions from outside the school to which teachers should present an alternative. But does that require a government monopoly of schooling? No. The need to protect children has been addressed by most Western democracies within the framework of publicly supported school choice.

In Spain, private schools are required to provide instruction on the basis of the principles of human and civil rights expressed in the national constitution. France requires that subsidized private schools—almost all of which are Catholic—provide instruction "with total respect for freedom of conscience." In practice, strange or dangerous doctrines have not been a problem in Europe, even though 70 percent of all students in countries like the Netherlands attend non-government schools using public funding.

The doctrines taught at some "Islamic schools" in Western Europe have rightly raised red flags. But these schools provide supplementary religious instruction—they have neither been funded nor regulated by the state. There is little evidence in Europe that non-government schools that receive public subsidies have taught intolerance or failed to develop civic virtue in their pupils. Indeed, one of the arguments in Europe for funding all-day Muslim schools that follow the national curriculum and employ certified teachers has been to create a mainstream alternative to the informal afternoon and weekend Koran schools run by Islamic fundamentalists with funding from Saudi Arabia and other outsiders.

Meanwhile, plenty of government schools are often not particularly accountable to the public. We suggest, therefore, that it would be more appropriate to be on our guard for unresponsive and irresponsible schools, of whatever structure, rather than assume that private schools are more likely to fall in this category. To the extent that socially subversive schools may exist, it is surely appropriate to protect children from them—without regard to who owns the building.

Unequal access?

In all countries, most poor families live near other poor families, and therefore send their children to schools with a core of students starting with low expectations for achievement. School assignments based on geographic residence, therefore, often produce glaring inequities. Another way to allocate educational opportunities is through standardized tests. But this also leads to school stratification.

A third option is to let students sort themselves, by parental choice. Choice can exacerbate or ameliorate unequal schooling, depending on how it is funded. If there is a refusal to let public funding follow students to alternate schools, as in most of the U.S., then parents with fewer resources, less energy, poorer information, or weaker ambition will often end up with inferior schools.

The only form of parental choice now possible in most of America is the highly impractical and costly option of relocating. Families with higher aspirations move to the suburbs to get away from bad public schools, resulting in ever-increasing segregation of neighborhoods as well as schools by ambition, class, and race. Public schools in the United States have now become more racially segregated than private schools.

But what about the charge that non-government schools will unfairly exclude racial minorities, low-income students, or others, because they are free to select their pupils? This is easily avoided by simple non-discrimination clauses, which are common in countries ranging from Belgium (where two thirds of students attend subsidized private schools) to Norway. Countries like Australia have also chosen to adjust the level of subsidies provided by the government to private schools according to the socioeconomic status of the pupils. The lesson to be learned from this varied experience is that educational equity is better served by funding approved private schools than by letting public school monopolies and family income play the major role in determining whether parents have a say in their children's education.

Choosing inferior schools?

In most countries, subsidized private schools are held to the same academic standards as public schools. Usually these standards are enforced by school inspections and high-stakes national examinations.

In Australia, subsidized schools receive a six-year approval whose renewal is contingent on inspections to determine whether staff are qualified and results satisfactory. Non-public schools in Belgium must submit to government inspection of the subjects taught, the level of instruction, and compliance with the country's strict language laws. The rules do not, however, prescribe teaching methods, which are entirely within the discretion of each school.

Hungary takes a particularly interesting approach to reconciling standards with school autonomy. The national curriculum sets a general educational framework, but leaves it up to individual schools to fill this in with specific courses and teaching methods. Schools submit their curricula to a "National Core Curriculum Bank" from which other schools, if unable or unwilling to develop their own approaches to the national framework, may draw. Curricula in the "national bank" are considered pre-approved and do not require review when any new school adopts them.

In Poland, all schools may choose between adopting a curriculum already approved by the Ministry of Education and developing their own. Schools must also work closely with parents to develop a program for moral education.

Subsidized schools in Sweden are held accountable by the fact that their pupils take national, standardized exams in math, Swedish, English, and civics. Danish private schools, while given extensive freedom to shape their curricula and teaching methods, are similarly accountable to parents for good results: Their national test scores in Danish, math, English, and elective subjects are made public.

Public schools can't compete?

Sweden encourages diversity and competition among public and private schools alike. Depending on where they live, parents may be able to choose, with public support, among local public schools, those of another community, and non-government schools of various sorts. Municipalities are free to decide how to allocate their education funding; most distribute it on a per-pupil basis to the schools chosen by parents.

Similarly, private schools are treated as an equal alternative by the Danish educational system, which allows considerable diversity even among the public schools in the same community. This "Scandinavian model" of even-handed competition among all sorts of schools has been implemented in Finland as well, where even parent-run schools can qualify for financial support from municipalities.

Threatening the rights of teachers?

Some countries require that teachers in subsidized private schools receive the same pay and protections as those in corresponding public schools. This is the case in Denmark, otherwise committed to allowing the most extensive freedoms to each school. Belgium requires its private and religious schools to pay their staffs at the same rate as staff of public schools (with the exception of members of religious teaching orders); this is true in New Zealand as well—a result of insistence by the teacher unions.

In Australia, by contrast, teacher salaries are set by private schools themselves, and may be above or below those negotiated by the unions for the public schools. Some Swedish municipalities set the salary levels, while others leave that up to individual schools, whether state-run or private.

What of that final concern: that taking government money might alter, water down, standardize, or otherwise damage the very qualities in private and religious schools that make them desirable in the first place? There is no question that public funding has led to a substantial loss of autonomy in some countries. This is something the U.S. would need to guard against carefully. Countries like Australia and Norway, however, have found ways to support private and religious schools without undermining their distinctive qualities.

The fact is, private schools in the United States are already subject to state laws that require them to be equivalent to public schools in certain aspects. The good news is, these requirements are usually interpreted flexibly, and there has been little government interference. U.S. courts have held that the distinctiveness of these schools must be respected, so regulation may not be overly intrusive.

This general understanding will help protect the autonomy of America's private educational institutions—particularly if it is defended by broad public opinion and activism against enforced homogenization. Under such conditions America's private and religious schools can thrive within the mainstream as they have thrived outside of it—and on a much larger scale.

Charles Glenn is a professor of education at Boston University. Jan de Groof is a member of the faculty of the Collège d'Europe. Together, they are authors of the study Finding the Right Balance: Freedom, Autonomy, and Accountability in Education.

UNIT 3

Striving for Excellence: The Drive for Quality

Unit Selections

Key Points to Consider

- Identify some of the different points of view on achieving excellence in education. What value conflicts can be defined?

- What are some assumptions about achieving excellence in student achievement that you would challenge? Why?

- What can educators do to improve the quality of student learning?

- Have there been flaws in American school reform efforts in the past 20 years? If so, what are they?

- Has the Internet affected the critical thinking skills of students? Defend your answer.

 **Links: www.dushkin.com/online/**
These sites are annotated in the World Wide Web pages.

Awesome Library for Teachers
http://www.awesomelibrary.org
Education World
http://www.education-world.com
EdWeb/Andy Carvin
http://edwebproject.org
Kathy Schrock's Guide for Educators
http://www.discoveryschool.com/schrockguide/
Teacher's Guide to the U.S. Department of Education
http://www.ed.gov/pubs/TeachersGuide/

The debate continues over which academic standards are most appropriate for elementary and secondary school students. Discussion regarding the impact on students and teachers of state proficiency examinations goes on in those states or provinces where such examinations are mandated. We are still dealing with how best to assess student academic performance. Some very interesting proposals on how to do this have emerged.

There are several incisive analyses of why American educators' efforts to achieve excellence in schooling have frequently failed. Today, some interesting proposals are being offered as to how we might improve the academic achievement of students. The current debate regarding excellence in education clearly reflects parents' concerns for more choices in how they school their children.

Many authors of recent essays and reports believe that excellence can be achieved best by creating new models of schooling that give both parents and students more control over the types of school environments available to them. Many believe that more money is not a guarantor of quality in schooling. Imaginative academic programming and greater citizen choice can guarantee at least a greater variety of options open to parents who are concerned about their children's academic progress in school.

We each wish the best quality of life that we can attain, and we each desire the opportunity for an education that will optimize our chances to achieve our objectives. The rhetoric on excellence and quality in schooling has been heated, and numerous opposing concepts of how schools can reach these goals have been presented for public consideration in recent years. Some progress has been realized on the part of students as well as some major changes in how teacher education programs are structured.

In the decades of the 1980s and 1990s, those reforms instituted to encourage qualitative growth in the conduct of schooling tended to be what education historian David Tyack once referred to as "structural" reforms. Structural reforms consist of demands for standardized testing of students and teaching, reorganization of teacher education programs, legalized actions to provide alternative routes into the teaching profession, efforts to recruit more people into teaching, and laws to enable greater parental choice as to where their children may attend school. These structural reforms cannot, however, in and of themselves produce higher levels of student achievement. We need to explore a broader range of the essential purposes of schooling, which will require our redefining what it means to be a literate person. We need also to reconsider what we mean by the "quality" of education and to reassess the essential purposes of schooling.

When we speak of quality and excellence as aims of education, we must remember that these terms encompass aesthetic and affective as well as cognitive processes. Young people cannot achieve the full range of intellectual capacity to solve problems on their own simply by being obedient and by memorizing data. How students encounter their teachers in classrooms and how teachers interact with their students are concerns that encompass both aesthetic and cognitive dimensions.

There is a real need to enforce intellectual standards and yet also to make schools more creative places in which to learn, places where students will yearn to explore, to imagine, and to hope.

Compared to those in the United States, students in European nations appear to score higher in assessments of skills in mathematics and the sciences, in written essay examinations in the humanities and social sciences, and in the routine oral examinations given by committees of teachers to students as they exit secondary schools.

What forms of teacher education and in-service reeducation are needed? Who pays for these programmatic options? Where and how will funds be raised or redirected from other priorities to pay for this? Will the "streaming and tracking" model of secondary school student placement that exists in Europe be adopted? How can we best assess academic performance? Can we commit to a more heterogeneous grouping of students and to full inclusion of handicapped students in our schools? Many individual, private, and governmental reform efforts did not address these questions.

Other industrialized nations champion the need for alternative secondary schools to prepare their young people for varied life goals and civic work. The American dream of the common school translated into what has become the comprehensive high school of the twentieth century. But does it provide all the people with alternative diploma options? If not, what is the next step? What must be changed? For one, concepts related to our educational goals must be clarified and political motivation must be separated from the realities of student performance.

Policy development for schooling needs to be tempered by even more "bottom-up," grassroots efforts to improve the quality of schools that are now under way in many communities in North America. New and imaginative inquiry and assessment strategies need to be developed by teachers working in their classrooms, and they must nurture the support of professional colleagues and parents.

Excellence is the goal: the means to achieve it is what is in dispute. There is a new dimension to the debate over assessment of academic achievement of elementary and secondary school students. In addition, the struggle continues of conflicting academic (as well as political) interests in the quest to improve the quality of preparation of our future teachers, and we also need to sort these issues out.

No conscientious educator would oppose the idea of excellence in education. The problem in gaining consensus over how to attain it is that the assessment of excellence of both teacher and student performance is always based on some preset standards. Which standards of assessment should prevail?

Classroom Crisis:
It's About Time

The new testing requirements are the latest addition to an ever-growing list of demands on teachers that steal time from academic instruction. Ms. Meek gives a play-by-play account of a day in a third-grade classroom. How many minutes can actually be spent teaching?

BY CLAUDIA MEEK

EDUCATION talk is everywhere. In a voter exit poll taken by the *Los Angeles Times* on 8 March 2000, both Democrats and Republicans listed education as their top concern.[1] Rivers of ink and torrents of bytes about education are flowing from the pens and keyboards of writers both in and outside the field. Commentators pontificate; researchers analyze; columnists criticize. Through it all, we teachers simply go to work each day and try to satisfy an increasingly broad array of social and academic expectations.

Amid this chorus of voices, one note is missing: the voice of the classroom itself. Concerns, philosophies, politics, persuasive public opinions, and methodologies of the day all converge in the daily learning environment of the classroom. In this small, educational Petri dish, the finite amount of time available collides with social and academic mandates, not the least of which are the broadened subject-area standards connected with high-stakes testing. In this article, I examine the conflict between available time and time demands in a third-grade classroom.

I will examine the subject of time in elementary school in two ways. First, I'll present data collected from my own third-grade public school classroom, buttressed by data from large-scale research published by the National Center for Education Statistics. Second, I invite readers to share the sequence of events during a real day in my classroom. This second strand of information goes beyond the data to reflect how elementary education is often *experienced* in today's schools and lends support to the all-too-common teacher refrain, "There's no time to teach!"

THE CASE STUDY CLASSROOM

Beginning with the 1999–2000 school year, I logged the minutes spent on various activities in my third-grade classroom. I divided the activities into two main groups: academic instruction and social services. Under the heading "social services" I placed all classroom activities that did not focus on an academic

subject. These fell into the following subcategories: fundraising, disaster preparedness, socialization, holidays, assemblies, regular interruptions (bells, morning announcements, etc.), and miscellaneous.

At the end of the academic year, I totaled the combined minutes from my logbooks. The yearly academic minutes allotted for instruction in my classroom exceeded those required by the California Department of Education.[2] However, the sum of classroom interruptions in all categories for the year amounted to 15,695 minutes — nearly 262 hours. When subtracted from the classroom minutes available, 30% of classroom time was spent on social services. Nearly one-third of all the time available for actually teaching the required academic subjects was absorbed by a crush of other responsibilities.[3]

THE TIME IT TAKES TO TEST

To be thorough in our review of classroom time use, I should mention a new and ravenous time-consumer: extensive test preparation and the actual time it takes to administer tests. These two activities draw on the same finite number of classroom minutes as social service activities and academic instruction.

Testing time has increased dramatically in recent years. Just five years ago, yearly testing in California elementary schools often took one week or less. At my school, the SAT-9 testing window was lengthened to three weeks during 1999-2000. Although learning did take place during this time through the review of subject matter, the school felt like it was in "suspended animation" until all tests were completed. Teachers were encouraged to give test reviews when students were not actually taking tests.

In addition to the SAT-9 testing, third-graders in this school district were required to take a district-generated set of assessment tests twice during the 1999–2000 school year. These assessments were given in addition to the normally scheduled subject-matter exams that coincide with curriculum being taught. The total time spent on student assessment generated outside the classroom by state and district mandates during 1999–2000 was approximately 32 hours. These 32 testing hours were in addition to the 262 hours of social service time cited above. Thus 294 hours in a single academic year were unavailable for instruction.[4] With these numbers in mind, we can begin to understand the time pressure felt by those in elementary school classrooms.

CAN 50,000 TEACHERS BE WRONG?

My study dealt with just a single classroom — my own — in a single state — California. Readers may well wonder if these findings are consistent with those across the nation. The National Center for Education Statistics reported the results of a large data set, collected from elementary schools in both public and private sectors in the U.S. The NCES report detailed the use of classroom time as it relates to teaching academic subjects. The sample of public school teachers numbered 53,008, and the data were gathered over three different school years: 1987–88, 1990–91, and 1993–94. The sample was stratified by state, by sector, and by school level. The report focused on first through fourth grade, and the information reflected data only from full-time, self-contained public school classrooms.[5]

The NCES data showed that the percentage of time spent on core curriculum generally does not vary by student, classroom, teacher, school, or community characteristics. Teachers who work with poor students or English-language learners spend the same amount of time teaching the core academic subjects as do teachers who work with more advantaged pupils. Teachers in the NCES study spent an average of 68% of school time teaching the core academic curriculum.[6] Of course, that means that 32% of classroom time is spent on activities that I have chosen to designate as social services. According to this body of data, there was little variation in the amount of time that teachers spent teaching core curriculum subjects in the classroom over the three years surveyed or across the United States.

BEYOND THE NUMBERS: IT'S A TEACHER'S LIFE

Numbers and studies. Data and details. These research tools demonstrate numerically that there is not enough classroom time to meet the broad array of classroom expectations. The expanded demands of testing raise the level of stress on students, teachers, and schools. But in the bare bones of research reporting, the meat is often overlooked. So here's the beef. Join me for a glimpse into my third-grade classroom, circa 2000.

It's already 7:15. I'm later than usual getting to the classroom this morning. I wanted to get a lot done before school. Ugh! This classroom smells horrible. I'll just plug in new room deodorants, open the windows, and boot up the computer. I need to make copies of those Valentine homework passes. It's a better gift than candy. Glad I got my other handout copies for

this week done last Friday. Oh, I want to write a Valentine's Day letter to the class myself. Better do that right now.

Okay, that sounds pretty good. Now I'll get on the copy machine before everybody gets here at 7:45. Quick, I'll check the Parent Resource Center copy machine first. No, it's not turned on. Should I wait or risk a long line in the teacher workroom for the other machine?

"Linda, how many in line?" Looks like about 10 minutes before I can make my copies. I'll have to come back. Don't forget the daily school bulletin and the attendance folder. I have to talk to the principal about the meeting for my new student, Brandon. The phone for his family seems to be disconnected. I'll try later. Oh no, I need to write out my monthly award certificates. That awards assembly is today. I'll start them this morning if I can make it back to the classroom before 8:15.

"Yes, Kathy, I'll review that new report card format for next year, the one showing the student performance standards." Maybe I can do that during recess. It needs to be passed along quickly to the other third- grade teachers. I don't have recess duty today, so maybe I can connect with the county special education people about Bryan. He needs a special classroom placement for next year.

"Good morning, Mrs. Beason. All the parents are putting their Valentine's party donations on the table in the classroom. Go ahead in. Yes, Tiffany is doing a great job on Accelerated Reader and is ahead of everyone in her challenge math. She can go ahead and take her computer test if you stay in the classroom with her. Yes, I'll be right back after I make these copies on the machine."

There's the usual buzzing crowd outside the classroom. It's funny how everything is so exciting to 8-year-olds. Valentine's Day is such a big deal. "Okay, kids, if you have Valentines or food, put it on the back table in the classroom. There's the bell. Go outside and line up for me, please."

"Hello Mrs. Morris. I can't conference now. Walk to the playground with me to pick up the class, and we'll talk about Mark. He hasn't been turning in his homework. Okay, kids, let's walk to the classroom. Yes, he has his binder, but his homework isn't in it. Keep checking his assignment sheet every night."

The classroom smells better now, but I have to shampoo those stains out of the carpet. Gross. "Class, please begin your morning language and math review. Perfect papers get a sticker."

Let's see. I need to collect money for yearbooks, plus those Valentine letters from parents, and homework. I also need those permission slips so I can take the Accelerated Reader contest winners to lunch with me on Friday.

"Who has their pizza permission slips signed?" It's so easy for them to remember the things they really want to do! Oh, and I need to remember the box tops for PTA.

"Kids, put your Valentines away for now. Our party will start at about 9:30." I wish we could have the party after lunch, but then we have the awards assembly. "First, we work, then we'll play." Didn't my grandmother say that?

Maybe I can at least get through our spelling words for this week. "Kids, please go to the word wall. This week all our words have a long e. How does the e get long?" I've got to hurry to get this done before recess. I want them to run off some of that sugar they'll have at the party so we can settle in afterwards. We really have a lot to cover today.

"Thanks for coming in, Mrs. Hill. Yes, I'll show you how to set up for the party back there. Just let me finish our spelling. Let's keep some of the cookies back for another time. Yes, Brittany can help you."

I'll use some of those letters written by parents as Valentines for our oral language lesson. We can set up the microphone. "Kids, after we distribute our Valentines and while we are eating, you may read your Valentines from your parents to the class. I'd like to read mine to you first to model what I expect you to do."

I need to get this party mess cleaned up. "Class, you need to be finished with your food in another five minutes for recess. Edgar, please take the trash can around the room."

I'll try to reach Brandon's family during recess. I've got to finish his paperwork for the meeting. Poor little guy; he's really trying hard. He's doing well in his small reading group, but he'll never pass those new grade-level competencies. Wish I could get in touch with his family by phone. I'll write a letter tonight if it's still disconnected.

There's the end of recess bell. I'll walk the kids to their PE class and check my lesson plans again. Maybe we can get back on track. "OK, boys and girls, line up for PE."

As the day in my third-grade classroom careened to a close, there was some academic time between 11 a.m. and lunch at 12:30 p.m. During that time, the class experienced five interruptions: two Valentine balloon deliveries, two intercom announcements, and one parent drop-in. A school awards assembly after lunch kept the students out of the classroom until afternoon recess at 2 p.m. At 2:15 p.m., there was time for a brief social studies lesson, and the class was dismissed at 2:34 p.m.

IN THE LAND OF BUREAUCRATIC FICTION

Education guidelines created at the state level can suggest that any number of minutes be spent on academics in elementary school classrooms. However, the California Department of Education assigns only *eight minutes a day* for housekeeping tasks in the classroom. Please! This time is to include collecting assigned homework, taking the roll, discussing upcoming school events, collecting money and notes from parents, writing behavior referrals, settling classroom disputes, dealing with health issues, responding to intercom calls or classroom visits by parents, and… need I go on? In addition, zero minutes are allotted by the state for electives, which theoretically should complement all the other functions that take place in public school classrooms.[7] From this brief look inside a third-grade classroom, one can see that the state-recommended academic minutes are simply bureaucratic fictions.

Furthermore, schools are free to arrange for any number of assemblies and fund-raisers. The social services we provide to children are enormously important. Assemblies that cover drug awareness and divorce issues, for example, help children and families in ways that perhaps no other social institution can. But these extensive social services take time away from teaching the academic curriculum.

The public and the politicians can also demand high test scores, and solid academic standards are the backbone of public education. But the current extensive academic standards require enormous amounts of time to teach. Which of our classroom social service activities should we eliminate to free the time needed to cover these standards?

The numbers don't add up. In reality, there is not enough classroom time to shoulder the academic, social service, and assessment missions that the public schools have accumulated. What can be done? That is another story. But we have taken the first step in our recovery program: we have recognized and articulated a serious problem. And it's about time.

NOTES

1. "The Message Behind the Votes," *Los Angeles Times*, 8 March 2000, p. A-20.
2. California Association of School Business Officials, *Education Code*, October 2000, section 11.21:46112.
3. Claudia Meek, "The Scoop on Schools: It's About Time" (Doctoral dissertation, American World University, 2001). Each of the six data logs generated from the 1999-2000 school year is unique. For instance, the first log reflects several large blocks of ongoing time absorbers, such as solving classroom disputes. Such interruptions were factored in at 10 minutes per day in a 180-day year. Likewise, morning announcements, housekeeping tasks, and bells that stop the flow of instruction are factored in at 20 minutes per day. Other logs simply record assemblies, fund-raisers, disaster drills, and so on as they occurred throughout the year.
4. Ibid., p. 40.
5. *Time Spent Teaching Core Academic Subjects in Elementary Schools: Comparisons Across Community, School, Teacher, and Student Characteristics* (Washington, D.C.: National Center for Education Statistics, Statistical Analysis Report, February 1997), pp. 8–10.
6. Ibid., pp. 12–13.
7. *State Mandated Instruction Time by Subject*. Information supplied to teachers by Hemet Unified School District, Hemet, California, 1990s to present. Each teacher is required to submit a detailed plan for instructional minutes at the beginning of the school year that reflects mandated minutes per academic subject. State department of education officials say that minutes are suggested, not mandated.

CLAUDIA MEEK is a third-grade teacher at Bautista Creek Elementary School, Hemet, Calif. (e-mail: claudon@pe.net).

From *Phi Delta Kappan*, April 2003, pp. 592-595. © 2003 by Phi Delta Kappa International, Inc. Reprinted by permission.

Needed: Homework Clubs for Young Adolescents Who Struggle with Learning

JOSEPH SANACORE

As we enter the new millennium, many young adolescents are demonstrating a greater need for support from the village. Demographic trends such as a high divorce rate, a rise in the number of homes with two working parents, and an increase in single parents who must work have resulted in home situations in which these students do not have a consistently available adult they can talk to about their daily stresses. As important, they do not have a consistently available resource to help them with homework assignments or, at least, to structure their homework environment. One way of responding to this problem is to organize homework clubs that support the individual needs of middle school students.

Homework Clubs Are Important

The expression "children home alone" conjures up an image of young people at the mercy of any unscrupulous person who wants to harm them. Certainly, unprotected children are increasingly at risk of being sexually abused, harassed, bullied, or otherwise mistreated. From an academic perspective, being home alone suggests that young teenagers might not be involved in thoughtful activities because they are spending too much time watching television, playing video games, socializing on the telephone, and engaging in other activities that do not extend or complement school-related goals. The learning that occurs in school usually needs reinforcement at home; a local homework club can provide the type of setting that supports the school's instructional priorities. An added benefit is that learning is taking place in a safe and caring environment.

Homework clubs are also important because they foster individualization of instruction. The class size in some schools can range from twenty-five to forty students, and these learning communities receive minimal support from paraprofessionals and volunteers. Obviously, this teacher-student ratio can diminish opportunities for responding to young adolescents as individuals. While attending a homework club, however, these learners can work with a caring adult who highlights their strengths and needs. To illustrate, a student who is struggling with reading might be expected to read a section of Avi's *The Fighting Ground* (1984) and discuss it in class the following day. Because this student is an American Revolution buff, the club teacher capitalizes on this strength by connecting the student's prior knowledge to the book's content. Then, they both engage in a variation of paired reading as they complete the assigned section of *The Fighting Ground*.

Homework clubs also help students to respond personally to assignments. When middle school learners are permitted to personalize homework activities, they are more likely to become intensely emotional and empathetic as they develop relationships with story characters. For example, historical fiction writer James Lincoln Collier recently talked with sixth graders at a Long Island middle school. Responding to a student's question, "What motivates you to write?" Collier said that he loves "to personalize history by performing an act of imagination, jumping out of this world and into the world of my characters. In a sense, I become the characters who lived during the period of time. I feel as they feel. I hear what they hear. I think as they think. I am there!" (Sanacore 1995). These thoughts of a writer could easily become the reflections of a reader, especially if the reader is supported by the club teacher. Not surprisingly, when middle-level learners respond personally to homework assignments, their interest and engagement increase.

Another important aspect of homework clubs is their sensitive response to the unique personalities of learners. A shy student who is unwilling to become involved in class discussion, role playing, Readers' Theater, or similar activities might be willing to participate in these activities in a club setting. When such participation does occur, the student develops confidence and competence, which he or she will probably bring back to the classroom. Similarly, individuals who are reluctant to share their literature response journals with the classroom community may feel more comfortable sharing their journals with a smaller number of students attending the club. These and other personality characteristics are more easily accommodated in homework clubs than in larger classroom environments.

The Homework Club: A Brief Description

Homework clubs are available in schools, churches, synagogues, libraries, and community agencies. They can take many forms and are given many titles, including "clinic," "center," "program," and "institute." Regardless of their format and title, their main intent is to support a school's efforts to help struggling learners succeed. For example, one after-school program is supervised by a teacher and a social worker who are paid through the school budget. In another setting, a school-university partnership has enabled undergraduate and graduate interns to work with middle school children from 3:30 to 5:30 PM, focusing on homework, school-related projects, and technology use. The program provides young adolescents with meaningful connections to college interns, and it also gives the interns valuable field experiences with the "real" world of education. This school-university partnership is codirected by a school administrator and a university supervisor. In both of these settings and in other well-structured after-school programs, teachers and their teaching assistants accept important responsibilities such as organizing appropriate instructional activities that are well matched with learners' strengths and needs, connecting these activities in a congruent way to classroom expectations, and evaluating the worth of these efforts.

Not surprisingly, students who struggle with learning are usually referred to a homework club by classroom teachers or special educators. Guidance counselors, administrators, and parents can also refer children to a club because they are failing, reading and writing below their potential, struggling in mathematics and science and other content areas, or lacking a structured homework environment at home. The importance of providing these individuals with a warm, caring milieu cannot be underscored enough.

When a student arrives at the club, he or she has a snack while the instructor reviews the homework assignment from school. After the club teacher and student develop a rapport, both work cooperatively to complete the assignment. Typically, learners attend the club on weekday afternoons or on Saturdays for one to three hours. Based on need, students should have options to rotate in and out of the program or to remain for the entire school year.

Key Elements of Effective Homework Clubs

Homework clubs certainly have a constructive purpose, and they are more apt to successfully support struggling learners when key elements are working in concert. These elements include, but are not limited to, the following guidelines:

Create Homework Assignments That are Interesting and Challenging

An important responsibility of classroom teachers is to give homework that extends students' thinking and simultaneously challenges them to enjoy related problem solving. A special

"Fresh Voices" report appeared in *Parade* magazine, addressing the topic "How We Can Make Our Schools Better." A sampling of students from throughout the United States wrote on the topic, "What I Would Change about My School." Interestingly, a fourteen year old boy provided insights about homework:

> In most of my classes, homework is like, "Read the chapter and answer the questions at the end." Boring. I'd like to use my mind a little more. Like in history in seventh grade, we were studying caravans, and the teacher had us write a journal as if we were in a trading caravan in ancient times, traveling from city to city. A lot more interesting and challenging. (Minton 1999, 4)

This young teenager's personal response echoes other students' feelings about homework, and collectively they suggest that stimulating assignments in all subject areas are more beneficial for learning than are boring, reductionistic activities that cause apathy toward learning.

Provide a Read-Aloud Experience During Every Club Session

One of the most powerful ways of influencing learners' understanding of text is to read to them each day. When we read aloud a book that we love and that we believe students will love, we provide a demonstration of reading fluency and enjoyment that they can observe and emulate. Short, Harste, and Burke (1996) believe that students benefit from read-alouds, which give exposure to book language, story patterns, and varied literature. This exposure nurtures students' interest in reading and expands their choices of books to read.

An experienced club teacher is well aware of the positive impact that read-alouds can have on all students, but especially those who struggle with learning. Read-alouds serve as scaffolds for individuals who are unable to complete their homework assignments independently or do not have access to resources in their homes. Whether read-alouds are incorporated into reading assignments or used during free time after homework is completed, these important literacy events increase the chances that students who struggle with learning will benefit in both short-term and long-term ways. This holds true in mathematics, science, social studies, language arts, and other curricular areas.

Run Alongside Struggling Learners

Similar to the intent of interactive read-alouds are conferences in which teachers read and write along with students. Drawing on Tharp and Gallimore's (1988) analogy of running alongside a child who is learning how to ride a bicycle, Bomer (1998) believes that reading and writing conferences with struggling literacy learners provide opportunities for working closely with these individuals. During conferences, the teacher reads and writes along with each learner while whispering cues and guiding interactive responses.

Although these scaffolded activities benefit learners in both immediate and lasting ways, running alongside learners is often confusing because quick decisions about guiding them need to be made in a natural, supportive manner. Bomer (1998) therefore suggests a cheat-sheet of guidelines that might be helpful for a while. These guidelines are intended for read-along conferences, but they also can be adapted for writing:

- Speak softly, gently. Think of yourself as a voice inside the reader's head—because you will be.
- Aim through the reading for meaning. Act as if [the student] is telling you something that's supposed to make sense, rather than acting as if the student is performing "reading." Say, "What'd you say?" or "He did what?" as you would to yourself if you read something that didn't make sense to you.
- If the reader stops, wait. After singing something silently to yourself, ask what she is thinking.
- One thing to ask is, "What would make sense?" or "What could that be?" This asks the reader to make a guess based on sense-making.
- Try as often as possible to figure out a way to keep the reader thinking through text… after you leave the conference. What could he do with a friend that would extend this learning?

These guidelines support a more focused interaction among the student, the text, and the club teacher. They also help the learner to gain insights that he or she can apply to other parts of the curriculum.

Supply the Homework Club with a Wide Variety of Resources

Another major support system for struggling learners is a library resource center that is part of the club. Having access to the center's materials will help them with their homework assignments as well as nurture their lifetime literacy. The resource center should include a diversity of materials, such as paperbacks, picture books, fiction and nonfiction works, poetry anthologies, comedies and dramas, large-print books, "how-to" manuals, audiobooks, bibliotherapeutic stories, illustrated books, multicultural sources, dictionaries, computer software, videotapes, newspapers, magazines, pamphlets, and artifacts (Sanacore 1997, 2000, 2002; Sanacore and Wilsusen 1995; Tiedt 2000).

Although these materials are beneficial for all students' learning, technological resources can also have a special impact on learners with special needs. These individuals might learn more effectively with such adaptive hardware as electronic communication aids with voice synthesizers and computers that scan and read aloud printed materials. Complementing these and other hardware adaptations are certain software products that can meet a range of special needs. For example, the *Language Experience Recorder* (Teacher Support Software) and *Write: OutLoud* (Don Johnston) are talking word processors, with the latter product providing the advantage of reading back students' writing by a nonjudgmental source. Also worth mentioning is *Storybook Weaver* (MECC), which is a multimedia resource that not only stimulates creative writing but also is useful across the curriculum. In addition, the *Student Writing Center* (The Learning Company) provides students with oppor-

tunities to produce documents (e.g., newspapers and reports), to incorporate graphics, and to make choices (Sanacore 1997).

Struggling learners, in particular, profit from a well-stocked resource center because they have immediate access to print and nonprint materials that might not be available in their homes. As important, students who attend the club are more likely to respond positively to their literacy learning and thus to use it for the rest of their lives.

Enhance Club Activities through Effective Staff Development

Whether the homework club is staffed by full-time or part-time, novice, veteran, or retired teachers, these individuals benefit from effective staff development. Specifically, they need exposure to activities that connect the classroom and club settings so that efforts to help struggling learners are well coordinated. Because coordination is the joint responsibility of club teachers, classroom teachers, and administrators, these professionals should use the staff development sessions to develop insights and strategies for helping young adolescents to complete their homework successfully. The focus of staff development is to create stimulating homework assignments that (*a*) extend classroom learning, (*b*) engage students in powerful read-alouds, (*c*) guide learners to read and write interactively, (*d*) provide opportunities for shadowing students during the act of reading and writing, (*e*) match individuals with appropriate resources, (*f*) invite learners to make choices that are personally interesting and satisfying , (*g*) encourage students to be reflective, and (*h*) motivate learners to evaluate their own progress.

These and other related areas can be covered successfully through a variety of staff development options, including full-day sessions, after-school workshops, and informal study groups. Another option for strengthening homework assignments is a variation of peer coaching, which involves mutual observations of the classroom and club teachers. Peer coaching is especially effective when the entire faculty "buys into" the process, when collaborative activity is highlighted, when the "coach" is the teacher being observed and the "coached" is the teacher observing, and when teachers become involved in cooperative activities that positively influence students' learning (Showers and Joyce 1996). Classroom and club teachers who engage in peer coaching are more apt to develop insights about how young teenagers respond to homework. Staff development options offer teachers comfortable outlets for learning to improve students' learning through stimulating homework activities.

Evaluate Students' Progress and the Effectiveness of Homework Assignments

The process and content of homework assignments can be a powerful or mediocre source of support for students' learning. Continuous communication between the classroom and club teachers may help determine the value of the assignments. By talking or writing to each other at least once a week, they have opportunities to elaborate on students' work and determine if the homework is responsive to students' strengths and needs. This type of congruent communication goes a long way in helping individuals who struggle with learning to understand the instructional connections between the classroom and club settings.

Regrettably, teachers are sometimes so busy that the important process of congruent communication is neglected. One way of resolving this problem is for classroom teachers to complete brief contact sheets concerning homework assignments. The following areas should be included on the contact sheets: date, student's name, objective(s), suggested resources and materials, recommended strategies and activities, and comments from the club teacher and student. Delivering the contact sheets to the club teacher and returning them to the classroom teacher are the student's responsibility.

As the classroom and club teachers communicate through discussion, contact sheets, or other means, they should highlight each student's pertinent accomplishments. To illustrate, a discussion might concern a rubric that was used to evaluate an individual's progress in a writing assignment. This year, such a discussion was observed, which focused on a variety of criteria for rating a student's expository writing. Cooperatively, the classroom and club teachers connected the rubric to the sixth grader's development of topic, plan of organization, elaboration of ideas, demonstration of sentence variety, use of language, and use of mechanics. This discussion helped the teachers realize that the student developed her topic imaginatively, organized her ideas logically, and developed her ideas fully through examples and explanations; however, she demonstrated minimal sentence variety, used incorrect language occasionally, and made errors in mechanics that, at times, hindered the clarity of the writing. At the end of this discussion, both classroom and club teachers developed better insights about the type of class work and homework that highlights the girl's writing strengths. Fortunately, rubrics are useful for evaluating children's progress in writing, reading, listening, talking, visualizing, and other important areas of communication. As important, they give students opportunities to evaluate their own learning.

Evaluating one's own progress is vital to the independence and success of struggling students. Regrettably, individuals who have experienced continuous failure do not have a clear sense of their strengths and needs. These individuals profit from sensitive classroom and club teachers who discuss with them the relationships among their effort, strategy use, and successful text interpretation. Walker (1992) suggests that these discussions be supported in a variety of ways, such as (a) inviting students to decide what artifacts are placed in their portfolios so they can evaluate their success in different instructional areas and determine their progress over time; (b) encouraging learners to use checklists to evaluate success in specific literacy activities (e.g., writing a summary of a story and deciding whether or not they considered elements of story grammar); and (c) guiding individuals to talk about their strategy use and related effort. Walker elaborates on this third suggestion by referring to a teacher who motivates students to connect their discussions of successful reading strategies and effort to key as-

pects of predictive reading. After reading stories, the students rate their predictions in relation to a chart.

> Assessments like this help struggling readers attribute their performance to intrinsic factors such as their own knowledge and skill at using strategies rather than to luck or easy materials.... As students identify and assess the problem-solving strategies they use, they can attribute their success to these strategies rather than to abilities they believe they don't possess. (29–30)

Walker's considerations are easily adapted to classroom and club settings, thus providing struggling learners with opportunities to develop confidence in evaluating their own progress. With positive experiences in the self-assessment process, these learners will probably continue to use it throughout their lives.

Secure Funding for the Club

Effective clubs need funding for personnel, professional development, resources, transportation, and other related items. The central office administration and board of education are key players in designating the budget for a homework club. If the school budget cannot pay for all club expenses, other sources should be investigated.

Specifically, administrators and teachers can work cooperatively with the PTSA to sponsor a resource drive. Through newsletters, coffee klatches, and other means of communication, the PTSA can encourage the community to donate functional hardware, software, and print and nonprint materials. The PTSA can also sponsor book sales and other events and can use profits to buy needed resources. Another potential source is local industry, which is well known for making donations of money and functional products in exchange for tax exemptions. Complementing these efforts are state and federal grants, whose financial support is useful for securing important materials and equipment. In addition, private foundations and philanthropic organizations are sources of support that can significantly enhance efforts to promote effective homework clubs.

Advocating for Homework Clubs

Today's demographic trends indicate disruptions in young adolescents' lives, and the homework club represents one positive response to this problem. A well-planned club provides students with a safe environment while it helps them extend school-related learning. Although most students benefit from the club setting, those who struggle with learning especially profit from the club's offerings and services. Learners who are at risk of failure are more apt to "slip through the cracks" in bureaucratic schools and stressed-out homes; conversely, their chances of being successful in the after-school club are increased because this environment supports individualized and small-group activities. Having positive experiences in the club, however, depends on important elements, such as stimulating homework assignments, powerful read-alouds, club teachers who read and write alongside children, a club library with a wide variety of resources, an updated staff, evaluative strategies that focus on students' progress and the effectiveness of their homework assignments, and adequate funding. When these and other key elements are orchestrated by genuinely caring educators, the homework club becomes an empowering source of support for helping individuals catch up with peers and become successful learners for the rest of their lives.

Key words: homework clubs, struggling learners, teacher development

REFERENCES

Avi. 1984. *The Fighting Ground*. New York: Lippincott.

Bomer, R. 1998. Conferring with struggling readers: The test of our craft, courage, and hope. *New Advocate* 12:21–38.

Minton, L 1999. How we can make our schools better. *Parade* 4.

Sanacore, J. 1995. Handing our students over to authors: Parents, teachers, and administrators supporting an effective visiting authors' program. *Journal of Reading* 38: 576–79.

_____. 1997. Reaching out to a diversity of learners: Innovative educators need substantial support. *Journal of Adolescent and Adult Literacy* 41:224–29.

_____. 2000. Promoting the lifetime reading habit in middle school students. *The Clearing House* 73:157–61.

_____. 2002. Struggling literacy learners benefit from lifetime literacy efforts. *Reading Psychology: An International Quarterly* 23: 67–86.

Sanacore, J., and S. Wilsusen. 1995. Success for young at-risk children: Treat them as we treat all children. *Reading and Writing Quarterly: Overcoming Learning Difficulties* 11:359–68.

Short, K., J. Harste, and C. Burke. 1996. *Creating classrooms for authors and inquirers*. Portsmouth, NH: Heinemann.

Showers, B., and B. Joyce. 1996. The evolution of peer coaching. *Educational Leadership* 53:12–16.

Tharp, R, and R. Gallimore. 1988. *Rousing minds to life: Teaching, learning, and schooling in social context*. Cambridge: Cambridge University Press.

Tiedt, I. 2000. *Teaching with picture books in the middle school*. Newark, DE: International Reading Association.

Walker, B. 1992. *Supporting struggling readers*. Ontario, Canada: Pippin.

Joseph Sanacore chairs the Department of Special Education and Literacy at the C.W. Post Campus of Long Island University, in Brookville, New York.

From *The Clearing House*, November/December 2002. © 2002 by Heldref Publications, 1319, Eighteenth St., NW, Washington, DC 20036-1802. Reprinted with permission of the Helen Dwight Reid Educational Foundation.

A Nation Deceived

Playing the blame game won't help at-risk kids, but universal preschool will

By Kenneth H. Maurer

Twenty years ago, the landmark report *A Nation at Risk* blamed educators for our failing economy and our failing students. The solution entailed raising standards, testing students and teachers, and holding educators accountable.

While *A Nation at Risk* reported the dismal results of students on standardized tests, no research was done to justify the blame placed on educators for the failing schools and the failing economy. Instead, we set almost unreachable national education goals, and now we have the No Child Left Behind Act (NCLB).

A follow-up study might well be titled *A Nation Deceived*. Over the past two decades, we have been deceived into thinking that all will be well in education if only we fix the teachers and the schools. Under this scenario, NCLB sounds like a rational solution. But in my opinion, it's not.

It's hard to argue with the law's basic tenets—increased student achievement, better teachers, and higher standards for all. Most people would agree these are good goals. And if all students were equal in all ways, NCLB might work wonders for our schools.

Unfortunately, though, that is not the case.

Special education students, for example, are labeled "special education" because they have learning or physical disabilities. Too many low-income students lack the social skills, the health care, and the natural learning opportunities that come from an upper- or middle-income environment. Nothing in the No Child Left Behind Act provides impoverished or special education students with the means to pull themselves up by their own bootstraps or to help overworked teachers perform miracles in their classrooms. Children will be left behind.

Good goals, bad execution

Do you believe all children come to school ready to learn? Do you believe all children have access to proper health care? Do you think all children have the social skills necessary to be successful in school?

Research supports the idea that students who are mentally, physically, and emotionally ready for first grade do much better academically than students who are not. One major component of the Goals 2000: Educate America Act, signed into law by President Clinton in March 1994, was that every child would be ready to enter first grade. That legislation

seemed to take into account some basic facts:

- Children are more likely than any other age group to be poor.
- Child poverty rates are climbing.
- Minority children are three times as likely to be reared in poverty as majority children.
- Poverty in early childhood has long-lasting negative consequences for cognitive development and academic outcomes.
- Our nation loses when human resources are lost because children do not reach their potential.

For President Bush and Congress, setting the goals for NCLB was the easy part. Achieving those goals will take much more work. We are no closer to making sure that no child is left behind in 2003 than we were in the late 1980s and early '90s.

Children need social skills, health care, and stimulating mental activities to be ready to learn in first grade. We can make that happen with programs for low-income children that provide early childhood education from birth through age 5. Children born into poverty-level families should receive free health care, day care, and education. The program should be modeled after the Carolina Abecedarian Project, which was designed to break the poverty cycle.

About the Project

The Abecedarian Project started in 1972 with 111 children from low-income families. They were divided into an experimental group of 57 children and a control group of 54.

Both groups received nutritional supplements and social service referrals for the first eight years of their lives. The 57 randomly assigned to the experimental group also received year-around, all-day educational child care and preschool programs that emphasized the development of cognitive, language, and adaptive behavior skills.

> ## If we want to raise educational standards for every child and increase student achievement, we have to help the children who need it most.

Researchers assessed cognitive achievement and other factors through a battery of standardized measures. When the students completed the early childhood program, they entered school. They were studied and tested again at ages 12 and 15.

In addition to nutritional supplements and social services, the Abecedarian intervention included child care and preschool educational programs from birth to age 5 for the experimental group. Each child had prescribed educational activities. The activities consisted of social, emotional, and cognitive areas of development. Language development received the most emphasis.

The study's major findings hold out hope that we can improve the educational achievement of most of our children if we are willing to

make the commitment. The findings included the following:

- Children who participated had higher cognitive test scores from the toddler years to age 21.
- Academic achievement in both reading and math was higher from the primary grades through young adulthood.
- Children in the program completed more years of education and were more likely to attend a four-year college.
- Participants were older when they had their first child, and mothers of children who participated in the program had higher educational and employment status than mothers whose children were not in the program.

The need for universal preschool

The way to accomplish the goals of NCLB is not through more testing and busing failing students in failing schools to different schools. It is to adopt the concept of universal preschool. We must help all children be ready to learn when they begin school.

The National Institute for Early Education research at Rutgers University says that society receives a $4 return for each dollar spent on high-quality preschool. Rutgers researchers conclude that children who receive nurturing care in small groups from well-trained teachers are less likely to need special education programs, less likely to smoke, more likely to attain higher levels of education, and more likely to earn higher salaries over their lifetime than those who do not. In addition, their mothers are able to find better-paying jobs and earn more in their lifetime when not having to worry about childcare, health care, or preschool for their children.

America is the richest country in the world. We can afford to offer ev-

ery child an environment that is safe, healthy, emotionally supportive, and cognitively stimulating. If we want to raise educational standards for every child and increase student achievement, we have to help the children who need it most. We have to understand that learning begins in infancy.

Americans have been deceived about the causes of education failure. *A Nation at Risk* blamed teachers and educators. Goals 2000 set an agenda but did nothing to make it happen. No Child Left Behind is based on a laudable goal but will have little or no effect on improving education in our country.

Our nation has been deceived into thinking that we can fix our youth by raising standards, testing students and teachers, and holding educators accountable. These actions will not work until all children are ready to learn when they arrive at the schoolhouse door.

We must stop blaming teachers and educators and accept the fact that our society is not doing enough for our nation's low-income youth. We must encourage our legislators and President Bush to adopt policies and programs that work to improve academic achievement based on research, not political rhetoric.

The war that we cannot afford to lose is around the corner and down the block. Year-round, all-day educational child care and preschool programs for low-income youth are our best weapons. When students in these programs reach first grade, they will be ready to learn. And when the majority of students come to school ready to learn, then we truly can raise standards and increase academic achievement.

Kenneth H. Maurer (kmaurer@schools. mtco.com) is superintendent of Metamora Township High School in Metamora, Ill.

April Foolishness:

The 20th Anniversary of

A Nation at Risk

A Nation at Risk famously declared a crisis in American education. Even today, 20 years after the report's release, we cling to its message, which Mr. Bracey shows to be as flawed as it was compelling.

BY GERALD W. BRACEY

TWENTY YEARS ago this month, James Baker, Ronald Reagan's chief of staff, and Mike Deaver, Reagan's close advisor, defeated Attorney General Ed Meese in a battle of White House insiders. Over Meese's strong objections, they persuaded President Reagan to accept *A Nation at Risk: The Imperative for Educational Reform*, the report of the National Commission on Excellence in Education. Secretary of Education Terrel Bell had convened the commission. In his memoir, *The Thirteenth Man*, Bell recalled that he had sought a "Sputnik-type occurrence" that would dramatize all the "constant complaints about education and its effectiveness" that he kept hearing. Unable to produce such an event, Bell settled for a booklet with 36 pages of text and 29 pages of appendices about who had testified before the commission or who had presented it with a paper.

Meese and his fellow conservatives hated *A Nation at Risk* because it did not address any of the items on President Reagan's education agenda: vouchers, tuition tax credits, restoring school prayer, and abolishing the U.S. Department of Education. Baker called those issues "extraneous and irrelevant." He and the moderates on the White House staff thought the report contained a lot of good stuff to campaign on.[1]

The President accepted the report, but his speech acknowledging it largely ignored the report's content and simply reiterated his own agenda. According to Bell, the speech was virtually identical to the draft of a Reagan speech that he had read and rejected the previous day. The *Washington Post* called

it a "homily." Bell tells of looking around as Reagan spoke and noticing that "Ed Meese was standing there with a big smile on his face."[2]

Despite Meese's sabotage, *A Nation at Risk* played big in the media. In the month following its publication, the *Washington Post* carried 28 stories about it. Few were critical. Joseph Kraft did excoriate conservatives for using the report to beat up on liberals without offering anything constructive. William Buckley chided it for recommendations that "you and I would come up with over the phone." The *New York Times* humor columnist Russell Baker contended that a sentence containing a phrase like "a rising tide of mediocrity" wouldn't be worth "more than a C in tenth-grade English." About the authors' writing overall, Baker said, "I'm giving them an A+ in mediocrity."[3]

Any students who were in first grade when *A Nation at Risk* appeared and who went directly from high school graduation into the work force have now been there almost nine years. Those who went on to bachelor's degrees have been on the job for nearly five years. Despite the dire predictions of national economic collapse without immediate education reform, our national productivity has soared since those predictions were made. What, then, are we to make of *A Nation at Risk* 20 years on?

The report's stentorian Cold War rhetoric commanded and still commands attention: "If an unfriendly foreign power had attempted to impose on America the mediocre educational performance that exists today, we might well have viewed it as an act of war" (p. 5).

By contrast, the report's recommendations were, as Buckley and others observed, banal. They called for nothing new, only for more of the same: more science, more mathematics, more computer science, more foreign language, more homework, more rigorous courses, more time-on-task, more hours in the school day, more days in the school year, more training for teachers, more money for teachers. Hardly the stuff of revolution. And even those mundane recommendations were based on a set of allegations of national risk that Peter Applebome of the *New York Times* later called "brilliant propaganda."[4] Indeed, the report was a veritable treasury of slanted, spun, and distorted statistics.

Before actually listing the indicators of risk, *A Nation at Risk* told America why those indicators meant that we were in such danger. Stop worrying so much about the Red Menace, the booklet said. The threat was not that our enemies would bomb us off the planet, but that our friends—especially Germany, Japan, and South Korea—would outsmart us and wrest control of the world economy: "If only to keep and improve on the slim competitive edge we still retain in world markets, we must dedicate ourselves to the reform of our educational system" (p. 7).

In penning this sentence, the members of the National Commission tightly yoked the nation's global competitiveness to how well our 13-year-olds bubbled in test answer sheets. The theory was, to be kind, without merit. A few, such as the historian Lawrence Cremin, saw these claims for the nonsense that they were. In *Popular Education and Its Discontents*, Cremin wrote:

> American economic competitiveness with Japan and other nations is to a considerable degree a function of monetary, trade, and industrial policy, and of decisions made by the President and Congress, the Federal Reserve Board, and the Federal Departments of the Treasury, Commerce, and Labor. Therefore, to conclude that problems of international competitiveness can be solved by educational reform, especially educational reform defined solely as school reform, is not merely utopian and millennialist, it is at best a foolish and at worst a crass effort to direct attention away from those truly responsible for doing something about competitiveness and to lay the burden instead on the schools. It is a device that has been used repeatedly in the history of American education.[5]

Alas, Cremin's wisdom was read only by educators—and not by very many of them, either. It certainly did not reach the policy makers who needed to absorb its message.

In fact, the theory propounded by *A Nation at Risk* became very popular in the late 1980s, when the nation slid into the recession that would cost George H. W. Bush a second term. One then heard many variations of "lousy schools are producing a lousy work force and that's killing us in the global marketplace." The economy, however, was not listening to the litany

and came roaring back. By late 1993 and early 1994, headlines over stories about the economy expressed energy and confidence: "The American Economy: Back On Top" (*New York Times*), "America Cranks It Up" (*U.S. News & World Report*), and "Rising Sun Meets Rising Sam" (*Washington Post*).

> # During the years after the publication of *A Nation at Risk*, critics of the schools not only hyped the alleged bad news but also deliberately suppressed the good news.

Of course, it was *possible* that the comeback of the U.S. economy had actually been spurred by true and large improvements in the schools. It was at least as possible as that school improvements after Sputnik in 1957 had put a man on the moon in 1969. If it was true, though, it was a national secret. In fact, the school critics denied that there had been any gains. Three months after the *New York Times* declared the American economy to be number one in the world again, Lou Gerstner, CEO of IBM, took to that paper's op-ed page to declare "Our Schools Are Failing."[6] One reads Gerstner's essay in vain for any hint that schools are on the way up.

Indeed, evidence abounds that Gerstner and other school critics, especially those in the first Bush Administration, strove mightily to keep the dire warning issued by *A Nation at Risk* alive, and they continue to strive today. In 2001 Gerstner was back in both the *Washington Post* and the *New York Times*. The CEOs of Intel, Texas Instruments, and State Farm Insurance all penned op-ed essays for national newspapers about the poor quality of schools, as did Secretary of Health and Human Services Tommy Thompson, former Sen. John Glenn, former Gov. Pete DuPont of Delaware, and former Secretary of Education William Bennett.

During the years after the publication of *A Nation at Risk*, critics of the schools not only hyped the alleged bad news but also deliberately suppressed good news—or ignored it when they couldn't actually suppress it. The most egregious example of suppression—that we know about—was the suppression of the Sandia Report. Assembled in 1990 by engineers at Sandia National Laboratories in Albuquerque, the report presented 78 pages of graphs and tables and 78 pages of text to explain them. It concluded that, while there were many problems in public education, there was no systemwide crisis. Secretary of Energy James Watkins, who had asked for the report, called it "dead wrong" in the *Albuquerque Journal*. Briefed by the Sandia engineers who compiled it, Deputy Secretary of Education and former Xerox CEO David Kearns told them, "You bury this or I'll bury you." The engineers were forbidden to leave New Mexico to discuss the report. Officially, according to Diane Ravitch, then assistant secretary of education, the report was undergoing "peer review" by other agencies (an unprecedented occurrence) and was not ready for publication.[7]

Lee Bray, the vice president of Sandia, supervised the engineers who produced the report. I asked Bray, now retired, about the fate of the report. He affirmed that it was definitely and deliberately suppressed.[8]

There were other instances of accentuating the negative in the wake of *A Nation at Risk*. In February 1992, a small international comparison in mathematics and science appeared.[9] America's ranks were largely, but not entirely, low, although actual scores were near the international averages. Secretary of Education Lamar Alexander and Assistant Secretary Ravitch held a press conference that garnered wide coverage in both print and electronic media. "An 'F' in World Competition," was *Newsweek's* headline. *Newsweek* had fallen for the hokum that high test scores mean international competitiveness. The *Washington Post* quoted Alexander as saying that the study's outcome was a "clear warning that even good schools are not properly preparing students for world competition."[10]

Critics would hammer the schools with this international study for years. In January 1996, for instance, a full-page ad in the *New York Times* showed the rankings of 14-year-olds in math. Out of 15 countries, the U.S. ranked 14th. "If this were a ranking in Olympic Hockey, we would be outraged," said the large-type ad. The immediate source of the ad was the Ad Council, but the sponsors were, in the order in which they were listed in the ad, the Business Roundtable, the U.S. Department of Education, the National Governors' Association, the American Federation of Teachers, and the National Alliance of Business.[11] Clearly, with friends like these, public schools needed no enemies.

Five months after the math/science study, another international comparison appeared, this one in reading. No one knew. *Education Week* discovered the study first, but only two months after the results were published and then only by accident. Robert Rothman, an *EW* reporter at the time, received a copy from a friend in Europe. American 9-year-olds were second in the world in reading among the 27 nations tested. American 14-year-olds were eighth out of 31 countries, but only Finland had a significantly higher score.

Education Week ran the story on its front page. *USA Today* played off the *EW* account with its own front-page piece. *USA Today's* article included a quote from Deputy Assistant Secretary of Education Francie Alexander that reflected the Bush Administration's handling of such good news. She dismissed the study as irrelevant. (I was told by someone in the Office of Educational Research and Improvement that Ravitch handed the results to a group of researchers in the office and told the group to make the study disappear. The study was conducted by an educational organization based in The Hague, so, unlike the federally funded Sandia Report, it couldn't be suppressed. The group of researchers produced about six inches' worth of reports but couldn't make the results go away.)

While *A Nation at Risk* offered a litany of spun statistics about the risks the nation faced, its authors and fellow believers presented no actual *data* to support the contention that high test scores implied competitiveness—only the most circumstantial of evidence. The arguments heard around the country typically went like this: "Asian nations have high test scores. Asian nations ['Asian Tigers' we called them then], especially Japan, have experienced economic miracles. Therefore, the high test scores produced the economic good times." Thus the National Commission on Excellence in Education—and many school critics as well—made a mistake that no educated person should: they confused correlation with causation.

The "data" on education and competitiveness consisted largely of testimonials from Americans who had visited Japanese schools. On returning from Japan, educational researcher Herbert Walberg said that many features of the Japanese system should be adopted here. "I think it's portable. Gumption and willpower, that's the key."[12] The believers overlooked cautionary tales such as Ken Schooland's *Shogun's Ghosts: The Dark Side of Japanese Education* or the unpretty picture of Japanese schools presented in the education chapters of Karel van Wolferen's *The Enigma of Japanese Power*.

How representative were the Japanese schools that these American visitors saw? No one knows for sure, but doubtless they saw only the good side. I once asked Paul George of the University of Florida about the difficulty of gaining entrance to any less-than-stellar Japanese schools. George has spent years in Japanese schools of various kinds. His reply was succinct: "Look, there are 27 high schools in Osaka, ranked 1 to 27. You can easily get into the top few. You would have a much harder time getting into number 12 or number 13. Not even Japanese researchers can get into number 27."

The proponents of the test-score theory of economic health grew quiet after the Japanese discovered that the emperor's palace and grounds were actually not worth more than the entire state of California, a bit of misinformation widely disseminated as fact in Japan in the Eighties. Japan has foundered economically now for 12 years. The government admits that bad loans from banks to corporations amount to more than 10% of its Gross Domestic Product. Some estimate the size of the bad loans as high as 75% of GDP. We now see headlines such as "The Sinking Sun?" (*New York Times*) and "A Second Decade of Economic Woes?" (*Washington Post*).

The case of Japan presents a counterexample to the idea that high test scores ensure a thriving economy. But there is a more general method available to test the hypothesis put forth in *A Nation at Risk* that high scores equal competitiveness. For this test, I located 35 nations that were ranked in the Third International Mathematics and Science Study (TIMSS) eighth-grade tests and were also ranked for global competitiveness by the World Economic Forum (WEF), the Geneva think tank. Among these 35, the U.S. was number one in 2001. Among all 75 countries that the WEF ranked in its *Global Competitiveness Report* 2001–2002, the U.S. was number 2, trailing Finland. But Finland did not take part in the first round of TIMSS in 1995. The rank order correlation coefficient between test scores and competitiveness was +.19, virtually zero. If five countries that scored low on both variables were removed from the list, the coefficient actually became negative.

A Nation at Risk fabricated its case for the connection between education and competitiveness out of whole cloth, but to make its case for the dire state of American education, it did provide a lot of statistics. It was the spin on these numbers that led Peter Applebome to characterize the report as propaganda. Consider these.

• "Over half the population of gifted students do not match their tested ability with comparable achievement in school" (p. 8). I have asked both commissioners and members of the commission staff to tell me where this statistic came from. No one knows. And, of course, it makes no sense because 20 years ago, the principal instruments for identifying gifted students were achievement tests.

• "Average tested achievement of students graduating from college is also lower" (p. 9). Another nonexistent statistic.

• "There was a steady decline in science achievement scores of U.S. 17-year-olds as measured by national assessments of science in 1969, 1973, and 1977" (p. 9). Maybe, maybe not. The National Assessment of Educational Progress (NAEP) was not originally designed to produce trends, and the scores for 1969 and 1973 are backward extrapolations from the 1977 assessment. In any case, the declines were smaller for 9- and 13-year-olds and had already been wiped out by gains on the 1982 assessment. Scores for reading and math for all three ages assessed by NAEP were stable or inching upward. The commissioners thus had nine trendlines (three ages times three subjects), only one of which could be used to support crisis rhetoric. That was the only one they reported.

• "The College Board's Scholastic Aptitude Tests demonstrate a virtually unbroken decline from 1963 to 1980" (pp. 8–9). This was true. But the College Board's own investigative panel described a complex trend to which many variables contributed. It ascribed most of the decline to changes in who was taking the test—more minorities, more women, more students with mediocre high school records, more students from low-income families.

When the standards for the SAT were set, the students who received 500 as an average score were members of an elite: 10,654 high-schoolers, mostly living in New England. Ninety-eight percent were white, 61% were male, and 41% had attended private, college-preparatory high schools. In 1982, the year A Nation at Risk's commissioners labored, 988,270 seniors took the SAT. Eighty-four percent were white, 52% were female, 44% had mothers with a high school diploma or less, 27% came from families with incomes under $18,000 annually, and 81% attended public schools. All of those demographic changes are associated with lower scores on any test. It would have been very suspicious if the scores had *not* declined.

• "Average achievement of high school students on most standardized tests is now lower than 26 years ago when Sputnik was launched" (p. 8). The commissioners could not have known if this were true for "most standardized tests." At the time, most companies that produced standardized tests did not equate them from form to form over time. Instead, they used a "floating norm." Whenever they renormed their tests, whatever raw score corresponded to the 50th percentile became the new norm. Only the Iowa Tests of Basic Skills (ITBS, grades 3–8) and the Iowa Tests of Educational Development (ITED, grades 9–12) were referenced to a fixed standard and equated from form to form, beginning in 1955. In order to examine trends in test scores over time, one needs a test that is referenced to a fixed standard

where each new form is equated to the earlier form. Among achievement tests, only the ITBS-ITED battery met this requirement.

It *was* true that on the ITED, scores were lower than when Sputnik was launched. Barely. The commissioners could have noted that the scores had risen for five consecutive years and that their statement about test scores and Sputnik didn't apply to most middle or elementary grades. The five-year rise had been preceded by a decade-long decline, which itself was preceded by a 10-year rise. Scores rose from 1955, a baseline year when the test was renormed and qualitatively changed as well, to about 1965. Scores then fell until about 1975, reversed, and climbed to *record high* levels by 1985 (something unnoticed or at least unmentioned by critics or the media).

It is instructive to examine what the nation was experiencing during the 10 years of falling test scores from 1965 to 1975. Just one year before the decline began, the Civil Rights Act of 1964 was passed, and 1965 opened with the Watts riots in Los Angeles. Urban violence then spread across the nation. The decade also brought us the Black Panthers, the Symbionese Liberation Army, Students for a Democratic Society, the Free Speech Movement, the Summer of Love, Woodstock, Altamont, Ken Kesey and his LSD-laced band of Merry Pranksters, the Kent State atrocities, and the 1968 Chicago Police Riot. Martin Luther King, Jr., Robert Kennedy, and Malcolm X were all assassinated. The nation became obsessed with and depressed by first the war in Vietnam and then Watergate. "Recreational drugs"—pot, acid, speed, Quaaludes, amyl nitrate—had become popular. If you remember the Sixties, the saying goes, you weren't there.

Popular books included such anti-Establishment tracts as *The Making of a Counter Culture*, *The Greening of America*, and *The Pursuit of Loneliness*. Books critical of schools included *Death at an Early Age*, *The Way It Spozed to Be*, *36 Children*, *Free Schools*, *Deschooling Society*, *The Death of School*, *How Children Fail*, *The Student as Nigger*, *Teaching As a Subversive Activity*, and, most influential, Charles Silberman's 1970 tome, *Crisis in the Classroom*.

Under these conditions of social upheaval, centered in the schools and universities, it would have been a miracle if test scores had *not* fallen.

When A Nation at Risk appeared, universities and education associations fell over themselves lauding it. The education associations said that they welcomed the attention after a decade of neglect. "We are pleased education is back on the American agenda," wrote Paul Salmon, executive director of the American Association of School Administrators. They also said, later, that they didn't want to appear defensive by challenging the report. They also said, much later and in private, that they were certain that, with all these problems in education, money would surely follow. They were wrong.

As for the universities, well, a crisis in our schools always presents a great opportunity for educational researchers seeking to liberate money from foundations and governments. *A Nation at Risk* was to the research universities as September 11 was to the arms and security industries.

The National Commission on Excellence in Education commissioned more than 40 papers that laid out the crisis. Virtually all of them were written by academics. The report acknowledged only one that was written by someone actually working in a school, and it was not a commissioned work. Harvey Prokop, a teacher in San Diego, wrote a critique of a National Commission seminar in his town. He called it "Intelligence, Motivation, and the Quantity and Quality of Academic Work and Their Impacts on the Learning of Students."[13]

Alas, nothing else is new and, indeed, we must recognize that good news about public schools serves no one's reform agenda—even if it does make teachers, students, parents, and administrators feel a little better. Conservatives want vouchers and tuition tax credits; liberals want more resources for schools; free marketers want to privatize the schools and make money; fundamentalists want to teach religion and not worry about the First Amendment; Catholic schools want to stanch their student hemorrhage; home schooling advocates want just that; and various groups no doubt just want to be with "their own kind." All groups believe that they will improve their chances of getting what they want if they pummel the publics.

It has been 20 years, though, since *A Nation at Risk* appeared. It is clear that it was false then and is false now. Today, the laments are old and tired—and still false. "Test Scores Lag as School Spending Soars" trumpeted the headline of a 2002 press release from the American Legislative Exchange Council. Ho hum. The various special interest groups in education need another treatise to rally round. And now they have one. It's called No Child Left Behind. It's a weapon of mass destruction, and the target is the public school system. Today, our public schools are truly at risk.

NOTES

1. Quoted in Terrel H. Bell, *The Thirteenth Man: A Reagan Cabinet Memoir* (New York: Free Press, 1988) p. 29.
2. Ibid., p. 131.
3. Joseph Kraft, "A Note to Conservatives: Come Off It," *Washington Post*, 3 May 1983, p. A-19; William F. Buckley, Jr., "The Obvious Solution: Tuition Tax Credits," *Washington Post*, 3 May 1983, p. A-19; and Russell Baker, "Beset by Mediocrity," *New York Times*, 30 April 1983, p. A-23.
4. Peter Applebome, "Dire Predictions Deflated: Johnny Can Add After All," *New York Times*, 11 June 1983, p. A-31.
5. Lawrence J. Cremin, *Popular Education and Its Discontents* (New York: Harper & Row, 1989), pp. 102–3.
6. Louis V. Gerstner, "Our Schools Are Failing: Do We Care?," *New York Times*, 27 May 1994, p. A-27.
7. Quoted in Julie Miller, "Report Questioning 'Crisis' in Education Triggers an Uproar," *Education Week*, 9 October 1991; and Diane Ravitch, letter to the editor, *Education Week*, 30 October 1991. The David Kearns quote comes from a personal communication from Sandia engineers, and the *Education Week* article stated that "Administration officials, particularly Mr. Kearns, reacted angrily at the meeting."
8. The report finally appeared in full in 1993 in the May/June issue of the *Journal of Educational Research* under the title "Perspectives on Education in America." Its authors were Sandia engineers C. C. Carson, R. M. Huelskamp, and T. D. Woodall.
9. Archie Lapointe, Nancy Mead, and Janice Askew, *Learning Mathematics* (Princeton, N.J.: Educational Testing Service, 1992); and Archie Lapointe, Janice Askew, and Nancy Mead, *Learning Science* (Princeton, N.J.: Educational Testing Service, 1992).
10. Mary Jordan, "Students Test Below Average in World, U.S. Fares Poorly in Math, Science," *Washington Post*, 6 February 1992, p. A-1.
11. *New York Times*, 31 January 1996.
12. Quoted in Keith B. Richburg, "Japanese Education: Admired but Not Easily Imported," *Washington Post*, 19 October 1985, p. A-1.
13. Harvey Prokop, "Intelligence, Motivation, and the Quantity and Quality of Academic Work and Their Impacts on the Learning of Students," a critique of the National Commission on Excellence in Education seminar, "The Student's Role in Learning," submitted to the National Commission on Excellence in Education, 1982.

GERALD W. BRACEY is an associate for the High/Scope Foundation, Ypsilanti, Mich., and an associate professor at George Mason University, Fairfax, Va. His most recent book is What You Need to Know About the War Against America's Public Schools *(Allyn and Bacon/Longman, 2003). He lives in the Washington, D.C., area.*

From *Phi Delta Kappan*, April 2003, pp. 616-621. © 2003 by Gerald W. Bracey. Reprinted by permission.

"OF COURSE IT'S TRUE; I SAW IT ON THE INTERNET!"

Critical Thinking in the Internet Era

Students use the Net as a primary source of information, usually with little or no regard as to the accuracy of that information.

By Leah Graham and Panagiotis Takis Metaxas

The Internet is revolutionizing research methods at colleges and universities around the world. Though it can be extremely useful to researchers, the Net presents a significant challenge in that it is quite different from traditional sources. The lack of uniform standards and the ease of access have made the Internet a powerful but uncertain medium. Substantial effort is required to adequately evaluate its information, and this may not always be apparent to users [5]. This is particularly challenging for students, as many have come to rely on the Net as a primary source of information without formal instruction about the difficulties involved. The Internet has gained a primary place in research methods, and it is vital that students become able to critically evaluate the information it provides.

Several solutions have been suggested to determine accuracy in Internet research. In [1], Jerry Campbell supports the Association of Research Libraries' plan to develop an Internet portal to "trustworthy" information. This portal would "promote the development of and provide access to the highest quality content on the Web." Many colleges have also adopted this approach by providing lists of approved online sources to students. While it appears to provide a practical alternative to information.coms that focus more on advertising than accuracy, this approach suffers from several drawbacks. First, it is impossible to continually monitor all the content found using these portals. Web sites change overnight and expand at exponential rates, and attempting to continuously verify every page of each lined site would be an incredibly time-consuming task. Clearly, this is not feasible, but it would be necessary to ensure the accuracy and timeliness expected of information found using a "scholar's portal." Additionally, this approach places the responsibility of evaluation on the Web masters of these portals. A more interactive approach that encourages users to develop critical-thinking skills would provide lasting value, while preventing them from becoming dependent on these portals for the correct answers.

Table 1. The survey scoring system.			
Score	Correct		Double-Checked
0	–		–
1	No		No
2	Yes	-or-	Yes
3	Yes		Yes

Developing other approaches requires a firm understanding of how students currently use the Internet for research. Consider the results of an informal questionnaire distributed by Angela Weiler in 1999 at SUNY College of Agriculture and Technology, Morrisville, NY. In response to a question asking how students would ascertain if online sources were accurate enough to be considered "a good source of information," 29% said they accepted Internet information regardless, with only 34% considering additional verification important [5]. These startling results confirm the importance of further study to provide specific information about students' online research practices. To address this, we developed a six-question survey administered to 180 Wellesley College students during the 2000–2001 academic year. Students' responses to this survey helped explain how college students, from different backgrounds, class years, and majors, react to information on the Internet.

Research Methods

Participants in this study were students from the "Computers and Internet" class; it was, in fact, their first assignment. Students were told the purpose of the survey was to understand how students conduct searches. The survey was divided into seven email messages. The first explained the process of responding to the survey and included a personal information questionnaire. The following six email messages each contained one question and asked students to report their answer and search strategies.

The survey was designed to answer three research questions:

- How strongly do students rely on the Internet for information?
- What claims are students more likely to believe?
- Who is most susceptible to misleading claims?

To identify students' reliance on the Internet, they were told to answer the questions in whatever way they wished. They were free to use any resource available, including visiting the library, and they were asked to report which search methods were used for each question.

The survey revealed the extraordinary confidence students have in search engines. If the question did not mention a Web site, almost all students immediately turned to a search engine. Many remained faithful to one search engine throughout the survey, even if it did not immediately provide the answer sought.

The six survey questions were used to determine students' ability to evaluate information, as well as their inclination to verify their responses. Four questions tested particular areas of misinformation: advertising claims, government misinformation, lobby group propaganda, and scams. Preliminary research indicated these areas could present a significant challenge to students. Two additional questions were used to determine if

Table 2. Median score by class year.

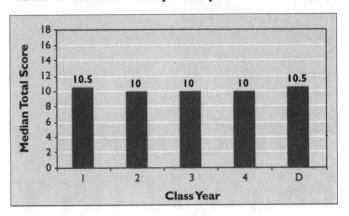

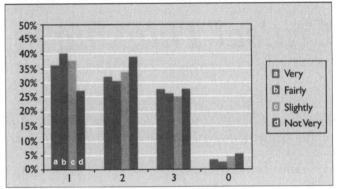

Table 3. Scores by confidence level.

students were more diligent about accuracy and verification when the information was easy to find.

Each response was given a score from 0–3, with 3 being the highest score. The scoring system placed equal weight on accuracy and the students' efforts to double-check responses (see Table 1). An optimal answer was therefore defined as a correct response confirmed in at least two sources. Other scores were categorized as follows:

A 0 indicates no response, a 1 an incorrect response that was not double-checked, and a 2 either a correct answer that was not double-checked or an incorrect response that was double-checked. The 2 category contains both types of responses, as dividing the category would require placing more importance on accuracy or verification. Neither of these attributes, when considered individually, wholly constitutes adequate research practices. As such, the 2 category remains the middle category for responses not entirely acceptable due to a lack of accuracy or verification.

Finally, to evaluate which groups of students are in greater need of assistance, students were asked to fill out a questionnaire asking for age, class year, and other factors. This data was matched with their responses to the survey questions.

Results

The findings were remarkable. Regarding students' reliance on the Internet, it became apparent that students are very eager to use the Internet—and only the Internet—in conducting research. Though the survey was not in any way limited to Internet resources, less than 2% of students' responses to all questions included non-Internet sources. Many of these responses also quoted online sources at some point. This finding emphasizes the importance of teaching good Internet research skills, as students rely so heavily on the Internet.

The survey also revealed the extraordinary confidence students have in search engines. If the survey question did not mention a particular Web site, almost all students immediately turned to a search engine. Many remained faithful to one search engine throughout the survey, even if it did not immediately provide the answer sought. This is particularly interesting since experts believe no single search engine captures more than 16% of the entire Internet. With all search engines combined, this only increases to 42% [2]. Additionally, students were asked a question to determine the extent of their understanding of search engines. Few students responded with any degree of awareness of the process by which search engines post results. This is distressing, as the reliability of search engines to faithfully and selflessly guide users to appropriate materials has often been questioned.[1]

The second research question about the types of information most problematic to students yielded disheartening results. Students were overwhelmingly susceptible to three types of misinformation—advertising claims, government misinformation, and propaganda—and somewhat susceptible to scam sites.

The two most successful misleading claims were advertising and government misinformation. To study the impact of advertising claims, students were asked: "List three major innovations developed by Microsoft over the past 10 years." The term "major innovation" was left vague, as Microsoft's innovative history is a widely debated issue. There are many opinions on the topic, and we expected students overall to discuss at least several.

However, 63% of students responded that Microsoft was responsible for many major innovations based on information from only one source. Almost all of these students immediately went to the Microsoft Web site and used the Microsoft Museum Timeline that details Microsoft's achievements—or at least, what Microsoft claims to be its achievements. Only 12% checked several sources and made more complete argument. Some 22% fell in between these two groups, receiving a score of 2. These results are intriguing in view of recent litigation against Microsoft that drew worldwide attention to its business practices and innovation efforts. Yet almost two-thirds of students responded without a shadow of a doubt that Microsoft was completely honest about its claims.

Government misinformation followed closely behind advertising claims. Students were asked: "Did the 1999 Rambouillet Accords allow NATO to operate in all of Yugoslavia or only in Kosovo?" (The correct answer—all of Yugoslavia—can be found in the actual document, though it is difficult to wade through its 82 pages. The complete text can be found online, but summaries and reviews are much more common. A frequently found summary is the U.S. Department of State Bureau of European Affairs fact sheet released on March 1, 1999, which implies that NATO presence is limited to Kosovo.[2]

A total of 62% of students said that NATO is limited to acting within Kosovo based on one source, and many listed the State Department memo as their only source. And 26% said the same thing but made some effort to double-check the information or happened to find the correct answer on the first attempt. Many students in this category stumbled on anti-NATO Web sites and reported that information without checking another less-biased source. Only 10% found the correct answer and verified it in two places.

Political lobbying groups are another common source of misinformation or half-truths. Students were asked to evaluate a claim made by getoutraged.com. This Web site is the work of an anti-smoking lobby, though it is officially copyrighted by the Massachusetts Department of Public Health. Students were asked: "Getoutraged.com says that tobacco is responsible for 30% of all deaths in the 35–69 age group. Would you cite this information in a research paper?" This statistic, taken from a pamphlet entitled "Growing Up Tobacco Free," is actually a projection made in 1992 on how many deaths tobacco will probably cause in the 1990s, but getoutraged.com lists this as if it were a proven fact [3]. The number of deaths was actually estimated to be closer to 20% by organizations such as the American Cancer Society and the U.S. Centers for Disease Control and Prevention.[3]

All future educational ventures must focus on teaching users the Internet is an unmonitored method of sharing information.

Despite this, 48% of students said they not only believed the statistic from getoutraged.com, but they would confidently cite it in a research paper. They did not attempt to find a corroborating source. Only 21% expressed reluctance to use this information after checking with additional sources, with 30% falling in between. What is most disturbing is that many of the students who readily believed this statistic realized the site was probably the product of an anti-smoking lobby, but the fact it was sponsored by the Massachusetts Department of Public Health reassured them. Students seemed to believe that because a source was cited and the Massachusetts government copyrighted the Web site, the statistic would naturally be accurate.

Fortunately, the results are not entirely dim. Students were much less susceptible to the scam Web site. They were asked to evaluate vespro.com's "revolutionary" product Vespro GHS containing Human Growth Hormone (hGH), an emerging medical treatment to combat the effects of aging. According to the Web site, this product will decrease body fat, reduce wrinkles, restore lost hair, and normalize blood pressure, among a variety of other benefits—an absolute miracle drug. This Web site provides quotes from medical journals that are generally taken out of context to support its claims. For instance, there is a quote from a 1989 article in the *New England Journal of Medicine* that seems to support the beneficial effects of hGH, though its conclusion simply states further research is necessary [4].

Students were asked: "Would you recommend Vespro Life Science's hGH product to a friend concerned about getting older?" Only 13% of the students immediately agreed to recommend this product without consulting another source while 35% conducted further research and reported they would not recommend the product without more information. And 52% of students received a score of 2. Though these results are not overly encouraging, they demonstrate that students remain skeptical of this type of information on the Internet.

The remaining two questions were used to determine students' inclination to verify information. The first question asked students to report the creator of Linux. The answer is easily found quickly online. The second question asked students to find the land area of Lisbon, Portugal. While this sounds elementary, it can take a tremendous amount of time to locate any answer on the Internet, and even longer to find a second source. For the easy Linux question, 78% of students reported the first answer they found, without verifying it from another source. For the more difficult Lisbon question, 75% of students reported the first answer they found without double-checking. It appears that students are just as likely to avoid verifying an answer, regardless of the time or effort needed to do so.

Finally, to determine which groups of students are more susceptible to misleading claims, responses to the personal information questionnaire were matched with answers to the six survey questions. Using class year, we hoped to see if students became better Internet researchers over the course of their years at Wellesley. The results indicate there was no significant difference in performance based on class year (see Table 2).

We then looked at self-reported confidence in their Internet searching abilities to determine if students who were more "Internet-savvy" were better able to critically evaluate information on the Internet. The categories available were very confident, fairly confident, slightly confident, and not very confident. Table 3 indicates the total number of scores (0–3) given to students in each confidence level. The distribution of scores for all questions is very similar for each confidence level. Only the "not very confident" group shows notable, though not overly large, differences. This suggests the confidence a student has in his or her ability to effectively search the Internet does not significantly affect the student's performance.

Conclusion

Clearly, students consider the Internet a primary source of information. The results presented here suggest many students have difficulty recognizing trustworthy sources, though perhaps the underlying problem is a lack of understanding of the Internet as an unmonitored source of information. All future educational ventures must focus on teaching users the Internet is an unmonitored method of sharing information. Specifically, this instruction should equip users to use search engines effectively, and this requires an awareness of their technological and financial constraints. This is not to recommend teaching students that all

search engines are devoid of useful information, but rather to promote a better understanding of the actual service provided by search engines.

Students are also not consistently able to differentiate between advertising and fact. Many responses to vespro.com mentioned that as the Web site was just trying to sell a product, its claims could not be readily believed. However, many of these same students immediately believed claims made by Microsoft on its commercial Web site. Students must understand that all information on the Internet is there for a reason, and it is vital to determine the purpose of the information when evaluating its accuracy.

The very small number of students who double-checked information is also concerning. It is commonly believed the triangle method—locating three independent sources that point to the same answer—produces the most accurate information. This approach does not differentiate a great deal between "good" and "bad" sites, but rather encourages users to double-check information regardless of the source. Students in this study seemed to have a great deal of confidence in their abilities to distinguish the good sites from the bad. Colleges themselves often encourage this attitude as they determine "good" or "trustworthy" Web sites to help students begin Internet search. While is is certainly useful to provide guidance, it is equally important to promote the development of critical thinking skills that will allow students to make use of the entire Internet, rather than a few approved sites.

Our findings also suggest that students across the board have similar difficulties in carefully evaluating information found on the Internet. Older students with stronger traditional research skills performed no better than other students, which suggests these skills are simply not sufficient when evaluating online information. In the past, the greatest problem facing researchers was finding information; now, with the advent of the Internet, the greatest problem is evaluating the vast wealth of information available. Students in this survey placed greater emphasis on the process of finding an answer than on analyzing the actual information. The difficulties students encountered suggest this practice is of little use in determining the accuracy of online information. It is therefore important to develop specific research practices for Internet searches that take the structure and purpose of the Internet into account.

As students continue to view the Internet as a primary source of information, without a significant shift in training methods, this problem will only worsen. It is vital that students better understand the nature of the Internet and develop an instinctive inclination for verifying all information. This will allow students to take advantage of the tremendous benefits provided online without falling prey to the pitfalls of online research.

Notes

1. See, for example, [2]; "Information Retrieval on the World Wide Web" (Gudivada et al., *IEEE Internet Computing 1,* 5 (1997, and "Searching the World Wide Web" (Knoblock, *IEEE Expert 12,* 1 (1997).

2. "Understanding the "Rambouillet Accords." Fact sheet released by the Bureau of European Affairs, U.S. Department of State, Washington, D.C.: www.state.gov/www/regions/eur/fs_990301_rambouillet.html

3. "Cigarette Smoking Related Mortality." Centers for Disease Control and Prevention. U.S., 1990. *Morbidity and Mortality Weekly Report 42,* 33 (1993); www.cdc.gov/tobacco/research_data/health_consequences/mortali.htm

REFERENCES

1. Campbell, J. The case for creating a scholar's portal to the Web: A White Paper. *Libraries and the Academy 1,* 1 (2001).

2. Introna, L. and Nissenbaum, H. Defining the Web: The politics of search engines. *IEEE Computer 33,* 1 (2000), 54–62.

3. Lynch, B. S. and Bonnie, R. J., Eds. *Growing Up Tobacco Free: Presenting Nicotine Addiction in Children and Youths.* National Academy Press, Washington, D.C., 1994.

4. Salomon, F. et al. The effects of treatment with recombinant human growth hormone on body composition and metabolism in adults with growth hormone deficiency. *New England J. Medicine 32,* 1 (Dec. 1989).

5. Weiler, A. Two-year college freshmen and the Internet: Do they really 'know all that stuff?' *Libraries and the Academy 1,* 2 (2001).

LEAH GRAHAM is a graduate of Wellesley College, Wellesley, MA. **PANAGIOTIS TAKIS METAXAS** (pmetaxas@wellesley.edu) is an associate professor of computer science at Wellesley College.

From *Communications of the ACM,* May 2003, pp. 71-75. © 2003 by Association for Computing Machinery, Inc. (ACM).

UNIT 4
Morality and Values in Education

Unit Selections

Key Points to Consider

- What is character education? Why do so many people wish to see a form of character education in schools?

- Are there certain values about which most of us can agree? Should they be taught in schools? Why, or why not?

- What can teachers do to help students become caring, morally responsible persons?

- Do you agree with Aristotle that virtue can and should be taught in shools? Explain.

 **Links: www.dushkin.com/online/**
These sites are annotated in the World Wide Web pages.

Association for Moral Education
http://www.amenetwork.org/

Child Welfare League of America
http://www.cwla.org

Ethics Updates/Lawrence Hinman
http://ethics.acusd.edu

The National Academy for Child Development
http://www.nacd.org

Morality has always been a concern of educators. There has possibly not been a more appropriate time to focus attention on ethics, on standards of principled conduct, in our schools. The many changes in American family structures in past years make this an important public concern, especially in the United States. We are told that all nations share concern for their cherished values. In addition to discerning how best to deal with moral and ethical educational issues, there are also substantive values controversies regarding curriculum content, such as the dialogue over how to infuse multicultural values into school curricula. On the one hand, educators need to help students learn how to reason and how to determine what principles should guide them in making decisions in situations where their own well-being and/or the well-being of another is at stake. On the other hand, educators need to develop reasoned and fair standards for resolving the substantive values issues to be faced in dealing with questions about what should or should not be taught.

There is frustration and anger among some American youth, and we must address how educators can teach moral standards and ethical decision-making skills. This is no longer simply something desirable that we might do; it has become something that we must do. How it is to be done is the subject of a national dialogue that is now occurring.

Students need to develop a sense of genuine caring both for themselves and others. They need to learn alternatives to violence and human exploitation. Teachers need to be examples of responsible and caring persons who use reason and compassion in solving problems in school.

Some teachers voice their concerns that students need to develop a stronger sense of character that is rooted in a more defensible system of values. Other teachers express concerns that they cannot do everything and are hesitant to instruct on morality and values. Most believe that they must do something to help students become reasoning and ethical decision makers.

What teachers perceive to be worthwhile and defensible behavior informs our reflections on what we as educators should teach. We are conscious immediately of some of the values that affect our behavior, but we may not be as aware of what informs our preferences. Values that we hold without being conscious of them are referred to as tacit values—values derived indirectly after reasoned reflection on our thoughts about teaching and learning. Much of our knowledge about teaching is tacit knowledge, which we need to bring into conscious cognition by analyzing the concepts that drive our practice. We need to acknowledge how all our values inform and influence our thoughts about teaching.

Teachers need to help students develop within themselves a sense of critical social consciousness and a genuine concern for social justice. Insight into the nature of moral decision making should be taught in the context of real current and past social problems and should lead students to develop their own skills in social analysis relating to the ethical dilemmas of human beings.

There is a need for teachers to develop principles of professional practice that will enable them to respond reasonably to the many ethical dilemmas that they now face. Knowledge of how teachers derive their sense of professional ethics is developing; further study of how teachers' values shape their professional practice is very important. Schooling should not only transmit national and cultural heritages, including our intellectual heritage; it should also be a fundamentally moral enterprise in which students learn how to develop tenable moral standards in the contexts of their own world visions.

The controversy over teaching morality deals with more than the tensions between secular and religious interests in society. We argue that the construction of educational processes and the decisions about the substantive content of school curricula involve moral issues as well.

One of the most compelling responsibilities of schools is that of preparing young people for their moral duties as free citizens of free nations. Governments have always wanted schools to teach the principles of civic morality based on their respective constitutional traditions. Indeed when the public school movement began in the 1830s and 1840s, the concept of universal public schooling as a mechanism for instilling a sense of national identity and civic morality was supported. In every nation, school curricula have certain value preferences embedded in them.

For whom do the schools exist? Is a teacher's primary responsibility to his or her client, the student, or to the student's parents? Do secondary school students have the right to study and to inquire into subjects not in officially sanctioned curricula? What are the moral issues surrounding censorship of student reading material? What ethical questions are raised by arbitrarily withholding information regarding alternative viewpoints on controversial topics?

Teachers cannot hide all of their moral preferences. They can, however, learn to conduct just and open discussions of moral topics without succumbing to the temptation to indoctrinate students with their own views.

Teaching students to respect all people, to revere the sanctity of life, to uphold the right of every citizen to dissent, to believe in the equality of all people before the law, to cherish freedom to learn, and to respect the right of all people to their own convictions—these are principles of democracy and ideals worthy of being cherished. An understanding of the processes of ethical decision making is needed by the citizens of any free nation; thus, this process should be taught in a free nation's schools.

What part ought the schooling experience to play in the formation of such things as character, informed compassion, conscience, honor, and respect for self and others? The issue of public morality and the question of how best to educate to achieve responsible social behavior, individually and collectively, are matters of great significance today.

Values: The Implicit Curriculum

A school's culture can help foster students' sense of personal and social responsibility.

Linda Inlay

Whether teachers intend to or not, they teach values. Teachers' behaviors are, in fact, moral practices that are deeply embedded in the day-to-day functioning of the classroom (Jackson, Boostrom, & Hansen, 1993). Likewise, a school's culture communicates values through the ways in which faculty, parents, and students treat one another and through school policies on such issues as discipline and decision making.

In his eight-year study of more than 1,000 classrooms, Goodlad found a "great hypocrisy" (1984, p. 241) in the differences between what schools espouse as values and what students experience. This disparity produces cynical students who don't take seriously what schools say about character (Postman & Weingartner, 1969).

> ### A ropes course can teach students mutual trust and foster group cohesion.

At River School, a charter middle school of approximately 160 students, we work hard to develop an entire school culture that teaches character through the explicit curriculum of reading, writing, and arithmetic and through an implicit curriculum of values—what Adlerian psychologist Raymond Corsini called the implicit four *R*s: responsibility, respect, resourcefulness, and responsiveness (Adler, 1927/1992; Ignas & Corsini, 1979). My introduction to this school-wide approach to character education began 30 years ago when school director and Catholic nun Sr. Joan Madden, who was collaborating with Corsini in implementing what they called Individual Education,

hired me as a teacher. She told me, "You are not teaching subjects. You are teaching who you are."

At River School, we rarely talk about character—nor do we have posters or pencils that trumpet values—because we know that the most effective character education is to model the values that we want to see in our students. We attempt to align every part of our school—from assessment to awards, from decision making to discipline—to encourage and foster students' character development. Our mission is to help students cultivate a strong sense of self through demonstrations of personal and social responsibility.

Fostering Personal Responsibility

We have barely spent a month in our school's new location when the fire alarm goes off. We have not yet established our safety protocols, and two of our students have pulled the fire alarm while horsing around, a typical middle school antic. Before I even get back to my office, the two students who pulled the alarm have voluntarily acknowledged the mistake that they made. They decide to "clean up their mistake" by apologizing to the affected people on campus, from the caretakers in the toddler program to the senior citizens in the Alzheimer's Center. One student voluntarily talks with the fire chief about her error. The mistake becomes an important lesson, as all mistakes should be.

These students are willing to be accountable for their actions. We view negative behavior as a sign of neediness, and we respond with positive contact, not just discipline of the behavior. Humans resist the diminution of spirit that comes with typical messages implying that they are "bad" or "wrong." These students have instead heard a call to responsibility:

> You made a mistake. To be human means making mistakes and learning from them.

> What do you think you should do to clean up this mistake?

Teachers focus on creating an atmosphere in which it is emotionally safe to make mistakes. We acknowledge when we have made a mistake and work hard not to get angry at students' mistakes. Within this emotionally safe terrain, we hold students accountable for their actions, allowing them to experience appropriate and natural consequences. Parents know, for example, that they are not responsible for bringing their children's forgotten homework to school.

The view of responsibility is the essential notion of our systems approach to character and relates to our underlying assumption about human beings. Humans are self-determining creatures; we have free will to make choices. Because of our ability to think, discern, and reflect, we want to make our own choices.

If humans have free will and the capacity to choose, then experiencing the consequences of "good" or "poor" choices is how humans learn to make choices. At the River School, we organize our school's curriculum and culture to provide many age-appropriate choices so that students learn, through trial and error, what works and what doesn't work for growing as independent learners and human beings.

The middle school years are about testing limits and shedding the old skin of the elementary school years, and we expect our students to cross boundaries as a way to learn about choice, consequences, freedom, and responsibility. Students say that they notice that our discipline system is different because we treat them like adults, even when they don't act like adults. We trust in our students' innate ability to make good decisions for themselves—with practice over time.

We define responsibility as an attitude that reflects a willingness to see oneself as cause, instead of victim. Students who see themselves as active rather than passive don't blame others. They see the mistake or the situation as the result of the choices that they have made. If the situation is out of their control, they see their responses to the situation as their own choice to be positive or to be negative.

This approach lessens extrinsic control, nurtures our students' intrinsic motivation to learn, and increases their self-confidence to meet and overcome challenges.

Fostering Social Responsibility

Self-determination is one side of human need; a sense of community and belonging is the other. Our vision of students developing fully as individuals cannot occur without the community being a safe place that accepts the different qualities of each individual. Particularly in middle school, we see students struggling to meet these two needs. They desperately want to belong, so they assume the external trappings and mannerisms of their peer group. At the same time, they try to break away from traditions and develop their individual identities.

To grow as individuals, students must believe that the school community accepts individual differences. One test of a school's effectiveness in teaching social responsibility is how well students treat those who are socially inept on the playground. Most of the time, our students respect one another. When they do not, the school community has opportunities to learn about making our school safe for everyone.

In preparation for the annual Thanksgiving feast, a student writes notes of appreciation on the placemats of each of her classmates.

Last year, for example, students were picking on a classmate who we suspected had a mild form of autism. With the student's consent, we devoted several team meetings to helping the school community understand why he sometimes stared at others or made odd noises. As a result of these conversations, students began to include him at lunch tables, lessened the teasing considerably, and defended him when teasing occasionally occurred. Such open conversations help each student become aware of how he or she makes a difference to every other student in school.

How do we teach *responsiveness,* this value of being responsible for one another? We begin with the recognition that we need to fulfill our students' needs for significance ("I matter") and for belonging (being part of a community) by structuring the school's culture so that we listen to students, take their concerns seriously, and depend on them.

We organize students into homeroom advisories in which the homeroom teacher is their advocate. The homeroom groups further divide into smaller "listening groups" that meet every other week with their teachers to share concerns and acknowledge successes. These meetings provide one of the ways in which we allow students to participate in solving problems in the school.

In one case, for example, someone was trashing the boys' bathroom. Student advisories discussed the problem, and one homeroom class volunteered to monitor the bathrooms throughout the day. Instead of the unspoken code of silence often practiced by middle schoolers, students reported the boy involved because they trusted that he would be treated with respect in the discipline process. In another case, students disliked some features of the dress code that had been developed by the student council and teachers. Students presented a proposal for changes at a staff meeting and did such an outstanding job of responding to the purposes of the dress code that the changes were approved.

We also take time to listen to students' ideas and questions as we develop the school's curriculum, modeling responsiveness by taking their concerns seriously. We follow the approach of the National Middle School Association (2002) to curriculum integration by asking students to develop their own questions for dealing with particular standards. The student question "What do you wish you could say but don't have the courage to say?" was the impetus for a unit last year that studied the First Amendment; various positions on evolution; and Galileo, Gandhi, Susan B. Anthony, and other figures who dared to take an unpopular stand.

Students who see themselves as active rather than passive don't blame others. They see the mistake or the situation as the result of the choices that they have made.

If a student has problems with a teacher, he or she can call on a facilitator to mediate a conference. The purpose of a facilitating conference with a teacher is not to question his or her authority or to find out who is wrong and who is right. The goal of the conference is common understanding; the teacher works to understand the student's point of view and the student works to understand the teacher's point of view. Earlier this year, for example, a student felt picked on by his teacher and asked for a conference. Following the protocol of the facilitating conference, the teacher began with an "invitation" and asked, "What do you want to say to me?" After the student spoke, the teacher rephrased what the student said, and after the teacher spoke, the student rephrased what the teacher said. Through this active listening format, each came to a better understanding of the reasons for the other's behavior, and their relationship and classroom interactions improved.

We use this same conference format with students, faculty, and parents. Facilitators for conflicts are usually the advisors or the principal, with new teachers learning these communication skills primarily through observation and special training during faculty meetings. In some situations, students facilitate their own conflicts in listening groups, or they ask teachers to allow them time to do so. Last year, for example, two students began harassing each other on Halloween, when one laughed at the other's costume. When their conflict came to a head four months later, a facilitating conference helped them come to a

resolution. They apologized to each other without being asked to and were friendly for the rest of the year.

Once understanding occurs, both sides can reach a solution together. Conflicts in the community become opportunities to learn how to deal with differences, to learn how to listen and solve problems. In this way, we empower our students to voice their beliefs and opinions more effectively. Whether expressing their beliefs and opinions about personal relationships, the dress code, or the First Amendment, students have to think through the logic and rationale of their position. This active engagement results in improved critical thinking skills, and the students develop a sense of responsibility for their community and their learning.

Students also learn that the community depends on them as they perform community chores, offer community service, and plan school meetings and events. When the school's environment meets students' needs for significance and belonging, students are more likely to cooperate with others and look toward the common good.

Throughout our school, the implicit message is clear: We deeply respect our students, not just because they are our students, but because all human beings have the right to be respected in these ways. The seminal ideas of our program are not new. We have simply translated them into practical, day-to-day applications embedded in the school setting so that the entire school's culture becomes our implicit curriculum. Everything that we do and say teaches character.

References

Adler, A. (1927/1992). (Trans. C. Brett.) *Understanding human nature.* Oxford, UK: One World Publications.

Goodlad, J. (1984). *A place called school.* New York: McGraw-Hill.

Ignas, E., & Corsini, R. J. (1979). *Alternative educational systems.* Itasca, IL: F. E. Peacock Publisher.

Jackson, P., Boostrom, R., & Hansen, D. (1993). *The moral life of schools.* San Francisco: Jossey-Bass.

National Middle School Association. (2002). NMSA position statement on curriculum integration [Online]. Available: www.nmsa.org/cnews/positionpapers/integrativecurriculum.htm

Postman, N., & Weingartner, C. (1969). *Teaching as a subversive activity.* New York: Delacourt Press.

Linda Inlay is Director of the River School, 2447 Old Sonoma Rd., Napa, CA 94558; linlay@nvusd.k12.ca.us.

From *Educational Leadership,* March 2003, pp. 69-71. Reprinted with permission of the Association for Supervision and Curriculum Development.

Defeating the "Hidden Curriculum"

Teaching Political Participation in the Social Studies Classroom

DAVID L. MARTINSON

Laments about the decline in citizen participation in the American political process seem to grow louder each year. Clearly the failure of large numbers of Americans to participate even minimally in the democratic process by voting is a matter of grave concern. It has been derisively noted, for example, that among the top twenty industrialized nations, the United States ranks "number one in oil… [and] natural gas consumption… [and] number one in lowest voter turnout" (Moore 2001, 174).

Critics often blame that sorry state of affairs on the nation's schools, especially the social studies classroom. Such expressions of anxiety, of course, are not new. In 1968, Langton and Jennings reported research that "showed that whether or not students had taken any civics courses was largely irrelevant to their levels of political knowledge, political interest, and interest in political media, political discussion, political efficacy, civil tolerance, political trust, and participatory orientation" (cited in Erikson, Luttbeg, and Tedin 1991, 148).

To emphasize that point, a number of critics cite the work of Richard Merelman, who argues that "American schools do not and cannot teach democratic values." More particularly, "order keeping seems to demand an authoritarian school environment that is inconsistent with the content and procedures required for the learning of democratic behaviors" (cited in Hennessy 1985, 197). Merelman argues that "discussing political values in the classroom invites controversy and division" (197).

According to proponents of this view, attempts by social studies teachers "to socialize students to democratic values are delegitimized by… [a] hidden curriculum" (Erikson, Luttbeg and Tedin 1991, 149). This "hidden curriculum" has been defined as "the informal and decidedly antidemocratic set of teaching practices and power relationships by which the school operates" (149). There is an all too obvious "disjuncture be-tween the democratic creed and what actually goes on in school… [which] tends to inhibit political learning" (149). Political satirist Michael Moore (2001) describes entering a public high school and realizing that he "was… walking into the halls of a two-thousand-plus inmate holding pen" (97).

A Vermont Town Meeting?

The Norman Rockwell ideal of American democracy is perhaps best represented by the image of the Vermont town meeting in which each resident assumes an active and informed role in the decision-making process. Informed and concerned persons meet to discuss and decide issues, and from an intelligent and often vigorous debate good public policy inevitably emerges. Livingston and Thompson (1971) make this point when they state:

> In traditional democratic theory, the essence of democratic procedure was held to be reasoned debate of alternative solutions to public problems. Democracy, thus conceived, offered a unique solution to the problem of conflict, a solution which would control conflict without seeking to eliminate it. The assumption was that public policies and the statutes which embody them will express a majority opinion which has itself resulted from a free and open debate of public issues and which continue to be open to criticism and discussion. Underlying this arrangement was the assumption that there is an objective moral order which human reason and discussion can discover. (24)

The citizenry, in effect, was made up of persons who were "rational, infinitely improvable... [beings] who could be trusted to govern... [themselves]" (Livingston and Thompson 1971, 34). It was just such a vision that was in Thomas Jefferson's mind when he "substituted 'the pursuit of happiness' for 'property' in the familiar Lockean triad that opened the Declaration of Independence.... [Jefferson] tied the new nation's star to an open-ended, democratic process whereby individuals develop their own potential and seek to realize their own life goals" (Foner 1998, 20).

Romance and reality, of course, do not always coincide. In the immediate context, the romantic view of an informed and active citizenry simply flies in the face of fact. Vincent Blasi argues that the "vision of active, continued involvement by citizens fails to describe not only the reality but also the shared ideal of American politics" (cited in Gilimor, Barron and Simon 1998, 8). As noted above, large numbers of citizens do not participate at all. Furthermore, the so-called marketplace of ideas in which concerned political partisans grapple in an effort to discover the truth is, according to political commentator Bill Moyers (1999), fast becoming "the verbal equivalent of mud wrestling" (411).

What accounts for what many perceive as the disintegration of the ideal of a democratic political process in America? Erikson, Luttbeg and Tedin (1991, 335–37) suggest four possible explanations for the current public apathy:

1. mass political incompetence
2. rational disengagement
3. elite manipulation
4. public contentment

Explanations 2 and 4 present particular food for thought for social studies teachers. According to the "rational disengagement" thesis, for example, "from a strict cost-vs.-benefit standpoint, one should not follow public affairs closely, since the investment would get one nowhere" (Erikson, Luttbeg, and Tedin 1991, 336). Put simply, perhaps individuals are not more active in the political process because rationally they have better things to do with their time. Does each citizen have a responsibility to become a C-SPAN "junkie"?

Similar—and in some ways interrelated—is the case vis-à-vis explanation 4: public apathy as public contentment. Perhaps individual citizens do not take a more active part in the political process because they are basically content with the manner in which the system currently functions. Paradoxically, in fact, it may be that "when many people do participate in politics, it is a distressing signal either that government has ignored public needs or that conflicts between societal groups are no longer being successfully resolved by political leaders" (Erikson, Luttbeg, and Tedin 1991, 337).

In short, social studies teachers need not view themselves as failures if every student in class is not motivated to become a reader of *Political Science Quarterly*. Teachers in secondary school biology classes do not deem themselves failures if all their students do not become medical doctors! Certainly few will question the need to motivate citizens to become more active in the political process, as "one can hardly applaud when people do not actively seek to protect... [even] their own interests" (Erikson, Luttbeg, and Tedin 1991, 338). What is required is perspective.

Adopting an "Aristotelian" Perspective

The social studies teacher might look to the Greek philosopher Aristotle for guidance in how to approach her task. Aristotle has been called a "down-to-earth thinker who emphasizes the positive and presents a full vision of a virtuous and happy person" (Merrill 1997, 32). Of particular relevancy in the context of this article is Aristotle's concern that one strive to achieve a mean or "balance... between thinking and acting in extreme ways" (32).

Fagothey (1976) observes,

> The... [Aristotelian] mean is not absolute but... relative [to each person].... [W]hat is the right amount for one would be too much or too little for another.... [For example], a temperate meal for a wrestler would be overindulgence for a dyspeptic, a generous gift from a poor man would be a stingy one from a rich man. (174)

Aristotle believed that we get into trouble when we move to extremes—although many have misunderstood what he was proposing. He certainly would not tell a judge, for example, that he should only be moderately concerned about justice (Fagothey 1976, 174). He would, however, suggest "that justice itself is a mean between lenience and severity" (174). Similarly, a teacher must keep control of his or her classroom. That ideal level of control, however, is the mean between anarchy and authoritarianism.

The social studies teacher must approach the task of developing active and responsible citizens with a similar attitude. Not every student in class is going to run for Congress in the future. How can the social studies teacher encourage the diverse group of individuals that make up a typical class to at least consider becoming more active participants in the political process? Three specific considerations are of importance:

1. The teacher must foster a classroom atmosphere in which the spirit of democracy prevails. Democratic values should be practiced, not just talked about.

2. Classroom instruction must be directed toward political/governmental questions and issues to which students can readily relate.

3. The role the mass media play in politics, the explosion in media technology, and the way the media interact with the democratic process must be examined in considerable depth.

Getting Beyond the "Hidden Curriculum"

In my senior year of high school, my social studies course was disastrous. The teacher apparently believed that students learned best under the constant threat of one of her extreme emotional outbursts. The atmosphere in her classroom went beyond authoritarian—it was totalitarian! I mostly discounted the experience because I had learned at home to know better. Others were likely not so fortunate. After all, "responsible citizenship is not easily learned in a dictatorship" (Gillmor et al. 1990, 646).

Several other social studies courses in my high school were taught by the football coach—not an uncommon occurrence (Erikson, Luttbeg, and Tedin 1991, 149). Whether or not we had a test on a Monday was once determined by whether or not the football team won a key game on Saturday. In fact, far too often social studies course are taught by "teachers… [who] are simply not intellectually prepared to effectively handle the discussion of complex political topics" (149). Add an authoritarian mindset to a lack of intellectual preparation, and anyone can see why the hidden curriculum is alive and well.

School administrators often are deeply concerned about avoiding conflict and controversy. But well-taught social studies courses invite conflict and controversy. A school superintendent in Florida, for example, responded to a survey by declaring that "the first priority of our school is to provide a safe environment" (Martinson and Kopenhaver 1992, 162). The same administrator asserted that "confrontation and controversy lead to unsafe conditions" (162). It is doubtful that such an individual will be excited about hiring social studies teachers who will facilitate a classroom experience where genuine learning about active citizenship in a democratic society becomes part of the socialization experience.

Making the Subject Matter Relevant

Another vivid memory I have about my high school social studies courses is the requirement that we memorize things. A certain amount of memorization is useful. Too often, however, what we were required to memorize was intellectually empty and trivial. One teacher, for example, required that we memorize the capital city of every state in the nation—and we did not get credit unless we spelled the city name correctly.

More useful might have been requiring that we be able to recite portions—in a reasonably contextually accurate manner—of U.S. Supreme Court justice Louis Brandeis's legendary opinion in favor of freedom of expression, from the case *Whitney v. California*. That, of course, was unlikely to happen because (a) my teachers were likely not familiar with it, and (b) it would have challenged the "hidden curriculum" that ran unbridled in my high school.

I believe that social studies teachers can use a technique that I have found useful in college-level ethics courses to make material relevant to the students. Students coming to my classes know little of even the basics of ethical decision-making. I try to stimulate their moral imaginations to recognize relevant eth-

ical issues (Jaksa and Pritchard 1994, 12–14). To do this, I talk about drivers who disobey posted speed limits except when a highway patrol officer is present. I suggest that ethical drivers are those who obey traffic laws even when a highway patrol officer is not present, because that is the ethical or right thing to do.

Students come up with all sorts of inventive reasons why it is okay for them to disobey posted speed limits. Some get angry with me for suggesting that they might not be ethical drivers. Many of them probably begin to think about ethics in a somewhat serious manner for the first time in their lives. I would never have reached that point had I begun the course with a discussion of Immanuel Kant's categorical imperative.

The number of topics that a teacher in a social studies course can approach in a similar fashion seems almost limitless. Instead of beginning a discussion of freedom of speech and press and the First Amendment by having students memorize the writings of Thomas Jefferson and James Madison, the teacher can ask them to consider whether student publications in their school should be genuinely free of administration/faculty censorship. The specific right of groups like the Jehovah's Witnesses to engage in door-to-door evangelization can provoke discussion. By addressing topics in this way, teachers may bring students to recognize the tension between majority power and minority rights in a constitutional democracy.

The Role of the Mass Media

For students to appreciate the political realities in America in a new century, they must have some understanding of the role the media play in the contemporary political process. It is no hyperbole to argue that

> [I]f, for example, the political process is being challenged—and changed—by the very way television covers political campaigns, students need to understand why that is happening. Why have them memorize Abraham Lincoln's Gettysburg Address if it would be impossible for Lincoln to be elected president in the television age? (Martinson 1993, 126)

Although there are still a few apologists who question the power of the media to significantly influence public opinion, that view has been largely discredited by social scientists who have seriously examined the question. That is not to say that the mass media have unlimited power. The "magic bullet" theory of media impact was rejected decades ago. But news media have considerable power to "influence… social and cultural situations, trends, and processes within our society" (DeFleur and Dennis 1998, 459). The media may be limited in their ability to induce a Democrat to vote for a Republican, but they may be instrumental in determining whether an individual decides to vote at all.

An excellent example of this more sophisticated understanding of media effects on the political process centers around what is labeled "agenda-setting theory." Agenda-setting theory suggests that the media may not be as influential in telling individuals what to think as in telling them what to think about. Researchers Iyengar and Kinder argue that "Americans' views of their society and nation are powerfully shaped by the stories that appear on the evening news" (cited in Baran 2001, 328). The audience is not told explicitly whom to vote for, but it is certainly influenced when told what are the most important issues in the campaign. McCombs and Shaw state,

> In choosing and displaying news, editors, newsroom staff, and broadcasters play an important role in shaping political reality.... [The audience members] learn not only about a given issue, but how much importance to attach to that issue.... The mass media may well determine the important issues—that is, the media may set the "agenda" of the campaign." (cited in Baran 2001, 327)

Some communication scholars advance what they label "media-intrusion theory" which holds that the "media have intruded into and taken over politics to the degree that... [the political process has] become subverted" (Baran and Davis 2000, 325). The media, particularly television, have "subverted politics by undermining political party control... [and] replaced parties in the election process" (326).

Social studies students will remain largely ignorant of the political realities of contemporary America if they do not appreciate the impact of the mass media on the political process. This means, of course, that social studies teachers must be genuinely informed about current mass communication research and theory. It is no longer sufficient that the social studies teacher read the morning newspaper and watch the evening news (Martinson 1993, 127).

Conclusions

By taking a realistic approach to the subject matter, social studies teachers can increase their chances of having a positive effect on students. The immediate goal should be providing a motivational experience. If the teacher can motivate future members of the silent majority to be just a little less silent, more vocal, and more willing to participate in the political process, he or she will have achieved an important educational goal.

As Austin Ranney once noted, "for most Americans, politics is still far from being the most interesting and important thing in life.... [What is really important] in their lives... [is] making friends, finding spouses, raising children, and having a good

time" (cited in Harwood 1999, 278). Social studies teachers are not going to change that. What social studies teachers can do, to paraphrase James Fallows (1996), is provide students with the motivation and tools that will allow them to participate more actively in public life (269). To accomplish this more limited but realistic end, social studies teachers must move beyond the "hidden curriculum" mentality, demonstrate the relevancy of the subject matter, and know and teach how the mass media and media technology affect the political process today.

Key words: social studies, political participation, voting, hidden curriculum, democracy, mass media

REFERENCES

Baran, S. J. 2001. *Introduction to mass communication: Media literacy and culture*. Mountain View, CA: Mayfield.

Baran, S. J., and D. K. Davis. 2000. *Mass communication theory: Foundations, ferment, and future*. Belmont, CA: Wadsworth.

DeFleur, M. L., and E. E. Dennis. 1998. *Understanding mass communication*. Boston: Houghton Mifflin.

Erikson, R. S., N. R Luttbeg, and K. L. Tedin. 1991. *American public opinion*. New York: Macmillan.

Fallows, J. 1996. *Breaking the news: How the media undermine American democracy*. New York: Pantheon Books.

Foner, E. 1998. *The story of American freedom*. New York: Norton.

Gillmor, D. M., J. A. Barron, and T. F. Simon. 1998. *Mass communication law: Cases and comment*. Belmont, CA: Wadsworth.

Gillmor, D. M., J. A. Barron, T. F. Simon, and H. A. Terry. 1990. *Mass communication law: Cases and comment*. St. Paul, MN: West.

Harwood, R. 1999. The alienated American voter: Are the news media to blame? In *Impact of mass media*, ed. R. E. Hiebert. New York: Longman.

Hennessy, B. 1985. *Public opinion*. Monterey, CA: Brooks/Cole.

Jaksa, J. A., and M. S. Pritchard. 1994. *Communication ethics: Methods of analysis*. Belmont, CA: Wadsworth.

Livingston, J. C., and R. C. Thompson. 1971. *The consent of the governed*. New York: Macmillan.

Martinson, D. L. 1993. Redirect secondary school journalism education by focusing on first amendment concerns. *Contemporary Education* 64(2): 125–27.

Martinson, D. L., and L. L. Kopenhaver. 1992. How school superintendents view student press rights. *The Clearing House* 65(3): 159–64.

Merrill, J. C. 1997. *Journalism ethics: Philosophical foundations for news media*. New York: St. Martin's.

Moore, M. 2001. *Stupid white men*. New York: Harper Collins.

Moyers, B. 1999. New news and a war of cultures. In *Impact of mass media*, ed. R. E. Hiebert. New York: Longman.

David L. Martinson is a professor in the School of Journalism and Mass Communication at Florida International University, in North Miami.

From *The Clearing House*, January/February 2003, pp. 132-135. © 2003 by Heldref Publications, 1319, Eighteenth St., NW, Washington, DC 20036-1802. Reprinted with permission of the Helen Dwight Reid Educational Foundation.

Implementing a Character Education Curriculum and Assessing Its Impact on Student Behavior

CLETUS R. BULACH

Many school officials seek reasons for the increase in violence in the public schools. Bullying behavior is thought to be one of the major causes (Bulach et al. In press, Bulach 2000). The two students who were involved in the Columbine High School shootings were often subjected to teasing, according to press reports. The student who killed other students at a Paducah, Kentucky, middle school was also the subject of frequent teasing by his peers. The school bully at a middle school in Cherokee County, Georgia, according to newspaper reports, struck a fellow student after exiting the school bus, causing that student's death.

Bullying behavior occurs outside the school setting as well. In an article titled "Bullies on the Rise," published in the *Atlanta Journal and Constitution*, 29 August 1999, Tammy Joyner reported. "Bullying—one of the most insidious and fastest-growing forms of workplace violence—is on the rise worldwide....

Clearly there is a need in our society and in school settings to curb violence and to have citizens and students practice behaviors that are of a more civil and moral nature than currently is the pattern. If students practice behaviors associated with forgiveness, sympathy, and kindness, bullying behavior should decrease. Some observers attribute the pattern of harmful behavior to the breakdown of the family and the lack of moral training in the home. As a result, more and more school systems are introducing curricula to address this concern. This training is often called "character education." The citizens of some school systems have objected to this process because the desired character traits are often in the eyes of the beholder, that is, one community may emphasize character traits that are not valued by citizens of another community. Consequently, school officials need to ascertain those characteristics that are valued by their community to avoid this problem. Further, they need to determine the extent to which the characteristics are present or lacking in the student body; if a characteristic is already present, there is no need to teach it.

Purpose/Problem Statement

The October 27, 1997 issue of *Business Week*, in addition to having a wealth of information on character education programs, posed two similar problems as follows: (1) Whose values should be taught? and (2) How can character be measured accurately? The purpose of my research was to address these two concerns, to describe a process for determining those traits that should be taught, and to develop a survey instrument to measure the degree to which behaviors associated with the identified traits are present or absent.

Bulach et al. define a character trait as an intrinsic attitude or belief that determines a person's behavior in relation to other people and in relation *to self* (In press). Characteristics such as sportsmanship, generosity, courtesy, and empathy would produce behaviors that would be easily observable in relation *to other people*. Character values such as persistence, motivation, self-respect, and self-control would produce behaviors related more to self that would not be so easily observable.

I conducted an extensive survey of parents, teachers, and clergy in a K–12 school system near Atlanta, Georgia, to determine the character traits valued by the community. I asked them to list those traits they thought should be taught in their school systems and analyzed the data for the frequency with which each trait was listed. Based on frequency data, I identified twenty-seven traits as valued by the community. I consolidated these into sixteen character traits because a number of them were similar. I then asked the teachers, parents, and clergy to rank the sixteen traits from most important to least important. I have described this process in more detail elsewhere (Bulach 1999).

Teachers and parents at all grade levels were in agreement on the three most important character values to teach: (1) respect for self, others, and property, (2) honesty, and (3) self-control/discipline. Members of the clergy chose the following top three: (1) perseverance/diligence, (2) motivation, and (3) empathy. The remaining thirteen values, ranked in order of importance, were as follows: cooperation, responsibility/dependability/accountability, integrity/fairness, kindness, forgiveness, perseverance/diligence/motivation, compassion/empathy, courtesy/politeness, patriotism/ citizenship, tolerance of diversity, humility, generosity/charity, and sportsmanship.

To accomplish the second purpose (develop an instrument), I asked 130 teachers (K-12) to list those behaviors they would see if a student modeled or did not model those character traits. Frequency data were again used to select behaviors that could be used in a survey to determine the presence or absence of these character traits.

The instrument provides a measure of ninety-six behaviors associated with sixteen character traits. It can be used to have teachers or students describe their perceptions of students' behavior on each of the items. In the pilot study (Bulach and Butler 2002) students (462) and teachers (130) responded to each of the ninety-six behaviors on a five-point Likert scale ranging from 1 (*never*) to 5 (*always*). For example, one of the behaviors is "They think it is okay to do something as long as they don't get caught." The instructions tell them to choose the response that comes closest to what they think other students do or think. Forty of the items are stated negatively and are reverse scored (see the appendix for a grouping of the ninety-six behaviors according to the character trait that they represent). All negative behaviors are italicized to assist with reading the data.

A Cronbach alpha was used to measure the internal consistency/reliability of the instrument. The reliability coefficient involving 222 high school students was .96, for 210 junior high school students it was also .96, and for 30 third grade students it was .97 (Bulach and Butler 2002).

The instrument has construct validity only for those behaviors identified for that character trait. It is possible that there are other behaviors associated with a character trait that were not measured. Consequently, a student could be honest on the five behaviors listed for honesty and be dishonest on some other behavior not measured by the instrument. A further constraint on validity is that students report only on what they think other students do or think. Their perception could be inaccurate.

Another factor that could affect the validity of the instrument could be the racial/ethnic composition of the student body. The racial composition of the students in this study was 39 percent Afro-American, 52 percent Caucasian, and 9 percent other. It appears that the instrument is a valid measure of student behavior in a racially mixed school or a Caucasian or Afro-American school. The instrument has not been used in a school with a large Latino or Asian population.

In the pilot study (Bulach and Butler 2002), I gathered data from both teachers and students. The students at the elementary level tended to be slightly more positive than teachers about students' behavior, whereas the reverse occurred at the middle and high school level—teachers were more positive than the students. The differences were slight, however, and were not statistically significant. I consider the student data a more valid measure of student behavior. Students are more likely than teachers to know what goes on in bathrooms, hallways, and buses, or when teachers' backs are turned. Brendtro (2001) reported that thousands of students are bullied and teased each day, and teachers intervene in only one out of twenty-five episodes. Either teachers do not see what is going on, or do not care! Data can be collected from both and compared, but I prefer to believe that teachers do not see what is going on and that that is why data should be collected from students and not teachers.

The instrument has been used in over 220 elementary, middle, and high schools. It does discriminate between students exposed to a character education curriculum and those who are not. Students who are exposed to a character education curriculum have more positive scores. For example, students in a Junior Reserve Officer Training Corps (JROTC) have significantly higher scores than students in the same school who are not in the JROTC program (Bulach 2002). JROTC students had a score of 3.43 on the character trait "courtesy/politeness" compared to the rest of the student body with a score of 2.65. The same pattern occurred for each of the other fifteen character traits. This finding should send a signal to school officials.

The change in emphasis for character education programs in the regular school setting versus the JROTC setting is very different. Character education programs in the regular setting tend to be knowledge or cognitively based while the JROTC curriculum tends to be behavior based. In the normal school setting, there tends to be a character word of the week or month and everyone devotes some time during the day to studying about that word. They may read stories or listen to songs that are examples of that word. For example, if the word were "dependable" they might listen to the song "Lean on me" by Al Jarreau or be asked to think of three words that describe dependability and share them. In the JROTC program, they might study what the word means, but the major emphasis would be watching for behaviors that indicate dependability. If they are not in formation, in class on time, do not bring their homework, etc. they receive demerits. Further, peer pressure from upperclassmen reinforces desired behaviors. According to Williams (2000), the desired behavior must be modeled by everyone if the character education program is going to be effective, and this does occur in this JROTC program. (Bulach and Butler 2002, 9)

Implementation Suggestions

An effective character education program involves the entire faculty, staff, parents, and community. Cooks, custodians, and bus drivers, as well as the teachers, parents, and community must be involved if student behaviors are to be positively affected. The current practice of designating a character trait of the week or the month is not working because a word such as "respect" has a different meaning for each person. The student receives mixed messages about the trait. The second problem is that many school systems teach all of the mandated character traits each year. If a system has twenty-five traits to cover and they are repeated each year, students will say, "We did that last year. They become bored with it and do not take it seriously. Consequently, there is very little change in the behavior of students, and most character education programs, although they may be meeting state mandates, are ineffective and take time away from the regular instructional program.

There are those who believe that character cannot be taught, but it can be caught (Bulach 2002). Students have to talk about the character trait and its implications, but they also have to see the behaviors modeled by the people in their daily environment. Instead of focusing on the word of the week or month, the focus should be one or two behaviors of the week. This could be reinforced by periodic discussions on why this behavior is important. The behaviors for each trait are listed in the appendix; each school could also create its own list of behaviors. For example, in the category of behaviors for "respect" is, "Students help to improve the appearance of school property." This behavior relates to "respect for property."

If the focus were on this behavior for the week, the faculty and staff would know what behaviors to look for. Students, teachers, faculty, and others who deface property, litter, and so forth would be seen by someone and would be called to task. This system would enable students to become peer enforcers of the behavior. Peer enforcement of behavior is one of the main features of the JROTC program.

Another feature of many character education programs that contributes to ineffectiveness is a curriculum guide. Teachers use the curriculum guide as a resource, and it is taught at a certain time of the day or week. This may cause some change in students' character, but for any significant change to occur, the curriculum must be infused throughout the entire school day. Parents and the community must also be involved to reinforce character outside the school. If the focus is on a behavior such as "improving the appearance of property" everyone will know what to look for. For example, cafeteria workers could look for food being thrown or litter on the floor, custodians could look for things left in the hallways and damage to restrooms, bus drivers could look for scribbling on the backs of seats, parents could look at the appearance of their child's room and so forth. When the focus is on behaviors, a curriculum guide becomes obsolete because time does not have to be spent teaching character traits; everyone is more likely to reinforce desired behavior all day long.

A third feature that leads to ineffectiveness in many character education programs is the assignment of responsibility for the program to a teacher or counselor. This person is given the responsibility to implement the program but does not have the power to make faculty follow it. Consequently, many faculty members do little to promote character education. Unless the school leadership takes an active role, teachers will pay lip service to the character education program, but will not really support it.

Lickona (1991) has compiled a document, available from the Character Education Partnership (800/988-8081), titled "The Eleven Principles of Character Education Effectiveness." A survey has been constructed from the eleven principles and can be used to determine how effectively the character education program has been implemented. Data from the eleven principles survey and the instrument described in this article would allow school officials to determine how well their character education program is being implemented (process evaluation) and whether their character curriculum is affecting student behaviors (outcome evaluation). Based on the data from these two instruments, school officials can modify their program as needed.

Conclusions

Implementing programs to improve student behaviors associated with character traits is a task well worth undertaking. Everyone in the school community should be involved and the process and progress should be evaluated. If the character education program is successful, bullying behavior and incidents of violence should decrease, because students will be more sympathetic, tolerant, kind, compassionate, and forgiving. As faculty and staff model the behaviors associated with the character traits, and as their behavior is "caught" by the students, an improvement in the climate and culture of the school is likely to occur. With these improvements in student behavior and school culture, the result should be improved student achievement and test scores, as well.

APPENDIX

Selected Character Values and Their Corresponding Behaviors

Respect for self/others/property

Students think about the feelings of other students.
Students take care of school property.
Students are positive about themselves.
Students act to improve the appearance of the school or other property.

Students do things that hurt other students.
Students do things that are not good for them.
Students think that sexual activity is okay.
Students use tobacco.
Students use drugs and/or alcohol.
Students believe that keeping your body dean is important.

Honesty

Students think it is okay to do something as long as they do not get caught.
Students take things that do not belong to them.
Students turn in money or things that have been lost if they find them.
Students tell the truth.
Students can be trusted.

Self-control/discipline

Students control themselves/behave when they need to.
Students do what the teachers ask them to do.
Students resist those things that are not good for them or that will get them in trouble.
Students are able to wait to get what they want.
Students pay attention in class.
Students let other students tell them what to do.
Students control their anger.

Responsibility/dependability/accountability

Students can be trusted to do what they say they will do.
Students make excuses for their actions or argue about the consequences.
Students do what the teacher asks without having to be reminded.
Students complete their classwork on time.
Students turn in their homework on time.
Students accept the consequences of their decisions/actions.

Integrity/fairness

Students go along with the most popular student instead of those who are not popular.
Students do what they are supposed to do.
Students let other students talk them into doing something that is wrong.
Students take advantage of other students if given a chance.
Students treat others the way they would want to be treated.
Students stand up or speak out for what they believe is right.

Perseverance/diligence

Students show determination when faced with a problem.
Students think about and plan their work.
Students give up when they fail or do not succeed.
Students finish an assignment within the allotted time.
Students are distracted when doing their work.
Students daydream, doodle, stare out the window.

Cooperation

Students help each other.
Students help the teacher.
Students fight with each other.
Students work well in groups.
Students argue with each other.
Students compromise to solve a conflict/problem.

Compassion/empathy

Students feel sorry for students who are having a problem.
Students pick on each other.
Students say/do things that hurt other students.
Students help a student who is being picked on.
Students listen to each other's problems.
Students comfort/console other students who have a problem.

Kindness

Students are nice to each other.
Students are nice to teachers and other adults.
Students say things about others that are harmful.
Students give compliments to each other.
Students are cruel to each other.
Students help students who have physical or mental disabilities.

Forgiveness

Students try to get even.
Students accept the mistakes of others.
Students are mean to someone because of something that person did to them in the past.
Students accept an apology to end a problem.

Patriotism/citizenship

Students are positive about their country.
Students are positive about the police.
Students are positive about the need for rules and laws.
Students care about their community.
Students care about their school.
Students volunteer their services to help where needed.

Tolerance/diversity

Students accept students who have a different religion.
Students make fun of ideas that are different from theirs.
Students accept differences of opinion.
Students make fun of students who are different.
Students accept students who are from a different race.
Students make an effort to understand students who are different.

Courtesy/politeness

Students interrupt when others are talking.
Students use cuss words or bad language.
Students call each other names.
Students say things like: thank you, pardon me, and so forth, when appropriate.

Students listen when someone is talking to them.
Students ignore other students.
Students talk back to teachers and other adults.

Generosity/charity

*Students are more concerned about themselves than
they are about others.*
Students want to help the less fortunate.
Students are willing to share what they have with others.
Students want to know what is in it for them.

Sportsmanship

Students get mad when they lose.
Students congratulate their opponents whether they win or lose.
Students quit trying if they know they are going to lose.
Students will cheat to win.
Students agree that "how the game is played" is more important
than winning.

Humility

Students care too much about their appearance, e.g., having
the right clothing, looking just right, and so forth.
Students brag about themselves.
Students want to be the center of attention.
Students put down other students.
Students act as if they are better than other students.
Students admit when they are wrong.

*Key words: character education, student achievement, curric-
ulum, discipline, student behavior*

REFERENCES

Brendtro, L. K. 2001. Worse than sticks and stones: Lesson from research on ridicule. *Reclaiming Children and Youth* 10(1): 47–49.

Bulach, C. R. 1999. So you want to teach values? *The School Administrator* 56(9): 37.

-----. 2000. *External factors that affect bullying behavior.* Paper presented at the Eastern Educational Research Association at Clearwa-
ter, FL, 17 February.

-----. 2001. A comparison of character traits for JROTC students versus
Non-JROTC students. *Education* 122(3): 559–63.

Bulach C. R., and J. Butler. 2002. A comparison of character values as
perceived by students and teachers at differing grade levels. *Journal
of Humanistic Education and Development* 41(3):200–14.

Bulach, C. R, J. P. Fulbright, R. Williams, and B. Doss. In press. Bullying behavior: What is the potential for violence at your school?
Journal of Instructional Psychology.

Lickona, T. 1991. *Educating for character: How our schools can teach
respect and responsibility.* New York: Bantam Books, 51.

Williams, M. M. 2000. Models of character education: Perspectives
and developmental issues. *Journal of Humanistic Counseling, Education, and Development* 39(1): 32–40.

*Cletus R. Bulach is an associate professor in the Department of
Educational Leadership and Professional Studies at the State
University of West Georgia, in Carrollton.*

THE MISSING VIRTUE

Lessons from dodge ball & Aristotle

Gordon Marino

Americans are inclined to ring the moral alarm and then hit the snooze button. After the latest moral crisis on Wall Street (I won't go into the sexual-abuse crisis), there were loud cries for more ethics classes. Not a bad idea, but if you are going to talk with students about ethics, which is something I do for a living, it helps to know where they are calling from. In the mid-sixties, Philip Rieff (*The Triumph of the Therapeutic*) apprized us of the fact that therapy had become the organizing motif in much of Western culture and, as a result, our understanding of moral character was shifting. Rieff was right. In the early eighties, the moral philosopher Alastair Macintyre (*After Virtue*) observed that for postmodern men and women, candor, rather than moral accountability, had become a cardinal virtue. Over the years, I have taken some soundings in my ethics classes and have been surprised to find that a cardinal virtue that everyone used to salute now evokes a shrug.

In *Nichomachean Ethics,* Aristotle invites us to think about the connection between moral character and happiness. He asks, Can you be happy and a cad? Definitely not. If that is the case, which moral virtues are essential to happiness? Before unveiling Aristotle's recipe, I press my students, "Which moral virtues do you believe are indispensable to the good life?" A hand shoots up; respect gets the first vote, then compassion, and this year, a sense of humor comes in the third. After a while, some of the more traditional virtues such as wisdom and justice are invited in. Honesty eventually makes it onto the blackboard without my prompts. Raising my voice and making a vee with my eyebrows, I nudge them, "Is there something missing?" Students look around puzzled, as if to say, OK, what's the trick?

"What about courage?" "Oh yeah, I guess so," is invariably the grudging response. Save for the two years that I taught at the Virginia Military Institute, I have never seen courage hit the top of the list. I hector my captive audience, "How can you be honest without courage? Truth telling, for example, only becomes difficult when there are unpleasant consequences for being honest." The

sermonette continues, "And if you can't bear the consequences, you will be unwilling to tell the truth."

I close with an object lesson. Suppose it is the end of the spring semester and you did not hand your paper in for your ethics class. The professor believes that, in the interest of fairness, all students ought to have the same amount of time to work on their term papers and so has promised to dish out an F to anyone who does not hand the essay in on time. The deadline is fast approaching. You planned to write your term paper when you were on break in Cancún, but you never got around to it. You are a junior, planning to apply to medical school in the fall. No paper, and you are sure to get a D in the course and torpedo your chances for admission. Still, there is hope. While the professor may be a martinet, he is also a trusting soul. You could easily get a few extra days if you told him you were suffering from mononucleosis or that your grandmother died. What will it be? Truth and consequences or a white, maybe gray, lie?

My students at Saint Olaf College are as morally earnest as any I have ever taught, but there can be no denying that the death rates of grandparents rise here at semester's end as much as they do at other campuses. Unless he is even more afraid of getting caught in a lie, the student who cannot control his fears will start working up a short story on deadline day. Again, trying to give a boost to the ancient virtue, I pace dramatically and repeat, "You can't be an honest coward." Usually delivered in midsemester, this is one of my better half-time speeches. Students seem to walk out of class thinking (if only for a few hours) that courage is essential to the life they aspire to, and I shuffle out speculating on how courage could ever have become an afterthought.

Courage was touted as a keystone virtue in the post–World War II era in which I grew up. It was then common to hear stories about boys who would not be allowed back into their homes until they faced down some bully. Television, movies, and popular literature emphasized the signal importance of grace under pressure. The president was famous for having penned a Pulitzer Prize–winner called *Profiles in Courage.* A quick study of the "self help" literature of the nineteenth century also hints that our ancestors thought of courage as the bedrock of moral character. Again, what prompted the demotion of courage?

Prior to the war in Vietnam, the values of the military were widely respected and well represented in the larger culture. The qualities that were imagined necessary for good soldiering were incorporated into our notions of an ideal moral life. But as many Americans came to see the military as misguided and worse, a pall was cast over traditionally martial virtues, such as honor and courage. At best, the teaching elite now thinks of the military as a necessary evil and the virtues associated with the guardian class have become déclassé. (It will be interesting see how the military's reputation fares after the second Gulf War.) As the subconscious reasoning goes, courage is good for people intent upon combat but useless for less primitive, more pacific people.

Aristotle, however, taught that we acquire virtuous dispositions by practicing the actions that we want to be disposed toward. In accord with Aristotle, our moralists today rightly recommend diversity workshops as a means to develop a tolerant disposition. Yet in most of our lives there is very little opportunity for getting practice in coping with physical fear. Indeed, last year after much dispute, dodge ball was bounced out of many public schools. Those who defended the game argued that it helped develope mettle. Those who argued against it noted that some students found big red balls being hurled at their skulls traumatic. Guess who won the debate? And yet, the ramifications of regarding courage as a moral elective are potentially catastrophic, not only for our ability to tell the truth, but for our foreign policy as well. A nation of people who cannot tolerate feeling afraid might be unduly inclined to send their subcontracted military into actions that will quiet the sources of their fears. Courage by proxy is no courage at all.

Gordon Marino *is a philosophy professor and the director of the Hong Kierkegaard Library at Saint Olaf College in Northfield, Minnesota.*

From *Commonweal*, April 25, 2003, pp. 12-13. © 2003 by Commonweal Foundation. Reprinted by permission.

Flunking Statistics

The right's disinformation about faculty bias

BY MARTIN PLISSNER

When William F. Buckley Jr. launched America's conservative movement half a century ago, the requisite foe came readily to hand. *In God & Man at Yale*, Buckley identified the university he had just left—and, by implication, the country's entire higher-education establishment—as the driving force behind "agnosticism and collectivism" in American life. The specter of radical leftists in control of the nation's campuses would invigorate Republican platforms and speakers for a generation.

Years later, Richard Nixon, as president, found a fresh antagonist for conservatives to demonize: the liberal media. As with Buckley, the choice had personal roots. The formative battles of Buckley's career had been with the Yale faculty; Nixon's were with the press. In the enemies lists compiled by Nixon's staff, journalists outnumbered all other categories, including college professors, by a ratio of nearly 3-to-1. Elevated by a master to great Satan for the right, the news media retain that status to this day. But now the previous Satan is back as well.

As often happens in Washington, the matter began at a think tank. The right-of-center American Enterprise Institute (AEI), in the August cover story of its *American Enterprise* magazine, claimed documentation beyond dispute of the left-wing hammerlock on American faculties. *AE*'s editor-in-chief, William Zinsmeister, in league with David Horowitz (best known for his ads in college newspapers calling on black Americans to show "gratitude" for all that white Americans have done for them) of the conservative Center for the Study of Popular Culture, sent student volunteers to boards of election to search out the party registrations of 1,843 college teachers at 21 institutions. For the cover story, Democrats, Greens and "Working Family" registrants were lumped under "L" for "parties of the left"; Republicans and Libertarians, meanwhile, were filed under "R" for "parties of the right." (Independents, who would seem under Zinsmeister's labeling scheme to merit a "C" for "centrist," were ignored.) The overall ratio of L's to R's reflected in the story's bar graphs was dramatic: 11-to-1.

Conservative pundits swiftly pressed Zinsmeister's numbers into service. "Cokie," quipped George Will to Cokie Roberts on ABC's *This Week* in late August, "Bright college years are here again. Millions of parents will be sending children and a lot of money to colleges this fall. But perhaps parents should cut out the middle men and send the money directly to the Democratic Party." College campuses, said Will, are "intellectually akin to North Korea." *The Wall Street Journal* followed up on its editorial page a few days later, weighing in with a piece titled, "One Faculty Indivisible—Even the Press Corps Isn't This Uniformly Liberal." And in a September *U.S. News & World Report* column, John Leo, who had sounded the same alarm months earlier without benefit of the *AE* numbers, wrote a sequel.

Now, you don't have to be conservative and paranoid to expect that a show of hands between liberals and conservatives among the nation's academics doesn't figure to be close. In politics, college towns are not generally found to be bastions of the right. But Zinsmeister's purported findings were something else again. At none of the campuses—which ran the gamut from Harvard, Brown, Stanford and Cornell universities to 10 state schools and a smattering of smaller colleges—did the parties of the left prevail by a ratio of less than 6-to-1. At 86 percent liberal on the Zinsmeister scale, the University of Texas at Austin (on whose board appointees of George W. Bush still reign) trailed by only a tad the University of California, Berkeley (91 percent liberal).

The findings look pretty compelling—but not when you look at them closely. In the University of Texas sample, for example, 28 of the 94 teachers came from women's studies—not exactly a highlight of any school's core curriculum or a likely cross section of its faculty. At the same time, none of the 94 was from the university's huge schools of engineering, business, law or medicine—or from any of the sciences. At Cornell University, it's the same story: 166 L's by the *AE* bar graphs, and only 6 R's. But not one faculty member in the entire sample taught in the engineering, business, medicine or law schools, or in any of the sciences. Thirty-three, on the other hand, were in women's studies—more than any subject, save for English.

The methodology employed is similarly slapdash at the other chosen campuses. Harvard's faculty of more than 2,000 is represented by 52 members from just three academic disciplines, all in the social sciences. More than half of the University of California, Los Angeles sample comes from just two disciplines: history and, once again, women's studies.

Issues of methodology, however, are really beside the point when it comes to finding demons for a movement to exorcise. What's required is a program for doing it. In Buckley's case, the program, at least with respect to private universities such as Yale, was simple: Let the rich alumni who fund the schools put their money on strike until the scorners of God and untrammeled private enterprise are eased out and no longer hired. The rich alumni, however, never got with the program. In the pages following its August cover story, *AE* provides one for the times. Attorney Kenneth Lee, a stalwart of the conservative Federalist Society for Law and Public Policy Studies, argues, "The simple logic underlying much of contemporary civil-rights law applies equally to conservative Republicans, who appear to face clear practices of discrimination in

American academia that are statistically even starker than previous blackballings by race."

It isn't often you hear one of the Federalist Society's strict constructionists embracing, with relish, a case relying on the "logic" of contemporary civil-rights law. But it gets better. After acknowledging a legal problem with his case—the 1964 Civil Rights Act does not specifically outlaw discrimination based on political party or ideology, as it does with respect to race and religion—Lee says the absence of statutory support doesn't bother him at all. The Rev. Jesse Jackson, he points out, seldom wins a case in court, but he "regularly

bludgeons opponents with the specter of exorbitant legal fees, a potential lawsuit loss and heaps of negative publicity unless they cave." Why shouldn't conservative thinkers on college faculties do the same? Jackson may have lost some of his luster as a role model for the left. Now he may be about to find a new role in life as a tactician for the right.

MARTIN PLISSNER, *the former political director of CBS News, is the author of* The Control Room: How Television Calls the Shots in Presidential Elections.

UNIT 5
Managing Life in Classrooms

Unit Selections

Key Points to Consider

- Describe some of the myths associated with bullying behavior. How do you see the reality of bullying? What do you think school policy and teachers in particular can do to control bullying?

- Prepare your own roadmap of how you would create positive and productive approaches to the classroom instruction of middle-school-age children. Summarize your ideas about what features would lead to effective classroom management in a given school system.

 **Links: www.dushkin.com/online/**
These sites are annotated in the World Wide Web pages.

Classroom Connect
http://www.classroom.com

Global SchoolNet Foundation
http://www.gsn.org

Teacher Talk Forum
http://education.indiana.edu/cas/tt/tthmpg.html

All teachers have concerns regarding the "quality of life" in classroom settings. All teachers and students want to feel safe and accepted when they are in school. There exists today a reliable, effective knowledge base on classroom management and the prevention of disorder in schools. This knowledge base has been developed from hundreds of studies of teacher/student interaction and student/student interaction that have been conducted in schools in North America and Europe. We speak of managing life in classrooms because we now know that there are many factors that go into building effective teacher/student and student/student relationships. The traditional term *discipline* is too narrow and refers primarily to teachers' reactions to undesired student behavior. We can better understand methods of managing student behavior when we look at the totality of what goes on in classrooms, with teachers' responses to student behavior as a part of that totality. Teachers have tremendous responsibility for the emotional climate that is set in a classroom. Whether students feel secure and safe and whether they want to learn depend to an enormous extent on the psychological frame of mind of the teacher. Teachers must be able to manage their own selves first in order to effectively manage the development of a humane and caring classroom environment.

Teachers bear moral and ethical responsibilities for being witnesses to and examples of responsible social behavior in the classroom. There are many models of observing life in classrooms. Arranging the total physical environment of the room is a very important part of the teacher's planning for learning activities. Teachers need to expect from students the best work and behavior that they are capable of achieving. Respect and caring are attitudes that a teacher must communicate to receive them in return. Open lines of communication between teachers and students enhance the possibility for congenial, fair, dialogical resolution of problems as they occur.

Developing a high level of task orientation among students and encouraging cooperative learning and shared task achievement will foster camaraderie and self-confidence among students. Shared decision making will build an *esprit de corps*, a sense of pride and confidence, which will feed on itself and blossom into high-quality performance. Good class morale, well managed, never hurts academic achievement. The importance of emphasizing quality, helping students to achieve levels of performance that they can feel proud of having attained, and encouraging positive dialogue among them leads them to take ownership in their individual educative efforts. When that happens, they literally empower themselves to do their best.

When teachers (and prospective teachers) discuss what concerns them about their roles (and prospective roles) in the classroom, the issue of discipline—how to manage student behavior—will usually rank near or at the top of their lists. A teacher needs a clear understanding of what kinds of learning environments are most appropriate for the subject matter and ages of the students. Any person who wants to teach must also want his or her students to learn well, to acquire basic values of respect for others, and to become more effective citizens.

There is considerable debate among educators regarding certain approaches used in schools to achieve a form of order in classrooms that also develops respect for self and others. The dialogue about this point is spirited and informative. The bottom line for any effective and humane approach to discipline in the classroom, the necessary starting point, is the teacher's emotional balance and capacity for self-control. This precondition creates a further one—that the teacher wants to be in the classroom with his or her students in the first place. Unmotivated teachers cannot motivate students.

Helping young people learn the skills of self-control and motivation to become productive, contributing, and knowledgeable adult participants in society is one of the most important tasks that good teachers undertake. These are teachable and learnable skills; they do not relate to heredity or social conditions. They can be learned by any human being who wants to learn them and who is cognitively able to learn them. There is a large knowledge base on how teachers can help students learn self-control. All that is required is the willingness of teachers to learn these skills themselves and to teach them to their students. There are many sound techniques that new teachers can use to achieve success in managing students' classroom behavior, and they should not be afraid to ask colleagues questions and to develop peer support groups with whom they can work with confidence and trust.

Teachers' core ethical principles come into play when deciding what constitutes defensible and desirable standards of student conduct. Teachers need to realize that before they can control behavior, they must identify what student behaviors are desired in their classrooms. They need to reflect, as well, on the emotional tone and ethical principles implied by their own behaviors. To optimize their chances of achieving the classroom atmosphere that they wish, teachers must strive for emotional balance within themselves; they must learn to be accurate observers; and they must develop just, fair strategies of intervention to aid students in learning self-control and good behavior. A teacher should be a good model of courtesy, respect, tact, and discretion. Children learn by observing how other persons behave and not just by being told how they are to behave. There is no substitute for positive, assertive teacher interaction with students in class.

This unit addresses many of the topics covered in basic foundations courses. The selections shed light on classroom management issues, teacher leadership skills, and the rights and responsibilities of teachers and students. In addition, the articles can be discussed in foundations courses involving curricula and instruction. This unit falls between the units on moral education and cultural diversity because it can be directly related to either or both of them.

A Profile of Bullying at School

*Bullying and victimization are on the increase, extensive research shows.
The attitudes and routines of relevant adults can exacerbate or curb
students' aggression toward classmates.*

Dan Olweus

Bullying among schoolchildren is a very old and well-known phenomenon. Although many educators are acquainted with the problem, researchers only began to study bullying systematically in the 1970s (Olweus, 1973, 1978) and focused primarily on schools in Scandinavia. In the 1980s and early 1990s, however, studies of bullying among schoolchildren began to attract wider attention in a number of other countries, including the United States.

What Is Bullying?

Systematic research on bullying requires rigorous criteria for classifying students as bullies or as victims (Olweus, 1996; Solberg & Olweus, in press). How do we know when a student is being bullied? One definition is that

> a student is being bullied or victimized when he or she is exposed, repeatedly and over time, to negative actions on the part of one or more other students. (Olweus, 1993, p. 9)

The person who intentionally inflicts, or attempts to inflict, injury or discomfort on someone else is engaging in *negative actions*, a term similar to the definition of *aggressive behavior* in the social sciences. People carry out negative actions through physical contact, with words, or in more indirect ways, such as making mean faces or gestures, spreading rumors, or intentionally excluding someone from a group.

Bullying also entails an *imbalance in strength* (or an *asymmetrical power relationship*), meaning that students exposed to negative actions have difficulty defending themselves. Much bullying is *proactive aggression*, that is, aggressive behavior that usually occurs without apparent provocation or threat on the part of the victim.

Some Basic Facts

In the 1980s, questionnaire surveys of more than 150,000 Scandinavian students found that approximately 15 percent of students ages 8–16 were involved in bully/victim problems with some regularity—either as bullies, victims, or both bully and victim (bully-victims) (Olweus, 1993). Approximately 9 percent of all students were victims, and 6–7 percent bullied other students regularly. In contrast to what is commonly believed, only a small proportion of the victims also engaged in bullying other students (17 percent of the victims or 1.6 percent of the total number of students).

In 2001, when my colleagues and I conducted a new large-scale survey of approximately 11,000 students from 54 elementary and junior high schools using the same questions that we used in 1983 (Olweus, 2002), we noted two disturbing trends. The percentage of victimized students had increased by approximately 50 percent from

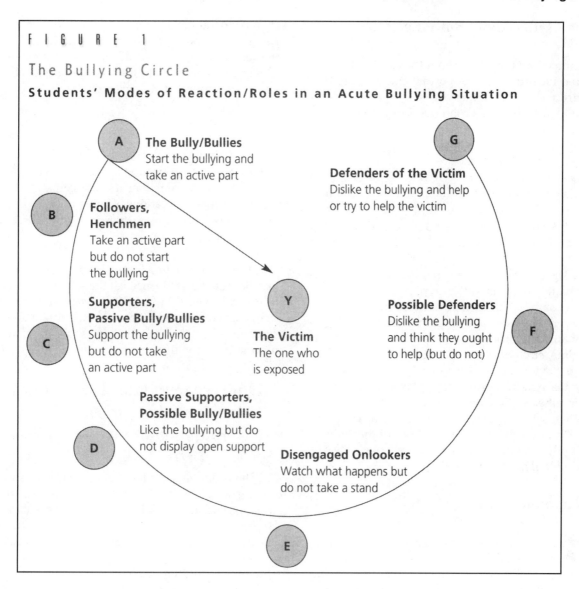

FIGURE 1

The Bullying Circle

Students' Modes of Reaction/Roles in an Acute Bullying Situation

A   The Bully/Bullies
Start the bullying and take an active part

B   Followers, Henchmen
Take an active part but do not start the bullying

C   Supporters, Passive Bully/Bullies
Support the bullying but do not take an active part

D   Passive Supporters, Possible Bully/Bullies
Like the bullying but do not display open support

Y   The Victim
The one who is exposed

G   Defenders of the Victim
Dislike the bullying and help or try to help the victim

F   Possible Defenders
Dislike the bullying and think they ought to help (but do not)

E   Disengaged Onlookers
Watch what happens but do not take a stand

1983, and the percentage of students who were involved (as bullies, victims, or bully-victims) in frequent and serious bullying problems—occurring at least once a week—had increased by approximately 65 percent. We saw these increases as an indication of negative societal developments (Solberg & Olweus, in press).

The surveys showed that bullying is a serious problem affecting many students in Scandinavian schools. Data from other countries, including the United States (Nansel et al., 2001; Olweus & Limber, 1999; Perry, Kusel, & Perry, 1988)—and in large measure collected with my Bully/Victim Questionnaire (1983, 1996)—indicate that bullying problems exist outside Scandinavia with similar, or even higher, prevalence (Olweus & Limber, 1999; Smith et al., 1999). The prevalence figures from different countries or cultures, however, may not be directly comparable. Even though the questionnaire gives a detailed definition of bullying, the prevalence rates obtained may be affected by language differences, the

students' familiarity with the concept of bullying, and the degree of public attention paid to the phenomenon.

Boys bully other students more often than girls do, and a relatively large percentage of girls—about 50 percent—report that they are bullied mainly by boys. A somewhat higher percentage of boys are victims of bullying, especially in the junior high school grades. But bullying certainly occurs among girls as well. Physical bullying is less common among girls, who typically use more subtle and indirect means of harassment, such as intentionally excluding someone from the group, spreading rumors, and manipulating friendship relations. Such forms of bullying can certainly be as harmful and distressing as more direct and open forms of harassment. Our research data (Olweus, 1993), however, clearly contradict the view that girls are the most frequent and worst bullies, a view suggested by such recent books as *Queen Bees and Wannabes* (Wiseman, 2002) and *Odd Girl Out* (Simmons, 2002).

Common Myths About Bullying

Several common assumptions about the causes of bullying receive little or no support when confronted with empirical data. These misconceptions include the hypotheses that bullying is a consequence of large class or school size, competition for grades and failure in school, or poor self-esteem and insecurity. Many also believe erroneously that students who are overweight, wear glasses, have a different ethnic origin, or speak with an unusual dialect are particularly likely to become victims of bullying.

All of these hypotheses have thus far failed to receive clear support from empirical data. Accordingly, we must look for other factors to find the key origins of bullying problems. The accumulated research evidence indicates that personality characteristics or typical reaction patterns, in combination with physical strength or weakness in the case of boys, are important in the development of bullying problems in individual students. At the same time, environmental factors, such as the attitudes, behavior, and routines of relevant adults—in particular, teachers and principals—play a crucial role in determining the extent to which bullying problems will manifest themselves in a larger unit, such as a classroom or school. Thus, we must pursue analyses of the main causes of bully/victim problems on at least two different levels: individual and environmental.

Victims and the Bullying Circle

Much research has focused on the characteristics and family backgrounds of victims and bullies. We have identified two kinds of victims, the more common being the *passive* or *submissive victim*, who represents some 80–85 percent of all victims. Less research information is available about *provocative victims*, also called *bully-victims* or *aggressive victims*, whose behavior may elicit negative reactions from a large part of the class. The dynamics of a classroom with a provocative victim are different from those of a classroom with a submissive victim (Olweus, 1978, 1993).

Bullies and victims naturally occupy key positions in the configuration of bully/victim problems in a classroom, but other students also play important roles and display different attitudes and reactions toward an acute bullying situation. Figure 1 outlines the "Bullying Circle" and represents the various ways in which most students in a classroom with bully/victim problems are involved in or affected by them (Olweus, 2001a, 2001b).

The Olweus Bullying Prevention Program

The Olweus Bullying Prevention Program,[1] developed and evaluated over a period of almost 20 years (Olweus, 1993, 1999), builds on four key principles derived chiefly from research on the development and identification of problem behaviors, especially aggressive behavior. These principles involve creating a school—and ideally, also a home—environment characterized by

- Warmth, positive interest, and involvement from adults;
- Firm limits on unacceptable behavior;
- Consistent application of nonpunitive, nonphysical sanctions for unacceptable behavior or violations of rules; and
- Adults who act as authorities and positive role models.

We have translated these principles into a number of specific measures to be used at the school, classroom, and individual levels (Olweus, 1993, 2001b). Figure 2 lists the set of core components that our statistical analyses and experience with the program have shown are particularly important in any implementation of the program.

Our research data clearly contradict the view that girls are the most frequent and worst bullies.

The program's implementation relies mainly on the existing social environment. Teachers, administrators, students, and parents all play major roles in carrying out the program and in restructuring the social environment. One possible reason for this intervention program's effectiveness is that it changes the opportunity and reward structures for bullying behavior, which results in fewer opportunities and rewards for bullying (Olweus, 1992).

Research-Based Evaluations

The first evaluation of the effects of the Olweus Bullying Prevention Program involved data from approximately 2,500 students in 42 elementary and junior high schools in Bergen, Norway, and followed students for two and one-half years, from 1983 to 1985 (Olweus, 1991, in press; Olweus & Alsaker, 1991). The findings were significant:

- Marked reductions—by 50 percent or more—in bully/victim problems for the period studied, measuring after 8 and 20 months of intervention.
- Clear reductions in general anti-social behavior, such as vandalism, fighting, pilfering, drunkenness, and truancy.
- Marked improvement in the social climate of the classes and an increase in student satisfaction with school life.

The differences between baseline and intervention groups were highly significant. The research concluded that the registered changes in bully/victim problems and related behavior patterns were likely to be a consequence of the intervention program and not of some other factor. Partial replications of the program in the United States, the United Kingdom, and Germany have resulted in similar, although somewhat weaker, results (Olweus & Limber, 1999; Smith & Sharp, 1994).

In 1997–1998, our study of 3,200 students from 30 Norwegian schools again registered clear improvements with regard to bully/victim problems in the schools with intervention programs. The effects were weaker than in the first project, with averages varying between 21 and 38 percent. Unlike the first study, however, the intervention program had been in place for only six months when we made the second measurement. In addition, we conducted the study during a particularly turbulent year in which Norway introduced a new national curriculum that made heavy demands of educators' time and resources.

Nonetheless, the intervention schools fared considerably better than the comparison schools. Surveys of the comparison schools, which had set up anti-bullying efforts according to their own plans, showed very small or no changes with regard to "being bullied" and a 35 percent increase for "bullying other students" (Olweus, in press). Because we have not yet analyzed the questionnaire information, we cannot fully explain this result, but it is consistent with findings from a number of studies showing that inexpert interventions intended to counteract delinquent and antisocial behavior often have unexpectedly negative effects (Dishion, McCord, & Poulin, 1999; Gottfredson, 1987; Lipsey, 1992).

Most students in a classroom with bully/victim problems are involved in or affected by the problems.

In the most recent (1999–2000) evaluation of the Olweus Bullying Prevention Program among approximately 2,300 students from 10 schools—some of which had large percentages of students with immigrant backgrounds—we found an average reduction by around 40 percent with regard to "being bullied" and by about 50 percent for "bullying other students" (Olweus, in press).

The Need for Evidence-Based Intervention Programs

Coping with bully/victim problems has become an official school priority in many countries, and many have suggested ways to handle and prevent such problems. But because most proposals have either failed to document positive results or have never been subjected to systematic research evaluation, it is difficult to know which programs or measures actually work and which do not. What counts is how well the program works for students, not how much the adults using the program like it.

Recently, when a U.S. committee of experts used three essential criteria (Elliott, 1999) to systematically evaluate more than 500 programs ostensibly designed to prevent violence or other problem behaviors, only 11 of the programs (four of which are school-based) satisfied the specified criteria.[2] The U.S. Department of Justice's Office of Juvenile Justice and Delinquency Prevention and other sources are now providing financial support for the implementation of these evidence-based "Blueprint" programs in a number of sites.

In Norway, an officially appointed committee recently conducted a similar evaluation of 56 programs being used in Norway's schools to counteract and prevent problem behavior (Norwegian Ministry of Education, Research, and Church Affairs, 2000) and recommended without reservation only one program for further use. The Olweus Bullying Prevention Program is one of the 11 Blueprint programs and the program selected by the Norwegian committee.

Norway's New National Initiative Against Bullying

In late 2000, Norway's Department of Education and Research and Department of Children and Family Affairs decided to offer the Olweus Bullying Prevention Program on a large scale to Norwegian elementary and junior high schools over a period of several years. In building the organization for this national initiative, we have used a four-level train-the-trainer strategy of dissemination. At Norway's University of Bergen, the Olweus Group Against Bullying at the Research Center for Health Promotion trains and supervises specially selected *instructor candidates*, each of whom trains and supervises key persons from a number of schools. The key persons are then responsible for leading staff discussion groups at each participating school. These meetings typically focus on key components and themes of the program (Olweus, 1993, 2001b).

The training of the instructor candidates consists of 10–11 whole-day assemblies over 16 months. In between the whole-day meetings, the instructor candidates receive ongoing consultation from the Olweus Group by telephone or through e-mail.

In implementing this train-the-trainer model in the United States with financial support from the U.S. Department of Justice and the U.S. Department of Health and Human Services, we have made some modifications to accommodate cultural differences and practical constraints. In particular, we have reduced the number of

Figure 2
The Olweus Bullying Prevention Program

General Prerequisite

- Awareness and involvement of adults

Measures at the School Level

- Administration of the Olweus Bully/Victim Questionnaire (filled out anonymously by students)
- Formation of a Bullying Prevention Coordinating Committee
- Training of staff and time for discussion groups
- Effective supervision during recess and lunch periods

Measures at the Classroom Level

- Classroom and school rules about bullying
- Regular classroom meetings
- Meetings with students' parents

Measures at the Individual Level

- Individual meetings with students who bully
- Individual meetings with victims of bullying
- Meetings with parents of students involved
- Development of individual intervention plans

whole-day assemblies to four or five and have granted greater autonomy to individual schools' Bullying Prevention Coordinating Committees than is typical in Norway.

So far, 75 instructor candidates have participated in training, and more than 225 schools participate in the program. Recently, Norway's government substantially increased our funding to enable us to offer the program to more schools starting in 2003.

We see Norway's national initiative as a breakthrough for the systematic, long-term, and research-based work against bully/victim problems in schools. We hope to see similar developments in other countries.

Notes

1. More information about the Olweus Bullying Prevention Program is available at www.colorado.edu/cspv/blueprints/model/BPPmaterials.html or by contacting nobully@clemson.edu or olweus@psych.uib.no.
2. The four school-based programs are Life Skills Training, Promoting Alternative Thinking Strategies (PATHS), the Incredible Years, and the Olweus Bullying Prevention Program. For more information

about the Blueprints for Violence Prevention's model programs, visit www.colorado.edu/cspv/blueprints/model/overview.html.

References

Dishion, T. J., McCord, J., & Poulin, F. (1999). When interventions harm: Peer groups and problem behavior. *American Psychologist, 54,* 755–764.

Elliott, D. S. (1999). Editor's introduction. In D. Olweus & S. Limber, *Blueprints for violence prevention: Bullying Prevention Program.* Boulder, CO: Institute of Behavioral Science.

Gottfredson, G. D. (1987). Peer group interventions to reduce the risk of delinquent behavior: A selective review and a new evaluation. *Criminology, 25,* 671–714.

Lipsey, M. W. (1992). Juvenile delinquency treatment: A meta-analytic inquiry into the variability of effects. In T. D. Cook, H. Cooper, D. S. Corday, H. Hartman, L. V. Hedges, R. J. Light, T. A. Louis, & F. Mosteller (Eds.), *Meta-analysis for explanation: A casebook* (pp. 83–125). New York: Russell Sage.

Nansel, T. R., Overpeck, M., Pilla, R. S., Ruan, W. J., Simons-Morton, B., & Scheidt, P. (2001). Bullying behaviors among U.S. youth: Prevalence and association with psychosocial adjustment. *Journal of the American Medical Association, 285,* 2094–2100.

Norwegian Ministry of Education, Research, and Church Affairs. (2000). *Rapport 2000: Vurdering av program og tiltak for å redusere problematferd og utvikle sosial kompetanse.* (Report 2000: Evaluation of programs and measures to reduce problem behavior and develop social competence.) Oslo, Norway: Author.

Olweus, D. (1973). *Hackkycklingar och översittare. Forskning om skolmobbing.* (Victims and bullies: Research on school bullying.) Stockholm: Almqvist & Wicksell.

Olweus, D. (1978). *Aggression in the schools: Bullies and whipping boys.* Washington, DC: Hemisphere Press (Wiley).

Olweus, D. (1983). *The Olweus Bully/Victim Questionnaire.* Mimeo. Bergen, Norway: Research Center for Health Promotion, University of Bergen.

Olweus, D. (1991). Bully/victim problems among schoolchildren: Basic facts and effects of a school-based intervention program. In D. Pepler & K. Rubin (Eds.), *The development and treatment of childhood aggression* (pp. 411–448). Hillsdale, NJ: Erlbaum.

Olweus, D. (1992). Bullying among schoolchildren: Intervention and prevention. In R. D. Peters, R. J. McMahon, & V. L. Quincy (Eds.), *Aggression and violence throughout the life span.* Newbury Park, CA: Sage.

Olweus, D. (1993). *Bullying at school: What we know and what we can do.* Cambridge, MA: Blackwell. (Available from AIDC, P.O. Box 20, Williston, VT 05495; (800) 216-2522)

Olweus, D. (1996). *The Revised Olweus Bully/Victim Questionnaire.* Mimeo. Bergen, Norway: Research Center for Health Promotion, University of Bergen.

Olweus, D. (1999). Norway. In P. K. Smith, Y. Morita, J. Junger-Tas, D. Olweus, R. Catalano, & P. Slee (Eds.), *The nature of school bullying: A cross-national perspective* (pp. 28–48). London: Routledge.

Olweus, D. (2001a). Peer harassment: A critical analysis and some important issues. In J. Juvonen & S. Graham (Eds.), *Peer harassment in school* (pp. 3–20). New York: Guilford Publications.

Olweus, D. (2001b). *Olweus' core program against bullying and anti-social behavior: A teacher handbook.* Bergen, Norway: Research Center for Health Promotion, University of Bergen.

Olweus, D. (2002). *Mobbing i skolen: Nye data om omfang og forandring over tid.* (Bullying at school: New data on prevalence and change over time.) Manuscript. Research Center for Health Promotion, University of Bergen, Bergen, Norway.

Olweus, D. (in press). Bullying at school: Prevalence estimation, a useful evaluation design, and a new national initiative in Norway. *Association for Child Psychology and Psychiatry Occasional Papers.*

Olweus, D., & Alsaker, F. D. (1991). Assessing change in a cohort longitudinal study with hierarchical data. In D. Magnusson, L. R. Bergman, G. Rudinger, & B. Törestad (Eds.), *Problems and methods in longitudinal research* (pp. 107–132). New York: Cambridge University Press.

Olweus, D., & Limber, S. (1999). *Blueprints for violence prevention: Bullying Prevention Program.* Boulder, CO: Institute of Behavioral Science.

Perry, D. G., Kusel, S. J., & Perry, L. C. (1988). Victims of peer aggression. *Developmental Psychology, 24,* 807–814.

Simmons, R. (2002). *Odd girl out.* New York: Harcourt.

Smith, P. K., Morita, Y., Junger-Tas, J., Olweus, D., Catalano, R., & Slee, P. (Eds.). (1999). *The nature of school bullying: A cross-national perspective.* London: Routledge.

Smith, P. K., & Sharp, S. (Eds.). (1994). *School bullying: Insights and perspectives.* London: Routledge.

Solberg, M., & Olweus, D. (in press). Prevalence estimation of school bullying with the Olweus Bully/Victim Questionnaire. *Aggressive Behavior.*

Wiseman, R. (2002). *Queen bees and wannabes.* New York: Crown.

Dan Olweus is Research Professor of Psychology and Director of the Olweus Group Against Bullying at the Research Center for Health Promotion at the University of Bergen, Christies Gate 13, N-5015 Bergen, Norway; olweus@psych.uib.no.

From *Educational Leadership,* March 2003, pp. 12-17. Reprinted with permission of the Association for Supervision and Curriculum Development. © 2003 by ASCD. All rights reserved.

BULLYING—
Not Just a Kid Thing

From "Students are just tattling" to "Boys will be boys," myths about bullying abound.

Doug Cooper and Jennie L. Snell

Bullying. The very word conjures up bad memories for many adults. Whether they were the target of bullying, used bullying behaviors themselves, or witnessed bullying toward others, many adults vividly recall incidents that happened 10, 20, or even 40 years ago. Perhaps because of these powerful memories, caring educators want their schools to be safe, respectful, and bully-free. They are not alone.

In the wake of school shootings and lawsuits brought against schools by victims of bullying, 11 state legislatures—California, Colorado, Georgia, Louisiana, Minnesota, Nevada, New Hampshire, Oklahoma, Oregon, Vermont, and Washington—have mandated that schools take active steps to reduce bullying. Although specific actions related to these mandates vary by state, many schools are finding that the most effective approach to bullying prevention is one that is inclusive of school staff, parents, students, and the community. Such approaches must also be comprehensive, with aligned policies and a research-based student learning component.

Since the late 1970s, Committee for Children, a nonprofit organization dedicated to helping schools address students' social and emotional development, has been conducting research and developing programs for educators, families, and communities to prevent child abuse, youth violence, and bullying (see www.cfchildren.org). Committee for Children's researchers, program developers, and implementation specialists

have learned from their work with many school districts to execute the early steps necessary for building a strong foundation to prevent bullying.

Uncovering Myths and Misconceptions

Bullying is so closely linked to childhood that it can easily be thought of as simply a child's problem. It is not. Adults play a major role depending on whether they ignore or work to prevent bullying. People who bully take advantage of an imbalance of power, such as greater physical size, higher status, or support of a peer group. Their bullying may take the form of face-to-face attacks with physical aggression, threats, teasing about perceived sexual orientation, or telling someone in a mean way that he or she can't play. Bullies often use behind-the-back behaviors, such as starting and spreading malicious rumors, writing hurtful graffiti, or encouraging others to exclude a particular child. Often, adults fail to take active steps to address the problem of bullying because they have the following misconceptions.

Everyone knows what bullying is. Bullying can often be difficult to distinguish from normal conflict and rough play. A study of the ability of lunchtime supervisors to distinguish students' play fighting, or "rough-and-tumble" play, from true aggression found that the adult supervisors were more likely to mistake aggression for play rather than the other way around (Boulton,

1996). In fact, they made errors in one out of four episodes. Adults need help recognizing bullying.

Boys will be boys. Many people perceive bullying as physical aggression—hitting, poking, or pushing—committed by boys. Bullying, however, is not limited to physical aggression or boys. Girls engage in bullying behaviors as much as boys do (Craig, Pepler, & Atlas, 2000). Some studies show that girls engage in more subtle forms of bullying, such as malicious gossip and social exclusion (Crick & Grotpeter, 1995). Other studies show that both boys and girls engage in all forms of bullying behavior.

> People who bully take advantage of an imbalance of power, such as greater physical size, higher status, or the support of a peer group.

Only a small number of children are affected. Just about every student in a school can be affected by and suffer from the long-term effects of bullying. By conservative estimates, 10 percent of school students are chronic targets of bullying, although the number may be higher (Perry, Kusel, & Perry, 1988). In addition, a school climate and culture of fear can affect more than just the students who are victims. Bullying often occurs away from adults, but students frequently witness bullying events (Hawkins, Pepler, & Craig, 2001). As bystanders, students are confused about what to do, and they fear becoming the next target.

Adults are already doing all they need to do. This misconception is one of the most challenging to overcome. First, adults might not know about bullying incidents. Many students who are targets of bullying do not tell adults. Second, students don't believe that adults will intervene even when they do report bullying. Playground observations of bullying support students' perceptions that adults rarely intervene (Craig et al., 2000). But when asked, teachers believe that they often intervene to stop bullying. Many reasons may exist for this mismatch between students' and adults' perceptions, such as adults not seeing the bullying, students not reporting it, or students not being aware of the follow-through actions that adults take after students report it. Whatever the reasons, it's clear that students believe that they need more help from adults than they are getting.

Students are just tattling. Some adults dismiss students' reports of bullying as tattling. This perpetuates students' beliefs that adults don't take reports of bullying seriously. Students and adults need to recognize and understand the difference between tattling (trying to get someone into trouble) and reporting (keeping someone safe). To counteract this misconception, adults need to be committed to listening attentively when students report bullying. Adults should gather information, take action to provide safety and assurance, and provide timely follow-up, such as checking in with the student to see whether the bullying has stopped.

Developing and Implementing Strategies

Uncovering bullying myths is an important first step. The next step is to develop and implement prevention strategies. Just as schools are familiar with installing smoke alarms, conducting fire drills, or developing earthquake and tornado preparedness procedures, schools should think through how to prevent bullying (Snell, MacKenzie, & Frey, 2002). Research shows that adults can reduce bullying among students by

taking an active role in creating and implementing prevention techniques (Olweus, 1993). Even without an extensive study of the phenomenon, school staff members can ask what they can do *before* they have a bullying problem—or before it grows.

Because bullying has a hidden nature, school staff members should begin their bullying prevention efforts by examining less-structured areas of their school, such as playgrounds and hallways, to improve student behavior through supervision and established guidelines.

Make Playgrounds and Hallways Safe

Recess provides students with rich opportunities for peer interaction and social skill development; recess play may even improve some students' ability to concentrate in the classroom (Pellegrini, 1995). However, students' reports and research observations show that bullying often occurs on the playground. Bullying also occurs in school hallways, on school buses, and in the cafeteria, because students interact informally in these locations, often with little supervision (Astor, Meyer, & Pitner, 2001). With bullying prevention in mind, adults should examine and make adjustments to adult supervision, established procedures, and guidelines for student behavior on playgrounds and in other less-structured environments.

> Students don't believe that adults will intervene even when they do report bullying.

Improve supervision. Although increasing supervision typically costs money, some low- or no-cost strategies make supervision more effective. For instance, provide training in "active supervision" for playground monitors and other staff who circulate through assigned areas. Give monitors a means of communicating, such as hand-held radios, to facilitate coordination across large spaces. Maintain an adequate adult-to-student supervision ratio. Encourage all school staff members to spend some time on the playground at recess to observe student behavior in an unstructured setting, to increase their

awareness of common recess problems, and to provide support for the recess supervisors' authority.

Woodway Elementary in Edmonds, Washington, for example, provided training for all of the school's stakeholders, including classroom teachers, custodians, playground supervisors, and office staff. The principal also hosted parent training in supervising play as part of the school's curriculum night. At Chautauqua Elementary in Vashon Island, Washington, bus drivers received extra training and helped develop behavioral expectations for riding on the bus.

Standing at the classroom doorway when students are changing classes provides hallway supervision and allows a teacher to greet students by name as they enter the classroom. Staff can convey tremendous caring by being present in the hallway and engaging in brief, informal conversations during transitions.

Develop specific routines. Establish clear guidelines for behavior and implement a schoolwide system for tracking, handling, and communicating about problems and disciplinary infractions. Teach rules to new students so that they learn the expectations and skills necessary for success.

To improve student behavior at recess, for example, teach and practice with students the transition routines for the beginning and end of recess. Teach common playground games to students in physical education class at the beginning of the school year and as a refresher in the spring. Provide sufficient play equipment for students in all grade levels. Assign new students "recess buddies" to help them make friends. For students who are less interested in traditional playground games, offer a range of activities, such as drawing or reading in a designated quiet area.

> Implement a schoolwide system for tracking, handling, and communicating about problems and disciplinary infractions.

Incorporate social-emotional learning. Balancing structured and unstructured playtime at recess provides students with the opportunity to practice and use their prosocial skills. Teach students ways to play fairly, form friendships, join group activities, include others, show respect, and manage emotions. Define each of these skill areas by helping students understand what each is, what each isn't, and what each looks like in action on the playground. Intervene and coach students when their behavior is inappropriate.

Implement a School Discipline Policy

Another way of getting started in bullying prevention is to write an anti-bullying policy that links bullying to the school's discipline policy. An effective written policy

- Declares the school's commitment to creating a safe, caring, and respectful learning environment for all students.
- Gives a clear definition of bullying and concrete examples of specific bullying behaviors.
- States consequences of bullying in the context of a school's discipline code.
- Provides students, parents, and school personnel with a common, concrete framework for recognizing and responding to bullying.

The most effective policies include input from different groups within the school community, such as students, teachers, playground monitors, and parents. Effective policies use clear, simple language to ensure that all students, parents, and staff understand them. Place a copy in the school handbook and in the information packets provided to all students and their families, and sustain the anti-bullying message throughout the school year.

Developing a policy can be a labor-intensive process, but the result is greater personal investment in the school community by staff, students, and parents (Rigby, 1996).

Learn More About Bullying

Learning more about bullying can help adults improve their ability to recognize bullying and to take action when it occurs. A school doesn't need to complete an extensive study of bullying before beginning to make school improvements, but it can simultaneously learn about bullying while taking preventive steps.

Thinking of bullying as a kid thing is a mistake. Students would solve the problem of bullying on their own if they had the skills, knowledge, and power to do so. But they don't have the power to correct the imbalance of power that characterizes bullying. Nor do they have the power to establish a strong foundation of bullying prevention in their school. They need the help of the adults in a school community.

Be vigilant and find ways for all the adult members of the school to work together to support one another's efforts in bullying prevention. Take a whole-school approach and work proactively both behind the scenes and in view of students to build a school climate and culture in which all members—students and adults—feel safe, respected, and included.

References

Astor, R. A., Meyer, H. A., & Pitner, R. O. (2001). Elementary and middle school students' perceptions of violence-prone school subcontexts. *Elementary School Journal, 101,* 511–528.

Boulton, M. J. (1996). Lunchtime supervisors' attitudes towards playful fighting, and ability to differentiate between playful and aggressive fighting: An intervention study. *British Journal of Educational Psychology, 66,* 367–381.

Craig, W. M., Pepler, D. J., & Atlas, R. (2000). Observations of bullying in the playground and in the classroom. *School Psychology International, 21,* 22–36.

Crick, N. R., & Grotpeter, J. K. (1995). Relational aggression, gender, and social-psychological adjustment. *Child Development, 66,* 710–722.

Hawkins, D. C., Pepler, D. J., & Craig, W. M. (2001). Naturalistic observations of peer interventions in bullying. *Social Development, 10,* 512–527.

Olweus, D. (1993). *Bullying at school.* Cambridge, MA: Blackwell.

Pellegrini, A. D. (1995). *School recess and playground behavior: Educational and developmental roles.* Albany, NY: SUNY Press.

Perry, D. G., Kusel, S. J., & Perry, L. C. (1988). Victims of peer aggression. *Developmental Psychology, 24,* 807–814.

Rigby, K. (1996). *Bullying in schools and what to do about it.* London: Jessica Kingsley.

Snell, J. L., MacKenzie, E., & Frey, K. (2002). Bullying prevention in elementary schools: The importance of adult leadership, peer group support, and student social-emotional skills. In H. Walker & M. Shinn (Eds.), *Interventions for academic and behavior problems II: Preventive and remedial approaches* (pp. 351–372). Bethesda, MD: National Association of School Psychologists.

Doug Cooper (dcooper@cfchildren.org) is a program developer and **Jennie L. Snell** (jsnell@cfchildren.org) is a child psychologist and researcher at Committee for Children, 568 1st Ave. South, Ste. 600, Seattle, WA 98104. Both helped create *Steps to Respect: A Bullying Prevention Program.*

From *Educational Leadership*, March 2003, pp. 22-25. Reprinted with permission of the Association for Supervision and Curriculum Development. © 2003 by ASCD. All rights reserved.

A Positive Learning Environment Approach to Middle School Instruction

School personnel need to reconsider young adolescents' needs and create a learning environment that contributes to positive behavior as well as academic achievement.

Peggy Hester, Robert A. Gable, and M. Lee Manning

Middle school teachers must be prepared to educate an increasingly diverse population of young adolescents (Manning, 1999/2000). Most of these students will respond positively to instruction, and will interact appropriately with both peers and adults. However, some students have persistent behavioral problems that, if unchecked, can intensify and become more complicated. It is critical to intervene early with these students; failure to do so puts the student at increased risk for conflicts with classmates, teachers, and family members (Asher & Coie, 1990; Patterson, Capaldi, & Bank, 1989; Webster-Stratton, 2000). That risk, in turn, is associated with academic problems. Indeed, mounting evidence indicates that a strong relationship exists between student academic performance and classroom conduct (e.g., Cantwell & Baker, 1987; Delaney & Kaiser, 2001; Kaiser & Hester, 1997). Research also demonstrates that students who do not perform well in class often have an increased incidence of discipline problems (Nelson, Scott, & Polsgrove, 1999). Other classroom factors, such as improper curricular placement, negative management styles, and ineffective instruction, can exacerbate an already difficult situation (Kauffman, 2001). Given these circumstances, it follows that school personnel need to reconsider young adolescents' needs and create a learning environment that contributes to positive behavior as well as academic achievement.

In recent years, various researchers (e.g., Dodge, 1993; Kaiser & Hester, 1997) have underscored the critical role that early intervention plays in preventing behavior problems in schools. While few persons would argue against the idea of prevention, educators sometimes unwittingly hinder efforts to address student learning/behavior problems (e.g., by withholding specialized supports until a student fails) (Kauffman, 2001). Prevention/ intervention is neither simple nor easy, and it often requires collaboration among various school personnel. It is important to recognize that the concept of "early intervention" is independent of a student's chronological age or grade level. Successful preventive intervention hinges on establishing a learning environment that supports students' positive and adaptive behaviors, identifying students who require more individualized programs, and determining ways to better serve all students. In the following discussion, the authors examine some common behavior problems in middle schools and then explore research-based implications for establishing a positive and supportive learning environment. Finally, they discuss the emergent role that school personnel play in promoting positive academic and behavioral outcomes for all students.

Understanding Young Adolescents' Behaviors

The current education scene in the United States is marked by changing demographics, declining resources, and increasing pressure to produce positive student outcomes. Despite these challenges, many schools have reported improvements in student performance. Yet, we know that some students suffer disproportionately from the consequences of these forces—academically, emotionally/behaviorally, or both.

What responses do young adolescents demonstrate, and what might be the underlying reasons for misbehaviors that impede instruction and socialization? How can educators convince young adolescents to assume greater responsibility for their own behavior?

What responses do young adolescents demonstrate, and what might be the underlying reasons for misbehaviors that impede instruction and socialization? How can educators convince young adolescents to assume greater responsibility for their own behavior? Assuming that the burden of appropriate behavior is a shared responsibility, how can middle school educators best promote positive behavioral responses?

Charles (2002) listed several categories of student misbehavior: 1) goofing off, 2) class disruptions, 3) defiance of authority, and 4) aggression. While the most serious offenses (e.g., physical assaults) are more likely to make headlines, teachers most often deal with far less significant problems such as non-compliance, calling out, and inattention. Although these problems may seem to be relatively innocuous, they routinely interfere with instruction and challenge teachers to come up with strategies and techniques in response (Charles, 2002).

In examining Charles's four categories of behavior, the most misunderstood problem is what Charles (2002) called goofing off—students sit idly, they talk to friends, and/or they fail to complete their work. The reasons for such behavior are many and varied. For example, whole-group instruction often fails to account for diverse student abilities. This can result in frustration and lead some students to withdraw from, or actively avoid, instruction. In other cases, the curricular content may lack relevance to students; or, it may be at odds with students' cultural and linguistic backgrounds (Cartledge et al., 2002). These and other factors can set the stage for what appears to be goofing off behavior.

Creating a Positive Middle School Learning Environment

Media headlines appear to suggest that schools today are hotbeds of aggressive and violent behavior. In fact, statistics show that these incidents, fortunately, occur very infrequently, and that schools remain the safest place for middle school students. Nevertheless, school personnel have a responsibility to recognize the effects of lesser yet more predictable misbehaviors on learning, and to take deliberate action to create a positive school environment. There is a growing consensus that a positive and safe learning environment is one that emphasizes cooperation, collaboration, and peaceful existence, and is one that is free from threats of psychological or physical harm—that is, an environment that reflects caring and concern for all students (Manning, 2000).

The current significance being attached to the school environment stems from several sources. First, several middle school documents (Carnegie Council on Adolescent Development, 1989; Jackson & Davis, 2000; Manning, 2000; National Middle School Association, 1995; Payne, Conroy, & Racine, 1998) underscore the benefits of a positive school environment on young adolescents' academic achievement and positive socialization. Second, a burgeoning amount of information on early adolescence suggests that 10- to 15-year-olds have a critical need for a positive atmosphere in which to socialize and learn (Manning & Bucher, 2001). Third, mounting recognition exists that schools must accept a larger responsibility to establish and strengthen positive interpersonal relationships between students and teachers, as well as among learners themselves (Kerr & Zigmond, 1986; Manning & Bucher, 2001).

Drawing upon the accumulated literature, we found evidence that effective learning environments usually:

- Recognize and accept the differences among young adolescents' physical, psychosocial, and cognitive development, and provide developmentally appropriate instruction

- Place value on gender, sexual orientation, cultural, and linguistic differences, and provide classroom organization and instructional approaches that account for these differences
- Provide curriculum that enhances young adolescents' acceptance of self and others, and that enables them to accept differences and similarities among people
- Provide instruction that ensures a high degree of academic engagement and success for all young adolescents
- Utilize management procedures that emphasize the idea that students constitute a community of learners, all of whom should accept (or be taught to accept) responsibility for their behavior
- Provide direct instruction to sub-groups or individual students who are unable or unwilling to comply with schedules and routines of instruction
- Recognize the importance of self-esteem and its influence on academic achievement, socialization, and overall personal development
- Encourage a sense of collaboration among students and educators
- Emphasize teamwork and trust, predicated on the principle that being fair to everyone means treating no two students exactly the same
- Recognize that each student brings diverse experiences to the classroom and possesses varied strengths and interests
- Help teachers teach more than academics so that students feel a commitment toward each other as well as a positive affiliation toward the school. (Manning & Bucher, 2001)

Table 1 summarizes strategies that teachers can use to prevent behavior problems among young adolescents.

Educators seeking to achieve positive educational outcomes face the challenge of making fundamental, systemic changes in schools. At the middle school level, education personnel must work to create environments that support young adolescents' social, academic, and emotional development and blunt the onset of behavior problems. Administrators and teachers can be made aware of the benefits associated with building-wide and classroom-level student supports and social interactions with parents, teachers, and peers. They also can recognize the importance of taking specific steps to rectify a problem situation (e.g., a focused intervention plan stemming from an assessment of behavior when so-called "universal supports" are not effective).

Specific Developmentally Appropriate Management Strategies

Creating school environments that are conducive to learning and positive behavior may require school personnel to redefine both the structure and culture of the school (e.g., Gable & Manning, 1996). In redefining the school environment to accentuate positive aspects of students' behavior, the focus shifts from dealing with inappropriate, unacceptable, or disruptive behavior to creating a setting that supports the learning and practice of more appropriate behavior. This is accomplished in various ways. Typically, educators reframe classroom and

Table 1

Proactive Strategies for Supporting and Maintaining Positive Student Behavior

CREATE A MIDDLE SCHOOL LEARNING ENVIRONMENT THAT SUPPORTS POSITIVE STUDENT BEHAVIOR

- Acknowledge and promote appropriate behavior throughout the day in all school settings (e.g., classes, advisory programs, and exploratories)
- Define behavioral expectations for appropriate school behavior
- Understand and plan for the effects of development on young adolescent behavior
- Teach students appropriate replacement skills for misbehavior so they have acceptable behaviors that serve the same function
- Affirm students' strengths, skills, and abilities—both academic and non-academic
- Acknowledge and support young adolescents' diversity of all types (e.g., developmental, cultural, gender, social class, and sexual orientation)

SUPPORT YOUNG ADOLESCENTS' SOCIALIZATION SKILLS

- Listen to young adolescents—their problems, concerns, and challenges
- Respond positively to student communication (e.g., respond to both verbal and non-verbal initiations)
- Use positive and nurturing affect (e.g., responsiveness, sensitivity) in interactions
- Teach positive social/communication skills so that students know positive, age-appropriate ways to interact
- Model appropriate social/communication strategies and build upon what the young adolescent says (e.g., expanding or seeking additional information)
- Teach developmentally appropriate conflict resolution skills for young adolescents acting angrily toward students and/or teachers
- Be consistent in implementing behavioral support strategies over time and in all settings, but take into account individual student strengths/weaknesses/differences

school rules/expectations for behaviors and directly teach all students specific expectations (Horner, 2000). Coupled with this strategy is the prolific use of positive affirmation (at least four times as many affirmations as there are acknowledgments of negative behaviors) with students adhering to these expectations (Lewis, Sugai, & Colvin, 1998). Some teachers have found it necessary to abandon longstanding practices (e.g., nagging or reprimanding students) (Shores et al., 1993), and instead directly engage students in interactions that support social/communication skills (Kaiser & Hester, 1997).

A review of the literature indicates that in order to create the most appropriate learning environment and apply the most effective classroom management practices, middle school educators should consider young adolescents' developmental characteristics. Ample evidence indicates that the behavior of young adolescents is affected by changes in self-esteem, as seen in greater desire for increased socialization, peer approval, and general social interaction (Manning, 1999/2000). These and other developmental characteristics can have a powerful impact on young adolescents' behavior. For example, a low self-esteem stemming from academic failure or subsequent peer rejection might cause a student to bully others in an attempt to feel more powerful. A strong need for peer approval might motivate

another student to disobey a teacher. Furthermore, a long-standing pattern of academic problems may lead some students to avoid (either passively or actively) tasks that they perceive to be irrelevant or too challenging. By understanding how overall development, along with specific contextual events, affect student behavior, teachers can better organize classes to promote opportunities for socialization and collaborative learning—both of which can benefit young adolescents, especially those from culturally and linguistically diverse backgrounds (Cartledge et al., 2002).

Effective middle school educators increase the predictability of daily routines. By providing clear schoolwide expectations and consistently acknowledging appropriate student behavior, teachers can eliminate a major obstacle to effective instruction—namely, the lack of stability and predictability over time. And, in establishing a stable teaching/learning environment, educators are able to make better use of limited instructional time, energy, and resources. In short, predictability in daily routines/expectations; consistency in implementation of intervention strategies; and proactive, systematic, and situational support of appropriate social/communication skills are fundamental to preventing student behavior problems (Colvin, Sugai, & Patching, 1993; Gable, Quinn, Rutherford, & Howell, 1998; Kerr & Nelson, 2002).

Most teachers recognize the importance of providing students with a structured classroom environment (e.g., Kerr & Nelson, 2002). Such a setting includes a clearly defined schedule, preparation for student transitions, delineation, and instruction in appropriate responses to adults and peers, along with regular opportunities for students to learn and practice positive social/ communication skills. Indeed, these classroom attributes are prerequisite to effective academic and nonacademic instruction (Kerr & Nelson, 2002; Reitz, 1994).

Effective middle school educators give clear instructions, demonstrate consistency, model behavioral expectations, and follow through on consequences. Research in classroom management demonstrates the value of offering precise instruction, spelling out the consequences for both compliance and non-compliance, and consistently implementing these procedures (e.g., Alberto & Troutman, 1999). The most successful teachers give simple, straightforward instructions so that students know exactly what is expected of them. Then, teachers follow through each and every time. Although teachers must recognize that different students have varying capacities to respond appropriately, failure to react in some way to inappropriate behavior gives the student tacit approval to repeat it. For example, if a student ignores a specific direction (such as, "Kevin, please pay attention to your own work"), the teacher might have to repeat the direction. If Kevin fails to respond to the direction the second time, the teacher might: 1) move into closer physical proximity, 2) verbally prompt him to comply with the direction, and 3) acknowledge the appropriate behavior of a classmate. If Kevin demonstrates the requested behavior, the teacher would praise his cooperation. While consistency and predictability are critical supports for all students, teacher expectations should reflect pupils' specific strengths and weaknesses. Teacher decisions regarding specific demands should be predicated on a careful review of all available information about the students. Educators can elicit positive behavior by encouraging students to participate actively in the rule-making process, to develop a rationale for specific rules/expectations, and to model behavior expectations for one another.

Unless a student is taught alternative strategies to accomplish a particular outcome (e.g., gain attention)—one that works better than the inappropriate behavior—he or she will likely persist in behaving inappropriately.

Effective middle school educators teach students appropriate replacement behaviors that serve the same function as the misbehavior. Absent more appropriate strategies, adults' attempts to address inappropriate student behavior sometimes are reactive and consist of some kind of punitive consequences (e.g., reprimands, time-outs, revoked privileges) (Conroy, Clark, Gable, & Fox, 1999). While these strategies temporarily

may serve to suppress an inappropriate behavior (e.g., calling out), they fail to teach students more acceptable replacement behaviors (such as raising one's hand in order to be acknowledged). Accordingly, there is a high probability that the misbehavior will recur. Unless a student is taught alternative strategies to accomplish a particular outcome (e.g., gain attention)—one that works better than the inappropriate behavior—he or she will likely persist in behaving inappropriately. Classroom interventions will be effective only to the extent that they successfully compete with and triumph over "existing contingencies" that support inappropriate behavior (e.g., calling out gains more attention than correct answers) (e.g., Gable, Quinn, Rutherford, & Howell, 1998; Mace, Lalli, & Lalli, 1991). Therefore, the traditional distinction between academic and non-academic instruction may need to be blurred, so that school personnel will routinely teach both academic and non-academic behavior (Gable, Hendrickson, Tonelson, & Van Acker, in press).

Knowledge of students' academic and non-academic needs can be gained in various ways. For example, by observing students throughout the day, teachers can identify "early warning" signs of problems and determine how best to intervene proactively and instructionally before the little problems escalate and become major challenges. Such a proactive approach to instruction (or to non-academic issues) may be applied to a group of students or to an individual, depending on the behavior. For instance, some young adolescents may lack the necessary skills to negotiate a particular social interaction (e.g., initiate a positive verbal exchange with a classmate). To successfully address this problem, students must be directly and systematically taught the appropriate social skills (Reitz, 1994), usually through teacher modeling, role play/behavioral rehearsal, and individual interaction sessions in which the student learns specific communication skills for interacting with others (Kaiser & Hester, 1997).

In that there are a range of possible skills to be taught, selection of specific skills should depend on which behavior best fits the situation and is most likely to be reinforced not only in the classroom, but also beyond it. Another criterion relates to efficiency—how much effort must go into teaching/learning behavior "X" versus behavior "Y." The more manageable both students and teachers perceive the instructional process to be, the greater the likelihood of a successful outcome (Gable et al., in press). Some skills that educators see as important may have little or no significance for students at home or in the community. We must acknowledge that fact to the student, underscore the need to make choices according to the setting, and teach students different skills for different settings. Indeed, such discrimination skills are a critical part of the socialization process. We know that these goals exceed the scope of traditional instruction. Nevertheless, teachers often discover that students' behavior improves as they experience greater feelings of success and higher rates of positive peer- and teacher-student interactions (Shores et al., 1993).

Effective middle school educators affirm positive behavior. Social reinforcement can be a powerful way to teach more acceptable behaviors. For example, specific praise can help facilitate everything from spelling and math skills to positive communication strategies and self-help skills (Alberto &

Troutman, 1999). Despite its documented effectiveness, teacher use of social reinforcement to acknowledge appropriate behavior and promote specific skills is often at such low rates as to be essentially ineffective (Gable, Hendrickson, Young, Shores, & Stowitschek, 1983; Shores et al., 1993). It is also important to recognize that neither praise nor punishment alone teaches students new behaviors (Kerr & Nelson, 2002). A positive comment or verbal command may signal that a certain consequence will follow a specific student response. But in no way does it ensure that the student will engage in the behavior if she or he does not know it, or if he or she sees it as less reinforcing than another response. In other words, direct instruction of a particular behavior, coupled with multiple opportunities to engage in it, can encourage students to engage in appropriate behavior over time and across settings.

Effective middle school educators teach developmentally appropriate socialization skills. In addition to structuring a classroom environment that affords students positive support, middle school educators can provide experiences that improve young adolescents' socialization skills. Changes in social characteristics and situations that normally occur during early adolescence can have a profound impact on young adolescents. Middle school educators are finding it increasingly useful to teach developmentally appropriate socialization skills, even though such skills are not part of their traditional instructional responsibilities. Socialization skills can be taught informally through friendships and social interaction under various conditions (e.g., cooperative learning activities) or formally through direct, systematic instruction. Sometimes, young adolescents may wish to work alone, and should be given the opportunity to do so. At other times, educators should encourage students to interact in more socially oriented situations. To do so, a teacher might allow students to choose their learning groups, and they might encourage students' social interaction through participation in extracurricular activities.

A shift in young adolescents' allegiance from adults (especially, parents and teachers) to peers and friends is a natural part of early adolescence, a change that warrants educators' understanding and acceptance. This shift in allegiance, accompanied by various peer pressures, becomes a powerful influence on young adolescents' daily socialization. Young adolescents' quest for freedom and independence also should be addressed as part of socialization skills instruction. In responding to this desire for increased freedom and independence, educators can provide students with routine opportunities to engage in decision making that reinforces the understanding that with freedom comes responsibilities. Once we recognize that students differ with regard to their repertoire of age appropriate social skills, it becomes easier to establish group-individual instructional priorities. School personnel can provide various students with opportunities to behave responsibly in specific ways and to demonstrate their growing capacity for self-control and self-management in safe and psychologically secure settings (Manning, 2002). Students who are unable or unwilling to demonstrate appropriate socialization skills will need additional instruction. Various traditional classroom management strategies, including the use of punishment, may exacerbate an already difficult instructional situation. Rather than teaching a student specific skills, the use of punishment can negatively affect adult-student relationships, causing students to avoid future interactions and, in turn, diminish the number of opportunities for teachers to demonstrate and reinforce appropriate behaviors. Furthermore, the use of punishment as a disciplinary tool can trigger in students feelings of anger, defiance, or a desire for revenge.

Recently, we observed a 6th-grade teacher working deliberately to build a positive, learner-centered classroom that would demonstrate that students could be managed without threats or punishments. She faced an especially difficult task because her students had learned during their previous school experiences to equate school with adult coercion, manipulation, and control. In seeking to change student perspectives on schooling, the teacher worked daily to promote positive teacher-student and student-student collaboration, and to encourage students to make appropriate decisions about their learning. To ensure active engagement and high rates of student success, she took steps to align curricular content and instruction with the academic interests and needs of her class. Although by no means a simple undertaking, the teacher found that, over time, the benefits of redefining a positive classroom environment were well worth her efforts. In the weeks that followed, students' overall perspectives toward schooling improved, consonant with their progress in both academics and socialization skills (Manning, 2002).

Concluding Remarks

Middle school educators today must deal with an increasingly diverse population of young adolescents (Manning, 1999/2000). Addressing the myriad challenges associated with students' diverse academic and social skills needs can consume a tremendous amount of time and energy. Effective middle school educators strongly support routine proactive approaches to improve student deportment as well as promote positive interactions between young adolescents and teachers. Without dismissing the significance of outside factors, the real burden of prevention/intervention rests with school personnel. Fortunately, the accumulated evidence clearly demonstrates that quality, sustained instruction can overcome virtually all potentially negative influences on student performance (e.g., socioeconomic status) (Greenwood, 2002). Such instruction should occur at the classroom and schoolwide levels. However, system-wide intervention means changing the school, the classroom, and the daily instruction in ways that teach, reinforce, and otherwise strengthen appropriate student behavior (e.g., Lewis et al., 1998). System-wide supports require that teachers establish nurturing classroom environments conducive to positive student behavior and successful academic performance. To accomplish that goal, school personnel must integrate the social, behavioral, and academic aspects of group-individual instruction. In all, a successful school environment reflects clear expectations, high rates of student engagement and academic success, and teacher acknowledgment of appropriate behaviors, as well as direct systematic instruction of positive behavior to replace disruptive behavior.

The authors have argued that middle school educators can exercise a tremendous amount of control over the nature and quality of daily instruction. Although by no means a simple undertaking, we must strive to support and nurture appropriate student behaviors in ways that account for their diverse learning and behavioral characteristics. It is reassuring to know that teachers are finding new ways to approach and interact with young adolescents to create conditions that are conducive to positive outcomes for all students.

References

Alberto, P. A., & Troutman, A. C. (1999). *Applied behavior analysis for teachers.* Upper Saddle River, NJ: Prentice-Hall.

Asher, S. R., & Coie, J. D. (1990). *The rejected child.* New York: Cambridge University Press.

Cantwell, D. P., & Baker, L. (1987). Prevalence and type of psychiatric disorder and developmental disorders in three speech and language groups. *Journal of Communication Disorders, 20,* 151–160.

Carnegie Council on Adolescent Development. (1989). *Turning points: Preparing American youth for the 21st century.* Washington, DC: Author.

Cartledge, G., Tam, K. Y., Loe, S. A., Miranda, A. H., Lambert, M. C., Kea, C. D., & Simmons-Reed, E. (2002). *Culturally and linguistically diverse students with behavioral disorders.* Arlington, VA: Council for Children with Behavioral Disorders.

Charles, C. M. (2002). *Building classroom discipline* (7th ed.). Boston: Allyn and Bacon.

Colvin, G., Sugai, G., & Patching, B, (1993). Precorrection: An instructional approach to managing predictable problem behavior. *Intervention in School and Clinic, 28,* 143–150.

Conroy, M., Clark, D., Gable, R. A., & Fox, J. (1999). A look at IDEA 1997 discipline provisions: Implications for change in the roles and responsibilities of school personnel. *Preventing School Failure, 43,* 64–70.

Delaney, E. M., & Kaiser, A. P. (2001). The effects of teaching parents blended communication and behavior support strategies. *Behavioral Disorders, 26,* 93–116.

Dodge, K. A. (1993). The future of research on the treatment of conduct disorder. *Development and Psychopathology, 5,* 311–319.

Gable, R. A., Hendrickson, J. M., Tonelson, S., & Van Acker, R. (in press). Integrating academic and nonacademic instruction for students with emotional/behavioral disorders. *Education and Treatment of Children.*

Gable, R. A., Hendrickson, J. M., Young, C. C., Shores, R. E., & Stowitschek, J.J. (1983). A comparison of teacher approval and disapproval statements across categories of exceptionality. *Journal of Special Education Technology, 6,* 15–22.

Gable, R. A., & Manning, M. L. (1996). Facing the challenge of aggressive behaviors in young adolescents. *Middle School Journal, 27,* 19–25.

Gable, R. A., Quinn, M. M., Rutherford, R. B., & Howell, K. (1998). Addressing problem behaviors in schools: Use of functional assessments and behavior intervention plans. *Preventing School Failure, 42,* 106–119.

Greenwood, C. M. (2002). Science and students with learning and behavior problems. *Behavioral Disorders, 27,* 37–52.

Horner, R. H. (2000). Positive behavior supports. In M. L. Wehmeyer & J. R. Patton (Eds.), *Mental retardation in the 21st century* (pp. 181–196). Austin, TX: Pro-Ed.

Jackson, A. W., & Davis, G. A. (2000). *Turning points 2000: Educating adolescents in the 21st century.* New York: Teachers College Press.

Kaiser, A. P., & Hester, P. P. (1997). Prevention of conduct disorders through early intervention: A social-communicative perspective. *Behavioral Disorders, 22,* 117–130.

Kauffman, J. M. (2001). *Characteristics of emotional and behavioral disorders of children and youth* (7th ed.). Upper Saddle River, NJ: Prentice-Hall.

Kerr, M. M., & Nelson, C. M. (2002). *Strategies for managing behavior problems in the classroom* (4th ed.). Upper Saddle River, NJ: Pearson Education.

Kerr, M. M., & Zigmond, N. (1986). What do high school teachers want? A study of expectations and standards. *Education and Treatment of Children, 9,* 239–249.

Lewis, T. J., Sugai, G., & Colvin, G. (1998). Reducing problem behavior through a school-wide system of effective behavioral support: Investigation of a school-wide social skills training program and contextual interventions. *School Psychology Review, 27,* 446–459.

Mace, F. C., Lalli, J. S., & Lalli, E. P. (1991). Functional analysis and treatment of aberrant behavior. *Research in Developmental Disabilities, 12,* 155–180.

Manning, M. L. (1999/2000). Developmentally responsive multicultural education for young adolescents. *Childhood Education, 76,* 82–87.

Manning, M. L. (2000). Child-centered middle schools: A position paper. *Childhood Education, 76,* 154–159.

Manning, M. L. (2002). *Developmentally appropriate middle level schools* (2nd ed.). Olney, MD: Association for Childhood Education International.

Manning, M. L., & Bucher, K. T. (2001). *Teaching in the middle school.* Columbus, OH: Prentice-Hall.

National Middle School Association. (1995). *This we believe: Developmentally responsive middle level schools.* Westerville, OH: Author.

Nelson, C. M., Scott, T. M., & Polsgrove, L. (1999). *Perspective on emotional/behavioral disorders: Assumptions and their implications for education and treatment. What works for children and youth with E/BD: Linking yesterday and today with tomorrow.* Arlington, VA: Council for Children with Behavioral Disorders.

Patterson, G. R., Capaldi, D., & Bank, L. (1989). An early starter model for predicting delinquency. In D. J. Pepler & K. H. Rubin (Eds.), *The development and treatment of childhood aggression* (pp. 139–168). Hillsdale, NJ: Lawrence Erlbaum.

Payne, M. J., Conroy, S., & Racine, L. (1998). Creating positive school climates. *Middle School Journal, 30,* 65–67.

Reitz, A. L. (1994). Implementing comprehensive classroom-based programs for students with emotional and behavioral problems. *Education and Treatment of Children, 17,* 312–331.

Shores, R. E., Jack, S. L., Gunter, P. L., Ellis, D. N., DeBriere, T. J., & Wehby, J. H. (1993). Classroom interaction of children with behavior disorders. *Journal of Emotional and Behavioral Disorders, 1,* 27–39.

Webster-Stratton, C. (2000). Oppositional-defiant and conduct-disordered children. In M. Hersen & R. T. Ammerman, (Eds.), *Advanced abnormal child psychology* (2nd ed., pp. 387–412). Hillsdale, NJ: Lawrence Erlbaum.

Peggy Hester is Associate Professor and Robert A. Gable is Professor, Early Childhood, Speech Pathology, and Special Education, and M. Lee Manning is Professor, Department of Educational Curriculum and Instruction, Old Dominion University, Norfolk, Virginia.

From *Childhood Education*, Spring 2003, pp. 130-136. © 2003 by the Association for Childhood Education International. Reprinted by permission of the authors.

The Rewards and Restrictions of Recess

Reflections on Being a Playground Volunteer

The experience strengthened my resolve to be a committed advocate for that little piece of free play permitted to children in an increasingly demanding, controlled, and tightly scheduled day.

Leigh M. O'Brien

I can hear them before I see them, as squeals of delight precede the group of 1st-graders set free from the confines of the school building. Then, they appear: a swirling mass of smiling, laughing, running children coming right toward me and toward that cherished half hour following lunch—recess! They play 4-square and basketball, jump rope, twirl Hula Hoops, and pursue an elusive soccer ball up and down the field. In essence, the children play. They often play chase, sometimes formalized as tag (as is technically required by the school). They swing; they toss leaves; they climb, and run, and slide. They chat with friends, comfort a peer who has fallen, and occasionally talk with a nearby adult. They have fun.

The Background

Last year, the principal at my daughter's school experienced difficulty in finding playground aides. At the same time, I was becoming increasingly concerned about the growing number of schools doing away with recess in the search for higher test scores. As most of us are aware, "plenty of people around the country are willing to sacrifice children's recess period to the voracious skills god" (Ohanian, 1999, p. 13). I sent the principal articles that offered support for her intention to keep recess intact. Wishing to practice what I preach, I also volunteered to be a recess "helper" for the year. That is why I spent approximately an hour and a half almost every Monday, from September through early June, watching, interacting with, supervising, consoling, disciplining, and otherwise "aiding" groups of 1st- to 3rd-graders as they enjoyed their recess time.

I found my experience as a playground helper to be fascinating and instructive—time well spent. And although not all

aspects of the experience were positive from my perspective, the experience did strengthen my resolve to be a committed advocate for that little piece of free play permitted to children in an increasingly demanding, controlled, and tightly scheduled day. Outside play provides a sense of freedom to explore and let one's imagination loose. A largely pressure-free, fun-filled time of unstructured physical activity is a welcome break from life's daily routines. Unfortunately, children's opportunities for outdoor play have decreased tremendously over the years. It makes me sad and angry that this is so. Obviously I was not (I *am* not) a dispassionate, objective observer in this matter, and in the following I will explain why.

The narrative that follows comprises relevant excerpts from the notes I took during and after the times I spent on site at the playground. I address the rewards as well as the restrictions of recess—from my perspective as well as the children's. My study was qualitative in nature. As a participant-observer, I sought to understand the situation by spending time on site, taking notes, talking with the "actors," reflecting, and trying to make meaning of what I was seeing, hearing, and feeling. Furthermore, my study is grounded in activism. My intent was and is to make sure recess is not abolished, despite the growing influence of those intently focused on academic skills, standards, and accountability. Recess provides one of the very few opportunities for children to speak and act relatively unfettered by adult expectations. Some have argued for a "third space" or "third discourse," where those who are often marginalized can act and speak freely (see www.indiana.edu/~jah/mexico/dgutierrez. html). This "third discourse promotes *counter-culture*, a peer culture that defines itself in opposition to official school structures" (Bingham, 2000, p. 431). In this space, school is made familiar, and students feel a sense of ownership over a part of it. On the playground, "what is most important is not content but *chatter*, not knowing but *dialogic being*" (Bingham, 2000, p. 431; italics added).

It has been suggested that teacher education programs could use recess as the perfect time and place to observe children's social behavior and ability to get along with others.

To me, this is the most important reason for maintaining recess. It is the non-adult-directed, counter-cultural "stuff" that is so rewarding for children—and so threatening to those who would maintain control at all costs. In recognition of this, I did my best to be there for the children, but only intervened if absolutely necessary, or if they requested that I do so. I find it very disturbing that many of the adults monitoring recess rather ruthlessly shut down any play that even hints at danger or "wildness." I know there are legitimate concerns about children being hurt and about potential litigation, but why can't we find a way to let children say, and do, and *be* what they want, just for one short half hour a day? Don't they need some sense of power in their world, some opportunity to make meaning of experiences on their own terms? In one study (Maxwell, Jarrett, & Roetger, 1999), children noted that recess was the *only* time of the day when they could make choices, and that to be able to do so made them feel respected.

What I Saw

October 30, 2000. High in the bright blue sky on this crisp and sunny fall day, a broad-winged hawk wheels silently as it searches for prey. Down below, it is anything but silent as the overlapping groups of 1st- through 5th-graders come out to play. I love to see children outside on a gorgeous day going full throttle with enjoyment!

November 6, 2000. It has been fun noting the kinds of things children love to do on the playground, some of them familiar from my long-ago childhood: 4-square, hopscotch, swings, chase, slides, and jump rope. The only things really new to me are the wonderful tire swings and the popularity of soccer, which both girls and boys literally line up to play.

It also has been rewarding to note the empathy that the children show their peers. Usually, with no adult intervention, even the "toughest" of kids is quick to comfort a peer who has been hurt, asking, "Are you okay?" or saying, "I'm sorry, I'm sorry."

I note there are loners, pairs, and cliques, the latter two groups sometimes inviolate, at other times, quite fluid in composition. There is single-gender play (e.g., boys playing football, usually just girls jumping rope or doing dramatic play) and mixed-gender play (e.g., the aforementioned soccer, chase, etc.)

November 20, 2000. Today, I noticed a focus on rules and negotiations in the children's play, typical of this age: "You're it—no tag-backs"; "Hey, that's not fair!"; "Why did you change the rules just when it was my turn?"; "Let's go play by ourselves!"

December 4, 2000. I had to skip a day today. I miss being on the playground; I miss the children! I find myself talking about it and them frequently, passionately. I've started thinking about adult hypocrisy, too. If we abolish recess, the message we send is that we think children are inferior beings. After all, adults are very vocal about their need for breaks from routine, yet we expect children to stay "on task" for the length of the school day!

January 8, 2001. It is the first day back after winter break. It has snowed a lot and the entire landscape looks and feels different, and the play is therefore different. In the snow, kids mostly slide down the hillside and run around, wrestling each other and trying to hide their snowballs from adults. I'm pleased that the school principal sends the kids outside despite the weather. I hear so often that children in other local schools can't go out if it's cold, rainy, muddy, snowy—typical winter weather in upstate New York!

January 22, 2001. Tamiqua*, a heavy-set African American 3rd-grade girl bused in from the nearby city school district, swings alone at the far end of the playground. I watch her, but am wary of intruding. Finally, Tamiqua comes over and stands by me without speaking. I say, "Hi. How are you doing?" and she quietly starts to cry. I attempt to comfort her, asking, "What's the matter? Are you lonely?" while she sniffles. Tamiqua nods her head, I put my arm around her, and then, fortunately, another girl notices and comes over to ask if Tamiqua wants to play. They go off together.

I say to an aide, "It's tough being a kid," and she replies, "She needs to bring her snow pants. She's reminded every day, but only brings them, like, one out of five days. She can't play on the field without them; I'm not really even supposed to let her come out, but I feel bad for her." Me, too, and I wonder how race and class affect the situation, as the school is almost entirely white and upper middle class.

January 29, 2001. Today, I wondered what these children are like in a different environment. Is the "natural" leader here also a leader in the classroom, or does the rough-and-tumble, wide-open nature of recess allow different kids and talents to shine? And what of the loner? Is s/he also by her or himself when inside? Are the pairs and cliques sustained inside? Some contend that recess is a great time for teachers to ascertain who are leaders and who are followers, and even who might be at risk of social ostracism. It has been suggested that teacher education programs could use recess as the perfect time and place to observe children's social behavior and ability to get along with others (Rike & Krueger, 2000). Of course, for us to do so would mean that recess would have to be considered important enough for teachers and prospective teachers to take part in, and that we would have to question the valuing of what we construct as "work" over that which we marginalize as "play." In my experience, this doesn't happen at too many schools past the pre-kindergarten level.

February 5, 2001. Today was interesting: Because the playground and field were icy, the kids had to stay in an extremely limited area (one snowy hill and the blacktop); there was more fighting, shoving, and so forth, and therefore more adult intervention.

I'm becoming increasingly troubled about what sometimes seems to be an over-inflated concern regarding safety, which often feels more like control to me. I tend to let kids go if they're having fun and not in immediate peril. The other adults (the paid aides) tend to stop any play with the slightest potential for danger, thereby seriously limiting the kids' creativity and fun. For example, the kids were sliding down a small, icy hill. Because it was deemed "too slippery" (isn't that the point?), they were told not to use it. Also, kids sometimes wanted to slide head-first or sideways; that, too, was prohibited. And snowballs, no matter how fluffy the snow, were verboten. The argument usually given to the kids had to do with safety—to me, as another adult, liability concerns were mentioned.

This situation reminds me of Foucault's notion of the panoptic, the all-seeing eye capable of watching all areas at once, thus ensuring compliance and control. This surveillance by an all-powerful, adult "gaze" regulates what is arguably the only time during the entire school day that the kids can truthfully call their own. I believe the aides' intentions are good, and I'm only a once-a-week volunteer, so I don't say anything; nevertheless, it troubles me.

February 12, 2001. It happened again today: The children were not allowed on the playground, but they were thrilled to be on the field, which was solid ice covered by a thin layer of snow. They quickly and cooperatively made an "ice skating rink" and an ice slide, and had great fun "skating" and sliding. After the 1st- and 2nd-graders played this way, with no problems, the 3rd-graders came out and had about 10 minutes of open-ended and creative play before a different aide restricted them, eventually moving all the children onto the blacktop. The kids, who had been smiling and saying "This is fun" about their play on the field, grumbled, but went.

The claim by some adults that they understand what children need allows us to construct and maintain control over children; a judgmental surveillance is thereby justified. At the school, the adults once again utilized their power to control and regulate. Unpredictability and complexity are thus denied, and children are limited to the possibilities that fit our construction of them (Cannella, 1997). I agree with Davey (2000), who writes, "Even when at play, our children tend to be monitored by adults who seem compelled to quiet their voices and still their bodies" (p. 31).

March 12, 2001. It's a sunny but cold day. Just a little over one week until the arrival of meteorological spring, but the playground is still covered in snow and ice. In fact, the playground proper is closed, so the kids play on the field (sliding down the hill, lobbing covert snowballs, skating on the "ice rink" once more) or on the blacktop.

I've started thinking about resistance: The adults, despite their attempts at control, are not all-powerful, and so the children often resist their attempts at disciplining, normalizing, and controlling. As has been found before (e.g., Willis, 1981) and

reiterated more recently (e.g., Butin, 2001), oppressed people with little power—and children by and large fit that description—find ways to assert their humanity, to strive for freedom. The resistance I've seen from children takes the form of circumventing adult rules by saying "We are playing tag," when in fact they are really running around wildly chasing each other; asking the more lenient or less informed aide (me) to weigh in on a questionable rule; or hiding behind a tree or going to the far end of the field in order to proceed with something "illicit." These and other covert activities provide opportunities, albeit limited ones, for children to assert themselves and their desire for less control and more freedom.

April 9, 2001. Last week the playground and field were still covered with snow. This week it's much warmer, with only sad, dirty piles of old snow left where it was plowed high. Miracle of miracles, the playground is open again and the kids are thrilled! Once more, swings, slides, and tunnels ring with delighted laughter. Flowers are pushing up around the edges of the playground. After a long, cold, snowy winter, spring is finally here.

April 23, 2001. Spring break was last week—the children come back to school on a very warm day, delighted to have full access to the playground. I notice today one of the benefits of outdoors mixed-age grouping (Katz, Evangelou, & Hartman, 1990). When the 2nd-graders come out, they often offer to share their extra strength and expertise (although not expressed in those words) by pushing the 1st-graders on the tire swings during the 10 minutes when recess periods for the two groups overlap. Both groups seem to benefit from this arrangement: the younger children get better pushes and more socialization; and the older children get to "strut their stuff" and be admired.

I talked with the principal today about my concerns regarding what I perceive as some rather harsh discipline approaches used by some aides, and about the lack of attention paid to verbal and emotional aggression. The latter concern was prompted by several 2nd-grade boys teasing my daughter, a child with special needs. I was also worried about how Ricardo*, a recent immigrant from Mexico just learning English, was treated by one aide. The principal was receptive, said she saw these situations as ongoing problems, and agreed to talk with the aides. We also discussed her problems in hiring and keeping well-qualified people willing to work (in the lunchroom and outdoors) for just two hours in the middle of the day.

We did not, however, discuss why it is that teachers are never present during recess time at this site, or why aides typically make minimum wage—and how addressing these issues might ameliorate some of the problems. We also did not discuss alternative models for utilizing aides—for example, if they were hired for the entire day, they could interact with children both indoors and out, thereby gaining both familiarity with the children and more respect. Nor did we specifically discuss the restrictions on rough-and-tumble play, which some researchers—and parents—feel is a necessity for boys' development. Although I did not notice any immediate changes, I was pleased to be heard and felt a little bit more hopeful about the future of play at this site.

I also used the opportunity to see if I might ask the kids what they liked and disliked about recess; I needed their insights to flesh out my reflections. I was granted permission, as long as I maintained the children's anonymity.

April 30, 2001. Today I began to ask the 1st-, 2nd-, and 3rd-graders, "What do you like about recess?" and "Is there anything you don't like?" My sample was small and completely "unscientific," although perhaps I could call it a "purposeful sampling" (Bogdan & Biklen, 1992). I simply approached children who weren't intensely involved in an activity and asked if they'd like to tell me how they felt about recess. Almost all said yes, although a few did not. (I did not press them for answers.) Some children noticed my note pad and pencil and approached me to ask what I was doing. Most of these children then wanted to share their thoughts.

May 7, 2001. As I've found to be the case with adults (e.g., O'Brien, 2000), most of the children were eager to answer my questions and tell their stories. They often asked me, "What are you doing?"; every third or fourth child followed that query by asking "Why?"

May 14, 2001. The opinions of the 28 children with whom I spoke largely jibed with my observations. That is, they love the openness and social dimension of swings, soccer, and the like. There seem to be some gender differences in terms of preferred play, broken down, largely, along traditional gender lines. Overall, boys seemed to prefer a little more active play and girls a bit more social play: boys play football and a rougher game of chase, when allowed; girls jump rope and play house/babies. Both genders like the swings, and both are often involved in impromptu soccer games. As we might expect, the focus of play appears to change with age; younger children engaged in more open-ended play and older children preferred games with rules. I observed some gender differences, in terms of dislikes; not surprisingly, no one seemed to like getting picked on or teased, and the children did not like being restricted in their play. I believe their comments highlight both the potential rewards and restrictions of recess.

May 21, 2001. I note a concern about gender and soccer: A 1st-grade boy tells me, "We played the boys versus the girls and won 9 to 0! And there were more girls!" I wondered how the girls felt, and why the teams were constructed according to gender, and what, if anything, the adults were doing—or should be doing—about the situation.

June 4, 2001. Today, the 1st-grade girls win the soccer game, 3-0. They're so excited! And I'm happy for them after the public gloating of the boys over their win the last time I was here. This was my last day on the playground. It was a fine day to end my brief stint as a volunteer recess aide. Maybe I'll do it again next year...

What I Felt/What I Learned

Volumes have been written about children's play (e.g., Fein & Rivkin, 1986; Frost, 1992; Johnson, Christie, & Yawkey, 1987; Piaget, 1962). Poems have been composed in praise of play. There is a United Nations Declaration of the Child's Right to Play. And child development experts are seemingly unanimous in their belief that play is an essential part of a child's day (e.g., Kieff, 2001). Researchers have even shown that a break such as recess, in part because of its multi-dimensionality, enhances children's well-being, as well as their social-emotional, physical, and cognitive development (e.g., Jarrett et al., 1998; Pellegrini & Davis, 1993). In summary, free, safe, relatively unrestricted play during recess is an essential requirement for helping children learn and grow.

During recess, children are learning the things that they need to know now and in the future. They're learning how to negotiate with peers to organize their play, how to make—and break—rules, how to read others' cues and respond appropriately, how to make and live with choices, how to solve problems, how to use their bodies in multiple ways, how to help and how to receive help, how to *be* who they are. Recess gives children the opportunity to be self-expressive in ways that no other setting can provide. Ultimately, recess can help children ask and attempt to answer what Ayers (2001) considers the essential question of education: Who am I in the world? Recess can and should help children develop a sense of agency, a sense of self.

Despite the above-mentioned benefits, the free play time found during recess is being inexorably cut back, even cut out of U.S. schools as a byproduct of a relentless drive to address academics and accountability (Alexander, 2000; Kieff, 2001; Noddings, 1992; Ohanian, 1999). Given my experience, I agree with Kieff (2001), who writes, "Instead of silencing the recess bell, administrators should make every effort to provide high-quality recess experiences for children" (p. 320). I believe that this "extra," like art and music, really needs more of our attention. Instead of *marginalizing* recess, we should do our best to *maximize* this important time.

If we think of recess as integral and essential to children's education, then we might ask, "What kinds of experiences are high quality? How can we ensure this is a beneficial time for *all* children, physically, socially, and emotionally? How can we best address issues pertaining to age, race, class, gender, ability, language, and other differences in this context? What kinds of negative experiences are occurring and how can we thoughtfully address them?" Moving into the wider societal context, we might investigate what has been said in response to questions about why work and play are seen as separate realms in the United States, with work valued and play devalued (e.g., Karier, 1973). How are these societal values related to our willingness to cut back and sometimes even do away with recess?

As can be seen by the adult attempts to circumscribe the children's play in the setting I described here, play is an artifact to be controlled and even suppressed when dominant forms are not exhibited. Therefore, I believe we also must ask ourselves, "How many and what kinds of choices can/should be provided? If restrictions are needed, how many/what kind/to what end? How can we make play areas safe without stifling children's choices, creativity, imagination, need to be powerful?" Furthermore, adults have labeled certain play "good" or "appropriate," versus that which they consider "bad" or "inappropriate." Thus, the freedom implied for young children within the construction of play often is an illusion. "Although the discourse may be to allow children to explore and make sense of their world, when the play behavior does not suit those who are in control, the voluntary activity is no longer allowed. Adults are really in control" (Cannella, 1997, p. 128). However, to open the "doors and minds" of children, recess needs to be unstructured time, with plenty of physical and psychological roaming space and a lack of imposed rules. We will lose our free thinkers, sensitive communicators, and safe outlets for self-expression if we continue to eliminate recess or severely curtail freedom during this time (Michaels, 2000). Thus, educators need to engage in serious discussion of these and similar issues.

Finally, building on the foregoing, we need to ask the big questions: For what purpose(s) do we educate? What is the role of adults vis-à-vis children's education, including play? Because of the time I spent as a playground volunteer this past year, I now *know* that schools need to consider the whole child and his or her development of agency and a positive sense of self. And I now *know* that children need adults who are thoughtfully and continually considering both the rewards and the restrictions of recess. The more time that adults respond attentively and generously to what they consider, the more that playgrounds will ring with the laughter of children playing freely, joyfully, and with their whole selves. The more they do so, the more educators can help children answer that most crucial question: Who am I in the world? We must—parents, educators, concerned citizens, even the children themselves—resist the trend toward limiting recess, and instead be tireless advocates for it; outdoor play is a necessity and the right of every child. Our advocacy for recess is one very important way we can support the "irrepressible possibility of humans" (Booth, 2001).

References and Resources

Alexander, K. K. (2000). Playtime is cancelled. In K. M. Paciorek & J. H. Munro (Eds.), *Annual editions: Early childhood education 00/01* (pp. 96–99). Guilford, CT: Dushkin/ McGraw-Hill.

Ayers, W. (2001, July). *The limits and possibilities of urban teaching.* Paper presented at a conference, University of Rochester, Rochester, NY.

Bingham, C. (2000). [Review of the book *Beyond discourse: Education, the self, and dialogue.*] *Educational Studies, 31*(4), 427–432.

Bogdan, R. C., & Biklen, S. K. (1992). *Qualitative research for education: An introduction to theory and methods* (2nd ed.). Boston: Allyn & Bacon.

Booth, E. (2001, July). *The John Washburn memorial lecture.* Paper presented at the Memorial Art Gallery, Rochester, NY.

Butin, D. W. (2001). If this is resistance I would hate to see domination: Retrieving Foucault's notion of resistance within educational research. *Educational Studies, 32*(2), 157–176.

Cannella, G. S. (1997). *Deconstructing early childhood education: Social justice and revolution.* New York: Peter Lang.

Clements, R.L. (Ed.). (2000). *Elementary school recess: Selected readings, games, and activities for teachers and parents.* Boston: American Press.

Davey, L. (2000). Recess and learning in Moscow. In R. L. Clements (Ed.), *Elementary school recess: Selected readings, games, and activities for teachers and parents* (pp. 30–33). Boston: American Press.

Fein, G., & Rivkin, M. (Eds.). (1986). *The young child at play: Reviews of research, volume 4.* Washington, DC: National Association for the Education of Young Children.

Frost, J. L. (1992). *Play and playscapes.* Albany, NY: Delmar.

Jarrett, O. S., Maxwell, D. M., & Dickerson, C., Hoge, P., Davies, G., & Yetley, A. (1998). The impact of recess on classroom behavior: Group effects and individual differences. *Journal of Educational Research, 92*(2), 121–126.

Johnson, J. E., Christie, J. F., & Yawkey, T. D. (1987). *Play and early childhood development.* New York: HarperCollins.

Karier, C.J. (1973). Business values and the educational state. In C. J. Karier, P. Violas, & J. Spring (Eds.), *Roots of crisis: American education in the twentieth century* (pp. 6–29). Chicago: Rand McNally.

Katz, L. G., Evangelou, D., & Hartman, J. A. (1990). *The case for mixed-age grouping in early education.* Washington, DC: National Association for the Education of Young Children.

Kieff, J. (2001). The silencing of recess bells. *Childhood Education, 77,* 319–320.

Maxwell, D. M., Jarrett, O. S., & Roetger, C. D. (1999, January). Recess through the children's eyes. Paper presented at the Conference on Qualitative Research in Education, University of Georgia.

Michaels, B. (2000). Art and recess. In R. L. Clements (Ed.), *Elementary school recess: Selected readings, games, and activities for teachers and parents* (pp. 70–74). Boston: American Press.

National Association for the Education of Young Children. (1997). *The value of school recess and outdoor play. A position statement.* Washington, DC: Author.

Noddings, N. (1992). *The challenge to care in schools: An alternative approach to education.* New York: Teachers College Press.

O'Brien, L. M. (1999). "I love Lydia": Mother as early childhood teacher educator. *Journal of Early Childhood Teacher Education, 20*(2), 105–119.

O'Brien, L. M. (2000, January). The transformative potential of woman-to-woman research. Paper presented at the 2000 Conference on Qualitative Research in Education, University of Georgia, Athens, GA.

Ohanian, S. (1999). *One size fits all: The folly of educational standards.* Portsmouth, NH: Heinemann.

Pellegrini, A. D., & Bjorkland, D. F. (1996). The place of recess in school: Issues in the role of recess in children's education and development. An introduction to the theme issue. *Journal of Research in Childhood Education, 11*(1), 5–13.

Pellegrini, A. D., & Davis, P. L. (1993). Relations between children's playground and classroom behavior. *British Journal of Educational Psychological Society, 63,* 88–95.

Piaget, J. (1962). *Play, dreams, and imitation.* New York: Norton.

Rike, E., & Krueger, A. (2000). Imaginative play and recess. In R. L. Clements (Ed.), *Elementary school recess: Selected readings, games, and activities for teachers and parents* (pp. 49–52). Boston: American Press.

Willis, P. (1981). *Learning to labour: How working class kids get working class jobs.* New York: Columbia University Press.

*This is a pseudonym

Leigh M. O'Brien is Director, Graduate (Inclusive) Early Childhood Education Programs and Associate Professor of Education, Nazareth College, Rochester, New York.

HOME FRONT

With America at war, schools struggle to help students understand the cause and effect of conflict

BY LAWRENCE HARDY

Liz Morrison can still see their faces, even after 12 years. And she still recalls the emotions she felt as she watched them board the plane for Paris—soldiers on the first leg of their journey to the Middle East and Operation Desert Storm.

"The guys were so *young,*" says Morrison, then a flight attendant on their 747 and now a high school history teacher in suburban St. Louis.

When the plane landed in France, the flight steward in charge of the cabin crew made a short but heartfelt speech. A Vietnam veteran, he said he received a hostile reception when he returned from Southeast Asia. "We will not allow you to be treated as I was treated," he said. Morrison cried, as did the other flight attendants and many of the soldiers. She vowed that she would always support the U.S. troops, wherever they were stationed.

Now working at Parkway South High School in Manchester, Mo., Morrison is not simply supporting the troops in the Middle East and hoping for their safe return. She is teaching about a crisis that has divided the country and split public opinion throughout the world. It is a difficult assignment, and educators cannot agree how to teach it. In large part, their approach ultimately depends on their political and pedagogical beliefs.

What is clear is that students want to be included in the discussion, whatever their teachers' views.

"The last thing they want to do is to be left out of it," says Susan W. Graseck, director of Choices for the 21st Century, a highly regarded high school current events curriculum developed by Brown University. "It's a very scary time. But it's a scarier time if you don't understand it too."

College students and their supporters rall[ied] for an antiwar protest at Hunter College in New York City on March 5—two weeks before the start of the second Persian Gulf war. High school students participated in similar protests as part of a national strike against U.S. military action in Iraq. As the nation drew closer to war in the Middle East, teachers across the country were trying to decide how to discuss the politically charged issue with their students.

Living with history

As this issue of *ASBJ* goes to press, a second Gulf War has begun. Myriad questions remain about the prosecution of war and the nature of a postwar Iraq. Doubtless, as you read this, many of these questions will have been answered, but one of the biggest questions—what will the war mean for the future security of the Middle East, the U.S., and the world?—may not be resolved for years to come.

"We're at a critical turning point right now in terms of the United States' place in the world, and the decisions we make are going to be with us for a long time," Graseck says. "We're creating history, and when you create history, you live with that history."

Teachers at all grade levels found themselves addressing the topic. In the early grades, they were mainly trying to reduce anxiety, particularly among students with family in the military. In middle school, some teachers were beginning to discuss the conflict itself. But it was in a high school that they could best engage their students. Interviewed in early March, while the nation teetered on the brink of conflict, high school teachers were taking different approaches to the difficult task of teaching about possible war.

Some teachers say they try not to let impressionable adolescents know how they feel about the controversial U.S. policy on use of force in Iraq. Others, representing various points on the political spectrum, say that while they present both sides of the issue, it is only right to let students know where they stand and to expose students to information that supports the teacher's deeply held beliefs. For some, that means emphasizing the virtues of American democracy and contrasting them with the oppressive nature of the Iraqi dictatorship and other totalitarian regimes. For others, it means exploring the devastating human costs to Iraq of Operation Desert Storm and the economic sanctions that followed.

"With all the injustice in the world and all the inequality and all the pain, I think it's very important that students know I care and am trying to do something about it," says Bill Bigelow, an Oregon high school teacher who opposes war with Iraq—and lets his students know it.

"One of the worst problems today is cynicism. It's kids feeling nothing can change. I want students to know that I don't believe this, that I operate on a different premise, that there is no inevitability to history to the extent that good things have happened because people have worked for them. And the same is true today."

Others argue that Bigelow's position—as well as that of teachers who support the war—runs counter to the schools' mission of producing independent thinkers, regardless of how much these teachers may strive to present both sides of the issue. "Remember, we're talking about children and adolescents here," wrote Jonathan Zimmerman, who teaches history and education at New York University, in the *Washington Post.* "They take their cues from adults with the authority to evaluate them. Once they sense the teacher's bias, any 'discussion' will inevitably assume the same slant."

Still others criticize Zimmerman's evenhanded approach to American history and current events, saying it is precisely because students are impressionable that teachers should guide them in understanding things such as the unique virtues of American democracy. Certainly, students should study the current Iraqi situation and debate various foreign policy positions, these educators say. But in the course of this or any other political discussion, when it comes to describing the bedrock values of the American political system, it's time to cast neutrality aside.

"I don't think you teach patriotism, but I do think it's important to give students an insight into the values of our democratic tradition," says William Damon, a senior fellow at the Hoover Institution and director of Stanford University's Center on Adolescence. "You teach the successes of our history as well as the failures. You try to be balanced about it. You do it in a way that helps [students] develop some pride in the heroic things their forefathers have accomplished."

A pragmatic approach

Morrison, the Missouri high school teacher, thinks the United States must confront Saddam Hussein at some point, even though she does not see evidence of an immediate threat. She compares Saddam's flaunting of the United Nations resolutions to Hitler's rejection of the Treaty of Versailles, which ended World War I and placed stringent restrictions on Germany's military. "People who violate treaties usually have an agenda," Morrison says.

'We're at a critical turning point... We're creating history, and when you create history, you have to live with history.'

—SUSAN GRASECK

Though she disagrees with some students about the danger posed by Saddam, Morrison accepted the views of students who wanted to participate in Books Not Bombs, a nationwide walkout of high school and college students opposed to war. And she used the discussion of the March 5 demonstration as a "teachable moment," talking to students about the meaning of civil disobedience and the importance of accepting the consequences. Schools across the country had a difficult time deciding how to deal with students who walked out of class, but Parkway South was fortunate—St. Louis had an ice storm, which cancelled school.

"That solved *that* problem," Morrison joked.

Enthusiastic and cheerful, Morrison takes a pragmatic rather than an ideological approach to teaching history. She uses the Brown University curriculum, a politically neutral program that enables students to debate various foreign policy options. But she also accepted a recent invitation from a peace group to have her students attend, as silent participants, a video conference with students from other schools in the United States and a school in Baghdad.

"If an opportunity comes up that I think is too good for my students to miss, I just go for it," Morrison says.

As it turned out, Morrison only had 10 minutes' notice before the conference started, and the group she was preparing for the event—her 11th- and 12th-grade Challenges to Democracy class—was not in session. So she had her ninth-grade American history class go instead and was surprised by their perceptiveness.

During the session, the Iraqi students seemed to answer the more innocuous questions extemporaneously; but when they were asked about their reaction to Sept. 11, they huddled in conference before offering a reply. Morrison said this made an impression on her ninth-graders.

"Their overwhelming reaction was that the kids in Baghdad were telling them what their country wanted [Americans] to hear," Morrison said. "I thought that was very interesting, because I hadn't scripted that [response]."

Debating the options

It's early March, and the war has not yet begun. The assignment for Sarah Roeske's Global Issues class is straightforward enough, but hardly simple: "We're going to be deciding whether we should go to war against Iraq," Roeske tells her class at Stafford High School near Fredericksburg, Va.

The students break into four groups to prepare their arguments for the next day's class. Like Morrison, Roeske has used Brown University's Choices curriculum to explore a number of issues, including economics, terrorism, and the conflict in the Middle East. For the current Iraq crisis, the university has created an abbreviated curriculum based on the format of its more in-depth programs. As in the regular curriculum, students research the subject and are presented with four policy options. They study each option and examine its goals, the policies needed to achieve those goals, the option's underlying beliefs, and various criticisms of the option.

Sometimes, Roeske asks students to defend policies they don't necessarily support. It helps them polish their critical thinking and debating skills, she explains. But her eight-period class has studied the Iraqi conflict extensively, and now Roeske wants the juniors and seniors to argue the positions they truly support—to create a fifth option based on their analysis of the other four.

Of the 15 students in the class, nine have parents who are either active duty or retired military personnel, but no active duty parents have been deployed to the Persian Gulf. Given such a high proportion of students from military families, it might be assumed that a majority would support the Bush administration's war plans. And, indeed, that is the case: Three of the four groups of students support war with Iraq, with varying conditions.

But the division is not between students from military families and those from civilian homes. It's between girls and boys. It's the class's three girls—two of whom have parents who are active duty or retired military—who strongly oppose a war.

"The Gulf War is so '91," the girls read from a poster that Roeske has asked each group to make. Then they explain their rationale.

"Saddam is a ruthless dictator, but he's not insane," says 11th-grader Katelyn Cowen. "He will not use weapons of mass destruction until he's provoked." And provoking Saddam, and much of the Muslim world, will only make the United States a bigger target for terrorism, the girls said.

When it comes time for questions, several students are quick to criticize the girls' position. "You said going in would make us a larger target for terrorism," says 12th-grader Travis Henty. "Last I looked, we were [already] a pretty big one."

Of the three groups of boys, Henty's group is the least enthusiastic about invading Iraq without a U.N. mandate. "We want to play every diplomatic card left before we play the war card," Henty says.

"What do you think of the stability of the region?" asks Cowen. "It's history."

The debate goes on, rapid-fire, for 40 minutes. Roeske serves as moderator, referee, and timekeeper, reluctantly limiting the number of questions so there will be time for all the groups to make their presentations.

Afterward, a few of the boys remain in the classroom and talk about what one dubs "the *awesomist* class."

"It's like we can debate, but we're still friends," one of the boys says.

"History can only take you so far, and in this class we're dealing with the current stuff," says 11th-grader Andre Jones. "I'm watching CNN and CSPAN, and I never used to do this.... I would stick to sports."

Roeske believes in keeping her political views to herself. "I'm not a moderate," she says. "I'm very much to one side, and my kids will never know what side I'm on." Actually, she *will* reveal her views, but only if students ask her after final exams are over.

After Sept. 11, Roeske took her class through a similar session on terrorism, but it was less of a debate because there was general agreement about the policies that should be pursued. The confrontation with Saddam is different. "The Iraq [question] is controversial, and because of that it's a much better teaching tool than 9/11 was," Roeske says.

One of Roeske's goals is to broaden students' minds and get them to look beyond their own experiences. "We're so insular, and I want the kids to look outside the US and not be so ethnocentric and look at things only from the American perspective," she says.

Questioning prevailing attitudes

Bigelow, the Portland High school teacher, also tries to get students to see things from a different perspective. Asked if his class is antiwar, he replies: "It's an antiwar course in the sense of wanting to give students the tools to be critical."

Despite his strong, and public, antiwar views, Bigelow presents both sides in class, even spending a period as President Bush, quoting from the parts of the State of the Union speech that dealt with Iraq and defending the president's policies. But he is most passionate about getting students to question prevailing attitudes.

At one point, he showed the class a Popeye cartoon in which Popeye is a U.S. Coast Guard officer fighting a marauding Arab

TEACHING ABOUT WAR

- "Facing Fear," a curriculum created by the Red Cross, includes a series of free lesson plans geared to children from kindergarten through high school. www.redcross.org/disaster/masters/facingfear
- The Web site for Educators for Social Responsibility, a non-profit group based in Watertown, Mass., advises teachers on "Eliciting Students' Thoughts and Feelings About War on Iraq." www.esrnational.org

TALKING WITH CHILDREN

- PBS has a Web site geared toward parents of young children called "Talking With Kids About War and Violence." The site includes advice from the late Fred Rogers on "Helping Children Deal with Scary News." www.pbs.org/parents/issuesadvice/war
- Judith A. Myers-Walls, a specialist at Purdue University in child development, has a Web site on talking with children about war and terrorism. www.ces.purdue.edu/terrorism

Other materials are available at:
- www.aboutourkids.org
- www.helping.apa.org
- www.aap.org/terrorism
- www.istss.org (Click on "Terrorism and Trauma," then "Information for the Public.")
- www.kidshealth.org (Click on "Parents," then "In the News.")
- www.nccev.org

called Abu Hassan. The cartoon is replete with stereotypes about dark-skinned, shifty, violent Arabs.

In an article for the Rethinking Schools Web site (www.rethinkingschools.org), Bigelow explained his purpose in showing the cartoon: "I wanted students to think about the framework that the media fashion for us—the purely bad guys and the purely good guys, the cleansing role of violence, the contempt for non-Western cultures, etc.," Bigelow wrote. "And I wanted them to recognize how we are often led to organize information about today's global conflicts, especially those in the Middle East, into these frameworks."

Bigelow also showed his class a video called "Greetings from Missile Street," which was made by a peace group that visited Basra in southern Iraq during the summer of 2000. In the film, ordinary Iraqis describe the lingering effects of Desert Storm and sanctions that the U.N. estimates contribute to the deaths of about 4,500 Iraqi children each month from malnutrition and preventable diseases.

"For the first time, they were able to imagine Iraqis as people other than Saddam Hussein and some kind of crazed militant flag-burners who are out to destroy America," Bigelow says.

While Bigelow criticizes U.S. policy and what he sees as the prevailing national mind-set from the left, others say it is the left itself that often distorts the discussion of U.S. history and current events. Too many educators responded to the 9/11 tragedy with a kind of "How have we hurt them?" approach, says Lucien Ellington, codirector of the Asia Program at the University of Tennessee at Chattanooga. The notion that poverty and degradation, somehow imposed by the West, are responsible for the growth of terrorism "is miseducation," he says, arguing that terrorism has more to do with the lack of economic and political freedom in many Arab societies.

Yet, as Ellington wrote in a Fordham Foundation article after 9/11, "the notion of accentuating positive versions of America or Western cultural exceptionalism is [considered] evil and politically reactionary. This applies to civic education, where the new buzzword among the social studies cognoscenti is 'global' not American citizenship."

Ellington, who worked on Jimmy Carter's 1976 presidential campaign, places his political philosophy as "somewhere between neo-liberal and neo-conservative." He says that, whatever his students' views, they must come to know America as a unique society in the history of the world.

"The historical master narrative should contain accurate information about our societal shortcomings yet can still be uplifting and inspirational for young Americans," Ellington wrote. "There is no contradiction between teaching accurate historical and political content and building a solid understanding of American patriotism and what it means to be a U.S. citizen."

Lawrence Hardy (lhardy@nsba.org) is an associate editor of American School Board Journal.

UNIT 6
Cultural Diversity and Schooling

Unit Selections

Key Points to Consider

- What is multicultural education? To what does the national debate over multiculturalism in the schools relate? What are the issues regarding it?

- How would you define the equity issues in the field of education? How would you rank order them?

- What are the ways that a teacher can employ to help students understand the concept of culture?

- Critique the slogan, "Every child can learn." Do you find it true or false? Explain.

 **Links: www.dushkin.com/online/**
These sites are annotated in the World Wide Web pages.

American Scientist
http://www.amsci.org/amsci/amsci.html

American Studies Web
http://www.georgetown.edu/crossroads/asw/

Multicultural Publishing and Education Council
http://www.mpec.org

National Institute on the Education of At-Risk Students
http://www.ed.gov/offices/OERI/At-Risk/

Prospects: The Congressionally Mandated Study of Educational Growth and Opportunity
http://www.ed.gov/pubs/Prospects/index.html

The concept of "culture" encompasses all of the life ways, customs, traditions, and institutions that a people develop as they create and experience their history and identity as a people. In the United States of America, many very different cultures coexist within the civic framework of a shared constitutional tradition that guarantees equality before the law for all. So, as we all have been taught, out of many peoples we are also one nation united by our constitutional heritage.

The civil rights movement in America in the 1950s and 1960s was about the struggle of cultural minorities to achieve equity: social justice before the law under our federal Constitution. The articles in this unit attempt to address some of these equity issues.

There is an immense amount of unfinished business before us in the area of intercultural relations in the schools and in educating all Americans regarding how multicultural our national population demographics really are. We are becoming more and more multicultural with every passing decade. This further requires us to take steps to ensure that all of our educational opportunity structures remain open to all persons regardless of their cultural backgrounds or gender. There is much unfinished business as well with regard to improving educational opportunities for girls and young women; the remaining gender issues in American education are very real and directly related to the issue of equality of educational opportunity.

Issues of racial prejudice and bigotry still plague us in American education, despite massive efforts in many school systems to improve racial and intercultural relations in the schools. Many American adolescents are in crisis as their basic health and social needs are not adequately met and their educational development is affected by crises in their personal lives. The articles in this unit reflect all of the above concerns plus others related to efforts to provide equality of educational opportunity to all American youth and attempts to clarify what multicultural education is and what it is not.

The "equity agenda," or social justice agenda, in the field of education is a complex matrix of gender- and culture-related issues aggravated by incredibly wide gaps in the social and economic opportunity structures available to citizens. We are each situated by cultural, gender-based, and socioeconomic factors in society; this is true of all persons everywhere. We have witnessed a great and glorious struggle for human rights in our time and in our nation. The struggle continues to deal more effectively with educational opportunity issues related to cultural diversity and gender.

The "Western canon" is being challenged by advocates' multicultural perspectives in school curriculum development. Multicultural educational programming, which will reflect the rapidly changing cultural demographics of North American schooling, is being advocated by some and strongly opposed by others. This controversy centers around several different issues regarding what it means to provide equality of opportunities for culturally diverse students. The traditional Western cultural content of general and social studies and language arts curricula is being challenged as Eurocentric.

Helping teachers to broaden their cultural perspectives and to take a more global view of curriculum content is something that the advocates of culturally pluralistic approaches to curriculum development would like to see integrated into the entire elementary and secondary school curriculum structure. North America is as multicultural a region of the world as exists anywhere. Our enormous cultural diversity encompasses populations from many indigenous "First Americans" as well as peoples from every European culture, plus many peoples of Asian, African, and Latin American nations and the Central and South Pacific Island groups. There is spirited controversy over how to help all Americans to better understand our collective multicultural heritage. There are spirited defenders and opponents of the traditional Eurocentric curriculum.

The problem of inequality of educational opportunity is of great concern to American educators. One in four American children does not have all of basic needs met and lives under poverty conditions. Almost one in three lives in a single-parent home, which in itself is no disadvantage, but under conditions of poverty, it often is. More and more concern is expressed over how to help children of poverty. The equity agenda of our time has to do with many issues related to gender, race, and ethnicity. All forms of social deprivation and discrimination are aggravated by great disparities in income and accumulated wealth. How can students be helped to have an equal opportunity to succeed in school?

Some of us are still proud to say that we are a nation of immigrants. In addition to the traditional minority/majority group relationships that evolved in the United States, new waves of immigrants today are again enhancing the importance of concerns for achieving equality of opportunity in education. In light of these vast sociological and demographic changes, we must ensure that we will remain a multicultural democracy.

The social psychology of prejudice is something that psychiatrists, social psychologists, anthropologists, and sociologists have studied in great depth since the 1930s. Tolerance, acceptance, and a valuing of the unique worth of every person are teachable and learnable attitudes. A just society must be constantly challenged to find meaningful ways to raise human aspirations, to heal human hurt, and to help in the task of optimizing every citizen's potential. Education is a vital component to that end. Teachers can incorporate into their lessons an emphasis on acceptance of difference, toleration of and respect for the beliefs of others, and the skills of reasoned debate and dialogue.

The struggle for optimal representation of minority perspectives in the schools will be a matter of serious concern to educators for the foreseeable future. From the many court decisions upholding the rights of women and cultural minorities in the schools over the past years has emerged a national consensus that we must strive for the greatest degree of equality in education as may be possible. The triumph of constitutional law over prejudice and bigotry must continue.

Education Is Critical to Closing the Socioeconomic Gap

Black leaders suggest how to improve the present economic and political status of blacks in America.

The Economic and Political Evolution of Black America

WARD CONNERLY

The old adage about the glass that is half empty also being half full has never been truer than it is with respect to the economic conditions of blacks in America. Gone are the days when being black was conterminous with being poor and disadvantaged. Instead, like other Americans, blacks now come in all economic shapes and sizes.

I distinctly recall, as a teenager growing up in a predominantly black neighborhood in the 1950s, being able to count on one hand the number of black families that could be characterized as economically successful. While few of the families in my neighborhood were living in poverty, that condition was only one or two paychecks away for most of them.

Today, at the dawn of the twenty-first century, not only is there a clearly defined and mushrooming black middle class, there is also a bustling corps of economic success stories of blacks with annual incomes of well over $100,000. In the immediate years ahead, as more blacks flock to private enterprise instead of relying on government jobs, the ranks of America's upper crust will predictably swell with blacks.

The part of the glass that is half empty involves millions of our fellow citizens who happen to be black and for whom the promise of America will be elusive. Their "blackness" is irrelevant to their condition. What accounts for their increasing distance from those who reside in the part of the glass that is half full is

their lack of education, their lack of marketable work skills, too many families that are broken and reliant on an unwed mother for financial support, and young males who have made the streets their home.

Add to this a culture of dependency on government and a belief that they are victims of a racist society, and one has a nearly complete explanation for the growing polarization of black America. One segment of black America is economically assimilating; another is not. The solutions are to be found in the very definition of the problems.

Ward Connerly is the founder and chairman of the American Civil Rights Institute.

The African-American Independent School and the Freedom of Choice

JOAN DAVIS RATTERAY

In the education of African Americans, black independent schools created by parents, teachers, community organizations, churches, and mosques have played a critical role in the economic uplift of the community. These schools have a long history of survival and contribution to the nation.

Little is known of their great work, but many well-known families have been nurtured by these schools. For example, the late jazz great Dizzy Gillespie attended the Laurinburg Institute in North Carolina; Alice Gresham Bullock, dean of Howard Law School, attended Boggs Academy in Georgia; Kathy

Hughes, founder of Radio One, Inc., attended Piney Woods School in Mississippi.

These schools are not designed to cater to the elite and the affluent. They have a rich tradition in helping families who are willing to make tremendous sacrifices in changing negative learning environments and placing their children in school settings that are able to provide more individualized attention in nurturing learning environments. These schools have a 200-year-old history in serving the academic, social, and cultural needs of generations of families who believe that much in traditional American schooling environments does not facilitate the growth and development of African-American students.

The creation of greater freedoms in the choice of educational alternatives is critical to closing the gap between socioeconomic differences in the community. Particularly in the twenty-first century, the African-American independent school continues to hold great promise as an alternative model in the education of African-American youth.

Today, nearly 70,000 African-American youths attend independent, community-based schools across the United States. These students constitute the second-largest group of African Americans outside the nation's public school systems, exceeded only by the number of African Americans enrolled in the nation's Catholic school systems.

A good education is a sound foundation for success.

There are over 400 independent black schools across America. They provide options in education for thousands of families who want to give their children incentives to succeed, pride in who they are and their accomplishments, and a feeling of self-worth and productivity.

African-American parents are faced with the challenge of whether it is wise to depend almost completely on government sponsorship of education or to balance that support with broader options from other educational environments. The independent black school has a long track record in the quest for independence in education. It should be seen as one of the great equalizers for positive change in the advancement of the educational, economic, and political condition of African Americans.

Joan Davis Ratteray is president of the Institute for Independent Education.

Two Worlds, Separate and Inherently Unequal

ROBERT W. ETHRIDGE

Affirmative action programs have enabled employers to hire individuals who reflect the race and gender of the market they are trying to cultivate. Companies, corporations, colleges, and universities have launched successful affirmative action campaigns to identify and hire well-qualified blacks at high levels within their organizations.

Salaries have been commensurate with the level of the position. Based on the analysis of the 2000 Census and more recent data, black incomes have never been higher, and black unemployment is at an all-time low among the middle- and

upper-middle-class blacks who are qualified.

Emphasizing education from an early age is an important part of parenting.

On the other hand, the median household income for black families fell in 2001; nearly 23 percent of black Americans were living below the poverty level that same year. To close the gap between middle-class blacks and those below the poverty level, training programs in computer usage and other technical areas

need to be funded at higher levels, so that single parents can afford to work full time.

All blacks should continue the push for upward mobility through affirmative action. Blacks need to become more politically active in both parties, so the agenda for the improved welfare of black Americans is uppermost on the minds of politicians. Multiracial coalitions should be formed to monitor the decision-making processes at all levels to ensure equity.

Robert W. Ethridge is president of the American Association for Affirmative Action.

The Polarizing of Black America

MILTON BINS

Both portraits of American blacks are correct, provided you let them stand alone as two separate and distinct descriptive statements. However, if you try to use the two portraits, as stated, to generate ideas about the serious and complex questions of how to advance the economic and political conditions of the American black, then you are immediately faced with some very difficult analytical and substantive problems.

The reason for the difficulty is that Portrait B states changes in the economic condition of American blacks for a single year, namely 2001, whereas Portrait A is a qualitative statement about the economic condition of black Americans at this point in time. Also, the assump-

tion that we are not somewhat integrated into the larger society and must continue to function and think as an isolated group just doesn't match up with the realities of black Americans today.

It is necessary for one to get out of the box created by the so-called Portraits A and B to offer some ideas on how to advance the economic and political conditions of the American black. First we must not allow ourselves to be viewed, described, or analyzed as isolated from what is happening in the larger society and to other Americans.

We are all becoming more polarized on the basis of socioeconomic status, educational backgrounds, technological skill levels, wealth creation, and competitive capabilities in an increasingly networked, global information-age economy. We must all be focused on our freedom, our economic agenda, and our collective interests and security as Americans, not as blocs or identifiable groups.

With respect to freedom, economic security, upward mobility, open access to all available opportunities, and nondiscrimination, no American can be left behind.

Milton Bins is the chief executive officer and chairman of the Douglass Policy Institute.

The Importance of Education and Other Goals

JOSEPH M. CONRAD JR.

I have given thought to this issue over the years, and I am certain that African Americans must come to a consensus establishing and prioritizing of quality-of-life goals for African Americans as a group, before we can expect to improve any condition we find ourselves in. To promote general advancement, all of us must be prepared to totally support this priority list of quality-of-life goals that will advance the group both in the long and short run.

African Americans must determine and prioritize these goals. My suggested list is first, education; second, economic development; third, home ownership; and fourth, health and safety. For me, these are the most important goals we should have as a group.

Education is first because knowledge is the power that frees and keeps one free. Ignorance is the shackle that permits the ignorant to be controlled by others. Economic development is second because a reliable income permits one to plan the future, a future that should include business ownership so we might own the jobs we need. Home ownership is third because it is the best and surest way to begin to acquire wealth. Health and safety is fourth because without these we will not be assured of our future.

Whatever goals we select we should support with everything we can muster, spiritually, politically, and economically. No politicians—black, white, brown, or red, Democrat, Republican, or independent—will be able to expect our vote, if these goals for African Americans are not political priorities for them. Each of these goals will have subgoals that are to be monitored, measured, and supported, just as are the main goals.

Once we are able to establish and prioritize quality-of-life goals for African Americans, we will have more than party labels to guide us. Our list of self-interest goals can be used to measure candidates, to determine to what degree they support the interests of African Americans, and then to guide us in our voting. Then and only then will African Americans experience economic and political advancement here in the United States and indeed in these Americas.

How can African Americans meet to formulate these priority goals? The various civil rights organizations might come together to help. In addition to protecting the civil rights gains of the past 50 years, these organizations might call together their counterpart organizations along with the various religious organizations and associations to develop these goals and criteria for monitoring their accomplishments.

With these goals as signposts for economic and political growth and development, African Americans might look to sustained advancement over the next 20 years.

Joseph M. Conrad Jr. is with the National Catholic Conference for Interracial Justice.

The Polarizing of Black America

LEMUEL BERRY JR.

The challenge set before African Americans and their advancement in today's economic and political environment is overwhelming. The environment many African Americans are confronted with today is not much different than that prior to and after the Civil Rights movement. Moving to the next level, in my humble opinion, requires diverse action, which would involve educational institutions, educational agencies, government, and community.

Initially, I believe the infrastructure of the African-American family must be improved. It is imperative that the matriarch and patriarch in the family provide a nurturing experience that exhibits the value of education, personal development, and sense of community. The African-American community must experience a major decline in young black males being incarcerated, while at the same time there must be an increase in graduation rates from high school and entrance into college.

The role of educational institutions must also be better organized and filled with support mechanisms for children. To this point, schools must employ better-qualified teachers who are knowledgeable of social and cultural differences. Too often, students of color are stigmatized because they do not fit the so-called normal student model. Furthermore, what person in his right mind can identify or justify what is normal in a society that is more diverse than any in the world?

Political leaders and government must also play a greater role in supporting community- and school-based programs that underwrite the core of developmental experiences, which directly influence a child and his respect for self, education, and community. A great deal is to be gained by American society if government plays a major role in correcting those unaddressed issues in the lives of African Americans.

Lemuel Berry Jr. is executive director of the National Association of African American Studies and vice president for academic affairs at the University of New England in Biddeford, Maine.

Voting Is the Key to Economic and Political Power

REP. MAXINE WATERS

We must begin owning our communities.

We must learn to save our money to invest in business opportunities, our children's education, and home ownership, even though lack of access to capital remains a major problem. Banks and financial institutions continue to redline, while predatory payday loan and check-cashing operators continue to prey on our communities. We must be able to implement the Community Reinvestment Act to force banks to invest in our communities.

We cannot continue having the highest unemployment rate (nearly twice that of whites), due to discrimination or lack of competitiveness, and the highest number of school dropouts. We must be prepared to take advantage of available opportunities and push education as our No. 1 priority.

To remove barriers to economic opportunity, our elected officials must have the clout to lead in legislating, deal making, and leveraging. Attaining and exercising political power begins in the voting booth.

In the most recent election, of the 20 million black Americans eligible to vote, only 4.8 million, fewer than one in four, actually went to the polls.

By not voting, we literally threw away our ability to influence elections in majority-white districts where our vote could decide the outcome. We abridged our power to negotiate with candidates in the 2004 presidential election and effectively neutralized black elected officials' power to negotiate for leadership roles in their respective elective bodies.

We must find a way to increase black voter turnout. This is the basis for economic and political power.

Maxine Waters represents California's thirty-fifth district in Congress. She is the founder and president of the Black Women's Forum.

For further reading, see "Proud Lion of Baltimore–The Life and Legacy of Frederick Douglass" on page 156 of The World & I, February 2003

"HE MAY MEAN GOOD, BUT HE DO SO DOGGONE POOR!":
A Critical Analysis of Recently Published "Social Conscience" Children's Literature

by Jonda C. McNair

"The Negro has met with as great injustice in American literature as he has in American life."

(Sterling Brown, 1933; 180)

Because literature is a sociocultural product, it provides a reflection of societal values, beliefs, and attitudes. Williams (1977) contends that literature also serves as a means by which to maintain the social order and the hegemony of dominant groups. In this article I will provide a critical analysis of recently published "social conscience" children's books, the majority of which perpetuate racial stereotypes and misrepresent African-American experiences and perspectives. According to Sims (1982), "social conscience" books are written mainly by white authors and directed mainly at white readers in an attempt to make them aware of the problems blacks face and to develop a social conscience. Before presenting the analysis of recently published social conscience books, I will offer a description of Sims's research.

"CULTURALLY CONSCIOUS" BOOKS

Sims (1982) conducted a content analysis of 150 children's books of contemporary realistic fiction featuring African Americans published between 1965 and 1979. She created the following typologies to categorize the books: "culturally conscious" books, "melting pot" books, and "social conscience" books. According to Sims, "the label culturally conscious suggests that elements in the text, not just the pictures, make it clear that the book consciously seeks to depict a fictional Afro-American life experience"[49]. *Mirandy and Brother Wind,* by Patricia McKissack, is an example of a culturally conscious children's book. Recurring features within culturally conscious books include language that "reflects the well known syntactic features of Black English," descriptions of skin colors, nicknames and names that are common with African-

American community, as well as its historical and cultural traditions (Sims, 1982; 68). According to Sims, "these books come closest to constituting a body of Afro-American literature for children"[49].

"MELTING POT" BOOKS

The "melting pot" books were those that ignored all racial differences among children, except for physical ones such as skin color. They were usually in the picture book format; otherwise readers would not know that the characters were black (Sims, 1982). An example of a melting pot book is *Mary Had a Little Lamb,* written by Sarah Hale and photo-illustrated by Bruce McMillan. This book is a contemporary reinterpretation of the well-known poem accompanied by photographs of an African-American girl. There are no textual changes, and if it weren't for the pictures, readers would likely assume that Mary was white. Recurring features within the melting pot books include nuclear families, standard English, and specific details indicating that, although, authors were making an attempt to be color-blind, they might have been "sometimes influenced by some unconscious internalized images of Afro-Americans partially resulting from the negative images of the past"[43]. Although the "melting pot" books ignored the "cultural distinctness" of African Americans, they were considered by Sims to be an improvement over the last typology, "social conscience" books, which I will explore in greater detail throughout this article.

"SOCIAL CONSCIENCE" BOOKS/STORY VARIATIONS

Sims writes, "in most cases the 'social conscience' books were created from an ethnocentric, non-Afro-American perspective which resulted in the perpetuation of undesirable attitudes"[18]. She also noted that many of the books within this typology were poorly written and frequently contained "happily ever after" endings, stereotypes, and implausible episodes. The social conscience books that Sims analyzed were contemporary realistic fiction in that they focused mainly on the civil rights era and had been written during that time period as well.

Awareness of Sims's work during the 1980s contributed to an increase in the number and proportion of culturally conscious books for children, written and illustrated by African-American authors and artists, later in the decade and into the 1990s (Miller-Lachmann, 1992). A generation of younger authors such as Rita Williams-Garcia, Sharon Draper, Christopher Paul Curtis, Karen English, and Andrea Davis Pinkney joined the pioneering and prolific older generation of Patricia and Fredrick McKissack, Virginia Hamilton, Walter Dean Myers, Eloise Greenfield, Elizabeth Fitzgerald Howard, Mildred D. Taylor, and others. During this era, fewer children's books by white authors and illustrators depicted African Americans in significant roles. Debates raged as to whether outsiders could present African-American characters effectively (Cooperative Children's Book Center, 1991; Rochman, 1993).

Concerns about the writer's background appeared to diminish by the end of the 1990s. However, the emergence of white authors writing about the African-American experience—often focusing on multiracial identity or relationships between blacks and whites past and present—raised questions about the reemergence of the self-conscious social conscience book. Had white writers and publishers learned anything from Sims's scholarship and the acclaimed works of African-American authors? Were these new books a recycling of the themes and stereotypes of previous works, or did they reflect a new understanding?

To find the answer, I analyzed 12 social conscience books for intermediate readers and young adults published between 1998 and 2002. Eight of the novels were historical fiction, while the remaining four were contemporary realistic fiction. As I read through the novels, I noted problematic aspects within the books and generated the following categories: stereotypes, active whites/passive blacks, beauty standards, language, and white perspective. In the remainder of the article, I will discuss the four story variations within the social conscience books that Sims examined, provide brief descriptions of the 12 recently published social conscience books, and explore the problematic aspects within them as well as the importance of teaching to conduct critical reading of texts.

Sims (1982) noted the following story variations within the social conscience books: (1) "School desegregation—marching into the lion's den," (2) "How to behave when the black folks move in" or "Guess who's coming to dinner?" (3) "Doing it the right way—working within the system," and (4) "Learning to get along with whites." It is interesting to note that the recently published books that could be categorized as social conscience books are remarkably consistent in regard to these four variations. For instance, *The Starplace,* which illustrates the first story variation, is a historical novel that takes place during the early 1960s in Quiver, a small town in Oklahoma. Celeste, an

African American, becomes the first black student to integrate the local junior high school. She is befriended by Frannie, a European American, who on a number of occasions stands up for Celeste when she is confronted with racial discrimination. Frannie and Celeste become friends partly through a mutual love of singing, and Frannie constantly describes her friend's voice in superlative terms.

Crossing Jordan, an example of the second variation, is the story of the friendship that develops between two girls. Jemmie, an African American, and Cassie, a European American, meet after Jemmie's family moves in next door. Cassie's father is a racist and builds a fence between his home and that of his new neighbors which, according to him, "even Michael Jordan couldn't see over"[2]. The ending of the story appears contrived and implausible. Cassie's father, who has expressed strong racist sentiments throughout the entire book, attends a potlock dinner with Jemmie's family. Although he had expressed anger at his wife for scheduling the event, he ultimately offers the following prayer: "Thank you Lord for food and friends"[140].

The Speed of Light illustrates the third social conscience story variation, "Doing it the right way." This story is set in the 1950s and is told from the perspective of Audrey Ina, an 11-year-old Jewish girl. Her father is attempting to help a black man who works for him obtain employment as a police officer. The story focuses on the anti-Semitism that Audrey Ina's family faces as a result of trying to "work within the system" and help Mr. Cardwell and his family.

Starfish Summer illustrates the fourth story variation, "Learning to get along with whites." In this contemporary story Amy is spending the summer at the beach with her aunt, and she wants to become friends with Crystal, who is initially hostile. Amy, a European American, learns that Crystal, an African American, is hesitant to become friends with her because the last friend whom Crystal met at the beach hurt her feelings and didn't return any of her letters. Although there was no racial conflicts, the book, in my opinion, is a social conscience book because Amy's main goal throughout the book seems to be solving Crystal's problem. Once she figures it out, she and Crystal become friends.

BRIEF DESCRIPTIONS OF THE REMAINING SOCIAL CONSCIENCE BOOKS

In order to provide contextual information for the remaining social conscience books that I will discuss throughout this article, I offer brief descriptions of them. *F Is for Freedom,* which takes place a decade before the Civil War, is the story of a young white girl who discovers that her parents are abolitionists and their home is a stop along the Underground Railroad. She takes an active role in helping a family of slaves to freedom. In *Bright Freedom's Song,* the main protagonist is a young white girl named Bright who discovers that her father, also an abolitionist, was once an indentured servant. Bright, too, begins to take an active role in helping to transport slaves to freedom in this story set several decades before the Civil War.

North by Night takes place in 1851 and through journal entries describes the experiences of a teenage white girl whose parents' home in Ohio is a station on the Underground Railroad. She befriends a runaway slave who is approximately her age and later takes the baby of this slave to freedom after the slave dies. *Stealing Freedom* is about a young black slave named Anna who travels on the Underground Railroad in hopes of being reunited with family members who have escaped to Canada. It too is set in the 1850s.

Darby takes place in South Carolina in 1926 and focuses on nine-year-old Darby, a white girl who wants to be a reporter. Darby is inspired to write because one of her closest friends, Evette, a black girl, is a talented writer. Darby eventually writes a story on racial equality for the local newspaper that creates controversy. *Jericho Walls* is set during the civil rights era, in 1957 in Alabama. It describes the experiences of Jo Clawson, a 12-year-old white girl who is the daughter of a preacher, and her friendship with a black boy named Lucas.

The two remaining novels, *Foreign Exchange* and *Zack,* are contemporary realistic fiction. *Foreign Exchange* is a collection of poems told from the perspective of several teenagers that focuses on the murder of a white girl named Kristen Clarke. *Zack* is the story of a biracial Canadian teenager with a Jewish father and an African-American mother who has never met his mother's side of the is family. Zack eventually decides to travel to Mississippi to meet his maternal grandfather.

PROBLEMATIC ASPECTS OF THE SOCIAL CONSCIENCE BOOKS

Sims (1982) writes, "The most telling criticism of white authors writing fiction about Afro-American experience has been that their own experiences growing up white in a society that confers automatic and inherent social superiority to that condition have determined the perspective from which they write"[12]. In their attempts to shed light on issues such as prejudice and discrimination, these authors, as Sims noted, "may mean good, [but] they do so doggone poor." Thompson and Woodard (1985) state, "The credentials of the writer who undertakes a book about blacks must include a black perspective based on an appreciation of black experience. Good intentions are not enough"[40]. According to Thompson and Woodard, the social conscience books "tend to reinforce the very attitudes they are trying to dispel"[41].

STEREOTYPES

Most of these 12 recent social conscience books contain both positive and negative stereotypes associated with African Americans. The depiction of blacks as musically gifted is an example of a positive stereotype. For instance, in *The Starplace,* Celeste's musicality is described as far beyond that of her schoolmates. After she sings in class for the first time, "no one seemed to be breathing"[63]. The music teacher thanks Celeste "in a voice like someone would use to thank a person who has just donated a lifesaving kidney to them. It was as though she was thanking Celeste not just for being wonderful, but for restoring her faith in music and even humanity itself, at least at the junior high variety"[63-64].

In *Crossing Jordan,* Jemmie's grandmother sings, "I am a wayfarin' stranger just traveling through this world of woe" while painting the fence[13]. She sings on at least three other occasions as well. In *Speed of Light,* Audrey Ina's housekeeper breaks into song while talking to family members and she "believed in signs"[23]. This belief in the supernatural constitutes another common stereotype, as demonstrated by the maid Abilene's belief in signs in *Jericho Walls:*

> "Look there," Abilene said. A bird fluttered against the window, staring in with darting eyes, then turned and flew back to a nest in the crook of our tree.
> "Now, what you know 'bout that! Y'all got a mockingbird in the neighborhood. Him flutterin' against the window that away means he's trying to bring good luck."[25]

Broderick (1973) noted in her book *The Image of the Black in Children's Fiction* that blacks were frequently depicted as both musically inclined and superstitious. Although some people may not view a focus on blacks' musical talents as offensive, according to Broderick (1973) "the cumulative impact" of portrayals such as those aforementioned "is to reinforce the misconception that all blacks have rhythm"[134].

Another disturbing feature of several of these recently published social conscience books is the tendency of the authors to describe how large African-American females are even when they are minor, insignificant characters. For instance, in *Zack,* the author describes two female relatives that Zack sees at a picnic: "Sharon was the widest woman I had ever seen. Her huge buttocks rose and fell like pistons as she walked. Rose was big too, but her sister-in-law made her look almost slender"[140]. In *Stealing Freedom,* the main character, Anna, describes her Aunt Mimi as "moving slowly because of her plumpness"[15]. She later describes a black woman with whom she lives while traveling on the Underground Railroad as "plump as a baked apple"[199]. This same woman "made a deep indentation in the mattress" when she climbed in bed with Anna, due to her "large form"[204].

It is interesting to note that one doesn't find any descriptions of large European-American females throughout the books. When descriptions focus solely on the size of large black women while ignoring the size of large white women, they begin to take on racial overtones. Would an African-American author be as likely to offer descriptions such as these considering the negative stereotypes of African-American women as obese? When one considers that the authors are white, the question becomes, "Are these overweight, superstitious characters who sing based on real-life individuals whom the authors know quite well, or do they simply reflect stereotypes associated with African Americans?"

ACTIVE WHITES/PASSIVE BLACKS

Another recurring aspect within these books is the active white standing up for the passive black. Although there is nothing wrong with whites working alongside blacks in the struggle for racial equality, something is seriously wrong with whites being depicted as active agents for change while blacks stand by passively. In *Speed of Light,* for instance, at a town meeting to discuss hiring a black police officer, Audrey Ina's father does all of the talking, while Mr. Cardwell, the prospective police officer, and his family stand at the back of the room and say nothing. In *The Starplace,* Frannie stands up for Celeste on several occasions while Celeste stands by passively. For instance, while Celeste is auditioning for a singing part, several students attempt to sabotage her performance by coughing, dropping notebooks, and giggling until Frannie "ran down and saved the day" by causing a disturbance of her own[129]. Her quick action forces several of the students to leave the audition so Celeste can sing without interruption. Celeste doesn't say or do anything other than stop singing and almost begin to cry.

On another occasion, Celeste is refused shoes, for sanitary reasons supposedly, at a bowling alley. According to Frannie, "Celeste's eyes were bright with embarrassment. I could feel her straining to escape back through the crowd, so I grabbed her by the sleeve to make her stay"[161]. Frannie then explains to the clerk that she and Celeste are at the bowling alley with the school. Again, Celeste doesn't stand up for herself.

In *Bright Freedom's Song,* the white protagonist, Bright, also appears to save the day by volunteering to transport a freed slave named Marcus along with other black slaves by wagon at night to a safe location on the Underground Railroad. Bright exclaims, "A Negro out at night all alone with a wagon hiding slaves?.... I have the best chance to get them away from here"[115]. Maybe it was dangerous for blacks to be alone traveling at night, but Marcus is a free, educated man who appears competent enough to transport slaves on his own. Consider Harriet Tubman, who most likely was alone at night many times with runaway slaves, yet she was one of the most successful conductors on the Underground Railroad.

BEAUTY STANDARDS

In several of these social conscience books, physical features associated with African Americans are depicted in a negative manner while the physical features associated with European Americans are described positively. For instance, when Bright, as a young child, sees a black slave hiding in the family's henhouse for the first time, she exclaims, "The devil is in the henhouse. I saw it. With two big eyes"[6]. Zack, a biracial teen, offers the following account of his African-American mother:

In spite of what Dad thought my mother wasn't beautiful. Her nose—which I had inherited, lucky me—was a little too prominent and broad, the curved nostrils too wide. But she was pretty, with velvety, black unblemished skin, big eyes and a deep honey-mooth voice.[26]

While zack insists his mother is pretty but not beautiful, which is itself puzzling, one is struck by his impression of her wide nostrils.

In *Foreign Exchange,* the girl who is considered the prettiest of all, Kristen Clarke, has blonde hair and blue eyes. The girls are jealous of her, and the boys, black ones included, think she is hot. Similarly, in *Crossing Jordan,* Cassie's sister is depicted as being "pretty as an angel," although the physical descriptions of her speak only of her long blonde hair[23]. Cassie is jealous of her sister, and even Jemmie, an African American, tells her "that sister of yours has the prettiest hair in the world"[38]. This statement is reflective of the author's ethnocentric standards. African Americans do not look on blonde hair in the same manner in which European Americans view it.

LANGUAGE

The dialogue of the black characters in several of these social conscience books was questionable and appeared inconsistent and culturally inauthentic. For instance, in *Bright Freedom's Song,* Marcus, the free and educated former slave, speaks in the following manner with Bright:

You do be right smart.... Yes, your papa and I have been friends for many years. I owe him my life and my freedom, the lives of my wife and others, too. And I believe that he owes me his freedom as well.... Slaves come in all sizes and all colors in some places, Missy.... Here and now, people like me be slaves. But white people have been slaves in the past. Some are still slaves, though they are not called by that name. The Children of Israel were slaves of the Egyptians until Moses led them out of bondage. Yes, your papa was once bonded. But I reckon it be your papa's place to tell you his side of this story. You better ask him.... I be not sure what I should tell one so young.[16]

Later in the same conversation Marcus begins to tell Bright about his own past.

I ran. As fast as I could I went, but men wearing face paint I had never seen caught me. One of them threw me over his shoulder. The next morning we came to his village. He spoke to me but I did not know his tongue. As I learned to do the hard and dirty work of his village, I learned to speak and understand his tongue. I was the slave of my father's enemies. The man who owned me made me work hard, but he did not beat me. From him, I learned that his people had killed my family.... I lived there for a few harvesttimes and grew to be a man. Then another people came in war to attack the village and killed my master. The winners of that war sold me to slavers.[17-18]

All of a sudden, Marcus is able to speak perfect "standard" English without the use of any "be's." Although it is common for educated African Americans to code switch depending on the context, Marcus's speech is notably different within the same context.

In *Crossing Jordan*, Jemmie frequently uses the word "girl" in her speech to begin and end sentences. Consider the following passage:

> "Do you like to run?"
> "Run? Girl, I don't run, I fly.
> Can't nobody beat me."
> "Bet I could."
> "Dream on, girl."[15]

While the word "girl" is used in this manner by some African Americans, it appears so much in Jemmie's dialogue throughout the book that it begins to sound culturally inauthentic. Just as Jemmie uses the word "girl" in her speech, her grandmother uses the words "Lord" and "child." There is a fine line between how some blacks talk and how some white authors think some blacks talk. However, it must be noted that blacks are linguistically diverse. Many African Americans speak "standard English" consistently while other African Americans, myself included, switch back and forth between "standard" English and black vernacular depending on the context.

WHITE PERSPECTIVE

There were numerous details within these social conscience books that I considered reflective of white perspectives. I am fully aware that whites are not monolithic; however, I believe that there are certain viewpoints that are more common among whites than people of color. For instance, in *Jericho Walls,* there is an episode involving *The Adventures of Huckleberry Finn* that seems troubling, implausible, and indicative of the white author's perspective. Jo, the white daughter of the preacher, introduces her friend Lucas to this book, and the two of them begin reading it together. Surprisingly, there is no discussion or dialogue between the two of them in regard to Mark Twain's repeated use of the word "nigger." I find it difficult to believe that during the 1950s in Alabama, Lucas would not have voiced any complaints about the constant use of the word. Although literary critics contend that Twain was being satirical, I doubt if these two children would have taken this into consideration. After reading the book, they decide to build a raft, and Lucas tells Jo that he wants to be Huckleberry, to which she replies, "You can't be Huckleberry.... You ain't white. You're colored, so you have to be Ole Jim"[79]. Lucas insists that he does not want to be Jim, and Jo responds by saying, "You shut up, Lucas! I say you gotta be Ole Jim"[79]. While aware of why Lucas might have wanted to be the main character instead of his black sidekick, the author doesn't seem to realize that the use of the word "nigger" may have been especially uncomfortable for a black person living during the era of segregation.

Zack contains a number of misconceptions. The author assumes that people of all races can pull themselves up by their bootstraps with hard work. Zack's father makes the following comment to his son as an explanation for why "the Jews are still around": "Because, when things get bad, the Jews don't sit around in bars... or loiter on street corners... moaning and complaining about being oppressed"[51]. This way of thinking implies that certain groups of people, such as African Americans, could do more to improve their condition with hard work, and it reflects the bias of the author, a European American. This belief in meritocracy is more common among European Americans than people of color. Although there is anti-Semitism in American society, Jews of European ancestry have the luxury of benefiting from white privilege, which offers them numerous advantages over other groups whose members can't "pass" for white.

Another characteristic of the white perspective is the depiction of whites as color-blind. Zack dates a white girl, and on one occasion she invites him over to her house. He asks her if her parents are aware that he is biracial, and she responds by telling him that they don't care. Zack visits her home and meets her parents without any problems.

In the novel-in-verse *Foreign Exchange,* Kwame, a black student, states, "I hope Jason, the guy I'm staying with,/Does not see me only in terms of black and white./I really hope he is color-blind"[96]. This statement is reflective of the author's point of view and not that of most African-American males, who are quite aware that Americans are not color-blind. Jensen (2001) states:

> At this moment in history, being color-blind is a privilege available only to white people. Non-white people do not have the luxury of pretending that color can be ignored. When an African American man is stopped on the street, he has to be conscious of what his color means to white police officers who may associate blackness with criminality.[20]

Another feature indicative of the white perspective is a superficial understanding of racism on the part of the authors. For example, in *The Starplace,* the story concludes:

> None of us—not one of our group—hung around Quiver after high school graduation. In fact, we scrambled out of there like we were being chased. After Celeste, we all understood deep in our bones that if a place refuses to be a launch pad for one person, it can't function as a launch pad for anyone.[213]

The author makes it appear as if the racism in Quiver was an anomaly that the good-hearted characters could choose to escape. I would argue, as do critical race theorists, that racism is a normal and permanent component of American life (Bell, 1992).

Another example of this treatment of racism appears in *Darby*. After Darby asks her mother if her great-granddaddy had owned any slaves, her mother replies:

Neither of your great-granddaddies ever did. Nobody in our family owned any property before the war. But the fact of the matter is that everybody working a farm had them. It was just the way. They lived from the land and to do that they needed help. There wasn't any sort of hate or anger involved, which is what everyone seems to have forgotten.[143]

At the same time as she seeks to absolve the family's ancestors, Darby's mother seems unable to make the important distinction between "help" and slave labor. She also fails to realize that racism is not necessarily about hate and anger, but instead is about a system of privileges that functions to the benefit of whites and to the detriment of blacks and other people of color.

Also indicating a white perspective is the tendency to allow black protagonists, usually slaves, to divulge their personal information and life stories to whites whom they hardly know. For example, in *Bright Freedom's Song,* Bright asks several personal questions of Marcus after meeting him for the first time. She tells him, "We are friends…. I would not say words that would take your freedom, I promise"[19]. Marcus responds by saying, "We are friends, little one…. I trust you to keep our secret"[19]. In *North by Night,* a pregnant slave named Cass confesses to Lucinda, a white abolitionist, that she is pregnant by her master, along with other personal information. Similarly, in *F is for Freedom,* a young white girl named Manda says to Hannah, a slave, "first tell me how you got away and what made you decide to try and go"[49]. Hannah then provides the details. Even in today's society, without the threat of being captured and returned to slavery, there are certain topics that many African Americans don't discuss in "mixed company," and it certainly seems unlikely that black slaves who were on the run would be as open and exhibit such blind trust in whites.

In a number of the stores in which African Americans are confronted with racial bigotry or discrimination, they are depicted as being totally forgiving of racism, as if passivity is the solution. In *Starplace,* Frannie's brother, Mitch, says to Celeste, "I'm not listening to her when she talks! She's got the wrong skin on!"117 Celeste responds by saying "Really Frannie, don't be hard on Mitch! I'll keep trying to win his confidence. Dr. King says peaceful resistance is the only way to open a closed mind and calm a fearful heart!"[122] In *Crossing Jordan,* Jemmie's mother becomes angry when she sees the fence that Cassie's father has put up between the two houses. Jemmie's grandmother remarks, "Leona, honey, let it go. Like Jesus says, turn the other cheek. Love thy neighbor"[8].

The last recurring feature reflective of white perspective is the portrayal of blacks as being content with substandard living conditions. In *Stealing Freedom,* when Anna speaks with slaves from other plantations, one of them states, "My master wasn't too bad"[104]. Another slave remarks, "Master Cahell, he fed us good"[105]. On another occasion, when Anna asks her father if the way they are treated as slaves is fair, her father responds by saying, "What is fair is up to the Good Lord, not to us"[44]. According to MacCann (1985), "this is a classic example of white perspective: the claim that blacks have no expectation of justice or a good life here on earth"[178]. In *F Is for Freedom,*

the slaves are made to eat in the closet for fear that they will be spotted by slave catchers. When they are told that they will have to eat in the closet, one of the slaves responds, "Your cooking's gonna taste as good in a closet as it does at your table. I know, 'cause we here can smell it…. Now quit your worrying about us, we're fine as beetles in a bottle full o'leaves"[80]. Unlike the authors of social conscience books, black writers of historical fiction such as Margaree King Mitchell, Christopher Paul Curtis, Patricia McKissack, Karen English, and Mildred D. Taylor depict African Americans, even those living under the direst circumstances, as people with pride, courage, and determination, not people to be pitied.

CONCLUSION

Considering the number of social conscience books that have been published over the last five years, it appears that there may be a resurgence of them. It is worth noting that Sims analyzed only contemporary realistic fiction, whereas most of the books that I analyzed are historical fiction, taking place around the Civil War or in the civil rights era. It is interesting to note that present-day white authors who confront racial issues within their books tend to focus on these two time periods. I would contend that a simplistic understanding of racism on the part of many white authors accounts for this, in that these periods are seen to highlight both the evils of racism and the potential for good-hearted whites to confront these evils.

Many of the problems Sims noted in books published between 1965 and 1979 are present in their recent counterparts. These include racial stereotypes, improbable episodes, contrived endings, literary mediocrity, and a heavy-handed presentation of the message or theme. Some of the books exhibit these flaws to a greater degree than others, as pointed out in the above sections. Hopefully, the fact that most of them were not well written and engaging will serve as a deterrent for young readers.

Although it may seem unfair and overly critical to pick out details, it is crucial to "read against" texts in order to uncover their hidden racial assumptions, however, subtle they may be. Children's books serve as a vehicle for socialization and the formation of values, beliefs, and worldviews. Hollindale (1988) states:

It might seem that values whose presence can only be convincingly demonstrated by an adult with some training in critical skills are unlikely to carry much potency with children. More probably the reverse is true: the values at stake are usually those which are taken for granted by the writer, and reflect the writer's integration in a society which unthinkingly accepts them. In turn this means that children, unless they are helped to notice what is there, will take them for granted too. Unexplained, passive values are widely shared values, and we should not underestimate the powers of reinforcement vested in quiescent and unconscious ideology.[12-13]

Most of these books perpetuate stereotypes, and all of them exhibit a European-American perspective of the black experience. Unfortunately, several of them received favorable editorial reviews. *Crossing Jordan* was selected as an American Library Association (ALA) Notable Book, while *Speed of Light* won the Sydney Taylor Award for the positive depiction of a Jewish experience. Although *Speed of Light* did show sensitivity to the Jewish experience, it was insensitive to the African-American experience. *The Starplace*, by far the worst of all the social conscience books, was described in *School Library Journal* as "a wonderful, well-written, multilayered novel with lots of appeal."

It is books such as these that induce African Americans to question the capability, if not necessarily the right, of white authors to depict accurately the black experience, although many people, mainly whites, become incensed and view this as a form of censorship. It is unlikely that social conscience books will ever disappear. Kohl (1995) contends that it is virtually impossible to shield children from all the problematic aspects of American society such as Barbie dolls, G.I. Joe toys, and racist children's literature. Therefore, it becomes necessary for educators and parents to help children develop a critical consciousness so that when they encounter books such as *The Starplace, Crossing Jordan,* and *Speed of Light,* they will not be manipulated into "an unconscious acceptance of their values" (Nodelman, 1996; 120–121). Nodelman writes, "rather than allowing ourselves to become immersed in a text to the point of accepting its description of reality as the only true one, we can define its values and so arrive at a better understanding of our own"[121].

REFERENCES

Bell, D. (1992). *Faces at the bottom of the well: The permanence of racism.* New York: Basic Books.

Broderick, M. (1973). *Image of the black in children's fiction.* New York: R. R. Bowker.

Brown, S. (1933). Negro character as seen by white authors. *Journal of Negro Education,* 179–203.

Cooperative Children's Book Center. (1991). *The multicolored mirror: Cultural substance in literature for children and young adults.* Fort Atkinson, Wis.: Highsmith Press.

Hollindale, P. (1988). Ideology and the children's book. *Signal* 55 (1): 3–22.

Jensen, R. (2001, January 5). Being color-blind does not offset innate advantages of white privilege. *Kansas City Business Journal.*

Kohl, R. (1995). *Should we burn Babar? Essays on children's literature and the power of stories.* New York: The New Press.

MacCann, D. (1985). Racism in prize-winning biographical works. In D. MacCann & G. Woodard (Eds.), *The Black American in books for children: Readings in racism.* Lanham, Md.: Scarecrow press.

Miller-Lachmann, L. (1992). *Our family, our friends, our world: An annotated guide to significant multicultural books for children and teenagers.* New Providence, N.J.: R. R. Bowker.

Nodelman, P. (1996). *The pleasures of children's literature.* New York: Longman.

Rochman, H. (1993). *Against borders: Promoting books for a multicultural world.* Chicago: ALA Publishing.

Sims, R. (1982). *Shadow and substance: Afro-American experience in contemporary children's fiction.* Urbana, Ill.: NCTE.

Thompson, J. & Woodard, G. (1985). Black perspective in books for children. In D. MacCann & G. Woodard (Eds.), *The Black American in books for children: Readings in racism.* Lanham, Md.: Scarecrow Press.

Williams, R. (1977). *Marxism and literature.* New York: Oxford Univ. Press.

CHILDREN'S BOOKS CITED

Ayres, K. (1998). *North by night.* New York: Dell Yearling.

Bell, W. (1998). *Zack.* New York: Aladdin.

Carbone, E. (1998). *Stealing freedom.* New York: Knopf.

Collier, K. (2002). *Jericho walls.* New York: Henry Holt.

Fogelin, A. (2000). *Crossing Jordan.* Atlanta: Peachtree Publishers.

Fuqua, J. S. (2002). *Darby.* Cambridge, Mass.: Candlewick Press.

Glenn, M. (1999). *Foreign exchange: A mystery in poems.* New York: William Morrow.

Gritz-Gilbert, O. (1998). *Starfish summer.* New York: HarperCollins.

Grove, V. (1999). *The starplace.* New York: Putnam.

Hale, S. (1990). *Mary had a little lamb.* New York: Scholastic.

Houston, G. (1998). *Bright freedom's song.* San Diego: Harcourt.

McKissack, P. (1988). *Mirandy and brother wind.* New York: Random House.

Rosen, S. (1999.) *Speed of light.* New York: Atheneum.

Schotter, R. (2000). *F is for freedom.* New York: Dorling Kindersley.

ABOUT THE AUTHOR

Jonda C. McNair, a former primary grade teacher, is currently a doctoral candidate in the School of Teaching and Learning at Ohio State University in Columbus.

From *Multicultural Review*, March 2003, pp. 26-32. © 2003 by The Goldman Group, Inc.

Twelve Ways to Have Students Analyze Culture

LYNDA R. WIEST

Schools serve increasingly diverse student bodies. They play an important role in helping students of different backgrounds learn to get along with one another both at school and in the community. Thinking critically about culture can help students toward that goal. In this article, I discuss a dozen ways educators can have students of any age reflect on culture and the intermingling of cultures.

Contemplate the value of diversity.

Students can think about what the world (and their lives) might be like if everyone were the same or very similar. They might write a short story about such a world. They can discuss or write an essay about ways that variety enriches or impairs their lives.

Define culture.

Culture can be a slippery concept. Have students try to define it. Ask if they belong to a culture. If so, which one? What makes it a culture? What are the pros and cons of being associated with a given culture? Can a person belong to more than one culture? If so, is this a good or bad thing, and why?

Students might come to realize that culture is a blend of factors, such as shared beliefs and ways of living, that link groups of people and frame the way that they view the world. Residents of a country or members of a tribe belong not only to their overarching culture, or macroculture, but they also belong to microcultures. These subcultures could be formed by common ethnicity, national origin (if different from the country of residence), socioeconomic status, religion, gender, age, sexual orientation, occupation, recreational interests, or other factors that groups of people may share.

Take another's perspective.

People tend to be egocentric. A most difficult and important thing to learn is an ability to see—to the degree possible—things from another person's perspective. Instructors may ask students to do a cultural immersion experience in which they participate, perhaps alone, in another culture for a brief period of time. They might attend a religious service that differs greatly from their own or join people of a different ethnicity or sexual orientation for a particular event. Students can describe the experience and how it felt to be a minority person in another culture. They can explain what they enjoyed, what they found difficult, and how they tried to negotiate the situation if it was uncomfortable.

Students might interview a person from another culture to gain insight into their life experience. Other activities may involve having students write an essay from the point of view of someone who differs from them culturally, or discussing an imagined experience of relocating to a culturally different region.

Analyze social behavior.

Examine the social behaviors of human beings, such as a tendency to congregate with others like oneself. Minority groups sometimes are criticized for being "separatist" and not mixing to a greater degree with members of the dominant culture. Students should reflect on their own habits. Most likely they spend much of their time with others who are similar to themselves in some manner, be it by ethnicity, gender, a shared pastime, or the like. Students can analyze why people tend to do this, the pros and cons, and if and why some groups (in particular, subordinate or marginalized groups) might be more likely to behave this way.

Speculate the meaning of observed actions and interactions.

What does it mean if a person winks at you? Is she interested in you? Did something get caught in his eye? Does she have a natural eye twitch? Considering various reasons for observed individual and group behaviors can help students think more broadly about people's intentions. A number of good books exist that discuss various cultural behaviors, including body language. Among these are *Do's and Taboos Around the World* and *Multicultural Manners: New Rules of Etiquette for a Changing Society*.

Students might brainstorm various interpretations of a picture or video clip they view together. In this way they might better understand the difficulty of assigning meaning to people's behavior and why written history, which is heavily interpretive and selective in nature, is necessarily subjective.

Interpret language.

Examine overt and covert meanings in terminology, grammatical constructions, and dialogue. What does a boy imply when he tells another boy he is "acting like a girl" or "throws a ball like a girl"? What does it mean to say two groups of people are like "cowboys and Indians"? Does language influence people's thought and behavior? Students can analyze language they hear in daily conversations, on television, in movies, or in song lyrics and that which they read in books or magazines.

Analyze and compare cultural customs.

Students can deconstruct their own cultural customs to interpret them in terms of historical roots, past and present significance, and evolution over time. They may realize that some customs have, or once had, a purpose, whereas others are more arbitrary.

By comparing customs, students may see cultural parallels. What similarities and differences exist between a belief in Hopi Kachinas and belief in an American Santa Claus or Easter Bunny? How does a Hopi belief that their people emerged onto the earth's surface through a hole in the Grand Canyon (a sipapu, or spirit hole) compare to a Christian belief in creationism? Are some beliefs or customs more valid than others? Students can develop understanding that "different" does not equate with "less than," and that customs are human constructions that influence world views and behavior.

Explore change in and alternatives to habitual behavior.

Discuss ways that customs have changed over time. For example, In what ways have wedding ceremonies changed in recent decades to reduce sexism in these rituals? Have church traditions changed over time to mirror societal change? How have students' family traditions changed over time and why? Can students identify customs, traditions, or typical behaviors in society, family, or friendship groups that they would like to change? Why, and is the change possible or likely?

These kinds of discussions will help students see that customs and behaviors are human constructs and choices that are subject to change. Students gain skill in creative thinking inclined toward seeing alternatives to group and individual behaviors. They also develop a belief in their individual and collective potential to effect change and have a tendency to be more flexible and solution-minded.

Examine sociotypes and stereotypes.

Sociotypes are characteristics that tend to be true across a particular group of people, such as the fact that most men have short hair. A stereotype, however, is applied to each member of a group. Assuming that all men have short hair, for example, might cause someone to mistake a long-haired male for a female.

Students can discuss where stereotypes originate (e.g., from a grain of truth, such as a sociotype) and how they are perpetuated (e.g., through jokes or the media). They can consider whether stereotypes are harmful or serve a purpose. Blonde jokes, for example, might be considered harmful because they create subconscious impressions of blondes as unintelligent, similar to stereotypical impressions of people with Southern accents. Some students might claim that stereotypes can be useful. A female might say that her notion that all men want, and can be aggressive about, sex is a safety measure because it causes her to avoid being alone with unfamiliar men. Another student might say stereotypes that are based on knowledge of specific cultures help a person make a "best guess" about appropriate initial interactions with persons of other cultures.

Identify sources of intercultural conflict.

Various types of conflict arise among different macrocultures (e.g., different nations) and microcultures (e.g., subgroups within a nation). Students can reflect on reasons for cultural conflict. What social, political, or other factors, for example, underlie conflict between the upper and lower classes?

Propose solutions to intercultural problems.

Students can exercise deep and creative thinking by generating possible solutions to problems that exist among different cultural groups. They might seek means for improving intercultural communication and understanding in general or in their own school or classroom.

Devise social action measures.

Students can brainstorm and plan specific social action measures to address some of their concerns about intercultural problems. They could then put a plan into action. Critical and creative thinking would arise naturally as students evaluate the progress of their projects and redirect them as needed.

Cultural knowledge is useful. Even more important is an ability and inclination to think critically and creatively. All students are quite capable of this type of thinking.

Students who delve into important issues concerning cultural difference will be better prepared to conduct their lives from a standpoint of knowledge and understanding.

Key words: culture, diversity; customs, perspective, language

REFERENCES

Axtell, R. E., ed. 1993. *Do's and taboos around the world.* Canada: John Wiley and Sons.

Dresser, N. 1996. *Multicultural manners: New rules of etiquette for a changing society.* Canada: John Wiley and Sons.

Lynda R. Wiest is a professor in the Curriculum and Instruction department at the University of Nevada, in Reno.

From *The Clearing House*, January/February 2003, pp. 136-138. © 2003 by Heldref Publications, 1319, Eighteenth St., NW, Washington, DC 20036-1802. Reprinted with permission of the Helen Dwight Reid Educational Foundation.

Language Differences or Learning Difficulties

The Work of the Multidisciplinary Team

Spencer J. Salend and AltaGracia Salinas

Maria moved to the United States from Mexico and was placed in Ms. Shannon's fourth-grade class where she sat quietly at her desk and kept to herself. Whenever directions were given, she seemed lost and later had difficulty completing tasks and participating in class discussions. During teacher-directed activities, Maria often either looked around to see what her classmates were doing and then mimicked them, or played with materials at her desk.

Ms. Shannon was concerned about Maria's lack of progress in developing English proficiency and her inability to pay attention and complete her work. Ms. Shannon thought Maria might have a learning disability and referred her to the multidisciplinary team to determine if she needed special education. The team organized the assessment process for Maria by considering the following questions:

- Who can assist the team in making decisions about Maria's educational program?
- What factors should the team consider in determining Maria's educational strengths and needs?
- What strategies should the team employ to assess Maria's educational strengths and needs?
- Should the team recommend a special education placement for Maria?

Educators often refer students like Maria for placement in special education (Ortiz, 1997). As Ortiz indicated, students learning a second language and students with learning disabilities often exhibit similar difficulties with learning, attention, social skills, and behavioral and emotional balance. As a result, multidisciplinary teams are increasingly working with educators like Ms. Shan-

non to conduct meaningful assessments and determine appropriate educational programs for a growing number of students whose primary language is not English.

Recommendations for Multidisciplinary Teams

Using the experiences of Maria and her teachers, this article provides recommendations for helping multidisciplinary teams accurately and fairly assess second-language learners and differentiate language differences from learning difficulties. The article includes six recommendations, as follows:

- Diversify the composition of the multidisciplinary teams and offer training.
- Compare student performance in both the native and secondary languages.
- Consider the processes and factors associated with second-language acquisition.
- Employ alternatives to traditional standardized testing.
- Identify diverse life experiences that may affect learning.
- Analyze the data and develop an appropriate educational plan.

These recommendations also can assist multidisciplinary teams in developing educational programs for second-language learners and in complying with the Individuals with Disabilities Education Act (IDEA), which states that students should not be identified as having a disability if their eligibility and school related difficulties are based on their proficiency in English, or their lack of opportunity to receive instruction in reading or mathematics.

Diversify the Composition of the Multidisciplinary Teams and Offer Training

IDEA requires that a multidisciplinary team of professionals and family members, with the student when appropriate, make important decisions concerning the education of students referred for special education. Initially, the team determines if students are in need of and eligible for special education services. When teachers refer second-language learners to the multidisciplinary team, the team frequently faces many challenges, such as differentiating linguistic and cultural differences from learning difficulties, and developing an appropriate educational program that addresses students' linguistic, cultural, and experiential backgrounds.

The composition and training of the multidisciplinary team are critical factors in determining the educational needs of second-language learners (Ochoa, Robles-Pina, Garcia, & Breunig 1999). Therefore, the team should include family and community members, as well as professionals who are fluent in the student's native language, understand the student and the family's culture, and can help collect and interpret the data in culturally and linguistically appropriate ways. The inclusion of these people allows the team to learn about the family's and the student's cultural perspective and experiential and linguistic background, and to assist in the determination of the origins of the student's learning difficulties. Team members can help determine what students' learning difficulties can be explained by sociocultural perspectives, experiential factors, and sociolinguistic variables.

The composition of multidisciplinary teams for second-language learners should include educators who are trained in assessing second-language learners and designing educational programs to meet their varied needs. Such membership may include English as a Second Language (ESL) teachers, bilingual educators, and migrant educators. Whereas ESL teachers offer instruction in English to help students build on their existing English language skills, bilingual educators teach students in both their native language and in English. Because bilingual educators are fluent in the family's native language, they can be instrumental in involving family and community members in the team process and in assessing students' skills in their native language. In the case of migrant students like Maria, the team also can benefit from the input of migrant educators, who provide individualized instruction to migrant students and serve as a liaison between the family, the school and the community (Salend, 2001).

For example, the multidisciplinary team assembled for Maria was expanded to include Ms. Garcia, a bilingual migrant educator who worked with Maria and her family in their home and had training and experience with the second language acquisition process, as well as in working with students from culturally and linguistically diverse backgrounds. Ms. Garcia worked with other members of the team to gather information about Maria's school, home-life and experiential background, to interact with and collect information from Maria, her mother, and other family members, to assess Maria's skills in Spanish, and to identify strategies to support Maria's learning.

The multidisciplinary team can foster the success of the process by working as a collaborative and interactive team (Chase Thomas, Correa, & Morsink, 2001; Salend, 2001). The collaborative and interactive nature of the team can be enhanced by agreeing upon goals, learning about each other's beliefs, experiences and expertise, understanding and coordinating each other's roles, being sensitive to cross-cultural perspectives and communication styles, establishing equal status relationships, and addressing differences directly and immediately. Successful teams adopt a problem solving approach and employ effective interpersonal and communication skills so that all team members feel comfortable identifying issues to be considered by the team, collecting and sharing information, seeking clarification from others, participating in discussions, and making decisions via consensus.

Multidisciplinary teams work with educators to conduct meaningful assessments and determine appropriate educational programs for a growing number of students whose primary language is not English.

Teams can enhance the effectiveness of the process for second-language learners by offering training to team members. Teams should provide this training to all school personnel, and it can help the team members be aware of the effect of sociocultural perspectives, experiential backgrounds, and linguistic variables on students' behavior and school performance. Team members also will benefit from training in employing culturally responsive instructional, behavior management and mental health interventions, understanding the second language acquisition process and the problems associated with the assessment of students from culturally and linguistically diverse backgrounds, and selecting and adapting assessment instruments (Salend, Dorney, & Mazo, 1997).

Teams often face mismatches between members of the team and second-language learners in terms of their different cultural, linguistic, and socioeconomic backgrounds (Gay, 2002).

- What is my definition of diversity?

- What are my perceptions of students from different racial and ethnic groups? With language or dialects different from mine?
- What are the sources of these perceptions?
- How do I respond to my students based on these perceptions?
- What kinds of information, skills, and resources do I need to acquire to effectively teach from a multicultural perspective?
- In what ways do I collaborate with other educators, family members and community groups to address the needs of all my students? (p. 4).

Thus, team members may find it helpful to engage in activities to examine their own cultural perspectives and consider how their cultural beliefs affect their expectations, beliefs, and behaviors and may differ from those held by students and their families (Cartledge, Kea, & Ida, 2000; Hyun & Fowler, 1995; Obiakor, 1999). Montgomery (2001) offered a self-assessment tool that team members can use to reflect upon their understanding of diversity. The tool includes the following questions:

Compare Student Performance in Both the Native and Secondary Languages

After multidisciplinary team members meet, they need to make a plan for assessment. The assessment plan for second-language learners should collect data to compare student performance in both the native and secondary languages. Team members can collect data relating to students' performance in both languages through the use of informal and standardized tests, language samples, observations, questionnaires, and interviews. These methods can be employed to examine students' language proficiency, language dominance, language preference, and code switching. Language proficiency relates to the degree of skill in speaking the language(s) and includes receptive and expressive language skills. Although proficiency in one language does not necessarily mean lack of proficiency in another language, language dominance refers to the language in which the student is most fluent and implies a comparison of the student's abilities in two or more languages. Language preference identifies the language in which the student prefers to communicate, which can vary depending on the setting. Code switching relates to using words, phrases, expressions and sentences from one language while speaking another language.

Collect data relating to students' performance in both languages through the use of informal and standardized tests, language samples, observations, questionnaires, and interviews.

Through observations, informal assessment, and interviews with Maria and her family members, the multidisciplinary team found out that Maria was proficient in Spanish but lacked proficiency in English. It was observed that when Maria spoke Spanish, she was expressive, used the correct tense and age-appropriate vocabulary, and understood all the communications directed to her. Whereas Maria used Spanish to initiate and maintain interactions with others in an organized and coherent manner, her English was characterized by the use of gestures and short, basic sentences to communicate. In addition, observations and interviews revealed that Maria preferred to speak Spanish in all settings, and that Spanish was the dominant language spoken at home, since Maria's mother did not speak English.

Consider the Processes and Factors Associated with Second Language Acquisition

The assessment process for second-language learners like Maria should recognize that learning a second language is a long-term, complex, and dynamic process that involves different types of language skills and various stages of development (Collier, 1995). Therefore, when assessing second-language learners, the multidisciplinary team needs to consider the factors that affect second-language acquisition and understand the stages students go through in learning a second language.

Because proficiency in a second language involves the acquisition of two distinct types of language skills, the team needs to assess students' basic interpersonal communication skills and cognitive/academic language proficiency. The former, the interpersonal skills are the social language skills that guide the development of social relationships (e.g., "Good morning. How are you?"). Even though they are relatively repetitive, occur within a specific and clearly defined context, and are not cognitively demanding, research indicates that they typically take up to 2 years to develop in a second language (Cummins, 1984).

Cognitive proficiency, on the other hand, refers to the language skills that relate to literacy, cognitive development, and academic development in the classroom. It includes understanding such complex academic terms as photosynthesis, onomatopoeia, and least common denominator. Because this proficiency does not have an easily understood context, and tends to be cognitively demanding, it often takes up to 7 years for children to develop and use these language skills. Since cognitive skills developed in one's first language foster the development of cognitive proficiency in one's second language, we must gather information on students' proficiency and educational training in their native language.

An analysis of Maria's English language skills indicated that she was starting to develop a mastery of interpersonal language skills and struggling in terms of her cognitive language proficiency. For example, Ms. Shannon reported that when Maria was given directions to perform a classroom activity in English, she had difficulty completing it. However, when the directions were explained in Spanish, she was able to complete the task.

In learning a second language, students go through developmental stages that team members should consider when evaluating students' learning.

In learning a second language, students also go through developmental stages (see Figure 1) that team members should consider when evaluating students' learning (Maldonado-Colon, 1995). Initially, second-language learners' understanding of the new language is usually greater than their production. Many second-language learners go through a silent period in which they process what they hear but refrain from verbalizing. This is often misinterpreted as indicating a lack of cognitive abilities, disinterest in school, or shyness. Once students are ready to speak their new language, their verbalizations gradually increase in terms of their semantic and syntactic complexity.

Observations of Maria in her class indicated that she was focusing on understanding via mimicking others and using visual and context clues, and that she communicated via pointing, physical gestures and the occasional use of one to three-word phrases. Therefore, the multidisciplinary team felt that she was functioning at the preproduction and early production stages of learning English.

The team should also be aware of other factors that may affect students and their developmental progress in maintaining their native language and learning their new language such as age, educational background, and language exposure. Students who have been educated in their native language often progress faster in learning a new language that those who have not had a formal education (Thomas & Collier, 1997). In addition, students may attempt to apply the rules of their first language to their second language, which can affect their pronunciation, syntax, and spelling (Tiedt & Tiedt, 2001). And as some students learn a second language, they may experience language loss in their native language. Similarly, children who simultaneously learn two languages from

birth may initially experience some temporary language delays in achieving developmental language milestones and some language mixing. These tend to disappear over time (Fierro-Cobas & Chan, 2001).

Figure 1. Stages of Second-Language Learning

1. **Preproduction or Silent period.** Students focus on processing and comprehending what they hear but avoid verbal responses. They often rely on modeling, visual stimuli, context clues, key words and use listening strategies to understand meaning, and often communicate through pointing and physical gestures. They may benefit from classroom activities that allow them to respond by imitating, drawing, pointing, and matching.
2. **Telegraphic or Early Production period.** Students begin to use two- or three-word sentences, and show limited comprehension. They have a receptive vocabulary level of approximately 1,000 words and an expressive level that typically includes approximately 100 words. They may benefit from classroom activities that employ language they can understand, require them to name and group objects, and call for responses to simple questions.
3. **Interlanguage and Intermediate Fluency period.** Students speak in longer phrases and start to use complete sentences. They often mix basic phrases and sentences in both languages. They may benefit from classroom activities that encourage them to experiment with language and develop and expand their vocabulary.
4. **Extension and Expansion period.** Students expand on their basic sentences and extend their language abilities to employ synonyms and synonymous expressions. They are developing good comprehension skills, employing more complex sentence structures, and making fewer errors when speaking. They may benefit from classroom literacy activities and instruction in vocabulary and grammar.
5. **Enrichment period.** Students are taught learning strategies to assist them in making the transition to the new language.
6. **Independent Learning period.** Students begin to work on activities at various levels of difficulty with heterogeneous groups.

SOURCE: *Creating Inclusive Classrooms: Effective and Reflective Practices* (4th ed., p. 91) by S. J. Salend, 2001, Columbus, OH: Merrill/Prentice Hall. Reprinted by permission of Pearson Education, Inc.

Employ Alternatives to Traditional Standardized Testing

As mandated by the latest reauthorization of IDEA, rather than relying solely on potentially biased, standardized tests, the multidisciplinary team should employ a variety of student-centered, alternative assessment procedures to assess the educational needs of students from culturally and linguistically diverse backgrounds accurately. Such assessment alternatives include performance-based and portfolio assessment, curriculum-based measurements, instructional rubrics, dynamic assessment, student journals and learning logs, and self-evaluation techniques (Salend, 2001). These assessment alternatives can provide the Multidisciplinary Team with more complete profiles of students like Maria including their academic strengths and needs, learning styles and the impact of the school environment on their learning.

In the case of Maria, the multidisciplinary team worked with Maria and Ms. Shannon to create a portfolio that showed that Maria's decoding and reading comprehension skills in Spanish were age appropriate. It also revealed that she reads phonetically, engages in self-correction, and uses context and semantic cues. These results were also confirmed by Maria's performance on a standardized Spanish reading test.

Identify Diverse Life Experiences That May Affect Learning

Many second-language learners have diverse life experiences that can have a significant effect on their learning. These experiences may include being separated from family members for extended periods of time (Abrams, Ferguson, & Laud, 2001). Identifying these experiences can help the team determine if students' learning difficulties are related to the existence of a disability or other experiential factors. Therefore, the team can use the guidelines in Figure 2 to collect information to determine if a student's difficulties in learning result from language, cultural, and experiential factors, acculturation, psychological and family traumas, economic hardships, racism, or lack of exposure to effective instruction.

Learning a second language is a long-term, complex, and dynamic process that involves different types of language skills and various stages of development.

Ms. Garcia was able to obtain information about Maria by speaking with Maria and her mother. Ms. Garcia reported that Maria had not had an easy life. She lived in a rural village in Mexico and sporadically attended a school that had limited resources. Maria traveled to the United States with her mother and her three siblings a year ago to join her father and two older brothers who had been working in the United States. Two other siblings remained in Mexico with the hope of joining the family when enough money could be saved to bring them to the United States. Two other siblings remained in Mexico with the hope of joining the family when enough money could be saved to bring them to the United States. However, within 6 months of living in the United States, Maria's parents separated; and her father returned to Mexico. Maria reported that she misses her life in Mexico and her siblings who are still living there.

Upon arriving in the United States, Maria's mother found a job working as a migrant farmworker. Because she doesn't speak English, did not attend school, and works long hours to make ends meet, Maria's mother finds it difficult to help Maria with her schoolwork and relies on Maria to help take care of the younger children, and to cook and clean. Maria's mother also said that although her children watch cartoons in English, the interactions in the home are in Spanish. Interactions with the family also revealed that the family has few links to and interactions with the community, and that their lifestyle parallels the traditions of Mexico.

Code switching relates to using words, phrases, expressions and sentences from one language while speaking another language.

This information was helpful to the multidisciplinary team in providing information regarding Maria's learning abilities. First, it revealed that Maria's learning ability may be related to the fact that she has not regularly attended school and that the school she attended in Mexico is very different form her current school. Second, Maria's mother relies on her to help around the house; and Maria has quickly learned to perform these roles, which shows that she learns by active participation and is viewed by her mother as responsible and independent. Third, Maria has had limited exposure to English, which affects her progress in learning English and performing in school.

Analyze the Data and Develop an Appropriate Educational Plan

After the team has collected the data, team members meet to analyze the data and make decisions about students' educational programs. For second-language learners, the analysis should focus on examining the factors that affect learning and language development, determining if learning and language difficulties occur in both languages, and developing an educational plan to promote learning and language acquisition. Damico (1991) offered questions that can guide the team in examining the data to assess the extent to which students' diverse life experiences and cultural and linguistic backgrounds serve as

Figure 2. Life Experience Factors and Questions

Length of Residence in the United States

- How long and for what periods of time has the student resided in the United States?
- What were the conditions and events associated with the student's migration?
- If the student was born in the United States, what has been the student's exposure to English?

Students may have limited or interrupted exposure to English and the U.S. culture, resulting in poor vocabulary and slow naming speed, and affecting their cultural adjustment. Trauma experienced during migration or family separations as a result of migration can be psychological barriers that affect learning. Being born and raised in the United States does not guarantee that students have developed English skills and have had significant exposure to English and the U.S. culture.

School Attendance Patterns

- How long has the student been in school?
- What is the student's attendance pattern? Have there been any disruptions in school?

Students may fail to acquire language skills because of failure to attend school on a regular basis.

School Instructional History

- How many years of schooling did the student complete in the native country?
- What language(s) were used to guide instruction in the native country?
- What types of classrooms has the student attended (bilingual education, English as a second language, general education, speech/language therapy services, special education)?
- What has been the language of instruction in these classes?
- What is the student's level of proficiency in reading, writing, and speaking in the native language?
- What strategies and instructional materials have been successful?
- What were the outcomes of these educational placements?
- What language does the student prefer to use in informal situations with adults? In formal situations with adults?

Students may not have had access to appropriate instruction and curricula, resulting in problems in language acquisition, reading, and mathematics.

Cultural Background

- How does the student's cultural background affect second language acquisition?
- Has the student had sufficient time to adjust to the new culture?
- What is the student's acculturation level?
- What is the student's attitude toward school?

Since culture and language are inextricably linked, lack of progress in learning a second language can be due to cultural and communication differences and/or lack of exposure to the new culture. For example, some culturesrely on the use of body language in communication as a substitute for verbal communication. Various cultures also have different perspectives on color, time, gender, distance, and space that affect language.

Performance in Comparison to Peers

- Does the student's language skill, learning rate, and learning style differ from those of other students from similar experiential, cultural, and linguistic backgrounds?
- Does the student interact with peers in the primary language and/or English?
- Does the student experience difficulty following directions, understanding language, and expressing thoughts in the primary language? In the second language?

The student's performance can be compared to that of students who have similar traits rather than to that of students whose experiences in learning a second language are very different.

Home Life

- What language(s) or dialect(s) are spoken at home by each of the family members?
- When did the student start to speak?
- Is the student's performance at home different from that of siblings?
- What language(s) or dialect(s) are spoken in the family's community?
- Is a distinction made among the uses of the primary language or dialect and English? If so, how is that distinction made? (For example, the non-English language is used at home, but children speak English when playing with peers.)
- What are the attitudes of the family and the community toward English and bilingual education?
- In what language(s) does the family watch television, listen to the radio, and read newspapers, books, and magazines?
- What is the student's language preference in the home and community?
- To what extent does the family interact with the dominant culture and in what ways?

Important information concerning the student's language proficiency, dominance, and preference can be obtained by soliciting information from family members. Similarly, the student's acquisition of language can be enhanced by involving family members.

Health and Developmental History

- What health, medical, sensory, and developmental factors have affected the student's learning and language development?

A student's difficulty in learning and acquiring language may be related to various health and developmental variables.

Source: Creating Inclusive Classrooms: Effective and Reflective Practices (4th ed.; p. 94–95) by S. J. Salend, 2001, Columbus, OH: Merrill/Prentice Hall. Reprinted by permission of Pearson Education, Inc.

Figure 3. Differentiating Instruction for Second-Language Learners

- Establish a relaxed learning environment that encourages students to use both languages.
- Label objects in the classroom in several languages.
- Encourage and show students how to use bilingual dictionaries and Pictionaries.
- Use repetition to help students acquire the rhythm, pitch, volume, and tone of the new language.
- Use simple vocabulary and shorter sentences, and limit the use of idiomatic expressions, slang, and pronouns.
- Highlight key words through reiteration, increased volume and slight exaggeration, and writing them on the chalkboard.
- Use gestures, facial expressions, voice changes, pantomimes, demonstrations, rephrasing, visuals, props, manipulatives, and other cues to communicate and convey the meaning of new terms and concepts.

- Preview and teach new vocabulary, phrases, idioms, structures and concepts through use of modeling, and hands-on experiences.
- Supplement oral instruction and descriptions with visuals such as pictures, charts, maps, graphs, and graphic organizers.
- Offer regular summaries of important concepts and check students' understanding frequently.
- Emphasize communication rather than form.
- Correct students indirectly by restating their incorrect comments in correct form.

Sources: Choice of Languages in Instruction: One Language or Two?, by A. Brice and C. Roseberry-McKibbin, 2001, *TEACHING Exceptional Children, 33*(4), pp. 10–16.

The Changing Face of Bilingual Education, by R. Gersten, 1999, *Educational Leadership, 56*(7), pp. 41–45.

Below the Tip of the Iceberg: Teaching Language Minority Students, by V. Fueyo, 1997, *TEACHING Exceptional Children, 30*(1), pp. 61–65.

explanations for the difficulties they may be experiencing in schools. These questions include the following:

- What factors and conditions may explain the student's learning and/or language difficulties (e.g., stressful life events, lack of opportunity to learn, racism, acculturation, and experiential background)?
- To what extent does the student demonstrate the same learning and/or language difficulties in community settings as in school and/or in the primary language?
- To what extent are the student's learning and/or language difficulties due to normal second language acquisition, dialectical differences, or cultural factors?
- Did bias occur prior to, during, and after assessment such as in the reliability, validity,and standardization of the test as well as with the skills and learning styles assessed?
- To what extent were the student's cultural, linguistic, dialectic and experiential backgrounds considered in collecting and analyzing the assessment data (e.g., selection, administration, and interpretation of the test's results, prereferral strategies, learning styles, family involvement)?

These questions also can guide the team in differentiating between two types of second-language learners (Rice & Ortiz, 1994), and planning appropriate educational programs for these students. One type of second-language learner demonstrates some proficiency in the native language but experiences difficulties in learning a new language that are consistent with the typical difficulties individuals encounter in learning a second language. Although these kinds of behavior are similar to those

shown by students with learning difficulties, these students' educational needs can best be addressed through participation in a bilingual education or an English as a Second Language (ESL) program.

The other type of second-language learner exhibits language, academic, and social behavior in the first and second languages that are significantly below those of peers who have similar linguistic, cultural, and experiential backgrounds (Ortiz, 1997). These students may benefit from a special education program and individualized educational programs (IEPs) that address their own linguistic, cultural, and experiential needs (Garcia & Malkin, 1993; Ortiz, 1997). Both types of second-language learners would benefit from the use of strategies for differentiating instruction presented in Figure 3.

Team members will benefit from training in employing culturally responsive instructional, behavior management and mental health interventions.

In the case of Maria, the multidisciplinary team determined that she did not have a disability. The assessment data led the team to conclude that Maria had age-appropriate decoding, reading comprehension, and speaking skills in Spanish and that her difficulties in learning English appeared to be related to the normal process of second-language acquisition and cultural and experiential factors. They also decided that Maria didn't qualify for special education services under the IDEA because her school-related difficulties were based on her lack of proficiency in English and the limited opportunities she has had to receive instruction.

The multidisciplinary team determined that Maria would benefit from the services of a bilingual educator because she needed to strengthen her native language skills to learn academic content and to provide a better foundation for learning English. They also recommended strategies for establishing home-school partnerships and communications, and encouraged her teachers to use cooperative learning strategies and the strategies in Figure 3. The team also developed a plan to collect data to examine the effectiveness of these intervention strategies on Maria's learning, language development, socialization, and her success in school.

Final Thoughts

The ability to acquire and use language has a great effect on students' learning behavior and educational performance. As a result, many second-language learners like Maria exhibit types of behavior that resemble students with learning difficulties and are referred to the multidisciplinary team. Because the team process may vary across school districts, educators need to consider how the recommendations can be incorporated into their assessment process to differentiate between language differences from learning difficulties, and to provide second-language learners with appropriate educational programs.

References

Abrams, J., Ferguson, J., & Laud, L. (2001). Assessing ESOL students. *Educational Leadership, 59*(3), 62–65.

Brice, A., & Roseberry-MeKibbin, C. (2001). Choice of languages in instruction: One language or two? *TEACHING Exceptional Children, 33*(4), 10–16.

Cartledge, G., Kea, C. D., & Ida, D. J. (2000). Anticipating differences—Celebrating strengths: Providing culturally competent services for students with serious emotional disturbance. *TEACHING Exceptional Children, 32*(3), 30–37.

Chase Thomas, C., Correa, V., & Morsink, C. (2001). *Interactive teaming: Enhancing programs for students with special needs* (3rd ed.). Columbus, OH: Merrill/Prentice-Hall.*

Collier, V. (1995). Acquiring a second language for school. *Directions in Language and Education, 1*(4), 1–12.

Cummins, J. (1984). *Bilingualism and special education: Issues in assessment and pedagogy.* San Diego, CA: College-Hill.

Damico, J. S. (1991). Descriptive assessment of communicative ability in Limited English Proficient students. In E. Hamayan & J. S. Damico (Eds.), *Limiting bias in the assessment of bilingual students* (pp. 157–218). Austin, TX: PRO-ED.*

Fierro-Cobas, V., & Chan, E. (2001). Language development in bilingual children: A primer for pediatricians. *Contemporary Pediatrics, 18*(7), 79–98.

Fueyo, V. (1997). Below the tip of the iceberg: Teaching language minority students. *TEACHING Exceptional Children, 30*(1), 61–65.

Gay, G. (2002). Preparing for culturally responsive teaching. *Journal of Teacher Education, 53*(2), 106–116.

Gersten, R. (1999). The changing face of bilingual education. *Educational Leadership, 56*(7), 41–45.

Langdon, H. W. (1989). Language disorder or difference? Assessing the language skills of Hispanic students. *Exceptional Children, 56,* 160–167.

Maldonado-Colon, E. (1995, April). *Second language learners in special education: Language framework for inclusive classrooms.* Paper presented at the international meeting of the Council for Exceptional Children, Indianapolis.

Montgomery, W. (2001). Creating culturally responsive, inclusive classrooms. *TEACHING Exceptional Children, 33*(4), 4–9.

Obiakor, F. E. (1999). Teacher expectations of minority exceptional learners: Impact on accuracy of self-concepts. *Exceptional Children, 66,* 39–53.

Ochoa, S. H., Robles-Pina, R., Garcia, S. B., & Breunig, N. (1999). School psychologists' perspectives on referrals of language minority students. *Multiple Voices, 3*(1), 1–13.

Ortiz, A. A. (1997). Learning disabilities occurring concomitantly with linguistic differences. *Journal of Learning Disabilities, 30,* 321–332.

Rice, L. S., & Ortiz, A. A. (1994). Second language difference or learning disability? *LD Forum, 19*(2), 11–13.

Salend, S. J. (2001). *Creating inclusive classrooms: Effective and reflective practices* (4th ed.). Columbus, OH: Merrill/Prentice-Hall.*

Salend, S. J., Dorney, J. A., & Mazo, M. (1997). The roles of bilingual special educators in creating inclusive classrooms. *Remedial and Special Education, 18,* 54–64.

Thomas, W. P., & Collier, V. P. (1997). *School effectiveness for language minority students.* Washington, DC: National Clearinghouse for Bilingual Education.

Tiedt, P. L., & Tiedt, I. (2001). *Multicultural teaching: A handbook of activities, information, and resources* (6th ed.). Boston: Allyn & Bacon.*

Spencer J. Salend (CEC Chapter #615), Professor, Department of Educational Studies, State University of New York at New Paltz.
AltaGracia Salinas, Special Education Teacher, Alexandria City Public Schools, Virginia.

Address correspondence to Spencer J. Salend, Department of Educational Studies, OMB 112, SUNY New Paltz, 75 South Manheim Blvd., New Paltz, NY 12561 (e-mail: salends@ newpaltz.edu).

**From the
Trenches**

The Evils of Public Schools

Edward G. Rozycki

> *He who passively accepts evil [is] as much involved in it as he who helps to perpetuate it. He who accepts evil without protesting against it is really cooperating with it.*
>
> —Martin Luther King

Introduction

My fifth-grade experience in Longfellow public school was a joy: a really educational experience.[1] Sixth grade was another story.

My sixth-grade teacher, Mrs. P., was much taken by my "artistic ability." One fine day she told me, "You're going to enter the Gimbel's Department Store Art contest on Healthy Living and win a prize!" I was somewhat flattered and excited at the thought that I would be permitted to while away several weeks of afternoons painting at a poster rather than following along the prescribed curriculum.

I began planning a poster on Healthy Living. What might I do? "Never you mind about that," said Mrs. P. "I have an old poster here you can just copy! Look! Isn't it wonderful?"

I was speechless. I was being told to do something that, even then, I recognized as deep-down dishonest. But the importunity was not coming, as it usually did, from classmates who were already seeing to my loss of innocence by teaching me—with full details—an obscenity a day. No, the temptation was coming from a member of that moral aristocracy, Teachers, who—my parents had drilled into me—were Ones Who Must Be Obeyed, Ones Who Knew Best What Was Good for Me.

I summoned up the courage to say that I didn't want to just copy someone else's work. Mrs. P. responded, "I'm

very disappointed in you. It's either paint this poster, or do arithmetic drills." So I painted.

With disgust and loathing I finished the poster. It was better than the original. Everyone admired it, especially She Who Had to Be Obeyed, Who Knew Best What Was Good for Me. The poster was hung in the front of the room for general approbation while awaiting shipment to the exhibition.

I don't know what came over me. A day after finishing that vile poster, right after lunch, I walked up to it and took a dish of black paint and spattered it onto the painting. I trembled, confused with the righteousness of my disobedience.

I hurried back outside believing no one had seen me. I was wrong. Carolyn N. was a witness. She ran to tattle to Mrs. P., who berated me as soon as I returned to class. She put me on a diet of four-place addition drills with no recess for two weeks. Strangely, she didn't call my parents and inform them of my "misbehavior." Dear, sweet Carolyn, at Mrs. P's behest, cleaned up the poster. It was submitted in my name. It won a prize. When my parents and Mrs. P. accompanied me to the awards ceremonies, they remarked on how indifferent I seemed to the honor.

No Special Fault

> *The Devil gets up into the belfry by the Vicar's skirts.*
> —T. Fuller, 1732

Clearly, such incidents are not restricted to public schools. I know, for example, of two private schools—one, of the ancient elite—where the headmasters sold drugs to the students. Only one of the headmasters was caught. In general, private education takes a quite different view of wrongdoing than the view that is promulgated in public schools.[2] Private education is thus, by its own definitions, not susceptible to the faults attributable to public education.

Even though parochial school kids no longer come home bearing tales of nuns wielding yardsticks in the classroom like Crusaders slaying heathen, students in those schools have recently told me that their teachers have used extended periods of class time to make them write letters supporting political agendas. The students were told to sign their parents' names without asking permission, even though the parents might well have opposed or taken no position on the political issue.

Corruption of educational mission is not unique to public education. But public schools do provide unique opportunities for corruption, for five interrelated reasons:

a. they are schools of last resort in a compulsory system;

b. this makes them susceptible to constraint by under-informed courts to institute procedures often contrary to good educational practice;

c. special, often emphemeral, interest groups can gain control over school practices by combing vociferousness with legal ingenuity;

d. not only naive idealists, but the weak-minded and pathologically sentimental, are seduced into assuming teaching positions that they—often with good reason—abandon at the rate of 10 percent per year nationally; consequently

e. the remaining educators do not possess sufficient sense of profession to risk opposing those whose efforts in the long run distort and demand the educational mission—for which no practical consensus exists—of the public school.

Educating(?) Peter

Hate Is Love. War Is Peace.
—George Orwell, *1984*

My memories of my sixth-grade artistic award were provoked by my recent reviewing—perhaps the tenth—of the video *Educating Peter* in a class of graduate students in education.[3] (I watch this video about twice a year.) The plot: An undersocialized, physically abusive white male child suffering Down syndrome is placed in a third-grade class with a teacher whose sole preparation seems to be rationalizing why onions are like peaches, if only you taste them the right way. The teacher, unable to handle Peter even with the help of what appears to be an extra adult, compels her students—with the complicity of school staff—to "take ownership of the situation." A few sessions of psychobabblic indoctrination help the third-graders to comprehend the causal complexities of Peter's behavior and their role in provoking it. This means that now it is expected that Peter's behavioral outbursts—

even the violent ones—will be interdicted by the students rather than by the teacher.

In an interview, the teacher explains how it is important, in this all-white school in Virginia, that her students learn to live with people different from themselves. She tells how by "raising her expectations"—one imagines her commanding her synapses to fire in unison, her dendrites to do drills—Peter is brought to make academic progress.

We see students reacting with shock and dismay to Peter's behavior. The adults in the video (and the narrator) assure us that these students are "learning to accept differences." There is no evidence for this remote probability. From the looks of things they could just as well be learning resignation in the face of power—both Peter's power and that of the adults who condone what to them as "normal kids" is forbidden.

The students, choked, kicked, pushed by Peter, are encouraged to rationalize, to declare that Peter has become their best friend, that Peter has taught them more than he himself has learned, that this has been just the peachy-keenest of classes. The students blush as they are interviewed, not being able—unlike the adults who provide them example—to suppress the natural embarrassment the innocent feel about deliberately mouthing what they believe to be false.

The film purports to take no sides in the controversy about inclusion but merely "tell a story." It is cleverly edited to produce a certain effect. I remember an earlier version I saw some years ago. It was different from the version I purchased from Ambrose Video Publishing. A crucial scene has been edited out.

In the early version, the boys are sitting outside in a field, Peter, unprovoked, kicks a boy—call him Johnny—square in the middle of the face. Here the cut occurs. Johnny, outraged, jumps on Peter. The teacher intervenes, and remonstrates with Johnny, who is moved off to the side. Splice here. Johnny cries to himself, unconsoled by an adult.

At the end of the year, we find Peter "accepted" into the group, having "fewer outbursts, mostly toward the end of the day."

In the present version, one sees the kick and then Johnny crying, alone and unconsoled. That he should not be consoled is inexplicable, assuming there are adults present. But knowing he has just been rebuked—which has been spliced out of the film—explains the lack of consolation. Johnny's isolation is part of his "punishment" for "fighting" back.

EDUCATING PETER: AS GRADUATE STUDENTS SEE IT

Party	Benefit Received	Kind of Benefit	Cost Suffered	Kind of Cost
Peter	Interaction with normal children	Immediate Substantial Intrinsic	Not treated as a moral being, a full person	Symbolic Immediate Intrinsic
Peter's Parents	Happier child at home Easier to live with	Immediate Substantial Intrinsic	Dependency on external support systems	Substantial Immediate Extrinsic
Student Featured in Video	Teacher approval	Immediate Substantial Intrinsic	Loss of academic learning	Substantial Immediate Extrinsic
	Learn tolerance	Remote Symbolic	Moral corrosion	Symbolic Immediate Intrinsic
Featured Student's Parent	Pride in school Approbation	Immediate Substantial Intrinsic	Child's loss of academic learning	Substantial Immediate Extrinsic
			Moral corrosion	Symbolic Immediate Intrinsic
Student Not Featured in Video	Learn tolerance	Remote Symbolic	Loss of academic learning	Substantial Immediate Extrinsic
			Moral corrosion	Symbolic Immediate Intrinsic
Non-Featured Student's Parent			Child's loss of learning	Substantial Immediate Extrinsic
			Moral corrosion	Symbolic Immediate Intrinsic
Teacher (Featured in Video)	Recognition	Immediate Substantial	Adjustment	Substantial Immediate
Principal (Featured in Video)	Recognition	Immediate Substantial		

At the end of the year, we find Peter "accepted" into the group, having—in the words of his teacher—"fewer outbursts, mostly toward the end of the day."

One of my students remarked that what the third-graders had accomplished was akin to changing a dangerous animal into a pet. Peter was exempted from normal discipline, clearly treated as possessing diminished responsibility, and given almost bizarrely effusive encouragement and reward for trivial accomplishments. He was "managed."

Immediate Costs and Remote, Improbable Benefits

My fame will be your consolation.

—Richard Wagner (to his betrayed wife)

The students who watched *Educating Peter* with me were asked to pay attention to four questions: What are the benefits of including Peter in the third-grade classroom? Who receives what kind of benefit? What are the costs of including Peter in the third-grade classroom? Who pays what kind of cost? The table on the previous page summarizes several years of responses from my graduate students.

What Cost "Charity"? What Cost "Justice"?

Everyone loves justice in the affairs of another.

—Italian proverb

It is not clear when we examine the chart whether or not it gives support to inclusion. Many costs and benefits go unperceived, so they do not come to be factored into political decisions to support or resist inclusion. But even allowing for a full disclosure of the costs and benefits assigned to each constituency of the school community, the lack of an *implementable* consensus on what the school is about obscures a clear choice. Yet those with power, the principal and the teacher, clearly tend to maximize their benefits and minimize their costs.

Supporters of public education—among whom I count myself—worry about the persistent and growing interest in vouchers and schooling arrangements that threaten the very existence of public schools. They need only watch *Educating Peter*, though, to understand where some of that impetus comes from.

Peter's education could be seen as a form of charity bestowed on the less fortunate. It is a debauched form of "charity," however, that comes through a compulsory system. Our courts have decided that the practice of inclusion is an improvement on justice. But the lopsided redistribution of scarce schooling resources—where the needs of some take precedence over the needs of many—may just bring about every child's educational starvation.

Notes

1. See Edward G. Rozycki, "Educational Assessment: Confusing Status with Achievement." *Educational Horizons,* Fall 1993, 7–10.
2. See Peter Cookson, Jr., and Caroline Hodges Persell, *Preparing for Power: America's Elite Boarding Schools* (New York: Basic Books, 1985).
3. *Educating Peter.* Home Box Office. VHS Tape. 20 minutes. (New York: Ambrose Video Publishing, 1993).

Edward G. Rozycki is a twenty-five-year veteran of the school district of Philadelphia. He is an associate professor of education at Widener University, Widener, Pennsylvania.

From *Educational Horizons,* Winter 2002, pp. 57-60. © 2002 by Educational Horizons. Reprinted with permission of the author.

**The
Cutting Edge**

Can Every Child Learn?

Gary K. Clabaugh

"The key element in teaching success isn't technical skill, more resources, or smaller classes; the key to success is higher expectations. Teachers will get more if they expect more. The mantra to chant daily is 'Every child can learn.'"

That's the tune that a lot of people are dancing to these days. George W. Bush and a remarkably diverse assortment of governors, national and state legislators, educational entrepreneurs, school superintendents, and ordinary, right-thinking Americans all assert, "Every child can learn." In fact, this overworked and underconsidered motto is as ubiquitous as dog doo on the public green.

Despite definitive research that points to nonschool factors as keys to school success, those embracing this motto implicitly dismiss the idea that "schooling failures" are really symptoms of social failures. They seem to believe that positive thinking can cancel out the educational consequences of the 20 percent poverty rate among U.S. children. They must believe that positive thinking can defeat our inner city infant mortality rate, which outstrips that of the Third World. They must imagine that positive thinking can help hundreds of thousands of U.S. youngsters who literally have no home where they can do their homework. (On an average night in D.C., for instance, homeless shelters contain 1,300 youngsters.[1]) They must suppose that positive thinking can cancel out the educational impact of long-term separation or divorce, experienced by 40 percent of all children born to post-1966 marriages—not to mention disruption in the stepfamily, the fate of one-third of those same kids.[2]

To hear the Pollyannas tell it, nothing can stand up to a strong conviction that "Every child can learn." When teachers believe this to the marrow of their being, all will be well.

Anyone, upon a little reflection, can see that this is humbug. Yes, most (but not all) children can learn to stay away from Mom when she's high or to keep out of the way of Mom's boyfriend when he's looking for someone to abuse. Sure, most (but not all) children can learn to wait until Mom is just high enough to say "yes" before asking her for food money. But few children can learn to do algebra, appreciate Shakespeare, or balance chemical equations if they are abused, scared, sick, hungry, or bereft of love and security. Under those circumstances, one can't even learn to read. They're too busy trying to survive.

Frankly, it's foolish to expect quality schoolwork from children in such situations. Even the most skillful teaching, up-to-date texts, clean and safe schools, and enlightened educational practices are relatively impotent in the face of these and similar difficulties. So let's forget about conquering all with wishful thinking and face the fact that social injustice and ferocious unfairness erode school effectiveness all across America.

For that matter, we can even question the literal truth of the claim that "Every child can learn." An exercise on the following page helps us think this through.

My skilled and experienced university colleagues specializing in special education assure me that there is only one thing listed that "every child" *might* be able to learn. That's to salivate on cue. They say only comatose children would probably be unable to learn to do this. They assure me, however, that many children can't learn to do *any* of these other things.

We see that the slogan is literally false. Then what can we make of its persistent use? Is the key to successful teaching, at least in some general sense, still higher expectations? Will teachers get more if they expect more? The answer plainly is *"No."*

So why is the motto ubiquitous? It's popular because claiming that "Every child can learn" shifts responsibility to educators and conceals the causes of school failure in ways useful to those in power. Can every child learn? Not in any sense that's meaningful to educators.

"EVERY CHILD CAN LEARN"

Testing the Slogan's Limits

Please respond to the following phrase completions, checking the box best reflecting your view. (Some examples share the same wording. Remember, though, *learning how* to govern one's impulses, for instance, is not the same thing as *learning to* govern one's impulses.)

Every child can LEARN THAT...	Strongly Disagree	Disagree	Undecided	Agree	Strongly Agree
I have a name					
2 follows 1					
Shoes can have shoelaces					
Thomas Jefferson was the third President of the U.S.					
I shouldn't act on impulse					
Chopin composed nocturnes for piano					
Every child can LEARN HOW TO...	**Strongly Disagree**	**Disagree**	**Undecided**	**Agree**	**Strongly Agree**
Recognize my name					
Imitate					
Spell my name					
Do long division					
Govern my impulses					
Perform Chopin nocturnes					
Every child can LEARN TO...	**Strongly Disagree**	**Disagree**	**Undecided**	**Agree**	**Strongly Agree**
Salivate on cue					
Play					
Tie my shoes					
Use long division as a tool					
Govern my impulses					
Be delighted by Chopin nocturnes					

Notes

1. "Bright Futures and Broken Dreams," The Children's Defense Fund, quoted by William Rasberry, column, *The Philadelphia Inquirer*, September 28, 1991, 8.

2. Gary Clabaugh and Edward Rozycki, *Understanding Schools: The Foundations of Education* (New York: Harper-Collins, 1990), 169.

Gary K. Clabaugh is a professor of education at La Salle University in Philadelphia, Pennsylvania. He directs La Salle's Graduate Program in Education and coordinates arts and sciences graduate programs.

UNIT 7
Serving Special Needs and Concerns

Unit Selections

Key Points to Consider

• Do you agree with Dr. Steven Strauss about the report on reading sponsored by NICHD? Why or why not?

• What can schools do to encourage students to read during the summer months? What can teachers do to encourage reading for pleasure throughout the school year.

• Describe life in an American suburban high school. What concerns do you have about student experience of this setting? If possible, use your own experiences as a guide.

 **Links: www.dushkin.com/online/**
These sites are annotated in the World Wide Web pages.

Constructivism: From Philosophy to Practice
http://www.stemnet.nf.ca/~elmurphy/emurphy/cle.html
National Association for Gifted Children
http://www.nagc.org/home00.htm
National Information Center for Children and Youth With Disabilities (NICHCY)
http://www.nichcy.org/index.html

People who educate serve many special needs and concerns of their students. This effort requires a special commitment to students on the part of their teachers. We celebrate this effort, and each year we seek to address special types of general concern.

People learn under many different sets of circumstances, which involve a variety of educational concerns both within schools and in alternative learning contexts. Each year we include in this section of this volume articles on a variety of special topics that we believe our readers will find interesting and relevant.

The journal literature thematically varies from year to year. Issues on which several good articles may have been published in one year may not be covered well in other years in the professional and trade publications. Likewise, some issues are covered in depth every year, such as articles on social class or education and school choice.

The special topics chosen for inclusion in this unit this year all relate to curriculum and instruction issues. They touch on concerns in teaching literacy skills and especially on concerns relating to the teaching of reading and teachers' grading policies as they relate to students' rights to privacy. In the first article Steven L. Strauss, M.D., provides an interesting critique of the National Reading Panel's research and findings. The panel's research was sponsored by the National Institute of Child Health and Human Development (NICHD). The second article in the unit, by Ann McGill-Franzen and Richard Allington, provides helpful suggestions for summer reading programs for students. Specific examples of what sorts of things teachers and administrators can do to encourage students to read in the summer are given. This relates to the frequent loss of learning by some students during the summer vacation. This clearly relates to the problem of how to increase the retention of reading skills between one school year and the next one.

Then, Dana Truby provides us with a summary of things we can do to hook students on reading series of books for children, which the students can learn to enjoy and hence improve their basic reading skills. The author provides a very good list of recommended series of books directed to children and adolescents.

Issues related to teaching children's literature are dealt with very well.

Next, Stephen J. Friedman reviews the findings of a very important U.S. Supreme Court case that considered certain classroom-related issues regarding students' rights to privacy in the classroom. He reviews the case of *Falvo versus Owasso Public Schools* in which a student and his family raised legal issues regarding certain controversial teacher grading policies in the classroom.

Finally, as she reviews two books on suburban America high schools, Kay Hymowitz finds fault with "good" schools. They may have all the trappings, but, Hymomitz says, they fail to spark their students' intellectual and moral imaginations. In particular she criticzes the teachers who attempt to "edutain" the students instead of teaching them.

Since first issued in 1973, this ongoing anthology has sought to provide discussion of special social or curriculum issues affecting the teaching/learning conditions in schools. Fundamental forces at work in our culture during the past several years have greatly affected millions of students. The social, cultural, and economic pressures on families have produced several special problems of great concern to teachers. Serving special needs and concerns requires greater degrees of individualization of instruction and greater attention paid to the development and maintenance of healthier self-concepts by students.

Challenging the NICHD Reading Research Agenda

The report of the National Reading Panel is touted as being based on a medical model of research. Offering a perspective from the field of medicine itself, Dr. Strauss examines the report and finds that it falls short on several of the most basic standards of good medical research.

BY STEVEN L. STRAUSS, M.D.

THE BEHAVIOR of the National Institute of Child Health and Human Development (NICHD) with regard to the production and dissemination of the report of its National Reading Panel is nothing short of scandalous. In fact, the scandal is of such enormity that it demands a full explanation.

The chief element of the scandal is the falsification of the panel's findings. This is immediately apparent when the panels' full report is compared with the short summary version offered for wide distribution. The full report acknowledges that there is scant evidence to justify the claim that phonics instruction leads to improved reading ability, noting that only some normal first-graders showed some gains. But the summary report falsifies the panel's own findings and asserts that phonics instruction correlates with improved reading ability in a number of areas all the way up to grade 6. Such distortions have been amply documented by Elaine Garan in her important new book and in these pages.[1]

Of course, it is the summary report that has been distributed to the media and to policy makers. Therefore, it should not be completely surprising to discover that the summary report was prepared, in part, by Widmeyer Baker, a public relations firm. This means that we can, quite accurately, think of the summary report as "PR," which certainly puts it in a different light. But it is more disturbing that the PR firm that contributed to the report is the same one employed by McGraw-Hill, a company with a substantial financial stake in the matter of the role of phonics in reading instruction.

But the scandal does not stop there. According to Garan—citing panel member Joanne Yatvin's minority report for the NRP—the sole reviewer of the phonics section of the NRP report was Barbara Foorman, a NICHD-funded researcher. And of the 38 articles included in the NRP's phonics meta-analysis, Foorman was the lead or secondary author of four. In other words, she contributed more than 10% of the articles reviewed by the NRP and was a reviewer of her own work.

The NRP meta-analysis was based on its version of a medical model of research that compares performance criteria before and after treatment. So, for example, just as a clinical researcher might compare pain level or muscle strength before and after treatment with drug X, so too did the studies reviewed by the NRP compare reading "ability" before and after phonics "treatment."

A recent series in the *British Medical Journal* reviewed the methodology behind an acceptable meta-analysis.[2] The authors specifically noted the importance of a thoroughly blind review of the studies, to the point of suggesting that articles be typographically reformatted so that the reviewers cannot identify the journal, authors, funding, or any other feature that could influence the review process. The authors of the *British Medical Journal* series pointed out that the quality of meta-analyses is significantly improved by such blinded methodology. The relevance of these concerns to Foorman's review is clear.

Foorman's NRP phonics studies are also open to serious criticism on their own terms. In at least two of the studies, Foorman refers to a set of 60 stimulus words that were used to test young readers before and after phonics instruction. Some of the words are labeled "regular," and others are labeled "exceptional." But no explanation is offered of how the stimulus words were assigned to one category or the other. Fundamentally, this oversight means that there is no way to tell for certain what Foorman means by "phonics."

Suppose Foorman's understanding of phonics is not the same as that assumed in the other studies included in the meta-analysis. Even worse, suppose that the various studies used mutually contradictory conceptions of phonics. Then the studies cannot be included together in a meta-analysis. But the NRP report does not indicate that anyone verified that all the phonics studies were studies of apples and not studies of apples and oranges.

This is not a hypothetical matter in the present situation. Foorman's stimulus words are, quite simply, confusing and incoherent from the point of view of phonics. I informally asked a group of teachers to divide Foorman's stimulus words into those that are regular and those that are not. I obtained nothing close to a consensus. Here are Foorman's 60 words. The "exceptional" words are marked with an asterisk.

nail	pure	last	chrome*
port	bowl*	rake	knack*
lord	rate	dine	putt*
pool	cram	chef*	warm*
born	camp	tart	wrong*
cone	led	leak	mint
whet*	botch	rack	neat
meek	neck	knit*	sew*
main	chord*	fake	shall*
site	phase*	fate	clutch
known*	norm	whop*	bold
shun	past	comb*	husk
fair	reel	heir*	lose*
dare	hose	link	blow
lime	word*	wrist*	share

In one of Foorman's NRP studies, first-grade children were tested before and after they received instruction on letter-sound relationships.[3] Some children received relatively more "letter-sound instruction," and others received relatively less. The authors of the study claimed that children who received relatively more letter-sound instruction showed significantly greater improvement on reading both regular and exceptional words than those who received relatively less letter-sound instruction.

In another of Foorman's NRP studies, she and her colleagues found that children who were given phoneme instruction performed significantly more accurately on reading regular words

than those who were not given such instruction and that children who were given onset-rime instruction performed significantly more accurately on exceptional words.[4]

But these conclusions are compelling only to the extent that we understand and accept what Foorman and her colleagues mean by "regular" and "exceptional." Unfortunately, no set of principles for making that distinction is provided. Consider, for example, the word *phase,* categorized by the authors as exceptional. Why is this word exceptional? It cannot be because of the final, silent *e* or the proceeding "long" vowel, since other words with this characteristic are regular, such as *rake, dine, fake,* and *fate.* It cannot be because of the pronunciation of the letter *s* as a voiced /z/ sound, since *hose,* also with a voiced /z/, is regular.

The only candidate is the initial digraph *ph.* But initial *ph* is unexceptionally pronounced /f/. Its exceptional status must thus be on the basis of some peculiar formal property, perhaps that the two letters together are pronounced as neither of the individual letters would be. But this also cannot be correct, since the digraph *sh* has exactly this formal characteristic, yet *shun* and *share* are judged to be regular.

Similar problems are encountered in the analysis of virtually every other exceptional word listed. To the extent that such problems remain unresolved, there is no reason whatsoever to accept any of the authors' claims. The claims are empty since we simply don't know what they are about. In turn, there is no reason to accept any of the NRP's conclusions that are based on an acceptance of such studies.

Indeed, the NRP report should be challenged to show where in its meta-analysis the panel scrutinized the studies for internal consistency and mutual compatibility. Of course, the panel did nothing of the sort, since, of all the criteria they used to decide which articles to include or exclude, nowhere is the quality of the study mentioned. All that mattered, ultimately, was that the authors claimed to have tested reading before and after phonics instruction. Quality was assumed simply because the study appeared in a peer-reviewed journal.

I am not a statistician, and I do not know whether 38 studies should be considered adequate for performing a meta-analysis of the type and scope carried out by the NRP. But let us suppose that it is. Consider then that these 38 studies were the entire amount that passed through the NRP's inclusion and exclusion filters and that the journals scanned were in fact all those published in English over a period of nearly 30 years. In other words, a global English language database spanning nearly three decades produced little more than one study per year that looked at phonics intervention with a study design deemed acceptable by the NRP.

This in itself is a very interesting finding, for it indicates that the educational research community did not consider such studies to be of very much importance and that the NRP "ignored the preponderance of research" in the field of reading and education, to quote James Cunningham's apt assessment of the NRP report.[5] Apparently, the panel members, mostly experimental scientists, felt that they knew better than the researchers in the field of reading itself regarding just what counted as clinically important. A similar attitude again found expression in a recent article in *Scientific American,* co-authored by Foorman, in which the authors badly declare that, if only student teachers were given a high-quality linguistics course on phonics, they would not have to be handed scripted lesson plans with formulaic drills on alphabetics.[6]

THE NRP VERSION of a medical model of research is, in fact, only a caricature of real clinical research in medicine. True, before a drug is approved, its efficacy must be demonstrated. But that is not all there is to clinical research. The researchers must be careful not to overstate their findings. And, furthermore, the drug under study must be shown to be relatively safe, no matter how effective it may be.

Suppose we accept that the phonics intervention studies indeed demonstrated improved "accuracy" or "fluency" of word reading. This is still a far cry from having demonstrated improved comprehension of novel, authentic text—certainly the gold standard for assessing any reading intervention.

In medicine, it has been clearly demonstrated that lowering blood pressure in hypertensive individuals reduces the risk of heart attack and stroke. Yet, even though some antihypertensive drugs, called calcium channel blockers, demonstrably lower blood pressure, they do not in turn reduce the risk of heart attack. Indeed, some antihypertensive medications pose health risks for individuals with asthma or depression. Others pose health risks for individuals with neuromuscular disease. Despite the potential benefit, the potential risk may be the overriding factor in deciding whether or not to use the drug at all.

A better medical-model analysis of phonics intervention than the one carried out by the NRP would at the very least include questions about potential risks. One might argue that there aren't any conceivable risks associated with phonics intervention, but that would at least acknowledge the full spectrum of issues involved in the assessment of interventions. The NRP report, as far as I can tell, did not even raise the question of potential risk, despite its touting of the "medical model."

But there is no doubt that a number of potential risks really do exist when children are exposed to intensive phonics. They spend less class time reading real books. To many, phonics exercises are boring and laborious, and persistent exposure to them might even turn off potential readers to the joys of reading. Overly "phonicsed" readers pay less attention to meaning. Overly "phonicsed" readers may be more likely to move their lips, which slows them down and thus compromises their construction of meaning. This list could no doubt be extended.

Two years ago, Reid Lyon, the reading research director of NICHD, testified before a congressional committee in support of President Bush's program of high-stakes testing and accountability as a means of raising reading achievement.[7] But where is the scientific evidence that high-stakes testing and accountability lead to improved reading ability? And, just as crucially, where is the evidence that they do so without risk? The answers to these questions were utterly and completely missing from Lyon's testimony, which is rather remarkable, considering the appeal to "science" that has justified the NICHD reading research agenda for more than a decade.

Indeed, there are anecdotal reports of serious mental health problems among schoolchildren as a consequence of the new climate of testing and accountability, so much so that a number of prominent child and adolescent psychiatrists and psychologists recently signed a petition demanding a moratorium on high-stakes testing.[8] In England, the National Union of Teachers recently voted to boycott the administration of that nation's high-stakes tests partly because evidence is accumulating that such tests pose a mental health risk to young people.

If NICHD were consistent in its declared principles, its representatives would testify before Congress that there is currently no scientific evidence that can justify the use of high-stakes testing and accountability. If it decided to study the matter first, as any scientist would advocate, and to request congressional funds for this purpose, then, in keeping with a medical model of clinical research, it would have to simultaneously request funds to study the potential risks. The decision to go ahead with high-stakes testing and accountability could then be made by weighing the risks against the benefits. The National Institutes of Health makes use of this model of research when it comes to almost everything—except reading.

Rather than employ an acceptable medical model of clinical evaluation, one that assesses both benefits and risks, the NICHD model is, in fact, a corporate-business model of assessment. The overriding priority of making a profit always outweighs both individual and social risks. That is why society as a whole has had to fight against corporate pollution of the environment, chronic structural unemployment, unsafe working conditions, exploitation of child labor, and so on. To the corporate-business mentality, these matters are risks to be dealt with only if forced to, since treating them threatens the maximization of profit. Likewise, NICHD's strange perception of an inflexible need for phonics and its public support for high-stakes testing and accountability have led the agency to neglect potential risks. Frankly speaking, this is not a medical model of clinical assessment, NICHD's claims notwithstanding.

NICHD's corporate connection is not merely conceptual. In fact, it is the basis for the entire scandal, a scandal in which NICHD's own research report is falsified when prepared for public consumption, a scandal in which the public is further beguiled with misleading allusions to science and a medical model of research that has supposedly allowed us to find out "what works." In a similar fashion, we have been told that nuclear power works, so we'll worry about disposing of the waste later.

NICHD's corporate connection was explicitly revealed by Duane Alexander, NICHD's director, in his presentation before Congress on the occasion of the release of the NRP report.[9] Referring to the panel's work, Alexander told the lawmakers that "the significance of these findings for the future literacy of this nation and for the economic prosperity and global competitiveness of our people is enormous." This comment deserves reflection.

The charge of the National Reading Panel was, according to Alexander, to "review the scientific literature reporting the results of research on how children learn to read and the effectiveness of various approaches to teaching reading." The charge did not include the economic goal of improving the literacy skills of

U.S. citizens in order to enhance the competitive edge of U.S. corporations in the global economy. Yet anyone who has followed the agenda of corporate America, as articulated by the Business Roundtable, knows that the current congressional urgency regarding literacy is about improving the skills of the U.S. workforce in order to make U.S. labor more productive, so that U.S. corporations will not fall behind their European and Asian competitors.[10]

Alexander's remarks follow from this agenda and from nothing else, since even ardent advocates of intensive phonics do not thereby automatically become cheerleaders for General Motors in its competition with Volkswagen or Toyota for a greater share of the automobile market. In fact, it is perfectly natural to imagine sincere advocates of intensive phonics who would wish instead to donate our new "scientific" understanding of reading to the rest of the world, so that we, as a generous and privileged people, could help wipe out the scourge of global illiteracy, no matter what effect this has on the competitive edge of "our" corporations.

Likewise, NICHD's claims about reading have no inherent bearing on the issue of high-stakes testing and accountability. One can be a sincere advocate of intensive phonics and still oppose the coercive pedagogical practices that follow from a regimen of high-stakes testing and accountability. But the real charge of NICHD and of the NRP is to promote the agenda of the Business Roundtable, which is among the nation's strongest and most influential advocates of high-stakes testing and accountability as a means of forcing "21st-century literacy skills" on the next generation of workers.

To view the findings of the NRP report as containing scientific information that will position U.S. corporations to better compete with their European and Asian counterparts is, in my opinion, also scandalous, especially when understood against the backdrop of the NRP's much-vaunted medical model. It is as if the productivity of labor depended crucially on a high level of visual acuity, and our scientists had discovered a new technique to improve visual acuity, which we were then going to distribute only to our own citizens and withhold from the rest of the world in order to maintain "our" competitive edge. Or imagine that our scientific laboratories discovered a cure for AIDS, but someone noted that the AIDS problem overseas represented a permanent drain on local economies, so that not providing the cure to these countries would enhance our competitive economic edge. No sane, ethical human being could accept this line of reasoning and withhold the treatment.

It is no wonder that the NRP report is shrouded in scandal. From the start, its true charge was shielded from the public. That charge—to increase the literacy skills of the U.S. work force in order to increase the competitive edge of U.S. corporations—is being sold to the public with such catch phrases as "literacy crisis," "scientifically valid," and "medical model." But the true charge views children as malleable cannon fodder in a global economic war. "More and more we see that competition in the international marketplace is in reality a 'battle of the classrooms,'" says Norman Augustine, former CEO of Lockheed Martin, former head of the Business Roundtable's Educa-

tion Task Force, and currently an education advisor to President Bush.[11]

The stakes are truly high in the struggle against this scandal. History can show us what happened—twice in the 20th century, in fact—when the battle between U.S. corporations and those of Europe and Asia reached a saturation point in the division of the world's markets. The issue is nothing less than the fight to prevent the next world war.

Notes

1. Elaine M. Garan, "Beyond the Smoke and Mirrors: A Critique of the National Reading Panel Report on Phonics," *Phi Delta Kappan,* March 2001, pp. 500–506; and idem, *Resisting Reading Mandates: How to Triumph with the Truth* (Portsmouth, N.H.: Heinemann, 2002).

2. Matthias Egger and Davey Smith, "Meta-analysis: Potential and Promise," *British Medical Journal,* vol. 315, 1997, pp. 1371–74; Matthias Egger, Davey Smith, and Andrew N. Phillips, "Meta-analysis: Principles and Procedures," *British Medical Journal,* vol. 315, 1997, pp. 1533–37; and Matthias Egger et al., "Bias in Meta-analysis Detected by a Simple, Graphical Test," *British Medical Journal,* vol. 315, 1997, pp. 629–34.

3. Barbara R. Foorman et al., "How Letter-Sound Instruction Mediates Progress in First-Grade Reading and Spelling," *Journal of Educational Psychology,* vol. 83, 1991, pp. 456–69.

4. D. W. Haskell, Barbara R. Foorman, and P. R. Swank, "Effects of Three Orthographic/Phonological Units on First-Grade Reading," *Remedial and Special Education,* vol. 13, 1992, pp. 40–49.

5. James W. Cunningham, "The National Reading Panel Report," *Reading Research Quarterly,* vol. 6, 2001, pp. 326–35.

6. Keith Rayner, Barbara R. Foorman, Charles A. Perfetti, David Pesetsky, and Mark S. Seidenberg, "How Should Reading Be Taught?," *Scientific American,* March 2002, pp. 84–91.

7. G. Reid Lyon, "Measuring Success: Using Assessments and Accountability to Raise Student Achievement," statement before the Subcommittee on Education Reform of the Committee on Education and the Workforce, U.S. House of Representatives, 8 March 2001.

8. Alliance for Childhood, "High Stakes Testing Position Statement," 25 April 2001, available on the Web at www.allianceforchildhood.org.

9. Duane Alexander, M.D., director, National Institute of Child Health and Human Development, testimony before the Labor, Health and Human Services, and Education Subcommittee of the Senate Appropriations Committee, U.S. Senate, 13 April 2000.

10. For a review of the business connection to the testing agenda, see Bess Altwerger and Steven L. Strauss, "The Business Behind Testing," *Language Arts,* vol. 79, 2002, pp. 256–62. Various Business Roundtable documents touching

on the subject are available on the Web at www.brtable.org, including "Workforce Training and Development," 1993; "Continuing the Commitment: Essential Components of a Successful Education System," 1995; "A Business Leader's Guide to Setting Academic Standards," 1997; Norman Augustine, Ed Lupsberger, and James Orr III, "A Common Agenda for Improving American Education," 1997; "An Introduction to the Business Roundtable," 1998; and "International Economic Crisis: Letter Hand-Delivered to the President, Leadership, and Congress," 1998. See also Edward B. Rust, Jr., Co-Chairman Business Coalition for Excellence in Education, Chair the Business Roundtable Education Task Force, statement before the Subcommittee on Education Reform of the Committee on Education and the Workforce, U.S. House of Representatives, 8 March 2001.

11. Norman R. Augustine, "A Business Leader's Guide to Setting Academic Standards," the Business Roundtable, www.brtable.org, 2 July 1997.

STEVEN L. STRAUSS, M.D., formerly on the faculty of the University of Maryland School of Medicine, is a neurologist in private practice in Baltimore and the author of Linguistics, Neurology, and the Politics of Phonics: Silent E Speaks Out *(Erlbaum, 2003). An earlier version of this article was presented at the annual meeting of the International Reading Association, San Francisco, May 2002.*

Bridging the Summer Reading Gap

By Anne McGill-Franzen and Richard Allington

June is fast approaching—you can feel the heat of summer in the hallways. Days are longer, attention spans are growing shorter, and everyone is ready for a break. Teachers are planning for their vacation time. Children are ready to shrug off the mantle of "student" for the three-month break, along with the backpacks, the math homework, and the quizzes and tests. But just because school is out, it doesn't mean that reading and learning should stop. Teachers know that many children can't afford to take such a long break. Young readers who don't continue to read over the summer—especially those who are reluctant or at-risk—are likely to lose crucial ground. One summer off can sometimes mean a whole school year of struggling academic performance.

Summer Reading Loss

Regardless of other activities, the best predictor of summer loss or summer gain is whether or not a child reads during the summer. And the best predictor of whether a child reads is whether or not he or she *owns* books. While economically-advantaged kids often have their own bedroom libraries, poor kids usually depend heavily on schools for books to read.

Understandably, summer reading loss or "summer setback" is a bigger problem for children from low-income families. Their reading achievement typically declines an average of three months between June and September, while that of typical middle-class students improves or remains the same. This means that a summer reading loss of three months accumulates to a crucial two-year gap by the time kids are in middle school, even if their schools are equally effective. It suggests that focusing *all* of our efforts on improving the schools isn't going to work.

Children need to read outside of school. Research clearly shows that the key to stemming summer reading loss is finding novel ways to get books into the hands of children during the summer break.

Libraries Fall Short

With schools and their libraries closed for the summer, public libraries might seem like a logical solution. However, those located in poor neighborhoods are often the first to close or restrict hours in a budget crunch. Even when public libraries are open, poor children may lack transportation. Research shows that public library use among poor children drops off when a library is more than six blocks from their home, compared with more than two miles for middle-class children.

Middle-class children might ride their bikes to the library, but poor kids often aren't allowed on the streets by themselves because it's considered too dangerous. And in rural areas, public libraries may be too far away for children to enjoy regularly. Hefty fines for late books can also deter children and their parents from using the public library. Families with little money to spare may not perceive a library that fines as "free."

We also know that teachers and librarians in the poorest communities, are the least likely to allow children to check out books because these schools can't afford to risk the loss of the few books they have. While economically-advantaged schools are able to buy multiple copies of favorite books, poor schools face serious limitations. High-poverty schools use what money they have to buy test-preparation packages, while middle-class schools buy books.

What Schools Can Do

Giving kids access to schools' book collections over the summer is an important start. We suggest these strategies:

1 *Allow students to check out school or classroom library books for the summer.* Staff the library one evening each week during the summer so that children can return the books they've read and select new ones.

2 *Sponsor school bookfairs.* Celebrate the book delivery on the last day of the school year. In schools serving low-income families, money might be allocated from the school budget or from federal program funds to pay for the books.

3 *Create a "Books for a Buck" program.* Recycle donated paperback books and books purchased at garage sales or library sales. At a dollar or even 25 cents apiece, books become more affordable to many children.

4 *Create an "honor library" that provides a steady supply of new and used paperbacks.* Place a cart outside the front doors of the school, or in another public place, where students can borrow books and leave books they've finished reading.

5 *Create a Summer School Voluntary Reading Program.* Make popular reading books available to summer school students to listen to, discuss and read, and take home to share with family and friends.

Motivation Matters

Limited access to books is only part of the reason for summer reading loss. While we know that the more children read, the better their fluency, vocabulary, and comprehension, it is less clear how to motivate children to read. Put simply, children whose reading skills are not strong—who have a history of less-than-successful reading experiences—simply aren't as interested in voluntary reading as are those children with a history of successful reading experiences.

Lower-achieving readers are typically asked to read books that are too difficult. Without books that can be read easily with good comprehension, these less-skilled readers will not improve. All of their cognitive energy is devoted to trying to figure out unknown words—which produces a dysfluent, word-by-word reading with little understanding of, or engagement with, the books in their hands.

These disjointed reading experiences fail to help children consolidate skills, and perhaps most significant, such experiences make children feel unsuccessful. They offer little incentive to persevere and, ultimately, participate in the world of readers. Children don't just need books; they need the right books. Providing children with books that fit—books that match their skill levels and their interests—is an important first step in encouraging voluntary reading.

Holding Their Ground

While the statistics on summer reading loss seem discouraging, there are answers. Studies suggest that children who read as few as six books over the summer maintain the level of reading skills they achieved during the preceding school year. Reading more books leads to even greater success. When children are provided with 10 to 20 self-selected children's books at the end of the regular school year, as many as 50 percent not only maintain their skills, but actually make reading gains.

Summer School Reading

In our current research, we are looking for the most effective ways to support the summer reading of children who struggle with high-stakes assessments and are at risk of failing their grade in school. Many of these children attend mandatory summer school, yet have few opportunities to read extensively in books that are at their level and about topics that truly interest them. Our work suggests that if children have opportunities to listen to, discuss, and read books on topics that they select, or books about characters that they love, they develop extensive background knowledge that can scaffold their independent reading and sustain their engagement. Summer school must provide interventions that accomplish these goals.

Getting the Books Out

School book collections are typically the largest and nearest supply of age-appropriate books for children. When teachers and school libraries can find ways to share books with students over the summer, the gains can be notable. This low-cost, low-intensity intervention obviously can't address the many and varied reading needs of all students. But it it is a starting point. With planning, there are simple ways to ensure that books become available to any child at any time of year—but especially in the summer, when the reading should be easy.

Anne McGill-Franzen and Richard Allington are education professors at the University of Florida. They can be reached via email at mcgillU-FL@aol.com. .

From *Scholastic Instructor*, May/June 2003, pp. 17-18, 58. © 2003 by Scholastic Inc.

A Fresh Look at **Series Books**

Ever-popular, series books can open the door to a lifetime of reading

By Dana Truby

What were your favorite books growing up? Chances are, there is a series book on your list. When Jim Trelease, author of *The Read Aloud Handbook* (Penguin, 2001), asked 2,887 teachers to name their childhood favorites, the one most often mentioned was the Nancy Drew series. Yet, Nancy Drew and her shelfmates, from the Hardy Boys to the Babysitter's Club, have long been shunned by teachers and scorned by many librarians.

Series books have been criticized as being "pernicious," "mindweakening," "addictive," "sensational," and above all, "formulaic." Even the best books of the genre have traditionally been seen as sub-literary. As Trelease points out, "The fear that Harry [Potter] and series books will corrupt the soul is at least as old as the Bobbsey Twins." How, then, are they good for children? For many kids, it's all about the pleasure of reading.

The conventional wisdom is that popular series books are valuable only in that they motivate reluctant readers. "Goosebumps or Fear Street is better than no reading at all," a parent of an 11-year-old said. "At least he's reading." And many parents and teachers feel the same. What they may be surprised to know is that real skill-building occurs when children read for pleasure, even when their choice of books leaves adults cold.

Reading for Pleasure

In her award-winning research on series books, Catherine Sheldrick Ross, a professor and dean at the University of Western Ontario, argues that series books help novice readers develop the reading pleasure that characterizes competent and committed lifelong readers. "The fact that so many of these committed readers have said that series books introduced them to the joy of reading," Ross writes, "suggests that the phenomenon of series book reading deserves a second look." She goes on to ask: "[W]hat gets children reading for the many thousands of hours necessary to produce the bulk of reading practice that creates confident readers?" The key seems to be taking pleasure in the experience of reading.

Practice Makes Readers

Research suggests what many teachers and habitual readers know—it takes practice to become a good reader (or cook, or tennis player) and the better you are at a skill, the more pleasure you are likely to derive from it. Certainly, kids know this. Avid readers, by the age of 12, can list numerous positive reading experiences. On the other hand, 40 percent of weak fourth-grade readers in a 1990 Texas study claimed they would rather clean their rooms than read. (Sad, but perhaps understandable, if success at room-cleaning seems attainable, and success at reading does not.) The cost of reading avoidance, however, is high. Children who read a lot by choice and enjoy it are far more likely to succeed at school than those who dislike reading.

Picking Your Own Books

In a recent discussion of series books, one third-grade teacher from Ohio said, with mock horror, that several of the girls in her class were devoted to the Olsen Twins books and always brought them for SSR (Sustained Silent Reading). Regardless of the "literary" value of such books, research is on the side of kids who follow their reading interests wherever they may lead. In *The Power of Reading* (Libraries Unlimited, 1993), Stephen Krashen makes a strong argument for the power of "free voluntary reading." This means, for Krashen, "putting down a book you don't like and choosing another instead. It's the kind of reading highly literate people do all the time." Readers learn to be better readers not through exercises and multiple-choice questions, but by reading lots of text that they find personally rewarding.

> Once a reader is hooked by a series, the books come with a guarantee of reading pleasure. Series books minimize the risks of reading.

This type of reading can help even the most disadvantaged readers. Jim Trelease cites a study of children who were severe dyslexics, yet managed to attain the highest levels of literacy (e.g., Ph.D.s, J.D.s). What set these children apart was that each developed a passionate interest in a particular subject that drove him or her to read. "In their extensive reading

8 Series for the Classroom

(Arranged from easiest to most difficult—approximately!)

1 *FROG AND TOAD* By Arnold Lobel. Two amphibians star in warm, funny stories about friendship. Great first series.

2 *JUNIE B. JONES* By Barbara Parks. Irrepressible, almost-six-year-old Junie is a read-aloud hit.

3 *A TO Z MYSTERIES* By Ron Roy. Dink, Josh, and Ruth Rose follow clues and solve fun mysteries.

4 *TIME WARP TRIO* By Jon Scieszka. Time travelers Fred, Sam, and Joe meet up with adventure.

5 *MAGIC TREE HOUSE* By Mary Pope Osborne. Travel the world from Egypt to the Amazon and beyond with brave, problem-solving siblings Jack and Annie.

6 *ZACK FILES* By Dan Greenberg. The humorous, fantastical scrapes of 10-year-old Zack. Good, silly fun.

7 *A SERIES OF UNFORTUNATE EVENTS* By Lemony Snicket. Orphans overcome adversity in this witty and enlightening series. Plenty to enjoy for kids, and inside jokes for adults.

8 *REDWALL* By Brian Jacques. Swashbuckling animal adventure tales set in Redwall Abbey. Magical, mystical, and the stuff of legends.

[on their subjects] they continually encountered material or words they already knew and had to filter from words they didn't know—which they also encountered. Thus they learned to skim, surmise, and conclude." Trelease adds, "This is the same thing accomplished by children who fall in love with a particular series of books."

Reading Begins With the Familiar

As this example shows, reading can lead us from the familiar into the unfamiliar. For many children, the first books they read on their own are picture books that were read aloud to them at home or at school. The words of a familiar story are the first words they learn to decode. The better readers know a story, the less they have to rely solely on the words in front of them to make meaning.

Similarly, studies of childhood reading habits consistently show that series books are the first extended texts for many young readers

and are an important transitional stage. They provide lessons in reading—how to sort significant details from the less significant ones, how to anticipate what may or should happen.

Series books, with their consistency of characters and highly patterned plots, provide young readers with the same reassurance of familiarity. Once a reader is hooked by a series, the books come with a guarantee of reading pleasure. "Series books minimize the risks of reading," Ross says, "which is probably particularly important for novice readers who have not yet developed confidence in their ability to make book choices."

What Teachers Say

One of the primary difficulties young readers have is choosing and getting started on a new book. Many teachers find that young readers find the process of selecting a book to read fraught with anxiety. "They find the library overwhelming, and wander back and forth, looking for advice or

for a book to jump off the shelf at them," says Jennifer O'Neil, a third-grade teacher at Chestnut Hill Academy in Philadelphia. "If they haven't developed a reading preference yet, series books really help," she adds. "It gives them somewhere to go for their next book. They like checking them off the list."

Reiko Finamore, a fourth-grade teacher at P.S. 116 in New York City, says that series books help give a new reader confidence, and learn "what it feels like to be a reader—to be hooked on a book." As one of O'Neil's third graders said, series books "keep you busy for a while."

Amy Talbot, a second-grade teacher at Medina Valley Elementary School in Castroville, Texas, says that series books are certainly the first chapter books her students attempt on their own. This year's hits are Junie B. Jones, Cam Jansen, and—most of all—Scooby Doo.

Laurie Pastore, a third-grade teacher at Concord Road Elementary School in Ardsley, New York, believes series books help to spur on her students' reading progress. "I watch children every year hook up with a popular series matched to their reading level and they stay with the series book after book, until they are ready to make the leap to harder texts."

Pastore finds series books helpful for teaching reading strategies. When they know a series well, Pastore says students don't have to work so hard simply decoding. "They can use their energy to develop an ability to retell the book in a concise way, or focus on discriminating between important and unimportant details." When students already know a character, for example, it is easier for them to make suppositions about that character's motivations. Pastore sums up: "I see kids using series books to finally make the connection between the literal text and the figurative meaning that lurks beneath the surface."

What Kids Are Reading

In Jennifer O'Neil's class, this is the year of Lemony Snicket. "They love him," she says. "For perhaps the first time, I have boys discussing literature on the playground." The runners-up for favorite series with O'Neil's students are Zack Files and Torquest.

Lemony Snicket is riding high in Finamore's class as well, where A to Z Mysteries and Jigsaw Jones are also popular. Finamore guides each of her students to choose his or her own book. "Then as a class we work on reading strategy, or story elements such as setting, and character." Pastore also has students read independently, but finds series books can create common ground, "where children begin to talk about literature together," she says. "I can pair up students who like a series and push them into new territory by asking them to think aloud. Usually this causes one or the other to consider the plot or the character in a new light, and it opens new possibilities for them as readers."

Perhaps one of the best arguments for series books is the love and dedication they seem to evoke in children. Asked what they liked about series books, children had lots to say: "Reading books in a series is like reading one huge book," said one boy. The class consensus: "Series books makes you want to keep on reading!"

Dana Truby is the senior editor of *Instructor*.

From *Scholastic Instructor*, May/June 2003, pp. 21-22, 62. © 2003 by Scholastic Inc.

Andy's Right to Privacy in Grading and the *Falvo versus Owasso Public Schools* Case

STEPHEN J. FRIEDMAN

About six years ago, *The Clearing House* published my article "Who Needs to Know That Andy Got a D?" (Friedman 1996). That was the first time that anyone had discussed the laws and professional standards that apply to the situation in which students are required to announce their grades aloud while the teacher writes them in the grade book. After summarizing the Family Educational Rights and Privacy Act (FERPA), I contended that the law was probably not applicable in classroom settings; rather, it addressed records kept by institutions (i.e. buildings and school districts). As it turns out, I was right—according to the Supreme Court of the United States. I would like to share the history of this case and offer a comment on the outcome.

Falvo versus Owasso Public Schools

In October 1998, Kristja Falvo filed suit in th U.S. District Court for the Northern District of Oklahoma on behalf of her three children, who experienced the practice of peers grading their schoolwork and announcing their grades aloud as they were recorded by the teacher. Of particular concern was one of her children, who had been identified as having a special educational need; announcing his grades proved humiliating. Prior to filing the lawsuit, she had asked district administrators and teachers to discontinue these practices, but they refused. Thus, she initiated a class action suit against the Owasso, Oklahoma, Public Schools. Wilfred Wright, Falvo's attorney, argued that rights guaranteed by FERPA and the Fourteenth Amendment were being violated.

In April 1999, Judge Terry Kern ruled in favor of the Owasso Public Schools. Karen Long, attorney for the schools, said, "We're pleased that Kern found the way that he did, that there is no privacy when grading" (Cooper, 1999). A letter written in 1993 by LeRoy S. Rooker, director of the Family Policy Compliance Office (FPCO) at the United States Department of Education, was influential; he argued that papers' being graded by other students are beyond the purview of FERPA because the grades are not being maintained by an educational agency or institution. In 1999, Rooker made a sworn declaration for the defense affirming that the letter stated the current position of the FPCO regarding this grading practice. Regarding the claim that Fourteenth Amendment rights were violated, Judge Kern followed a three-part test that has been applied in similar cases. That there is, in fact, an expectation of privacy is the first part of the test; Kern ruled that the case did not pass this test. He did not view the grades in this case as "highly personal" matters worthy of constitutional protection.

The Appeals

Falvo filed an appeal with the Tenth Circuit Court of Appeals in Denver. In his brief on behalf of Falvo, Wright (2000) argued that privacy in grading can be expected under FERPA. "The U.S. Department of Education concurs that once the student calls out the grade and it is received by the teacher a legal duty exists not to publicly disclose the information. However, the District Court would allow students call out their test grades. Yet this begs the question: how can the law allow the teacher to publicly disclose the test grade, if upon *receipt* of the audible grade information, the teacher is under a legal duty not to disclose the information? Falvo maintains that since a legal duty exists to protect the grade information, the teacher cannot require the student to announce that which is protected" (4–5).

The circuit court justices were persuaded, as Justice Murphy (2000) wrote:

> The grade the correcting student places on the paper is also "maintained," because that student is preserving the grade until the time it is reported to the teachers for further use. In sum, the grades which students mark at the teacher's direction, on each other's homework and test papers later reported to the teacher are "main-

tained… by a person acting for [an educational] agency or institution."

This interpretation of FERPA is consistent with Congress' intent to protect from disclosure grades in a teacher's grade book…. This court therefore concludes that the District Court erred when it resolved that the grading practice did not offend FERPA because the grades at issue did not constitute "education records" protected by that statute. (24–25)

This opinion also indicated that because the Rooker letter and declaration "lack sufficient reasoning, fail to account for the breadth of FERPA's language, and indicate the FPCO's somewhat cursory and purely hypothetical consideration of the issue before this court, the interpretation of FERPA offered in those documents is not persuasive" (22). However, the district court's ruling that there was no violation of rights guaranteed by the Fourteenth Amendment was affirmed.

The Owasso Public Schools appealed the circuit court's decision to the Supreme Court. In support of Owasso, the National Education Association (NEA) and the American Federal of Teachers (AFT) filed an *amicus* brief stating:

NEA and AFT are nationwide employee organizations—with memberships of approximately 2.6 million and one million, respectively. A substantial majority of NEA and AFT members are employed as teachers in public school districts throughout the United States. These members—with the approval of their employing school districts—routinely use the grading practice that is at issue in this case—*i.e.,* the practice of allowing students to grade one another's homework and quizzes as their teacher goes over the answers aloud in class. (1)

Other educational groups including the National School Boards Association, Oklahoma Education Association, and Reporters Committee for Freedom of the Press wrote briefs on behalf of Owasso. John Krumboltz, a professor at Stanford University, offered the following in his *amicus* brief in support of Falvo:

The vast majority of teachers do not use this harmful practice, but the minority who do use it are taking unnecessary risks with the welfare of children…. Teacher efficiency and performance are actually diminished by the practice because valuable class time is spent recording scores instead of learning new material. Besides, it is neither desirable nor necessary for every student paper to be graded…. Arguments that peer grading is some type of long-standing and honored educational practice are nonsense. There is no evidence in the educational literature that the peer grading described here even takes place in the public schools, let alone that it could have some beneficial consequences.

… Clearly the teacher's grade book is an educational record, not a private diary. (3–4)

The case was argued again in November 2001, with Falvo's attorney reaffirming the contention that the educational records that are the focus of this case are covered by FERPA, arguing again that records that have been revealed (as students call out their grades) cannot logically be concealed. The attorney for Owasso argued that the record is not maintained until such time that the teacher writes it in the grade book and therefore is not protected.

The Court found in favor of the Owasso Public Schools, 9–0. In delivering the opinion of the Court on February 19, 2002, Justice Kennedy indicated that interpreting educational records to cover classroom work would "impose substantial burdens on teachers across the country" and would "force teachers to abandon other customary practices, such as group grading of team assignments" (4).

For all these reasons, even assuming a teacher's grade book is an educational record, the Court of Appeals erred, for in all events the grades on students' papers would not be covered under FERPA at least until the teacher has collected them and recorded them in his or her grade book. We limit our holding to this narrow point, and not to decide the broader question whether the grades on individual student assignments, once they are turned in to teachers, are protected by the Act.

The judgment of the Court of Appeals is reversed, and the case is remanded for further proceedings consistent with this opinion. It is so ordered. (5)

Case closed, right? Most of the article that I wrote in 1996 focused on professional guidelines that point in a different direction for teachers, and the Supreme Court's decision has not altered that view.

Previously I addressed only the matter of students' announcing their scores. This case also involves "peer grading," which might be judiciously used by teachers in the early stages of learning, for example, peer editors helping each other improve their drafts before the final products are submitted to the teacher. But this would not entail grading at all. Students might be capable of providing formative feedback or perhaps even scoring their peers' minor homework assignments, but only teachers should be grading students. Similarly, a nurse might take a blood pressure reading, but the doctor is the one who evaluates the information. This is an important distinction that should be made in future discussions of these issues; thus I will generally refer to peer grading, which is consistent with the rhetoric used throughout the case, even though I recoil at the idea. Do we really mean to say that students can competently grade each other? If so, what is the teacher's role in the assessment process?

The Court held to a narrow view that might be consistent with the wording of FERPA. But fulfilling one's professional responsibilities is another matter. It has to do with building trust between one who holds power and one who doesn't. It has to do with erring on the side of caution if the professional is not sure how the patient, client, or even student is feeling. It has to do with affording fundamental respect to anyone seeking help. Many teachers have these feelings for their students and truly merit the label "professional." Even after this ruling, they will continue to treat their students as they always have—respectfully. Prior to the decision, many teachers with whom I shared the details of the case reacted with shock—"I thought that was already illegal!"

Alternative Assessment

The arguments forwarded by Owasso, NEA, and AFT seem to rest on the assumption that these practices are necessary if learning is to occur. Again, some teachers seem to find alternatives. Many of the assignments that teachers now record in their grade books can be treated as opportunities for the students to practice without the worry of being graded. Teachers should explain the reasons for practicing prior to the test. But this should not be too difficult to "sell"; after all, these are numerous real-world examples from which to draw. The student driver, for example, practices extensively before taking the road test and finally obtaining a driver's license. The process of practicing helps learners discover their strengths and weaknesses so that they can improve. This encourages perhaps the best kind of assessment—the ability to self-assess.

Other benefits accrue. Students can feel comfortable learning from their mistakes as opposed to being constantly held accountable in the grade book. Further, it is difficult for teachers to administer high-quality assessments consistently. Although teachers might be gathering a great deal of grading data, what is its quality? Consider student-corrected papers. Was the scoring accurate? If homework assignments are used to help determine the final grade, who actually did the work? If confined to relatively few instances, assessments can be developed that result in reliable scores. Conditions for testing can be controlled, and ultimately teachers can be fairly confident that they have good data on which to base grading decisions. Until we make more extensive use of traditional assessment concepts in the classroom and become better acquainted with their benefits and pitfalls, I will be unconvinced of the need to embarrass students.

And how are all those grades used that many teachers so meticulously gather? In a study in which we were able to interview a group of high school teachers, some interesting perspectives were shared. One teacher lifted her grade book in dramatic fashion and confessed that gathering so much grading data was a source of frustration. She mentioned that the grade book used in her district did not have nearly enough room for all the grades she recorded. We asked: "How do you use all these grades to assign final grades?" Some teachers said that it took a significant amount of time and a calculator. Another "confidently said that she really didn't need all those grades anyway because she could estimate [final] grades and not be off by 'more than half a grade per student'" (Friedman and Truog 1999, 39).

Are schools places where students go to learn or teachers go to teach? Ideally, these should coexist. The NEA and AFT worked with the National Council on Measurement in Education to draft the *Standards for Teacher Competence in Educational Assessment of Students* (1990) which states, "Teachers will be aware that various assessment procedures can be misused or overused resulting in harmful consequences such as embarrassing students [and] violating a student's right to confidentiality... " (32). The position taken by the NEA and AFT in this case appears to run counter to this standard as does Owasso's choice to appeal the circuit court's decision. Their stances seem to align better with the mission statement of the AFT (2000), which emphasizes the welfare of its members; students are not mentioned. Interestingly, though, the *amicus* brief submitted by the NEA and AFT focuses on students' grading each other's work. But this case also involves having students announce their grades aloud. Where do they stand on this, the most reprehensible aspect of the case?

Justice Scalia chided Falvo's attorney at the oral arguments for attempting to elicit sympathy for Falvo's son, who only received 45 minutes of speech therapy each week. Students should tough it out; it is a rite of passage—the path to manhood. It seems illogical to structure inclusive settings in schools for children with special needs and then treat them in this manner. Are we laying a trap or trying to help?

It is one thing for children to be cruel to each other "on their own time"; it is quite another for schools to sanction it (though many districts provide guidelines for student behavior beyond the school day). Some students will likely feel uncomfortable when the responsibility of grading a peer's paper is thrust on them or they are asked to announce their grades (see Campbell 1989). Certainly the issues become much more complex if the peer is a friend (or less than friendly) and judgment is involved. Even some very capable students do not wish to make public their academic prowess. This is especially true of students in middle school, who are experiencing changes in so many aspects of their lives that they could do without one more thing to make them feel self-conscious.

How would teachers who choose to subject their students to these practices feel if placed in a similar position? A few years ago, I presented on this topic at the annual meeting of the National Association of Secondary School Principals. At the beginning of the presentation, I handed out a five-item quiz containing questions related to current topics in the news—items that most reasonably attuned citizens should be able to answer. After giving the attendees a few minutes to complete the quiz, I recited the answers aloud asking them to score their own papers. Then I said that I was interested in their performance—"Those that got them all right, please raise your hands." I paused just long enough to gauge reaction and watch a few nervous glances exchanged. I then announced that this was just an experiment; after all, my topic was "Ethical Issues When Testing and Grading Students." Why the nervous glances? Even in this relatively trivial assessment setting, I had the sense that I was asking something that had the potential to embarrass someone.

After the district court's ruling, I asked an attorney for the University of Wisconsin system why, as a college professor, I couldn't require my students to announce their grades. He said it would probably violate FERPA. When I told him about the ruling, there was a long pause, after which he said that my students simply wouldn't allow it. For students, perhaps being treated with respect comes with age.

Finally, the Court's decision probably is consistent with the letter of the law, which was my sense in 1996 based on a layman's reading of FERPA. Still, the issues that Falvo's attorney raised loom large—How can teachers conceal that which has been revealed? The Supreme Court seems to be primarily concerned about the "burdens" placed on teachers. What about the burdens placed on students? These practices might be legal, but they are unprofessional.

Key words: privacy, student rights, Family Educational Rights and Privacy Act, grades, educational professionalism

References

American Federation of Teachers (AFT). 2000. *Mission statement.* Retrieved from <http://www.aft.org>.

American Federation of Teachers, National Council on Measurement in Education, and National Educational Association. 1990. Standards for teacher competence in educational assessment of students. *Educational Measurement: Issues and Practice* 9 (4): 30–32.

Campbell, M. K. 1989. The long walk: Truly an invasion of privacy. *Religion and Public Education* 16 (3): 419–22.

Cooper, S. 1999. Owasso family loses lawsuit on schools' grading practice. *Tulsa World* Retrieved 28 April from <http://www.tulsaworld.com>.

Friedman, S. J. 1996. Who needs to know that Andy got a D? *The Clearing House* 70 (1): 10–12.

Friedman, S. J., and A. L. Truog. 1999. Evaluation of high school teachers' written grading policies. *ERS Spectrum* 17 (3): 34–43.

Krumboltz, J. 2001. *Brief of Counsel of Counseling Psychology Training Programs as Amicus Curiae in Support of Respondent.* Case No. 00-1073.

Murphy, M. 2000. *United States Court of Appeals for the Tenth Circuit—Falvo v. Owasso Independent School District.* Case No. 99-5130.

National Education Association and American Federation of Teachers. 2001. *Brief for the National Education Association and the American Federation of Teachers, AFL-CIO as Amici Curiae Supporting Petitioners.* Case No. 00-1073.

Supreme Court of the United States. 2002. *Owasso independent school dist. no. 1–011 v. Falvo* (00-1073) 233 F.3d 1203, reversed and remanded. Retrieved from <http://supct.law.cornell.edu/supct/html/00-1073.ZO.html>.

Wright, W. K. 2000. *Appellant's opening brief to United States Court of Appeals for the Tenth Circuit—Falvo v. Owasso Independent School District.* Case No.98-C-765-K.

Stephen J. Friedman is a professor of educational measurement and statistics at the University of Wisconsin-Whitewater.

From *The Clearing House*, November/December 2002, pp. 62-65. © 2002 by Heldref Publications, 1319, Eighteenth St., NW, Washington, DC 20036-1802. Reprinted with permission of the Helen Dwight Reid Educational Foundation.

OBSERVATIONS

Tales of Suburban High

Kay S. Hymowitz

WHEN AMERICANS think about public education, they tend to see a stark divide. On the one hand, there are the failed school systems of our big cities, blackboard jungles where drugs abound, gangs rule the hallways, and dropouts outnumber the barely literate graduates. On the other hand, there are the shining, achievement-oriented public schools of the suburbs, the institutions that have led so many middle-class parents to flee New York City for Westchester or Chicago for Highland Park. In these greener pastures, public education seems to be working fine: students do not have to pass through metal detectors each morning, most of them go on to college, and their parents (according to opinion surveys) are basically content.

The problem with this picture, as we have learned in recent decades, is that, despite their obvious advantages, all is far from well in suburban schools. In 1983, the National Commission on Excellence in Education cautioned that, across the country, SAT scores were flat, and students were falling behind their peers in other nations. College professors began to gripe about incoming students who, even with sterling records in high school, had never heard of the Re-

naissance, or thought Winston Churchill was a Civil War general.

Compounding these pedagogic worries have been concerns about the often poisonous social and moral environment of the high schools in more prosperous communities. After two teenagers turned Columbine High School in Colorado into a killing field in 1999, just about every suburban district in the country began fretting about potential violence. Many launched curriculums to combat sexual harassment, to root out homophobia, to discourage cattiness among girls, and, of course, to stop bullying among boys, the supposed root cause of the massacre at Columbine. More recently, cheating has become an issue, especially with the temptations posed by the Internet. In one much-publicized scandal, a biology teacher at a high school in suburban Kansas City discovered that 28 of her students had downloaded whole sections of their term papers. But when the teacher tried to fail the offenders, the superintendent and parents refused to back her up, apparently seeing nothing remarkable in the transgression. As one student told the chastened teacher, "We won."

That matters are as bad as these instances suggest is amply confirmed by two new books that take us inside the

classrooms of today's suburban high school: Elinor Burkett's *Another Planet: A Year in the Life of a Suburban High School** and Denise Clark Pope's *Doing School: How We Are Creating a Generation of Stressed-Out, Materialistic, and Miseducated Students*.† Burkett, an astute journalist with many previous books to her name, introduces us to Prior Lake High School outside Minneapolis, an overwhelmingly white, middle-class school that sends its better graduates to state universities. The pseudonymous Faircrest High School described by Pope, a lecturer at Stanford's School of Education, is located in a "wealthy California suburb," and is a more diverse institution. Though a third of its students are lower-income Hispanics, Filipinos, or blacks, it also boasts more National Merit scholars than Prior Lake, and more Ivy League aspirants.

For all their differences, both institutions are considered "good" schools. They feature plenty of Advanced Placement (AP) courses, college-hungry kids, and attentive teachers, and their facilities are so fine that one parent in Burkett's account, observing plans for a new school complete with archery and golf ranges, quipped that it looked more like a sports-entertainment complex. The question is: what exactly are these "good" schools good *at*?

AN INSTRUCTIVE place to start is with the teachers. In dress, demeanor, and interests, many of the pedagogues at Prior Lake High School can hardly be distinguished from the hormonal crew they are supposed to be educating. There is the math teacher who brags to his students that he has read only two books in his life, one about highschool football and the other about Elvis Presley. There is the English teacher, with bleached hair and a "Tommy" shirt (because "kids love brand names"), who performs card tricks for his students and regales them with stories about his lost career as a basketball player. And there is the memorable Sandra Sterge, an English teacher—I think—who makes constant sexual innuendos in class, calling attractive male students "hotties" and joking about spending the weekend with them at the Day's Inn.

I say I *think* Sandra Sterge is an English teacher, but it is hard to tell. She sees her role as making sure students "are happy and feel like they belong," which seems to boil down to keeping them entertained. We do not see this former beauty queen instructing students in grammar, essay-writing, or literature—the subjects traditionally associated with her profession. Instead Burkett shows her to us teaching public speaking with a "lip-sync unit," an exercise in which students rap songs with lyrics such as "I like big butts and I cannot lie" and "I'm long and I'm strong and I'm down to get the friction on."

Nor is Sterge alone at Prior Lake in using popular culture as a tool for... well, it is unclear for what. During study hall, students watch the melodramatic psychobabble of *The Maury Show*. The English department insists that students study *The Scarlet Letter*—the movie, not the book. Other teachers show educational fare like the cross-dressing Dustin Hoffman in *Tootsie*.

Keeping students properly diverted is also a key part of the program at Faircrest High in California. Especially striking is Pope's depiction of American-history classes. In one of them, the teacher as-

signs only two projects for the entire semester, so that the students can, in her words, focus "in-depth" and become "experts." As a practical matter, this means that aside from watching a few videos about World War II, they spend most of their time listening to each other's "brief, disconnected reports on... topics as varied as the history of the automobile or the life of Lucille Ball." Another history teacher begins a unit on the 1960's by dressing in a tie-dyed shirt and lighting incense.

As for Faircrest's elite AP course in American history, its chief distinction seems to be higher production values. Eve Lin (as Pope calls one of the school's star students) worked for 250 hours on her part of an "intensive" group research project. Pope describes the culmination of this effort, a presentation in which the members of the group, wearing NASA name tags and T-shirts, escort their classmates into a darkened room decorated with twinkling stars. Through several scene and costume changes, they take the class on makeshift rockets, show film clips about space travel, and, using cardboard cones and Styrofoam cups, demonstrate how the Apollo 13 crew managed to fix their damaged spacecraft—all of this while the music from *Star Wars* blasts in the background. The teacher pronounces the show "magnificent" and gives the group an A+.

Not all the teachers at Prior Lake and Faircrest confuse education with entertainment. Some are serious and demanding, and they attract the most motivated students. But almost all of these exceptional teachers seem to be tired soldiers from a different era, readying themselves for retirement. One math teacher at Prior Lake, a veteran of 27 years, drives her calculus students so hard that they get perfect scores on the AP test at twice the national rate. While most students at the school do a total of two or three hours of homework a week, hers do more than that for her class alone.

But with no school-wide policies on matters like tardiness, plagiarism, and grading, even the most conscientious teachers find themselves without support, and sorely tempted to compromise their standards. Sick of excuses for unfinished homework, they hand out work-

sheets to be completed in class and hold special study groups before each test, resigned to the fact that their students will cram the past month's assignments into a single all-nighter. The hard-driving calculus teacher at Prior Lake compares her school to East Berlin before the wall fell, a place where "nobody did much work because rewards bore little relationship to merit."

WHAT MAY be the saddest part of these accounts is that the students at Prior Lake and Faircrest are not the least bit engaged by the "edutainment" that increasingly dominates their curriculum. To the contrary, they are often contemptuous of their chummy, "with-it" teachers. Eve Lin walks away from the NASA demonstration knowing that her A+ does not add up to much. "All that work for a one-hour performance.... I think people really underestimate what students can do." Others are disgusted by the condescension they constantly experience in the classroom. "She thinks she redefines cool," says one student of Sandra Sterge, the lip-sync queen. "I'm embarrassed for her. Can't she behave like an adult?"

Still, unlike their inner-city peers, the vast majority of these middle-class kids accept their tiresome four years as fate, a necessary prelude to college, which is itself a necessary prelude to a good paycheck. They do not play hooky, threaten teachers, or get into knife fights. Rather, they size up the situation and treat high school like a game, knowing what it takes to win. As one girl tells Burkett, "You can get all A's without learning anything."

This is what Pope means by "doing school," and it takes many forms. Students sign up for courses that include a lot of group projects and then befriend smarter, more conscientious classmates who will perform most of the work. They try to be "interactive," as they sometimes put it, asking a question every few minutes to impress the teacher even as they sit at their desks doing homework for the next class. They whine that a test was too hard, even—or especially—if they know it was not. They try to win over teachers by asking how their training for the marathon is going or whether they enjoyed a weekend date. "I have no interest in the personal lives of the teachers," one girl says of the young man who teaches her government course, "but it's a game, and Mr. Carr is losing."

Whenever possible, they also pick teachers who are reputed to be easy graders or who assign journals or "creative writing" instead of research papers or tests. One of the five "ideal students" whom Pope follows in her book chooses to write her English report on Cesar Chavez—not for reasons of political commitment but because she has saved an A paper about him that she wrote in middle school. They use Cliffs Notes and log onto sparknotes.com to get summaries of the books they are supposed to read, and if such resources do not provide enough help, they cheat.

In all of this, moreover, the students are actively aided and abetted by their parents. In an interview with the *Atlantic Monthly*, Burkett said that nothing shocked her more about Prior Lake than the attitude of the parents, who see themselves not as the allies of the teachers and administrators but as their children's agents. If a teacher is too academically demanding, they lobby to get their child transferred to another class. If junior's grades flag, they demand extra-credit work to let him bring them up. And they gripe: "Why isn't my child getting a higher grade?" "My son never got a B before." As Burkett writes of Prior Lake, "I didn't meet one teacher there demoralized by the low pay. But I met dozens of teachers demoralized by abusive parents who were not willing to let them do their jobs by holding kids to higher standards or by making them work."

Their authority undermined at every turn—not least by their own behavior— teachers find that order in their classrooms is pretty much dependent on adolescent whim. After being called to task for runaway talking, one girl at Prior Lake protests, "It's not my fault, I have ADHD [Attention Deficit Hyperactivity Disorder]." A special-ed student whose disability gives him the right to copies of a teacher's lecture notes feels free to sleep during class. At Faircrest, when several students pull down their pants and moon their classmates, a teacher can do nothing more than tell them to "cut it out."

One of Pope's subjects, a talented but underchallenged student named Michelle, finds herself paired for a project with a class slacker who failed the last test and had not done the reading since the fall, when she lost her textbook. Just as Michelle begins their joint presentation, her partner saunters out of the classroom to go to the bathroom. Michelle presents the material as her classmates take notes. "Slow down!" they yell. "Shit, you weren't supposed to write a book!" The teacher pleads, "Be nice" and "No swearing," but no one listens.

IN HER inability to make sense of these chaotic scenes, Denise Clark Pope unwittingly illustrates how little our self-styled education experts have to tell us about the problems of suburban schools. She views Faircrest through the prism of ed-school cliché. Such schools, she argues, are too focused on achievement and competition, and give short shrift to cooperative learning—even as her examples demonstrate that the latter approach simply leaves the better students to carry the weaker ones. She also suggests, contradictorily, that they do not provide enough opportunities for individualized learning—even as Faircrest students choose paper or research topics that let them get away with as little original work as possible.

Pope is right to object to the cynicism of the game the schools ask their students to play, but she offers no vision of what an educated person should look like. Her chief concern is that young people become "passionately committed" to learning; *what* they learn seems to be a matter of indifference. As she sees it, a Faircrest student who adores her Mexican dance class and another who is deeply involved in his community-service project are models of educational excellence.

Elinor Burkett, who comes to her subject with fewer preconceptions and more curiosity, provides a fresher picture of the suburban high school. But she is no more able than Pope to explain what she has so astutely observed. Indeed, as their two accounts make clear, *none* of the usual suspects takes us very far in assigning blame for the stubborn mediocrity of schools like Prior Lake and Faircrest.

Multiculturalism certainly does not play much of a role; Burkett notes that most of the assigned books are by white males. Nor are the educators at these schools sophisticated enough to have been corrupted by postmodernism— most have not heard of Faulkner, much less Foucault. Burkett makes a strong case for the woeful influence of the religion of self-esteem, but this too seems insufficient. Indulgent as they may be at times, teachers and parents alike do set real goals for the students. At both schools, caffeine-driven, sleep-deprived teenagers have date books crammed with lab-report assignments, church activities, tennis practice, theater and band rehearsals, student-council meetings, and part-time jobs. Finally, the schools impose a measure of order and discipline. Administrators search students' cars, test them for drugs, send them home for wearing T-shirts with provocative messages, and even take them to task for hanging out with the wrong people.

Why, then, do so many middle-class Americans now act as if education is nothing more than a "game"? The ultimate culprits no doubt lie deep in our national character, and most of all in our relentless pragmatism, which here expresses itself in the inability of a single adult in this educational universe to offer a broader view. Along with any serious commitment to subjects like English and history, the idea of education as a way to sharpen mental discipline, to cultivate higher cultural interests, or to teach civic principles has simply disappeared. The course offerings at Prior Lake include journalism, theater, stress management, and "death education" (which includes field trips to a cemetery and an undertaker), and educators now refer to activities like student council and football as "co-curricular" rather than "extra-curricular."

WHEN EVERYONE accepts that education is simply a means to acquire a McMansion and an SUV, the distinction between reading a classic novel and producing an entertaining video dissolves, especially if both efforts are rewarded with a coveted A. When students see teachers standing in front of them lighting incense or nodding approvingly during student presentations about *I Love Lucy*, it is perfectly understandable if they conclude that these adults have nothing serious to offer them, and are undeserving of their respect.

In a discussion of Thomas Jefferson during an honors class at Prior Lake, students demand, "How is this relevant to my life?" When the subject is the Electoral College, they complain, "Why do we have to learn this?" To some extent, this is just typical adolescent provocation. But the truth is, their teacher, an amiable but vapid young man whose literary taste has never evolved beyond John Grisham, does not have the slightest idea how to answer them—how to explain, that is, the importance of some-

thing like citizenship, which does not impinge directly on their immediate wants and needs.

But teenagers are not simply looking to be amused and flattered. At the end of her book, Burkett is surprised to run into one class goof-off who, after graduation, had enlisted in the Marines. He finished basic training with a perfect score on his final exam. "In boot camp," he tells her, "they kick your butt if you don't try your hardest."

Most graduates of our suburban high schools must wait until after graduation—if then—to experience satisfaction of this sort. The education they receive during the decisive years of adolescence not only fails to spark their intellectual and moral imaginations, it hardly even

tries. Instead it aims to produce students like Eric, a top academic achiever at Prior Lake, highly regarded by his teachers. "My belief is that every part of life is a game," he tells Burkett. "The question is: what can I get away with before it's a problem."

---

* HarperCollins, 336 pp., $26.00.

---

†Yale University Press, 240 pp., $24.95.

KAY S. HYMOWITZ *is a contributing editor of* City Journal *and the author of* Ready or Not: What Happens When We Treat Children as Small Adults.

UNIT 8

The Profession of Teaching Today

Unit Selections

Key Points to Consider

- What is "expertise" in teaching? Be specific; use examples.

- Describe the learning needs of new teachers in terms of curriculum, instruction, assessment, management, school culture, and the larger community. How important is maintaining order?

- How would a teacher education program that is based on the premise of developing novice teachers as "transformative" urban educators place student teachers in urban classrooms?

- Why do teachers leave the profession? What can be done to solve schools' staffing problems?

 **Links: www.dushkin.com/online/**
These sites are annotated in the World Wide Web pages.

Canada's SchoolNet Staff Room
http://www.schoolnet.ca/home/e/

Teachers Helping Teachers
http://www.pacificnet.net/~mandel/

The Teachers' Network
http://www.teachers.net

Teaching with Electronic Technology
http://www.wam.umd.edu/~mlhall/teaching.html

The task of helping teachers to grow in their levels of expertise in the classroom falls heavily on those educators who provide professional staff development training in the schools. Meaningful staff development training is extremely important. Several professional concerns are very real in the early career development of teachers. Level of job security or tenure is still an issue, as are the concerns of first-year teachers and teacher educators. How teachers interact with students is a concern to all conscientious, thoughtful teachers.

We continue the dialogue over what makes a teacher "good." There are numerous external pressures on the teaching profession today from a variety of public interest groups. The profession continues to develop its knowledge base on effective teaching through ethnographic and empirical inquiry about classroom practice and teachers' behavior in elementary and secondary classrooms across the nation. Concern continues about how best to teach to enhance insightful, reflective student interaction with the content of instruction. We continue to consider alternative visions of literacy and the roles of teachers in fostering a desire for learning within their students.

All of us who live the life of a teacher are aware of those features that we associate with the concept of a good teacher. In addition, we do well to remember that the teacher/student relationship is both a tacit and an explicit one—one in which teachers' attitude and emotional outreach are as important as students' response to our instructional effort. The teacher/student bond in the teaching/learning process cannot be overemphasized. We must maintain an emotional link in the teacher/student relationship that will compel students to want to accept instruction and attain optimal learning. What, then, constitutes those most defensible standards for assessing good teaching?

The past decade has yielded much in-depth research on the various levels of expertise in the practice of teaching. We know much more now about specific teaching competencies and how they are acquired. Expert teachers do differ from novices and experienced teachers in terms of their capacity to exhibit accurate, integrated, and holistic perceptions and analyses of what goes on when students try to learn in classroom settings. We can now pinpoint some of these qualitative differences.

As the knowledge base of our professional practice continues to expand, we will be able to certify with greater precision what constitutes acceptable ranges of teacher performance based on more clearly defined procedures of practice, as we have, for example, in medicine and dentistry. Medicine is, after all, a practical art as well as a science—and so is teaching. The analogy in terms of setting standards of professional practice is a strong one. Yet the emotional pressure on teachers that theirs is also a performing art, and that clear standards of practice can be applied to that art, is a bitter pill to swallow for many. Hence, the intense reaction of many teachers against external competency testing and any rigorous classroom observation standards. The writing, however, is on the wall: The profession cannot hide behind the tradition that teaching is a special art, unlike all others, which cannot be subjected to objective observational standards, aesthetic critique, or to a standard knowledge base. The public demands the same levels of demonstrable professional standards of practice as are demanded of those in the medical arts.

Likewise, we have identified certain approaches to working with students in the classroom that have been effective. Classroom practices such as cooperative learning strategies have won widespread support for inclusion in the knowledge base on teaching. The knowledge base of the social psychology of life in classrooms has been significantly expanded by collaborative research between classroom teachers and various specialists in psychology and teacher education. This has been accomplished by using anthropological field research techniques to ground theory of classroom practice into demonstrable phenomenological perspectives. Many issues have been raised—and answers found—by basic ethnographic field observations, interviews, and anecdotal record-keeping techniques to understand more precisely how teachers and students interact in the classroom. A rich dialectic is developing among teachers regarding the description of ideal classroom environments. The methodological insight from this research into the day-to-day realities of life in schools is transforming what we know about teaching as a professional activity and how to best advance our knowledge of effective teaching strategies.

Creative, insightful persons who become teachers will usually find ways to network their interests and concerns with other teachers and will make their own opportunities for creative teaching despite external assessment procedures. They acknowledge that the science of teaching involves the observation and measurement of teaching behaviors but that the art of teaching involves the humanistic dimensions of instructional activities, an alertness to the details of what is taught, and equal alertness to how students receive it. Creative, insightful teachers guide class processes and formulate questions according to their perceptions of how students are responding to the material.

To build their aspirations, as well as their self-confidence, teachers must be motivated to an even greater effort for professional growth in the midst of these fundamental revisions. Teachers need support, appreciation, and respect. Simply criticizing them while refusing to alter social and economic conditions that affect the quality of their work will not solve their problems, nor will it lead to excellence in education. Not only must teachers work to improve their public image and the public's confidence in them, but the public must confront its own misunderstandings of the level of commitment required to achieve teacher excellence. Teachers need to know that the public cares about and respects them enough to fund their professional improvement in a primary recognition that they are an all-important force in the life of this nation. The articles in this unit consider the quality of education and the status of the teaching profession today.

What New Teachers Need to Learn

Addressing the learning needs of new teachers can improve both the rate of teacher retention and the quality of the teaching profession.

Sharon Feiman-Nemser

Abrochure advertising a summer institute on mentoring new teachers features a well-dressed teacher standing at the chalkboard. The text reads,

> She has been teaching for three years. Her students really like her. She's dedicated. She's energetic. She's creative.... She's quitting. (Michigan Education Association, 2000)

The message inside the brochure is clear: If this third-year teacher had had a well-trained mentor, she would still be teaching.

The brochure illustrates an emerging consensus among U.S. educators and policymakers that the retention of new teachers depends on effective mentors and induction programs. More states are mandating induction programs than ever before, and many urban districts offer some kind of support to beginning teachers, usually in the form of mentoring.

Still, the overall picture is uneven. Most policy mandates lack an understanding of the learning needs of beginning teachers and of the resources required to create effective programs. Too often, induction programs offer only short-term support to help new teachers survive their first year on the job.

These induction programs generally aim to increase retention by providing emotional support to new teachers. Although this goal is important, it stops short of realizing what powerful induction programs

can accomplish. Keeping new teachers in teaching is not the same as helping them become good teachers. To accomplish the latter, we must treat the first years of teaching as a phase in learning to teach and surround new teachers with a professional culture that supports teacher learning.

Learning to Teach

The early years of teaching are a special time in a teacher's career, different from what has gone before and what comes after. No longer student teachers in someone else's classroom, beginning teachers are on their own, faced with the same responsibilities as their experienced colleagues.

Beginning teachers get hired, often late, and arrive a week before school starts for the year to set up their classrooms and prepare for students. Everything is new: where to put the desks, what to do on the first day and every day after that; who the students are; what their families are like; and what interests, resources, and backgrounds students bring to the classroom. For the novice, the questions are unending: What am I supposed to teach? How will my students be tested? What will their test scores say about me as a teacher? What does the principal expect? Am I supposed to keep my students quiet, or do my colleagues understand that engaged learning sometimes means messy classrooms and active students? And after the first weeks of school, how can I find out what my

students really know, deal with their diverse learning needs, and ensure that everyone is learning?

These questions represent a major learning agenda. They embrace issues of curriculum, instruction, assessment, management, school culture, and the larger community. They go well beyond maintaining order, which most perceive as the primary concern of beginning teachers.

Before novices begin teaching, they go through an initial phase of learning. In a preservice program, they can acquire subject-matter knowledge, study the learning process and students' cultural backgrounds, and acquire a beginning repertoire of approaches to planning, instruction, and assessment. But we misrepresent the process of learning to teach when we consider new teachers as finished products, when we assume that they mostly need to refine existing skills, or when we treat their learning needs as signs of deficiency in their preparation. Beginning teachers have legitimate learning needs that cannot be grasped in advance or outside the contexts of teaching.

What exactly do new teachers need to learn that they could not have learned before they began teaching? In the New Teacher Induction Study, an examination of three well-regarded induction programs in the United States, we asked mentors, principals, and new teachers to reflect on this question. Their responses reflect the special learning needs of beginning teachers (Feiman-Nemser, Carver, Katz, & Schwille, 1999; Feiman-Nemser & Parker, 1993).[1]

The Learning Curve

New teachers need to learn situationally relevant approaches to their subject matter. As one teacher remarked,

> I need to learn to teach subject matter in a way that students are going to get it, not necessarily the way the teacher's manual says to do it.

Standards documents also offer new challenges. One mentor called the district's curriculum standards "a thick foreign language book" that had to be interpreted before beginning teachers could learn to integrate standards into their teaching and not treat standards and teaching as separate tasks.

Each new teacher's learning agenda is also intimately bound up with the personal struggle to craft a public identity. As Featherstone (1993) points out,

> The new teacher is constantly on stage and urgently needs to develop a performing self with whom he or she can live comfortably. (p. 101)

One principal explained that new teachers' understanding of performance needed to include "the nitty-gritty things like transitions and momentum."

New teachers need to learn how to think on their feet, size up situations and decide what to do, study the effects of their practice, and use what they learn to inform their planning and teaching (Ball & Cohen, 1999). New teachers also have to learn to teach in a particular context. For example, one mentor in our study commented,

> Most of our teachers come to the district having little or no concept of what it means to live and be in an urban situation.

With such a large learning agenda, is it any wonder that these early years of teaching represent a period of survival and intense discovery, when the learning curve is steep and emotions run high?

By most accounts, new teachers need three or four years to achieve competence and several more to reach proficiency. If we leave beginning teachers to sink or swim on their own, they may become overwhelmed and leave the field. Alternatively, they may stay, clinging to practices and attitudes that help them survive but do not serve the education needs of students. A high-quality induction program should increase the probability that new teachers learn desirable lessons from their early teaching experiences.

To take new teachers seriously as learners, we must not give them the same responsibilities as veteran teachers or assign them the most difficult classes. With new teacher learning as our goal, induction becomes an educational intervention that addresses new teachers' learning needs while helping them develop a principled teaching practice.

A Process of Enculturation

In addition to being novices to the practice of teaching, new teachers are also newcomers to a particular school community. What kind of organization and culture are new teachers being inducted into?

The induction literature reflects a strong emphasis on adjustment (Griffin, 1987). Phrases like "learning the ropes" and "eased entry" suggest that induction is about helping new teachers fit into the existing system. Even if we object to the passivity of the new teacher that such formulations imply, we still need to think about who is "teaching the ropes" and what they are teaching. What implicit and explicit messages do new teachers receive about teaching in this school and district? How do interactions with colleagues, supervisors, and students strengthen or weaken new teachers' disposition toward students' learning and the new teachers' motivation to continue developing as teachers? Whether the early years of teaching are a time of constructive learning or a period of coping, adjustment, and survival depends largely on the working conditions and culture of teaching that new teachers encounter.

The story of beginning teaching usually revolves around several themes: reality shock, the lonely struggle to survive, and a loss of idealism. Eddy (1969) portrays some of these themes in an early study of new teachers in poor urban schools. She describes how new teachers face difficulties and turn to veteran teachers for advice:

> The solutions offered by the old-timers stress the importance of keeping pupils quietly occupied and forcing them to respond to the activities of the teacher, even if several days, weeks, or months are required to drill them in routines of acting out their subordinate role in the classroom. (p. 18)

When the situations do not improve, new teachers may find some comfort in ascribing their difficulties to traits in pupils or parents or in blaming the administration. Finding support for those views in older colleagues allows new teachers to "maintain a professional identity even when they fail to teach pupils in ways that enable them to achieve" (p. 118). Thus, Eddy concludes, experienced teachers indoctrinate new teachers with attitudes, behaviors, and values that they have defined as appropriate for teachers working in an education bureaucracy.

Painful to read, this study underscores the influential role of colleagues in shaping new teachers' professional stance and practice. As new teachers try to make sense of what is going on in their classrooms, the explanations and advice they encounter, especially from more experienced colleagues, affect their attitudes. Unfortunately, the models and messages available to the new teachers in Eddy's study only served to perpetuate the systemic inequities that still plague education.

Imagine this different induction scenario, based on data from the New Teacher Induction Study.[2] Fern is a beginning teacher in an urban elementary school that faces restructuring because of consistently low performance and administrative troubles. A districtwide initiative has reorganized schools into grade-level teams. Guided by lead teachers, teams are responsible for selecting instructional materials and learning activities, tracking each child's progress, keeping parents informed, and working with students until they meet that level's exit standards.

Although the teacher community is close-knit, the school is not an easy place to begin teaching. First, the redesign process is stressful and uncertain. Second, Fern is anxious about her classroom management skills and believes that her students' behavior is out of control.

Although her official mentor offers material resources for her curriculum and affective support to bolster her confidence, Fern's management difficulties undermine her sense of effectiveness. Fortunately, she receives direct help from a colleague. During an evaluation conference for a special education student, the speech teacher assigned to Fern's grade-level team notices her stress and offers to help. Several times a week, she comes to Fern's classroom, where she works directly with students who are having difficulty and quietly intervenes when student behavior is too disruptive. While Fern focuses on instruction, the speech teacher helps her maintain order by intervening with individual students as needed.

Fern credits the intervention, which continues for about six weeks, with effecting a marked improvement in her students' behavior. Eventually, the speech teacher stops coming on a regular basis, but the assistance has had a positive effect on both Fern and her students. As the year progresses, Fern feels comfortable seeking assistance from other teachers on her team, especially a veteran 3rd grade colleague who shares valuable experience about working with parents. With her team members' ideas about management and instruction, Fern feels less in survival mode and more able to concentrate on instruction.

Historically, schools have not been set up to support the learning of teachers, novice or veteran (Sarason, 1990). The typical organization, which Little (1999) refers to as "individual classrooms connected by a common parking lot" (p. 256), keeps teachers separated from one another, reinforcing their isolation and sense of autonomy. Without easy access to one another, teachers may feel reluctant to share problems or ask for help, believing that good teachers figure things out on their own. Even if teachers do get together, they may not know how to engage in productive talk about teaching and learning. Often concerns for comfort and harmony lead teachers to minimize differences in philosophy or practice and avoid asking for evidence or offering an alternative perspective.

Clearly, schools vary in their openness to innovation and experimentation, their capacity for collaboration around curriculum development and student assessment, and their commitment to shared standards and critical conversation.

We cannot assume that grade-level teams or other school structures automatically provide a forum for addressing new teachers' learning needs. Without the school's explicit endorsement of induction as a shared responsibility and a professional culture that supports collaboration and problem solving, new teachers may still find themselves alone with their questions and problems. Nor can we assume that assigned mentors have the time and the expertise to help novices improve their teaching and their students' learning, or that mentoring can make up for inappropriate teaching assignments. When staffing needs and teacher contracts work against appropriate and responsible placements for beginning teachers, induction support is at best a band-aid.

If, on the other hand, schools make assignments that fit new teachers' backgrounds and interests, provide easy access to resources and practical expertise, and offer regular opportunities for substantive talk about teaching and learning, then new teachers will feel supported by a professional community where all teachers are learners.

Quality Induction

New teachers long for opportunities to learn from their experienced colleagues and want more than social support and instructions for using the copying machine. New teachers want to discuss curriculum implementation, get ideas about how to address specific students' needs, and gain insight from colleagues with experience in their subject areas (Johnson & Kardos, 2002). Providing emotional support is not as valuable as helping new teachers learn to create safe classroom environments, engage all students in worthwhile learning, work effectively with parents, and base instructional decisions on assessment data.

Mentoring

The goal of new teacher learning should define the mentor's role and practice. Mentors often offer help only if the new teacher asks; they don't think of new teachers as learners and themselves as their teachers. When learning to teach is the goal, however, mentors become teachers of teaching, not buddies or local guides.

In many ways, mentoring is an unnatural activity for teachers. Good classroom teachers are effective because they can pull off a seamless performance, monitor student understanding, and engage students in important ideas. But good classroom teachers may not know how to make their thinking visible, explain the principles behind their practice, or break down complex teaching moves into components understandable to a beginner. Nor do they necessarily know how to design an individualized curriculum for learning to teach that is tailored to the specific strengths and vulnerabilities of a particular novice in a specific context.

Serious mentoring oriented around new teacher learning is a professional practice that can be learned. Strong induction programs offer mentors more than a few days of initial training. They provide ongoing opportunities for study and problem solving as mentors carry out their work with new teachers. To learn to mentor in educative ways, mentor teachers need opportunities to clarify their vision of good teaching, to see and analyze effective models of mentoring, to develop skills in observing and talking about teaching in analytic, nonjudgmental ways, and to learn to assess new teachers' progress and their own effectiveness as mentors.

By taking the professional development of mentor teachers seriously, induction programs increase experienced teachers' capacity for critical conversation and joint work, key elements in the creation of authentic professional learning communities. The investment in mentor teacher development also means that induction programs help renew and retain experienced teachers by casting them in new roles as school-based teacher educators.

Using Standards

Because national and state standards reflect visions of good teaching, they can serve to shape conversations about instruction. When we help new teachers assess their progress toward standards, we induct them into professional habits of inquiry and norms of accountability. In the Santa Cruz New Teacher Project, for example, mentors help new teachers identify areas of strength and areas of needed growth using a self-assessment tool (New Teacher Center, 2002) linked to the California Standards for the Teaching Profession. Early in their first year of teaching, new teachers create an individual learning plan that identifies particular development activities designed to improve the new teacher's knowledge and skills. Across the two years of the induction program, regular formative assessments provide the mentors and new teachers with useful data in determining how new teachers are doing, what they need to work on, and how much progress they are making.

The Challenges

Understanding induction as an enculturation process means recognizing that working conditions and school culture powerfully influence the character, quality, and outcome

of new teachers' early years on the job. Even the best induction programs cannot compensate for an unhealthy school climate, a competitive teacher culture, or an inappropriate teaching assignment.

If we take seriously the influential role of school organization and culture on new teachers' stance toward students and on their teaching ideology and practice, we ensure that beginning teachers have easy access to appropriate resources, on-site guidance and coaching, and regular opportunities to work on problems of teaching and learning with experienced, committed teachers.

And if we take teaching seriously as the learning profession, we will foster new teacher learning in a strong professional culture that promotes teacher learning across all experience levels. When we meet their learning needs, new teachers can reach their full potential—not only by staying in the profession but also by improving learning for all students.

Endnotes

1. The New Teacher Induction Study was sponsored by the National Partnership for Excellence and Accountability in Teaching with funds from the U.S. Department of Education, Office of Educational Research and Improvement, and by the Walter S. Johnson Foundation.

2. Daniel Katz constructed this scenario.

References

Ball, D., & Cohen, D. (1999). Developing practice, developing practitioners: Toward a practice-based theory of professional education. In G. Sykes & L. Darling-Hammond (Eds.), *Teaching as the learning profession: Handbook of policy and practice* (pp. 3–32). San Francisco: Jossey-Bass.

Eddy, E. (1969). *Becoming a teacher*. New York: Teachers College Press.

Featherstone, H. (1993). Learning from the first years of classroom teaching: The journey in, the journey out. *Teachers College Record*, 95(1), 93–112.

Feiman-Nemser, S., Carver, C., Katz, D., & Schwille, S. (1999). *New teacher induction: Programs, policies, practices*. Final Report. East Lansing, MI.

Feiman-Nemser, S., & Parker, M. (1993). Mentoring in context: A comparison of two U.S. programs for beginning teachers. *International Journal of Educational Research, 19*(8), 699–718.

Griffin, G. (1987). Foreword. In G. S. Griffin & S. Millies (Eds.), *The first years of teaching*. Chicago: University of Illinois, Chicago.

Johnson, S. M., & Kardos, S. (2002). Keeping new teachers in mind. *Educational Leadership, 59*(6), 13–16.

Little, J. W. (1999). Organizing schools for teacher learning. In G. Sykes & L. Darling-Hammond (Eds.), *Teaching as the learning profession: Handbook of policy and practice* (pp. 233–262). San Francisco: Jossey-Bass.

Michigan Education Association. (2000). Educational Testing Service presents a mentoring institute [Brochure]. East Lansing, MI: Author.

New Teacher Center. (2002). *Continuum of teacher development*. Santa Cruz, CA: Author.

Sarason, S. B. (1990). *The predictable failure of educational reform*. San Francisco: Jossey-Bass.

Sharon Feiman-Nemser is Mandel Professor of Jewish Education at Brandeis University, where she also works in teacher education. She may be reached at Mailstop MS037, 415 South St., Waltham, MA 02454; snemser@brandeis.edu.

The Teacher Shortage: Myth or Reality?

by Richard M. Ingersoll

Few educational problems have received more attention in recent times than the failure to ensure that elementary and secondary classrooms are all staffed with qualified teachers. Education researchers and policymakers have told us again and again that severe teacher shortages are confronting our elementary and secondary schools. At the root of these problems, we are told, is a dramatic increase in the demand for new teachers, resulting primarily from two converging demographic trends: increasing student enrollments and increasing teacher turnover due to a "graying" teaching force. Shortfalls of teachers, the argument continues, are forcing many school systems to fill teaching openings by lowering standards.

The prevailing policy response to these school staffing problems has been attempting to increase the supply of teachers. In recent years a range of initiatives have been implemented to recruit new candidates into teaching. Among these are career-change programs, such as "troops-to-teachers," designed to entice professionals into mid-career switches to teaching and Peace Corps-style programs, such as Teach For America, designed to lure the "best and brightest" into understaffed schools. Many states have instituted alternative certification programs, whereby college graduates can postpone formal education training and begin teaching immediately. Financial incentive, such as signing bonuses, forgiveness of student loans, housing assistance, and tuition reimbursement, have all been instituted to aid recruitment. The "No Child Left Behind Act," passed in winter 2002, provides extensive federal funding for such initiatives.[1]

Over the past decade I have undertaken a series of research projects on teacher supply, demand, quality, and shortages.[2] In this article I will briefly summarize what the data tell us about the realities of school staffing problems and teacher shortages. In my research I adopt an organizational perspective: my view is that looking at these problems from the perspective of the organizations—the schools and districts—where these processes occur is necessary in order to fully understand them. From this perspective, I argue, the data show that such recruitment efforts, however worthwhile, will not solve the teacher-staffing problems schools face. Indeed, I conclude that these efforts are largely a case of the wrong diagnosis and the wrong prescription.

The Project. My primary data source for this research was the nationally representative Schools and Staffing Survey (SASS) and its supplement, the Teacher Followup Survey (TFS), both conducted by the National Center for Education Statistics of the U.S. Department of Education. SASS is the largest and most comprehensive data source available on the staffing, occupational, and organizational aspects of schools. To date, four independent cycles of SASS have been completed: 1987–88; 1990–91; 1993–94; and 1999–2000. Each cycle of SASS administers survey questionnaires to a random sample of some 53,000 teachers and 12,000 principals from all types of schools and from all fifty states. In addition, one year later, the same schools are again contacted, and all those in the original teacher sample who had moved from or left their teaching jobs are given a second questionnaire to elicit information on their departures. This latter group, along with a representative sample of those who stayed in their teaching jobs, comprises the Teacher Followup Survey. The TFS is the largest and most comprehensive data source on teacher turnover, attrition, and migration in the United States.

What do these data tell us about school staffing problems and teacher shortages?

The Importance of Teacher Turnover for School Shortages. The data show that the conventional wisdom on teacher shortages, although partly correct, also errs in important ways. Consistent with shortage predictions, the data show that the demand for teachers has indeed increased. Since 1984, student enrollments have increased, teacher retirements have also increased, most schools have had job openings for teachers, and the size of the elementary and secondary teaching work force has increased. More important, the SASS data tell us that substantial numbers of schools with teaching openings have experienced difficulties filling their positions with qualified candidates.

But the data also show that the demand for new teachers and subsequent staffing difficulties are not primarily due to increases in student enrollment and teacher retirement. Most of the demand and hiring is simply to replace teachers recently departed from their positions; moreover, most of this teacher turnover has little to do with a "graying work force."

Teaching is an occupation with chronic and relatively high annual turnover. One of the best-known sources of national data

Figure 1

Percentage of annual employee turnover and percentage of annual teacher turnover

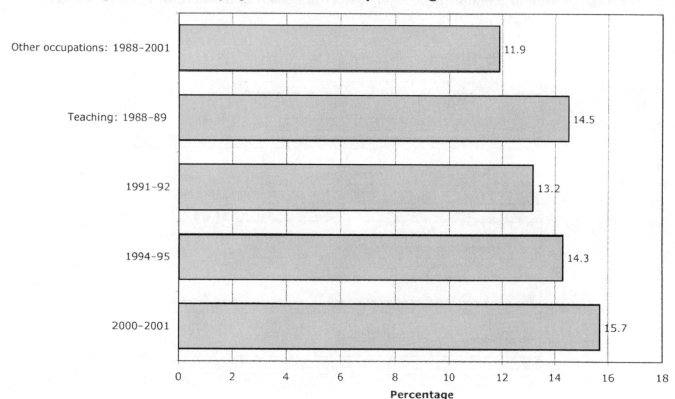

on rates of employee turnover, the Bureau of National Affairs, has shown that nationwide levels of total employee departures for a range of occupations and industries have averaged a stable 11.9 percent per year for the past decade.[3] In contrast, the TFS data show that teaching has a relatively high annual turnover rate: 14.5 percent in 1988–89; 13.2 percent in 1991–92; 14.3 percent in 1994–95; 15.7 percent in 2000–2001 (see fig. 1).[4]

Two types of teachers are included in these data on total turnover: *movers,* defined as those who move to teaching jobs in other schools, and *leavers,* defined as those who leave the teaching occupation altogether. Total teacher turnover is split fairly evenly between the two groups. Cross-school migration does not decrease the overall supply of teachers, because departures are simultaneously new hires. As a result, it seems reasonable to conclude that teacher migration does not contribute to the problem of staffing schools and to overall shortages. From a macro and systemic level of analysis, this conclusion is probably correct, and for this reason educational researchers have often de-emphasized or excluded movers. However, from an organizational-level perspective and from the viewpoint of managers, movers and leavers have the same effect—either situation results in a vacancy, which usually must be filled. Hence, research on employee turnover in other occupations and organizations and data such as those from the Bureau of Na-

tional Affairs almost always include both movers and leavers, and for this reason I include them here.

It is also important to note that teaching is a relatively large occupation: it represents 4 percent of the entire civilian work force. There are, for example, more than twice as many K–12 teachers as registered nurses and five times as many teachers as either lawyers or professors. The sheer size of the teaching force, combined with the relatively high annual turnover of the teaching occupation, means that there are relatively large flows into, through, and from schools each year. The image these data suggest is a revolving door.

Of course, not all teacher or employee turnover is a bad thing. Those who study organizations and occupations in general have compiled an extensive research literature on employee turnover.[5] On the one hand, researchers in this tradition have long held that some employee turnover is normal and efficacious in a well-managed organization. They tie infrequent turnover of employees to stagnancy in organizations; effective organizations usually both promote and benefit from limited turnover by eliminating low-caliber performers and bringing in "new blood" to facilitate innovation. On the other hand, researchers in this tradition have also long held that high employee turnover is both the cause and effect of performance problems in organizations.

Figure 2

Percentage of annual teacher turnover, by selected school characteristics (2000–2001)

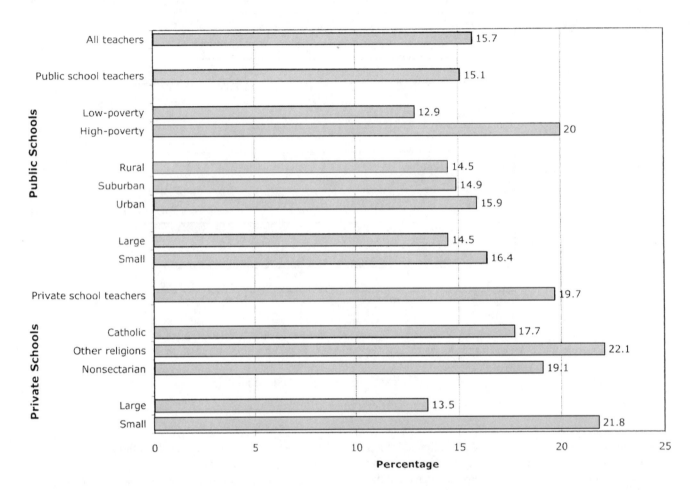

From an organizational perspective, employee turnover is especially consequential in work sites like schools, whose "production processes" require extensive interaction among participants. Such organizations are unusually dependent upon commitment, continuity, and cohesion among employees and, hence, especially vulnerable to employee turnover. From this perspective, then, high teacher turnover matters not simply because it may indicate sites of potential staffing problems but because of its relationship to school performance. Moreover, from this perspective high teacher turnover is of concern not only because it may indicate underlying problems in how well schools function but also because it can be disruptive, in and of itself, to the quality of school cohesion and performance.

However, although the data show that teaching has relatively high turnover, the data also show that the revolving door varies greatly among different kinds of teachers and different kinds of schools. As found in previous research, SASS data show that teaching loses many of its newly trained members long before the retirement years.[6] I used these data to calculate a rough es-

timate of the cumulative occupational attrition of teachers in their first few years of teaching. The data suggest that after just five years, between 40 and 50 percent of all beginning teachers leave teaching altogether.

Moreover, the data also show that the revolving door varies greatly among different kinds of schools, as illustrated in Figure 2. For example, high-poverty public schools have far higher turnover rates than do more affluent public schools. Urban public schools have slightly more turnover than do suburban and rural public schools.

Private schools have higher turnover rates than public schools, yet there are large differences among private schools. On one end of the continuum lie larger private schools, with among the lowest average turnover rate: about 13.5 percent, close to what is found in other occupations. On the other end of the continuum lie smaller private schools. The turnover rates of smaller private schools have the highest average levels: about 22 percent. The turnover rate in these schools is almost double the national average for many other kinds of employees.

Figure 3

Percentage of school teachers giving various reasons for their turnover (1994–95)

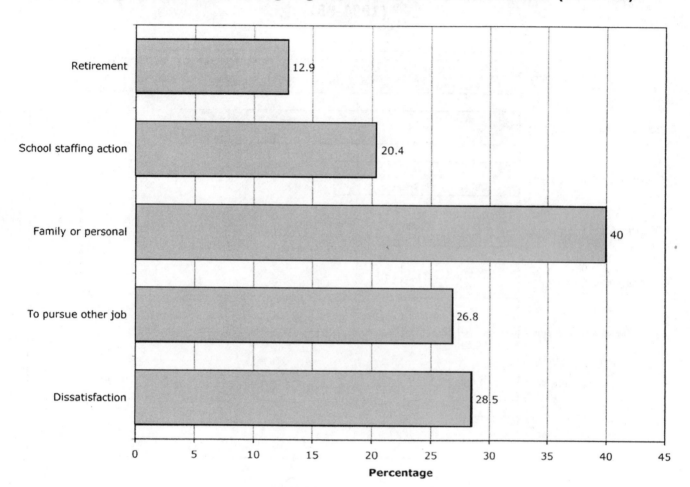

These data raise important questions: Why do teachers depart at relatively high rates, and why do these rates differ so dramatically between schools?

The Sources of Teacher Turnover. To answer these questions I conducted extensive advanced statistical analyses of the data from different SASS/TFS cycles to determine which characteristics of teachers and schools correlate with the likelihood of teacher turnover, and I also closely examined data on the reasons teachers themselves give for their turnover. I found considerable consistency among these different types of data and among different cycles of the survey. In Figure 3, I summarize the principal findings from these different analyses.

Contrary to conventional wisdom, retirement is not an especially prominent factor. The latter actually accounts for only 13 percent of total turnover.

School staffing cutbacks due to layoffs, terminations, school closings, and reorganizations account for more turnover than does retirement. These staffing actions more often result in migration to other teaching jobs than in abandoning teaching altogether. However, the data also show that staffing actions, like retirement, account for little of total teacher turnover.

A third category of turnover, personal reasons, includes departures for pregnancy, child rearing, health problems, and family moves. They account for more turnover than either retirement or staffing actions, and the data also show that these motives are common to all schools.

Finally, two reasons directly related to the working and organizational conditions of teaching are, together, the most prominent sources of turnover. Far more turnover results from such factors than from retirements. Almost half of all departures report as a motivation 1) job dissatisfaction or 2) a desire to pursue better jobs, different careers, or improved career opportunities, in or out of education.

Teachers who leave because of job dissatisfaction most often link their departure to low salaries, lack of support from administration, discipline problems, and lack of influence over decision-making. Interestingly, several factors stand out as not serious enough to cause much turnover from schools: large class sizes, intrusions on classroom time, and insufficient plan-

Figure 4

Percentage of school teachers giving various reasons for their dissatisfaction-related turnover (1994–95)

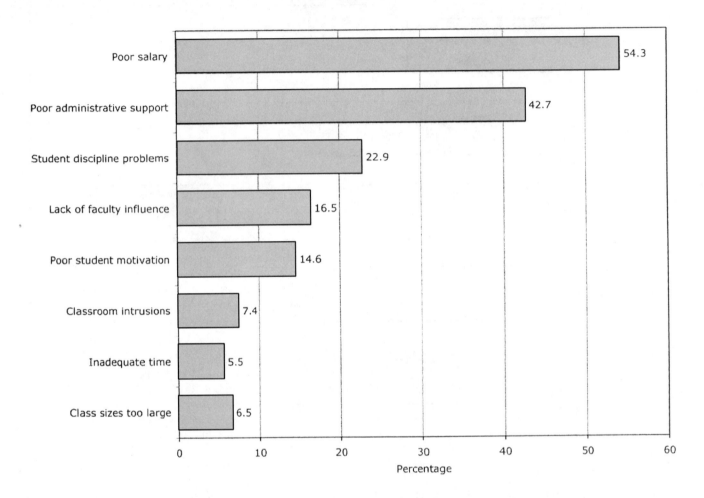

ning time (see Figure 4). These latter findings are important because of their implications for policy.

Implications. It is widely believed that two converging demographic trends—increasing student enrollments and increasing teacher retirements—have led to school staffing problems and, in turn, lowered educational performance. In response, school districts, states, and the federal governments have developed a variety of recruitment initiatives designed to bring more candidates into teaching.

The data suggest, however, that these efforts, perhaps worthwhile, will not by themselves solve school staffing problems. The data suggest that these problems are not primarily due to shortfalls resulting from increases in student enrollment or in teacher retirement. In contrast, the data suggest that school staffing problems result from a revolving-door syndrome: large numbers of teachers departing from teaching for reasons other than retirement. In short, the problem is not primarily shortages, in the conventional sense of too few teachers being recruited

and trained; rather, the problem is turnover: too many teachers departing prior to retirement.

This distinction is important because of its implications for educational policy. Supply-and-demand theory holds that where the quantity of teachers demanded is greater than that supplied, there are two basic policy remedies: increasing the quantity supplied or decreasing the quantity demanded. Teacher recruitment, an example of the former approach, has been and continues to be the dominant approach to addressing school-staffing inadequacies. However, this analysis suggests that recruitment programs alone will not solve schools' staffing problems, if they do not also address the problem of teacher retention. States such as California, where reductions in class size have strained the supply of new teachers, pose exceptions. But for just such reasons, California must, like other states, pay more attention to retention. In short, recruiting more teachers will not solve the teacher crisis if large numbers of such teachers then leave. The image that comes to mind is that of a bucket rapidly losing water because of holes in the bottom.

Pouring more water into the bucket will not solve the problem if the holes are not first patched.

One strategy suggested by the data for plugging these holes is increasing teacher salaries, which are, not surprisingly, strongly linked to teacher turnover rates. Increasing salaries is, of course, expensive, given the sheer size of the teaching force.

A second factor suggested by the data is increased support from school administrations, especially for new teachers. Supportive measures could range from ensuring sufficient classroom supplies to providing mentoring for new teachers. The latter is crucial; life for beginning teachers has traditionally been described as a sink-or-swim proposition, and as the data show, turnover is especially high among new teachers.

A third factor suggested by this analysis is enhanced faculty input into school decision-making. Other data from SASS indicate that, on average, teachers have little say in many key decisions concerned with and affecting their work.[7] But these data also indicate large variations among schools, and those where teachers are allowed more input into decisions that affect their jobs have less turnover.

Reduction of discipline problems is a fourth factor tied to teacher turnover. The data tell us that, regardless of the background and poverty levels of the student population, schools vary dramatically in the degree of student misbehavior and again, not surprisingly, that schools with significant student misbehavior problems have significant teacher turnover. One factor tied to both student discipline and teacher turnover is how much decision-making influence teachers themselves have over school policies concerned with student behavioral rules and sanctions: schools where teachers say they are allowed more input into these kinds of issues witness less conflict between staff and students and less teacher turnover.[8]

The data do not suggest that plugging holes through such changes will be easy. But from the perspective of this analysis, schools are not simply victims of inexorable demographic trends, and the management and organization of schools play significant roles in both generating and solving school staffing problems. The data suggest that improvements in such aspects of teaching would contribute to lower turnover rates, in turn diminish school staff problems, and, hence, ultimately aid school performance.

Notes

1. For a review of these initiatives, see Eric Hirsch, Julie Koppich, and Mike Knapp, *Revisiting What States Are Doing to Improve the Quality of Teaching: An Update on Patterns and Trends* (Center for the Study of Teaching and Policy, University of Washington, 2001).

2. See Richard M. Ingersoll, "The Problem of Underqualified Teachers in American Secondary Schools," *Educational Researcher* 28 (1999): 26–37 (available at <http://www.aera.net/pubs/er/arts/2802/ingsoll01.htm>); Richard M. Ingersoll, "Teacher Turnover and Teacher Shortages: An Organizational Analysis," *American Educational Research Journal* 37, no. 3 (2001): 499–534; and Richard M. Ingersoll, "The Teacher Shortage: A Case of Wrong Diagnosis and Wrong Prescription," *NASSP Bulletin* 86, no. 631 (summer 2002): 16–30.

3. Bureau of National Affairs, "BNA's Quarterly Report on Job Absence and Turnover," *Bulletin to Management* (Washington, D.C.: Bureau of National Affairs, 2002).

4. The 2000–2001 teacher turnover data in figures 1 and 2 are preliminary estimates. As of fall 2002, the 2000–2001 TFS had not yet been entirely released by NCES. However, these figures are consistent with similar data from the earlier cycles of the TFS.

5. See W. A. Mobley, *Employee Turnover: Causes, Consequences and Control* (Reading, Mass: Addison-Wesley, 1982). See also James Price, *The Study of Turnover* (Ames, Ia.: Iowa State University Press, 1977).

6. See Richard Murnane, Judith Singer, John Willett, J. Kemple, and R. Olsen (eds.), *Who Will Teach? Policies That Matter* (Cambridge, Mass.: Harvard University Press, 1991).

7. Richard M. Ingersoll, *Who Controls Teachers' Work? Power and Accountability in America's Schools* (Cambridge, Mass.: Harvard University Press, 2003). Available at <http://www.hup.harvard.edu/catalog/INGWHO.html>.

8. Ibid.

Richard M. Ingersoll is Associate Professor of Education and Sociology at the University of Pennsylvania. This piece draws from a longer article published in the Fall 2001 issue of the American Educational Research Journal.

Developing Novice Teachers as Change Agents:
Student Teacher Placements "Against the Grain"

By Sheila Lane, Nancy Lacefield-Parachini, & JoAnne Isken

Introduction

Efforts at reforming urban schools have often revolved around choosing the "right" formulaic programs or providing sufficient funds to repair schools. However, too little attention has been paid to staffing schools with competent teachers who desire to stay and effect reform. Finding ways to educate student teachers and novice teachers at these schools so they see themselves as capable of generating substantive change has been difficult. How does a university assist student teachers at urban sites to become both competent and empowered while simultaneously learning to teach?

Feiman-Nemser (1990) has described conceptual orientations in teacher education as "cluster[s] of ideas about the goals of teacher preparation and the means for achieving them" (p. 1). She describes a "critical orientation" as one that "combines a progressive social vision with a radical critique of schooling. On the one hand, there is optimistic faith in the power of education to help shape a new social order; on the other, there is a sobering realization that schools have been instrumental in preserving social inequities" (p. 6). Yet, a teacher education program committed to reforming urban schools with student teachers becoming "critical educators" faces several dilemmas when placing student teachers. One dilemma is the shortage of "model" guiding[1] teachers in urban schools. According to Haberman (1993), only 5–8 percent of the current teachers in urban schools are considered outstanding teachers. A second dilemma is that there are many potential guiding teachers in urban schools whose conceptual orientation about students and learning differs from that of the university. These guiding teachers create a classroom model that often contradicts the beliefs of the student teachers. A third dilemma is that most teachers in urban schools do not conceive of their role as being a change agent: "… in Goodlad's (1990) recent survey of pre-service programs nationwide, only 5 percent of student and faculty respondents, when questioned about the role of teachers in schools, alluded to the idea that the teacher could be an agent for change" (Goodlad as cited in Cochran-Smith, 1991, p. 281). A fourth dilemma is that most models of the guiding teacher-student teacher relationship are unidirectional, based on the transmission concept of a mentor-mentee relationship where there is just one learner and one teacher. Within this traditional apprenticeship model, the novice is rarely encouraged to think critically or question the practices of the expert. A thoughtful university's goal, on the other hand, must be to develop teachers who "… view knowledge and situations as problematic and socially constructed rather than as certain" (Zeichner & Liston, 1987, p. 288).

As teacher educators who place student teachers solely in urban settings, we contend that novice teachers need to develop feelings of "ownership" so they feel empowered to transform the urban educational setting rather than feel defeated by it. The question, then, is this: How does a teacher education program based on the premise of developing novice teachers as "transformative" urban educators (Giroux, 1986) place student teachers in urban classrooms?

We sought to investigate this question by examining the placement of our student teachers in two urban schools. Cochran-Smith (1991) reports findings from having placed student teachers with cooperative teachers who were "… themselves struggling to teach against the grain" (p. 285), and who believed strongly in the teacher's role as reform agent. She found that: "Despite their inexperience, student teachers do learn about teaching against the grain when they talk with experienced teachers within a collaborative context where questions are urged, answers are not expected, and the tentative forays of beginners are supported" (p. 285). Because of the dilemmas described earlier, as well as the "critical orientation" of our teacher education program, we however found ourselves in a situation different from the one Cochran-Smith discussed. We placed a group of student teachers at two urban elementary schools with guiding teachers who were not strong proponents of reform and possessed beliefs different from the critical orientation of the teacher education program. Instead, the student teachers were reform-minded and encouraged to work collaboratively with their guiding teachers. Thus, they were differently placed "against the grain" (Cochran-Smith, 1991). Data were collected on these student teachers over the academic year, and it emerged that they had a substantial impact on the practice of their guiding teachers. This led to further inquiry on two main questions: Do certain student teacher placements engender critical reflection on the part of both student teachers and guiding teachers? What everyday practices are challenged by these kinds of placements?

This research was conducted by the three of us: two principals at urban schools (both schools with over 95 percent of students eligible for a free or reduced lunch) in which the focal student teachers were placed and a university faculty member serving as university liaison from UCLA's Graduate School of Education and Information Studies Center X Teacher Education Program. The principals also headed a team of student teachers who student taught at their school sites. The principals conducted a weekly seminar for the student teachers; the university liaison participated in the seminar as well, and also observed the student teachers regularly. While student teaching, both students and guiding teachers wrote in interactive journals regularly, thus encouraging reflection and questioning by both. In addition, after their first year, beginning teachers continued meeting with the university liaison, participating in seminar and [writing] their Master's Portfolio. These journals and portfolios as well as interviews were selected as data over the last five years.

Believing that not all of the guiding teachers would have the same critical orientation as that of Center X and the student teachers, the principals exhorted the student teachers to question the practices of their guiding teachers. Student teachers were expected to develop their strong theoretical principles into a practice consistent with their conceptions of how their students learn. The principals, university liaison and student teachers all read literature about the common pressure in urban schools, an institutional pressure, to conform to the "norms" of the school or get pushed out (Weiner, 1993). In order to counter this pressure, student teachers were pushed to examine and confront their beliefs continually, and were charged to help their guiding teachers to do the same. Thus, their reflections during student teaching were not only about their practice, *but were about how they believed their practice was affecting their guiding teachers.* They were expected to develop strong enough principles so they could continue this conceptual orientation during their first year of teaching, and thus were expected to challenge the practices and beliefs of their schools.

At both schools, at the end of the first year, it was found that the preservice teachers had become change agents for their guiding teachers in terms of implementing changes and thinking about practice. This finding fueled additional study and analysis to flesh out the conditions under which our students effect change in their placements.

The Program

UCLA's Graduate School of Education and Information Studies' Center X Teacher Education Program's aim is to nurture "critical (transformative) pedagogues": urban teachers who challenge the conditions they find and feel empowered to change them. The program works solely with urban schools, and supports their students in the field for two years: the first year while earning their teaching credential, and the second as a full-time teacher in an urban school. Student teachers are encouraged to employ sociocultural teaching methods and to become social change agents in their schools and communities, and to view cultural and linguistic diversity as an asset to teaching and learning. During the second year, while teaching, students return for university seminars and classes and write a Master's Portfolio. One of our teachers, "Maria," reflected on the uniqueness of this teacher education model during her first year teaching in an urban school:

> *When I see or hear about new teachers implementing classroom strategies that they adopt from their teacher education programs, I find myself thinking that they have been brainwashed. They have not had to question or struggle with their identities as teachers; they just do what their program tells them to do. These teachers do not have ownership over the strategies they implement.*

During both years, students are continually encouraged to question and reflect on their practice and link their practice to theory. They examine how their everyday actions reflect a socially just philosophy. They also examine the underlying political and economic forces which work to maintain the status quo at their school sites. The program stresses the five components Bennett (1995) describes as "... a model of preparing teachers for diversity: ... selection, understanding multiple historical perspectives, developing intercultural competence, combating racism, and teacher decision making" (Bennett as cited in Ladson-Billings, 1999, p. 223).

Existing Research

Limited research exists around guiding teachers (Ariav & Clinard, 1996; Ganser, 1997; Hamlin, 1997). Cochran-Smith's (1991) study emphasized the effects of cooperating teachers on student teachers, although she did find that, as a result of the frequent discussions and reflections, the role of the cooperating teachers was "much more extensive than the demonstration and evaluation of teaching strategies" (p. 305). Hamlin (1997), in an extensive study, found changes in supervising teachers as falling in four categories: learning "... new ideas and activities... ; review/reinforcement of techniques... ; reflection and analysis of current teaching practices; and renewed excitement about teaching" (p. 81). Ariav and Clinard (1996) found some additional benefits: supervision gave the teacher an opportunity to observe her children, which gave her a "... different perspective on their personalities" (p. 10). These studies also found that teachers enjoyed the opportunities for discussions not common at their schools, and learning how to be more reflective. Ganser (1997) surveyed both cooperating and mentor teachers and also found them describing the benefits of working with a student teacher. Those benefits included increased thinking about long-range planning, and a kind of professional rejuvenation. One mentioned that he/she became more tolerant of mistakes as a result. While these studies reveal a willingness on the part of guiding teachers to be reflective, there's no evidence that reflection led to actual change in their practice.

Vann (1988–89) has a broader point of view and suggests that the entire urban school often benefits from hosting student teachers: "To neglect an opportunity to place a student teacher in a situation that could improve student performance and indirectly contribute to a strengthening of the entire staff and school in the process [through involving guiding teachers in a reflective process] would be irresponsible" (p. 60). D. Kagan (1992) discusses student teacher placements in which the guiding teacher and student teacher do not have the same conceptual orientation and argues that "... growth on the part of the guiding teacher may also occur in these settings because cooperating teachers need to be prepared to discuss opposing beliefs rather than demand blind conformity" (p. 163).

In addition, Kagan states that student teachers would benefit from such placements because they "... were more likely to examine and reconstruct their own beliefs if they were confronted with cooperating teachers whose beliefs were different from their own" (p. 157). She emphasizes: "cognitive dissonance may be necessary for novices to confront their own beliefs and images and acknowledge that they need adjustment... Student teachers need to understand that benefits may accrue from immediate discomfort" (p. 163). The idea that placements of this nature stimulate critical, reflective practice by both the guiding teacher and the student teacher is also supported by Tom (1985): "... to make teaching problematic is to raise doubts about what, under ordinary circumstances appear to be effective or wise practice... the objects of our doubts might be typical ways teachers respond to classroom management issues, customary beliefs about the relationship of schooling to society, or ordinary definitions of teacher authority—both in the classroom and in the broader school context" (p. 37).

The extent to which these studies focused on urban sites is not clear. As well, the conceptual orientation of the guiding teachers vis a vis the supporting academic institutions is not clear. This suggested to us a need to conduct research solely in urban sites. Further, student teachers ought to learn to teach in urban sites, despite the shortage of "model" guiding teachers. More research is needed; this study is an attempt to fill this gap.

Part Two:

How Do Guiding and Student Teachers Work Together?

Most conceptions of the relationship between guiding teachers and student teachers envision a forward moving linear relationship, that of the mentor training the mentee, the expert training the novice. In many traditional models, student teachers are placed with mentor classroom teachers and are expected to imitate and replicate their practices. These kinds of linear learning relationships in a traditional apprenticeship model have been questioned and reconsidered by Lave and Wenger (1991). Wenger (1998) conceptualized a relationship as a more dynamic one, one of "changing participation and identity transformation in a community of practice" (p. 11). In line with this, we are researching the premise of a possible conceptual change in the relationship between the guiding teacher and the student teacher to a kind of cognitive apprenticeship, where both would be involved in "sense-making" as a part of a dialogical relationship, one in which both parties could have an equal effect on the other (Shor, 1992). Murrell (2002) describes a "community teacher" as one prepared through "the immersion of candidates in a rich context of collaborative activity and inquiry" (p. 16). He emphasizes that student teachers need to develop "a situated understanding of people, principles, and context" (p. 17). Gaining what Murrell calls a "cultural learning perspective" (p. 16) will help them in their development as change agents during their cognitive apprenticeship in a community of practice.

This "against the grain" student teaching model focused on preparing teachers "... not just for the mechanics of their occupation... but to develop in them intellectual habits of reflection on their calling... that are the mark of a professional continually engaged in self-improvement" (Goodlad, p. 38 as cited in Yost, 1997). As a part of the "against the grain model," the student teacher and guiding teacher wrote to each other in an interactive journal which contained questions and answers from both the guiding teacher and the student teacher, as well as reflections from both. During these interactions, which are a part of the data, they were making their thinking visible. This kind of dialogue, envisioned by Zeichner (1993), where student teachers and their guiding teachers are looking at how their "... everyday actions challenge or support various oppressions and injustices relate[d] to social class, race, gender, sexual preference, [and] religion... [can become] a central part of teachers' reflections" (p. 14). In a traditional transmission model, this rich interaction would not take place; instead, student teaching would be looked at mainly as a kind of training model in techniques and methods.

Ladson-Billings (1999) also described a model teacher education program with a critical orientation, one in which "the emphasis on understanding race and racism is not a goal in itself but, rather, a means for helping students develop pedagogical options that disrupt racist classroom practices and structural inequities" (p. 237). Building on this literature, we developed our research agenda, which examined how our students "disrupted practices" at their school sites while they student taught or were in their first year of teaching as well as how their guiding teachers were changed as a result of their interaction.

Methods and Data Sources

We selected and analyzed data on all of the student teachers and their guiding teachers. Each year, because of a shortage of "model" guiding teachers, a subset of three to five student teachers in the cohort was placed "against the grain." After identifying themes in the data, we selected some robust examples for further analysis of that theme.

Data came from interactive dialogue journals student teachers and guiding teachers kept during the student teaching experience. In addition, student teachers wrote weekly reflections and lesson analyses. Guiding teachers, principals and student teachers were interviewed. Videotaped lessons were analyzed as well. During their second year in the program, students wrote master's degrees portfolios which included analyses of their practice and reflections on theory and practice, which were analyzed. In addition, field observations by the university liaison and the principals were analyzed. Three to five interactions between students and guiding teachers and from first year teachers were selected for further study because they revealed a reflective interactive dialogue between guiding teacher and student teacher or revealed an action plan for change by teacher participants. From that population, one teacher and her student teachers were studied for five years. A case study is being written about this teacher; excerpts are included here.

A systematic analysis of the data was conducted and we coded the data. Initial analysis of data was based on Hamlin's (1997) four categories of change in supervising teachers: learning new ideas and activities; review/reinforcement of techniques; reflection and analysis of current teaching practices; and renewed excitement about teaching (p. 81). However, we found these categories inadequate in describing the development of the teaching ideas of the guiding teachers as well as those of the student teachers. We identified patterns of practice in which commitment to effecting change emerged: grouping students; community building; and social justice projects that demonstrated the development of teacher agency. These themes were transformed during different stages of teacher development. *For student teachers,* we coded the work for new ideas posed during their student teaching experience. *For the guiding teachers,* we studied ideas tried from novice teachers that challenged their own practice. *For the full time first year urban teacher,* we focused on ideas tried that challenged practices of the school in which they were teaching. As a part of examining teacher agency, specific statements were examined for personal pronoun referents, e.g. "I'm planning on trying that."

To derive final conclusions, data were examined to define major categories and patterns and to answer research questions (Yin, 1989). Facts and information from the different methods of data collection were triangulated to seek convergences from two or three independent sources. Efforts to arrive at the same meaning by at least three independent approaches [were] used (Stake, 1985). The effect of the change factor was examined from entries in the student teacher-guiding teacher's interactive journals, from teacher and principal interviews, and from other writings.

Results/Educational Importance

The main finding that emerged from the study was that the student teachers became change agents and had an impact on the practice of guiding teachers at the schools. The student teachers had such strong beliefs that they did not waver even when confronted by guiding teachers with differing conceptual orientations. Rather than being co-opted by the "grain," they changed the "grain." Vignettes from the writings of the participants, both guiding and student teachers, indicate the efficacy of the student teachers. These student teachers continued to be studied the following year, during their first year of teaching. Their commitment to remain agents of change are clearly described in reflective writings in which they describe ways in which they challenged the practices of their schools.

One key result was that the relationship between the student teachers and guiding teachers was, in fact, bi-directional and recursive. Clark and Peterson (1986) described the relationship between teacher behavior, student behavior, and student achievement as circular and not linear. The data in this study reveal the same circular relationship between preservice teacher behavior, student behavior and achievement, and guiding teacher behavior and achievement. Each one's behavior affected the behavior and interactions of the other. However, in the case of these preservice teachers, the classroom experiences and dialogue constructed by the preservice teachers and the guiding teachers resulted in strong changes in the guiding teachers, both in teaching practice and in thinking in a social justice framework.

Discussing effective staff development, Wilson and Berne (1999) described several characteristics of successful programs: "is collaborative, providing opportunities for teachers to interact with peers… incorporates constructivist approaches to teaching and learning; recognizes teachers as professionals and adult learners" (Abdal-Haqq, 1995, as cited in Wilson & Berne, p. 175). They emphasized that teachers have little experience engaging in "professional discourse" so they can develop "critical collegiality." However, in the current study, because the guiding teachers were working with student teachers and thus were viewed as "experts" by the surrounding school community, they may have been more willing to engage in the kind of professional, "critical" interactive discourse that eventually resulted in changes in their points of view towards their students. These changes in their conceptual orientations about their students were reflected in changes in their practice. One example of this change was their seeing students as being capable of work in small groups, which they were unable to acknowledge before having a student teacher in their classroom.

Three main sites of change emerged in the dialogue journals: one based on grouping children in the classroom; one based on building community in the classroom; and one based on opposing the practices at school sites. Those areas are exemplars in which the conceptual orientation that novices brought to the setting was contradictory to the practices of the guiding teachers or the school.

Grouping Children/Challenging Practices of the Guiding Teacher and School

One guiding teacher whom we have been studying longitudinally, began the 1996–1997 school year, the first year of our study, by informing her student teacher that group work, even pairing students, did not work with her fifth grade students because they were "*incapable*" of engaging in this kind of work; she mainly taught directed individual lessons from textbooks to her students. Seven months later, on April 21, 1997, she wrote to her student teacher in their interactive journal: "Hats off to you for taking the challenge of cooperative groups! You did a great job of choosing assignments, or projects, that eased the students into the roles of their groups." Two weeks later, on May 5, 1997, she wrote: "I can't stress enough how you've been able to convert me over to being a believer in cooperative groups. You've done an EXCELLENT job of organizing and structuring the activity. All your hard work has truly paid off."

During the following school year, the guiding teacher changed her own practice to become more constructivist. An interview with the principal (one of the researchers in this study) revealed that during this school year, this teacher began planning integrated units with her student teachers, which involved group work as their base. Over the next two years, she and her student teachers gradually incorporated themes into these jointly planned units involving social justice, using art by Diego Rivera and other artists who made social statements in their work. The principal emphasized that all of this was new for this teacher, and reflected a renewed excitement about teaching. This teacher continued to sustain this constructivist pattern during the 1998–1999 school year. She involved herself in team teaching and wrote supportive comments to her student teacher about using group work. During the 1999–2000 school year, there was no dialogue between this guiding teacher and student teacher in the dialogue journal about grouping issues that was *not* supportive of small group work.

Another participant, a first year teacher, reflected on her issues with grouping and taking ownership during her first year of teaching in an urban school, after she had completed her student teaching. She was under pressure by others at her site to conform to the norms of the school and stop using groups, but she didn't waver in her beliefs. She wrote: "Other teachers recommended eliminating my groupwork and concentrating on direct instruction, focusing on 'the basics.' My philosophy that children learn by constructing meaning by interactions with others and engaging in meaningful tasks negates this concept of students passively learning. Fellow teachers tell me that English Language Learners are the hardest to teach—that they have just given up. I will not accept that as a reason for non-participation and failure. I encourage them and attempt to make conversations and dialogues as comfortable and authentic as possible."

Building Community/Challenging Practices of the School and Guiding Teacher

Another recurring theme that emerged involved building community in the classroom. Two student teachers during the 2000–2001 school year introduced ideas that challenged their guiding teachers' notions of classroom activity. One student teacher wrote:

When I first observed my guiding teacher's classroom, I noticed the children did not ask a lot of questions. I challenged my guiding teacher to come up with ways to have the children talk more, share, and ask each other questions. I think it came down to encouraging and asking more about the students' home life. My guiding teacher has been challenged to see home more as a resource. He has seen results from activities that have fo-

cused on home and students' lives. I think he is realizing that, although structures and schedules are important, spontaneity and freedom in their writing can also be valuable.

Here, the student teacher was explicitly challenging his guiding teacher to think about his practice in new ways. The student teacher was encouraged to write about this and reflect on his "mission" to his university field supervisor (who was also the principal at his school). This kind of challenge and support is unusual for a teacher education program.

The second student teacher wrote in a similar vein about her relationship with her guiding teacher: "I have challenged him with the activities I have put forth in the community building in the morning. I present activities that require him (guiding teacher) to participate also. I give students journal prompts to write about after sharing time. When we had the journal prompt: 'I feel sad when,' the journal entries shocked my guiding teacher. It opened a new world for him to know his students were feeling this way. I think it scared him to see his students talk about things that scare them or sadden them."

A first year teacher reflected about a difficult challenge she faced in her third grade class of eighteen students. She decided to challenge the practices of the school. Some students, because they were Jehovah's Witnesses, were prohibited from observing Christmas. She wrote:

It made me think about how different each of my students was and it opened my eyes to the lives they [the children] led outside of the classroom. The question of whether or not we would participate in the Christmas Assembly was on every student's mind. We had three class meetings about the assembly where we talked about why it would be difficult to participate. The students who wanted to perform were very understanding about the situation we faced since we had three students who did not celebrate Christmas. We needed to put community first to demonstrate its importance in our classroom. Together we decided to value the beliefs of our classmates and not participate in the assembly.

Remaining Questions/Further Research

Developing change agency in teachers as the mission of teacher education has implications for changing the structure of teacher education programs. Further research should examine how to identify guiding teachers who are open to interactive dialogue with their student teachers, and thus perhaps interested in examining their practice. In addition, the extent to which guiding teachers need special training to engage in effective dialogue/reflection should be investigated.

Besides trying to define the characteristics of teachers who may hold differing conceptual orientations, but still be open to changing their practice, we need to examine the significance of the settings (Zeichner & Liston, 1987). Perhaps the settings influenced these interactions. Some questions that can be examined: What are the kinds of settings (school sites, communities) that help shape teachers' beliefs? What is the influence of principals? Some of the change we observed in teaching practice may have resulted from the direct charge the student teachers received from their university field supervisors (the principals and university liaison) and the entire teacher education program's philosophy. The student teachers' mission was to reform the schools while learning how to teach children in urban schools. As documented above, the student teachers took this charge seriously.

Another reason for some of the changes in the practice of the guiding teachers may result from a close working relationship with the principals at the participating schools who had special knowledge about the setting: the principals also ran the seminars on teaching for the student teachers. Sometimes, universities undervalue principals of urban schools, viewing them as "the enemy" instead of partners and try to bypass them instead of work with them. However, principals can contribute to the knowledge of both the student teachers and university personnel. "By virtue of that unique school-based perspective, the principal can observe the student teacher with knowledge of the classroom setting and environmental conditions that the university supervisor simply does not have" (Vann, 1988–89, p. 61). Thus, principals could fill in the needed information about the community to enhance the practice of the student teachers. In addition, Vann discusses other special knowledge of the principal as the instructional leader of the school. Vann advocates the need for regular meetings among the university supervisors, the student teachers and the principal. Perhaps the teachers were open to change because of the strong university-school partnership and the close working relationship with the principals that existed at these schools. Thus, linking with school principals in innovative university-school partnerships can work to effect change in urban schools even when those schools have guiding teachers with contradictory conceptual orientations.

A commitment to empowering novice teachers who meet the highest standards for urban schools raises additional questions. Can novice teachers meet these standards if they student teach with teachers whose beliefs are contradictory to the conceptual orientation of the novice? How does the university have to change its program to meet the challenges posed by these dilemmas? Does the university need to ask new questions about the appropriateness of certain teachers as guiding teachers, such as: Which teachers will be willing to listen and engage in an open discussion about their beliefs? What are the characteristics of a guiding teacher that would support this "critical" model? Are most guiding teachers and schools changed by the experience of working with student teachers in these ways?

Conclusion

In the situations cited, guiding teachers appeared to change their practices. The student teachers became "change agents" in part by engaging their guiding teachers in dialogue about how students learn and how best to facilitate their learning. By confronting and reconstructing their own beliefs, the student teachers were able to define their social justice, critical agenda and develop their own conceptions of equity for their students, all of which they conveyed to their guiding teachers with the knowledge that this might spark a lively interactive dialogue.

The student teachers' focus on grouping students and building community in the classroom were the ways they communicated their social justice agenda in their daily practice. Since grouping students is based on a philosophy of how students learn, it is not surprising that this issue became a recurrent concern and area of difference and discussion between student teachers and their guiding teachers.

Cochran-Smith (1991) has stated that in most preservice programs "the role of the teacher as an agent for change is not emphasized, and students are not deliberately socialized into assuming responsibility for school reform and renewal" (p. 285). Instead, "student teachers are encouraged to talk about 'relevant' and technical rather than critical or epistemological aspects of teaching" (p. 285). Zeichner and Liston (1987) elaborated on this issue: "… a great deal of inconsistency exists between the role of teacher as professional decisionmaker,… and the dominant role of teacher as technician, one our society and its institutions seek to maintain" (p. 304).

Thus, a key element in a new "critical pedagogy-oriented" student teaching model, where urban student teachers challenge the conditions they find and feel empowered to change them, is the weekly teaching seminar in which student teachers critically reflect on their experiences with their peers and university educators. In seminar, the issues named by Tom are the kinds of problems that the student teachers discuss, and where they are urged to *raise them again* with their guiding teachers. Smyth (1989) submits that the benefits of such discussions at school sites as well as at the university are "mutually reinforcing… so that both preservice and inservice teachers are able to support one another in the effort to reclaim the classroom… " (p. 7). By following the critical pedagogy model, student teachers and first year teachers were explicitly encouraged to become more than technicians, to become agents of social change, and this commitment was manifested in their practice and interactions with their guiding teachers and their schools. This kind of goal, where both student teacher and guiding teacher challenge structural inequities in the system, has not been explicitly fostered by most teacher education programs.

The needs of urban schools and the diversity of their environments, both the student body and the teachers, demand creative measures which can use this richness in diversity to better educate all participants. Teacher preparation programs can work with urban educators to open an authentic dialogue that emphasizes reform.

Note

1. The Center X program refers to those full time veteran teachers who agree to mentor student teachers as guiding teachers. In other programs, they call them cooperating teachers or supervising teachers.

References

Ariav, T. & Clinard, L. M. (1996, June–July). Does coaching student teachers affect the professional development and teaching of cooperating teachers? A cross-cultural perspective. Paper presented at the International Conference on Teacher Education, Natanya, Israel.

Clark, C. C. & Peterson, P. L. (1986). Teachers' thought processes. In M. C. Wittrock (Ed.), *Handbook of research on teaching* (3rd Edition), pp. 255–296. New York: Simon & Schuster Macmillan.

Cochran-Smith, M. (1991). Learning to teach against the grain. *Harvard Educational Review, 51* (3), 279–310.

Feiman-Nemser, S. (1991, January). Conceptual orientations in teacher education. Issue paper 90–2, RIE. Lansing, MI: National Center for Research on Teacher Education.

Ganser, T. (1997, March). The contribution of service as a cooperating teacher and mentor teacher to the professional development of teachers. Paper presented at the annual meeting of the American Educational Research Association, Chicago, IL.

Giroux, H. (1986). Authority, intellectuals, and the politics of practical learning. *Teachers College Record, 88* (1), 22–40.

Haberman, M. (1993). Predicting the success of urban teachers. *Action in Urban Education, 15* (3), 1–5.

Hamlin, K. (1997). Partnerships that support the professional growth of supervising teachers. *Teacher Education Quarterly, Winter*, 77–88.

Hollingsworth, S. (1989). Prior beliefs and cognitive change in learning to teach. *American Educational Research Journal, (26),* 160–189.

Kagan, D. (1992). Professional growth among preservice and beginning teachers. *Review of Educational Research, 62* (2), 129–169.

Ladson-Billings, G. (1999). Preparing teachers for diverse student populations: A critical race theory perspective. In A. Iran-Nejad & P. D. Pearson (Eds.) *Review of research in education, 24,* (pp. 211–247). Washington, DC: American Educational Research Association.

Lave, J. & Wenger, E. (1991). *Situated learning: Legitimate peripheral participation.* Cambridge, UK: Cambridge University Press.

Murrell, P. C. Jr. (2002, April). Community teachers: Promoting teaching in culturally, linguistically, and racially diverse urban schools and communities. Paper presented at the annual meeting of the American Educational Research Association, New Orleans, LA.

Shor, I. (1992). *Empowering education.* Chicago: University of Chicago Press.

Smyth, J. (1989). Developing and sustaining critical reflection in teacher education. *Journal of Teacher Education, 40* (2), 2–9.

Stake, R. (1985). Case study. In *Research, Policy and Practice. World Yearbook of Education.* New York: Nichols Publishing Company, pp. 277–285.

Tom, A. R. (1985). Inquiring into inquiry-oriented education. *Journal of Teacher Education, 36* (5), 35–44.

Vann, A. S. (1988–1989). Student teachers and the building principal… The missing link. *Action in Teacher Education, (4),* 59–62.

Weiner, Lois (1993). *Preparing teachers for urban schools: Lessons from thirty years of school reform.* New York: Teachers College Press.

Wenger, E. (1998). *Communities of practice: Learning, meaning, and identity.* New York: Cambridge University Press.

Wilson, S. & Berne, J. (1999). Teacher learning and the acquisition of professional knowledge: An examination of research on contemporary professional development. In A. Iran-Nejad & P. D. Pearson, (Eds). *Review of research in education, 24,* pp. 173–209). Washington, DC: American Educational Research Association.

Yin, R. K. (1989). *Case study research: Design and methods.* Newbury Park, CA: Sage.

Yost, D. S. (1997). The moral dimensions of teaching and preservice teachers: Can moral dispositions be influenced? *Journal of Teacher Education, 48* (4), 281–292.

Zeichner, K. M. & Liston, D. P. (1987). Teaching student teachers to reflect. *Harvard Educational Review, (57),* 23–48.

Zeichner, K. (1993). Connecting genuine teacher development to the struggle for social justice. *Journal of Education for Teaching, 19* (1), 5–20.

Sheila Lane is director of special projects with the Center X Teacher Education Program at the University of California, Los Angeles; Nancy Lacefield-Parachini is administrator for Professor Development with District F of the Los Angeles Unified School District; and JoAnn Isken is principal of Moffett Elementary School, Lennox Elementary School District, Lennox, California.

From *Teacher Education Quarterly*, Spring 2003, pp. 55-68. © 2003 by Teacher Education Quarterly. Reprinted by permission.

From the Trenches

Preparing Teachers for Public Schools: Just More Cannon Fodder?

Edward G. Rozycki

PART I: A DISAPPOINTED TEACHER

I received this letter from a reader responding to an **educational HORIZONS** column I had written on the unreasonable expectations imposed on teachers.[1]

> … All of my life, I dreamed of becoming a teacher. After raising my family, I went to college to earn my teaching certificate. We sacrificed (monetarily and emotionally) for many years as I had to commute over two hours each day while moonlighting as a waitress, mom, wife, etc. Finally, I graduated cum laude with a B.S. in Secondary English from _____ University! Wow! The world is my oyster, right? I secured a teaching job at one of the junior high schools in my hometown. I swore all of my prayers had been answered!…
>
> There are no words to describe my feelings as the school year began. I can tell you that I quit 184 times that year. I am so disappointed and ashamed of wasting so much money and time on a teaching degree that is now my demise. To make matters worse, I thought my frustrations were because of my own ignorance, so I earned my master's degree in Education of Exceptional Learners K–12, hoping to learn to "cope" with what was expected of and blamed on me, as a teacher.
>
> After ten years, I am so burned out I could cry, and usually do. The thought of a new school year, new

IEPs, new ridiculous requests, parents, etc., just about puts me over the edge.…

> As a young (in years teaching), yet old (in age) teacher, my colleagues consists of a) "I have years until I can retire" or b) "I couldn't care less." They laugh at my frustrations and tell me to just "chill." My family thinks teaching is the best thing since sliced bread: "Off all summer? I don't even want to hear you!" Yet, I feel the hurt, and I know in my heart that I have changed more, become more calloused, less believing, more cynical than I have in my entire lifetime. In my opinion, teaching is impossible for someone who still has feelings and values and believes in education the way I always have. How very, very sad.…
>
> —A. J., Smalltown, U.S.A.

In the courses I teach at Widener University for graduate-level teacher administrator certificate candidates, I pose the question, "Why do many drop out of teaching?" and show them this letter. I explain to them that, unlike the case in the medical profession, law enforcement, and the military, prospective teachers are seldom exposed to the more unpleasant aspects of the intended occupation before they encounter them on the job. Indeed, in many preparation programs the down-side of employment in public education is ignored completely. Or what is worse, preparers of teachers not infrequently insinuate that if anything is wrong with the schools, it is the fault of present job-holders, whom the present aspirants in their classes—through messianic dedication and whiz-bang new methods—will soon replace.

"Are you really sure this is the profession for you?" I ask my students. "Perhaps what you learn in this course will help you find out."

I tell my students at Widener that their last in-class assignment will be to compose a letter offering support and suggestions to A. J.[2] Their varied responses show interesting patterns: older aspirants in the process of job change, as well as experienced teachers, tend to be sympathetic. Surprisingly—considering the sloganeering often heard to the contrary—in their letters these older people often suggest: "Lower your expectations!" "Not everybody can learn everything!" "Some kids aren't ready: it's not your fault!"

Younger persons with no teaching experience often become upset at the letter and suggest that the writer has emotional or even mental problems. Their end-of-term suggestions (although modified somewhat by what they have learned in the course) tend to be even crueler.

One young teacher with some experience in elementary education chided me, "You shouldn't show newcomers this letter. It will disillusion them. How can you expect people to go into teaching if they know about things like this? Prospective teachers need idealism: it is a very precious thing."

"Do you mean that it is important," I replied, "to be ignorant and naive to be a professional educator? Should we have ignorant and naive doctors, nurses, police, and military personnel as well? Would this make them better?" I continued by pointing out that in all likelihood half the people in the room would drop out of teaching within five years or sooner and I felt compelled to arm them with something other than ignorance and naiveté to help them struggle to survive in the profession.

The Vise of Ideology

Unfortunately there seem to be more than a few of my confreres in education who hold opinions similar to those of my fourth-grade teacher: people must be duped into becoming public school teachers. Rather than learning how organizational problems impact their classrooms and how to go about dealing with them (such knowledge being abstemiously parceled out even in courses for prospective administrators), would-be teachers are given to believe that the academic success of their students is primarily, if not solely, a matter of teachers' personal knowledge, skills, and dispositions. Accrediting bodies often base their approval on this specious doctrine.

Just in case would-be teachers might actually be tempted to become the kind of reflective educators they are sometimes told they should be, they are required to manifest allegiance to the latest fashion in educational ideology in various ways that subtly threaten their grades, dignity, and self-esteem should self-reflection yield nonconformity. Dogmatic, thought-controlling professors are far more likely to ambush a student beginning teacher preparation at a purportedly "secular" university than they would at an openly professed religious institution.

In many states thirty years ago, one had to be ready to "Stamp Out Nonbehavioral Objectives!" to secure a position as a teacher or professor. Then came "Basic Competencies" and "Generic Teaching" and "Outcomes-based Education" as the incantations required to prove suitability for hiring. One should not imagine that any real demonstrations of intellectual acuity or competence were required for any of these terms. They were passwords into the club.

It would be unwise to invoke "stupidity" at this point and turn our attention to other matters. It is much more productive of insight to assume a rationality hidden behind the pursuit of unprofessed goals. It is the political vulnerability of teacher-educators in our society that underlies the reluctance to prepare teacher-candidates with anything beyond a myopic technique-focus: Knowledge, Skills, & Dispositions. You will find professional organizations promulgating this myopia; the teacher dropout rate—13 percent per year—gives the lie to its adequacy.[3]

With rhetorical wind no longer billowing the sails of "Outcomes-based Education" or even "Effective Schools," the current shibboleths are "Best Practices" and "Constructivism."

The Best Practices Mythology

Ask your doctor, "What are the best practices in medicine?" Ask your plumber, "What are the best practices in plumbing?" I suspect that, unless they are very tactful people, they will laugh at you. But they might be nice and ask you in return, "Best practices for what purpose? Under what special conditions?" If you are really lucky, they might ask you," What's wrong with just good practices? Why would we want to incur the costs of identifying 'best practices' in advance of knowing the special circumstances that help determine what best practices are?"

Once, while chairing a search committee, I asked a visiting candidate about the dissertation she had completed at a prestigious university. She replied that in her experimental design, two classes were taught using "Best Practices" and two other, similar in every other feature, used other than Best Practices. The results? No difference in academic performance between the four classes. However, she went on, there were some interesting indicators for future study.

I pressed, "Did you comment on your results as possibly indicating that whatever it was you identified as 'Best Practices' might have failed?" "No," she insisted. "That wouldn't be a valid conclusion. Best Practices couldn't have failed."

I try to teach my students to evaluate claims by first asking what kind of evidence would settle them. Second, I tell them, they should consider whether is it plausible that anyone would have assumed the costs of getting that evidence. One finds very few education claims established with such care. I continually insist that my graduate students make a very simple but important distinction in their dissertations. Survey replies may show, for example, that group work is *perceived* to be effective. But these same surveys do not establish that group work *is, in fact,* effective. This distinction is routinely ignored, not only in educational research, but in social science research generally—and abetted by purported "postmodern" theorists who claim that the distinction between group perception and fact is passé.[4]

Constructivism: the New Scientism?

For several years I had been hearing students and colleagues drop the word "constructivism" into their conversation without paying much attention to it. I assumed it was just a belated recognition of Immanual Kant's contribution that many of the objects of experience may be partially the contributions of the way our minds work; e.g., cause, space, and time, for example, are not "out there" in the world, but somehow a result of how we interface with what is "out there."[5]

Awakening one cold winter's day from my philosophical slumbers, however, I realized that "constructivism" had clearly become the shiniest, newest slogan in education. I was interviewing a candidate—again, from a prestigious university—for a position at Widener. One of the committee members asked him, "What is your philosophy of education?" (Since this is my area of interest, I seldom ask just anyone that question: I expect too much for an answer.)

"I am a constructivist," came the reply.

I asked, "How does being a constructivist make your teaching different from someone who is not a constructivist?"[6]

Thus spake the applicant: "As a constructivist I am concerned that students understand what they are learning. Other kinds of teachers just give out grades."

I went looking for some sources on constructivism.[7] I found a website on "Epistemological Contructivism," featuring Ernst von Lagersfeld's basic definitions of radical constructivism.[8] I present one example here for your consideration: *Knowledge is not passively received either through the senses or by way of communication, but is actively built up by the cognizing subject.*

A cursory analysis easily shows us that von Lagersfeld cannot—by his own lights—know his principle. He invokes an underlying principle of mutual exclusion to rule out (by fiat, it appears) that knowledge is received through the senses or by communication, but certainly no such conclusion can be reached by an finite number of cognitions within experience.[9] Other critiques have far more damning things to say about this kind of rhetorical folderol.[10]

Constructivism is a term used to refer to a highly contentious and disagreed-upon, to say the least, mélange of concepts.[11] The debate around it is a morass of conflicting positions and assorted jabberwocky. Constructivism is not at all a coherent theory that should be foisted off on students as though it were in indisputable scientific foundation for pedagogical practice.

What is a prospective teacher to do? One can arm oneself to be sensitive to linguistic games and not to let oneself be upset by verbalisms. But where does one obtain that kind of preparation? Nowadays, hardly anywhere. Besides, it is very hard to keep a clear mind when one's institution is caught up in the accreditation game.

PART II: THE ACCREDITATION GAME

Fifty years of Gallup polling seem to support an interesting thesis: the firmness of a person's conviction that American schools fail because American teachers fail is inversely related to the evidence that person has for that conviction.[12]

So, the logic goes, to ensure good schools, we must ensure good teachers. To ensure good teachers, teacher training institutions should be accredited. Accreditation assures the public that what a college says it is training its teachers to do, is, in fact, what it is training them to do.

Up to a point, an accreditation requirement need not be unreasonable. All states provide accreditation, being very careful not to impose religious or philosophical restrictions on the teacher training institutions. State evaluations merely require each institute to show that, within the framework of its own mission and philosophy, it has the resources allocated to carry out the teacher training program it purports to have. What is important to note here is that teacher training institutions are not assumed to share any common goals.

Imagine a country, Erewhon, that sets all its clocks against a central clock: time units must be standardized, functioning must be reliable, people *must care* that such uniformity is available. State certification is Erewhon before there was a central clock. National accreditation assumes there is such a central clock: a science of pedagogy, a consensus on goals. But is there? It appears not.[13]

National accreditation is somewhat more demanding than state accreditation. For example, TEAC, the Teacher Education Accreditation Council, presses institutions applying for accreditation to show that they gather evidence regularly to determine whether the program in fact achieves the intended results. However, let us suppose that TEAC, rather than the applicant institution, also had the authority to define what constitutes acceptable evidence; this proviso would clearly be a much greater philosophical imposition than what the states now require.

In any event, bigger, well-funded schools see accreditation demands as a plus. Accreditation drives out institutions that can't afford the process or its requirements and thus reduces competition—provided people know or care whether teachers have come from accredited preparation programs. Of course, educators don't like to publicly admit they think about beating out competition. It seems far nobler to talk of "improving teacher education."

I recently spent more than eight hours with a consultant in small-group sessions focused on the program and unit approval requirements of the National Council for Accreditation of Teacher Education (NCATE). After careful listening and questioning I came to three conclusions.

1) If the institution pursuing NCATE accreditation is after competitive advantage, then the 85 percent initial approval rate indicated by the consultant (with an additional 13 percent approved on the second go-round) provides little competitive advantage. In particular, it is unlikely that accreditation will increase income sufficiently during the short period before

competitors acquire similar accreditation to justify the substantial expenses of the accreditation process.

A subsidiary consideration is the number of non-accredited programs from numerous ephemeral colleges and universities that grab some of the certification market. Many states actually encourage such entrepreneurship. The viability of such enterprises argues against accrediting organizations' claims that their approval is considered vital by employers.

2) What NCATE may in fact be offering is collusion in delusion: education departments can wrangle back a share of the tuition their home institutions siphon off each year to fund activities dearer to the trustees' hearts. "You say you meet our requirements, we'll agree with you; so long as you pay our [hefty] fees."

Can you imagine a medical school's licensure depending on its ability to show that—irrespective of circumstances—patients treated by its graduates show improvement in their well being? Yet NCATE requires evidence that—irrespective of circumstances—schoolkids taught by a program's graduates show scholastic improvement. For example, the 2002 Edition of NCATE Professional Standards indicates:

> Candidates develop and demonstrate proficiencies that
> support learning by all students as shown in their work
> with students with exceptionalities and those from diverse ethnic, racial, gender and socioeconomic groups
> in classrooms and schools.[14]

Luckily, this is only the top-level "target" requirement. Being unsuccessful is acceptable—as it should be for any race of beings yet to achieve divinity. What the teacher candidate at a school angling for such approval can expect is a lot of activity, pursued with breathless anticipation, that in the long run may contribute little to their long-term job survival.

The Teacher-Shortage Myth

Reconsider the sad lot of A. J., whose letter we read at the beginning of this essay. Clearly a dedicated, idealistic person, she was no doubt exposed in her long years of training to many of the nostrums and gimcracks that constitute knowledge at the Hogwarts School of Witchcraft and Wizardry, those special spells and potions that enable ordinary schoolteachers to offset the effects of poverty, abuse, and addiction and make each and every student, irrespective of physical, mental, or social condition, a first-rate, world-class scholar, pushing to the limits of his or her potential to achieve excellence.

But what if A. J.'s failure is more a matter of her working conditions than of the circumstances of her preparation? What if her loss resulted not so much from the sumulacra of science she encountered as a trainee as from her principal's emphasis on maintaining daily attendance rather than dealing with even the most outrageous classroom disruption (for instance, by suspending the culprits); with her persistent public humilation; with student threats and acts of intimidation? This puts a very different face on what can and must be done to help teachers teach and students learn.

In the summer of 1965 I took special training in the New Math. I was well paid and fed, received an interesting review of all the mathematics I had studied as an undergraduate, but ultimately obtained nothing I could use back in the junior high school where I taught. My biggest problem was getting my ninth-graders to stop fighting and sit down. When they did calm down somewhat it seemed that their attention was more readily focused on the opposite sex than on the fact that multiplication was distributive over addition.

If Richard Ingersoll's research is correct—that working conditions rather than lack of preparation drive teachers away from the public schools—then we might do well to examine whether these same conditions can account for students' poor performance.[15] My years of classroom experience tell me that poor working conditions for teachers are poor learning conditions for children.

But the leaders of our professional educational organizations and of our colleges and universities are far from our public school classrooms. Their strategies and manipulations to capture a piece of the teacher-preparation dollar explain not only their byzantine interconnections with accrediting agencies but also why the prospective teacher, whose pre-service career they readily control, serves both as the test for their educational experiments and as the scapegoat for failure.

Notes

1. See my column, "What Can a Teacher Do: Two Myths of Responsibility," *Educational Horizons* 79 (4): 158–161; available at <http://www.newfoundations.com/EGR/WhatCanTeacherDo.html>.
2. I have lost the original e-mail document in which this letter was sent. I have only the version I edited to preserve anonymity. I would appreciate hearing again from the person who sent me this letter to find out what has happened over this intervening time.
3. Richard M. Ingersoll, "Teacher Turnover and Teacher Shortages: An Organizational Analysis," *American Educational Research Journal* 37, no. 3 (2001): 499–534.
4. For an expanded version of this argument, see my column, "What Works? Under What Conditions? And Who Really Cares?" *Educational Horizons* 81 (2).
5. Thus, Nietzsche's comment that our brains are the constructions of our brains.
6. This is a trick question to see if the respondent knows enough to answer that only under certain conditions need commitment to a theory manifest itself in behavior. They don't normally catch this—an indicator of an incomplete education.
7. An interesting one is Andrew Elby, "What Students' Learning of Representations Tells Us About Constructivism," available at <http://www2.physics.umd.edu/elby/papers/constructivism/representatios.htm>.
8. <http://pespmcl.vub.ac.be/CONSTRUC.html>.
9. I tell you that cyanide is poisonous and show you a reference in the *U.S. Pharmacopoeia*. You feed it to your spouse, nonetheless. As a constructivist your defense in court is that

since you received the information only via communication, you did not know cyanide was poisonous.

10. See Martin A. Kozloff, "Constructivism in Education: Sophistry for a New Age," available at <http://people.uncw.edu/kozloffm/ContraConstructivism.html>.

11. For an unemotional review, see Peter Slezak, "A Critique of Radical Social Constructivism," available at <www.arts.unsw.edu.au/.../stsstaffhomepages/pslezak_site/Article%20Liks/Slezak-Soc%20Constructivism.pdf>.

12. A number of these surveys are available on Phi Delta Kappa's website at <http://www.pdkintl.org/kappan/kaindex.htm>.

13. See Lawrence Baines, Wade Carpenter, and Gregory Stanley, "Generic Engineering: The Standardization of Teacher Education," *Journal of Thought* Summer 2000: 35–44.

14. Professional Standards for the Accreditation of Schools, Colleges and Departments of Education, 2002 edition (Washington: National Council for Accreditation of Teacher Education), 27.

15. Ingersoll, "Teacher Turnover."

Edward G. Rozycki is a twenty-five-year veteran of the school district of Philadelphia. He is an associate professor of education at Widener University, Widener, Pennsylvania.

From *Educational Horizons*, Spring 2003, pp. 107-111. © 2003 by Edward G. Rozycki. Reprinted by permission.

UNIT 9
A Look to the Future

Unit Selections

Key Points to Consider

- What might be the shape of school curricula by the year 2020?

- What changes in society are most likely to affect educational change?

- How can schools prepare students to live and work in an uncertain future? What knowledge bases are most important? What skills are most important?

- What should be the philosophical ideals for American schools in the twenty-first century?

 **Links: www.dushkin.com/online/**
These sites are annotated in the World Wide Web pages.

Goals 2000: A Progress Report
http://www.ed.gov/pubs/goals/progrpt/index.html

Mighty Media
http://www.mightymedia.com

Online Internet Institute
http://www.oii.org

There are competing visions as to how persons should develop and learn. Yet there is great hope in this competition among alternative dreams and specific curriculum paths that we may choose to traverse. In this, all conscientious people are asked to consider carefully how we may make more livable futures for ourselves and others. This is really an eternal challenge for us all. We will often disagree and debate our differences as we struggle toward what we become as people and as cultures.

Which education philosophy is most appropriate for our schools? This is a complex question, and we will, as a free people, come up with alternative visions of what it will be. Let us explore what might be possible as more students go on the Internet and the wonder of the cyberspace revolution opens to teachers and students. What challenges can we expect in using the technology of the cyberspace revolution in our schools? What blessings can we hope for? What sorts of changes need to occur in how people go to schools as well as in what they do when they get there?

The breakthroughs that are developing in new learning and communications technologies are really quite impressive. They will definitely affect how human beings learn in the very near-term future. While we look forward with considerable optimism and confidence to these educational developments, there are still many controversial issues to be debated in the early years of the twenty-first century; the "school choice" issue is one. Some very interesting new proposals for new forms of schooling, both in public schools and private schools, are under development. We can expect to see at least a few of these proposals actually tried.

Some of the demographic changes and challenges involving young people in the United States are staggering. Ten percent of all American teenage girls will become pregnant each year, the highest rate in the developed world. At least 100,000 American elementary school children get drunk once a week. Incidence of venereal disease has tripled among adolescents in the United States since 1995. The actual school dropout rate in the United States stands at 30 percent.

The student populations of North America reflect vital social and cultural forces at work to destroy our progress. In the United States, a massive secondary school dropout problem has been developing steadily through the past decade. The next decade will reveal how public school systems will address this and other unresolved problems brought about by dramatic upheavals in demographics. In the immediate future, we will be able to see if emergency or alternative certification measures adopted by states affect achievement of the objectives of our reforms.

At any given moment in a people's history, several alternative future directions are open to them. North American educational systems have been subjected to one wave after another of recommendations for programmatic change. Is it any wonder that change is a sensitive watchword for persons in teacher educa-

tion on this continent? What specific directions it will take in the immediate future depend on which recommendations of the reform agenda are implemented, which agencies of government (local, state/provincial, and federal) will pay for the very high costs of reform, and which shifts in perceived national educational priorities by the public will occur that will affect fundamental realignments of our educational goals.

Basic changes in society's career patterns should also be considered. It is estimated that in the United States the average nonagricultural worker now makes a major job change about five times in his or her career. The schools will surely be affected, indirectly or directly, by this major social phenomenon. Changes in the social structure due to divorce, unemployment, and job retraining efforts will also have an impact. Educational systems are integral parts of the broader social systems that created them; if the larger social system experiences fundamental change, this is reflected in the educational system.

In the area of information science and computer technologies applicable for use in educational systems, the development of new products is so rapid that we cannot predict what technological capacities may be available to schools 20 years from now. We are in a period of human history when knowledgeable people can control far greater information (and have immediate access to it) than at any previous time. As new information-command systems evolve, this phenomenon will become more and more meaningful to all of us.

The future of education will be determined by the current debate concerning what constitutes a just, national response to human needs in a period of technological change. The history of technological change in all human societies since the beginning of industrial development clearly demonstrates that major advances in technology and breakthroughs in the basic sciences lead to more rapid rates of social change. Society is on the verge of discoveries that will lead to the creation of entirely new technologies in the dawning years of the twenty-first century. All of the social, economic, and educational institutions globally will be affected by these scientific breakthroughs. The basic issue is not whether schools can remain aloof from the needs of industry or the economic demands of society but how they can emphasize the noblest ideals of free persons in the face of inevitable technological and economic changes. Another concern is how to let go of predetermined visions of the future that limit our possibilities as free people. The schools, of course, will be called upon to face these issues. We need the most enlightened, insightful, and compassionate teachers ever educated by North American universities to prepare the youth of the future in a manner that will humanize the high-tech world in which they live.

All of the essays in this unit can be related to discussions on the goals of education, the future of education, or the development of curriculum.

DREAMS
of a livable future

Democracy, ecology, and cultural vitality depend on a new economic vision for the world

By almost any measure, multinational corporations have failed spectacularly on their promise of fostering global democracy and prosperity. That's why people all across the planet—from villagers in India to students in North America—are stepping up to challenge the abuses of big business. While corporate power is deeply entrenched, this new economic democracy movement is fueled by a fresh set of strategies about how people can regain power. —The Editors

By Paul Hawken

I was recently asked to give a talk in Melbourne, Australia, to a group of businesspeople to make a case for sustainable development. I watched them gorge on roast chicken and chocolate mousse and chardonnay and coffee, and by the time I got up to speak I didn't think they wanted what I was going to serve. They were full. Instead of answering, I posed the opposite question: I asked them what the business case is for worldwide endemic poverty, for double-glazing the planet with greenhouse gases. I asked them how it came to pass that we created an economic system that tells us it's cheaper to destroy the earth than to take care of it. Why do we get economic signals that are antithetical to our deeply held values and common sense? Why do we separate the benefits of industrial development to some from the cost to others? Why do our deepest aspirations for goodness, for inclusion and generosity not cumulate into a peaceful and equitable society? In short, I asked them why we live in two worlds instead of one.

ALL PUBLICLY HELD corporations live a lie. They believe that we reside in a world where capital has the right to grow and that that right is a higher right than the rights of people to their culture and what we hold in common. There is something incalculably wrong with this view. You can't get to sustainability from an economic model that strives first and foremost to increase the amount of money large corporations have. You can't get there if you're destroying the world's local economies. You can't get

there if you are McDonald's and spend $2 billion a year to get children to eat your junk food. We cannot correct environmental problems if we don't correct the assumptions that cause them. Most of the world's economy and the behavior of the world's governments are under the control of corporations. Corporations are striving to increase their control; at the same time, the world is increasingly out of control. There is a direct connection.

This new weight of corporate colonization is having disastrous results. Bechtel in San Francisco, Suez, and Vivendi of France want to privatize water the world over. Novartis, Du-Pont, Monsanto, and Bayer-Aventis want to control 90 percent of the germ plasm of 90 percent of the caloric food intake of the world. These are companies that make toxic aniline dyes, animal hormones, artificial sweeteners, explosives, and pesticides. Ted Turner said that in the end there will only be two media companies in the world, and he wants to have a stake in one of them. Rupert Murdoch agrees and wants to be the other. McDonald's opens up 2,800 restaurants a year, and even the U.S. government has said that the doubling of childhood obesity and alarming growth in diabetes in the past 20 years is due to fast food. Right now one out of every five meals in the United States is fast food, and they want that to be the case everywhere in the world. Coke says that it has achieved 10 percent of the total liquid intake of the world, and its goal is to go to 20 percent. Or is it 30 percent? These are absurd and devastating goals for corporations.

Our M.B.A. President and His CEO Sidekick

Why the White House is no friend of corporate reform

By ARIANNA HUFFINGTON

One of the main reasons the Bush administration has been so reluctant to rein in corporate America is that they are so much a part of it, with a vice president who was a CEO, three former CEOs who hold cabinet-level positions, two dozen ambassadors who are former CEOs or company chairmen, a president who is the first commander-in-chief with an M.B.A., and a domestic agenda no deeper than tax breaks for friends.

Fittingly, both the president and the vice president have been caught in the rising tide of corporate scandals. Last year it was revealed that both Harken Energy, while President Bush was on its board, and Halliburton Corporation, while Vice President Cheney was its CEO, had created subsidiary shell companies in offshore tax havens.

White House spokesman Dan Bartlett explained that Harken's off-shore entity wasn't designed to evade taxes, it was meant to enhance "tax competitiveness." Press secretary Ari Fleischer argued that the reason Bush's Houston-based Harken went Caribbean was a "moot" question because the oil and gas exploration company never made any money on its dealings in the Cayman Islands.

During Cheney's time as Halliburton's CEO, there was a dramatic increase in the number of Halliburton subsidiaries registered in tax havens: from 9 in 1995 to 44 in 2000. And it was accompanied by a no less spectacular drop in Halliburton's federal taxes: from $302 million in 1998 to less than zero—an $85 million rebate—in 1999.

At the same time they were hard at work stiffing U.S. taxpayers, Cheney and the Dallas-based Halliburton were happily nursing at the public teat—the company, which builds and maintains energy facilities, recived $2.3 billion in government contracts and another $1.5 billion in government financing and loan guarantees.

It would have been nice to hear what Cheney had to say about all of this, but he began making himself very scarce—especially to the media—right around the time in May 2002 when reports first surfaced that the Securities and Exchange Commission was looking into Halliburton's accounting practices from the Cheney era.

Of course, Cheney's reluctance to talk to reporters is understandable, given what has come to light about his heretofore highly touted tenure at Halliburton, including the questionable accounting procedures, the off-shore subsidiaries, and the revelation that the company did business with Iran, Libya, and—despite Cheney's denials—Iraq. It's his very own Axis of Profits.

But to be fair, Halliburton did end up giving a little something back to America—in the form of $2 million worth of fines for consistently overbilling the Pentagon while Cheney was CEO. In one case they charged $750,000 for work that actually cost them only $125,000. Despite all this, the company has continued to be awarded massive government contracts, including a 10-year deal with the Army that, unlike any comparable arrangement, comes with no lid on potential costs. I guess it really does help to have friends—and ex-CEOs—in very high places.

I do not believe that any Fortune 500 company can be sustainable, but there are definitely things that transnational corporations can do to help society and the environment. They can:

- Get out of our schools.
- Get out of our stomachs.
- Get out of our government.
- Get out of our rivers, oceans, and forests.
- Get out of our skies and soils.
- Get out of our seeds and the human genome.

Until corporations understand that they are spearheading a kind of commercial fascism, they're going to find that resistance will grow. It's fascist in the sense that it is an attempt to create a meta-order for people, with the assumption that a small group of people know better than the larger group; therefore, the large group does not have to be consulted. Whether it was Marxist Leninism or Mussolini, fascism has always been informed by the vanity that a few know more than the many—for their "own good." What is the World Trade Organization trying to bring to the table? Rules, order. What is the Free Trade Area of the Americas treaty trying to do? Rules, order. But whose rules? Whose order? What process? In *The Lexus and the Olive Tree*, Tom Friedman, an advocate of globalization, wrote: "The hidden hand of the market will never work without a hidden fist. McDonald's cannot flourish without McDonnell Douglas.... And the hidden fist that keeps the world safe for Silicon Valley's technologies to flourish is called the U.S. Army, Air Force, Navy, and Marine Corps."

TRADE IS GREAT. Trade is civilizing. Trade is not the issue. The question is who sets the rules and who enforces them. What will the shape of the relationships be among nations, regions, peoples, companies, markets, and the commons which support all life on earth?

It will come down to some very simple questions in the end. Do we want democracy and self-determination, or do we want oligarchic institutions? Do we want a world of uniformity where the road from every airport to every city center looks like every strip mall in the world? Do we want another world than the one envisioned by Monsanto, Wal-Mart, and Disney? Do we want our 9-year-old girls being lured by dolls with happy meals into McDonald's to end up with Type II diabetes? Or do we want strong regional and native cultures proud of their heritage, devoted to their land, committed to true development and the future of their children? In short, do we want a world structured by rich, mostly white men, or a world that is an expression of the fabulous qualities of all human beings?

The ENVIRONMENTAL movement must become a HUMAN RIGHTS movement.

The corporatization of the world is creating a loss of diversity. The degree to which the corporate world order tries to enforce a one-size-fits-all formula to the planet's media, culture, agriculture, and dietary habits is going to be seen in hindsight as just as much of a criminal act as the deracination and slaughter of the indigenous peoples of the Americas or the enslavement of Africans. We look back at those things now and feel ashamed. We will look back at what we're doing right now, and we'll see it for what it is: a violation of humanity. The very same companies that invoke sustainability have business models that destroy people and life. We will, I predict, in our lifetime, convict corporations of crimes against humanity.

A Nigerian tribal chief once said, "If you don't share your wealth with us, we will share our poverty with you." It is less expensive to share our wealth than to continue this extravagantly self-centered system we call corporate capitalism. This is not the most economical system. The idea that sustainability costs more is upside down and backwards. It costs less to maintain the earth in real time.

A world where 20 percent of its people get less than 1 percent of its resources, where nearly a billion go to bed hungry, a world torn by strife, riddled by greed, controlled by small, petty men bankrolled by large transnational corporations is not cheap.

WE KNOW HOW TO transform this world to reduce our impact on nature by severalfold, how to provide meaningful, dignified living-wage jobs for all who seek them, and how to feed, clothe, and house every person on earth. What we don't know is how to remove those in power, those whose ignorance of biology is matched only by their indifference to human suffering. This is a political issue. It is not an ecological problem. The way to save this earth is to focus on its people, and particularly those people who pay the highest price: women, children, communities of color, the localized poor. The sustainability movement—with-

out forsaking its understanding of living systems, resources, conservation, and biology—must move from a resource flow model of saving the earth to a model based on human rights, the rights to food, the rights to livelihood, the rights to culture, community, and self-sufficiency. The environmental movement must become a civil rights movement, a human rights movement. Without that, it will simply be a failed white man's movement from the North.

Sustainability has to be about improving the quality of life of all people on earth and honoring all forms of life.

The world is waiting for answers, and right now the main providers are fundamentalisms, whether they be political, religious, or economic. But we have to rebel against that which oppresses our imagination and our ability to dream to realize that not only is another world possible, but that we have the means at hand here and now to create it. Is it too late? Yes, it's late, but people never change when they are comfortable. The world is anxious. Author Margaret Drabble wrote, "When nothing is sure, everything is possible." We have nothing to fear. The worst is happening right now. Helen Keller once said, "This is a time for a loud voice, open speech, and fearless thinking. I rejoice that I live in such a splendidly disturbing time."

I WAS RECENTLY ASKED by a journalist, "Aren't you just dreaming?" I replied, "Absolutely I'm dreaming; somebody's got to dream in America." The dreams of a livable future aren't coming from George Bush and Dick Cheney, and it is our right to dream. It is something we owe our children's children. A dream is a gift of the future, and the future is begging.

I dream of having a U.N. arms control and inspection team coming to the United States to remove assault weapons from the hands of all National Rifle Association members. I dream of another U.N. team shutting down the 15,000 chemical plants in this country that are essentially biological weapons waiting to happen. I dream of my country living up to its legal treaty commitments and getting rid of weapons of mass destruction. I dream of a United States that actually has an energy plan; a climate plan, not a midterm election plan; a water plan to get rid of the pollutants in our riparian corridors and streams; a biodiversity plan; a plan to eliminate poverty and illiteracy; a plan that ensures that no child here or anywhere goes to bed hungry.

I once gave a talk at an elementary school to third graders, and I told them that there are a billion people in the world who want to work and can't work. A girl raised her hand and said, "Is all the work done?"

I dream of getting my government back, a country of, by, and for the people. I dream of a country that is big enough to say it is wrong; that can be remorseful and say it's sorry for the suffering it's caused First Peoples, African Americans, Hispanic Americans, Asian Americans, and people in other lands that we have wronged; a country big and generous enough to build new schools in inner cities and act with decency in the world.

To quote Uruguayan novelist Eduardo Galeano, "I dream about a time when the world will no longer be at war against the poor but against poverty; when the weapons industry will have no choice but to declare bankruptcy; when nobody will die of hunger, and the street children will not be treated as if they were trash because there will be no street children, because a black woman will become president of Brazil and another black woman president of the United States and an Indian woman president of Guatemala."

These dreams are pipe dreams unless we act politically. As David Orr says, "We have great ideas; the right wing does politics. We are cozy in our niches; they are in power. We are titillated about being right; they are busy being in control." I dream that we will become a political movement, not simply one called by the name of a color, but by the name of an ideal. What shall we call it?

LET'S NOT SPEND so much time on the big villains. It is not the Ken Lays or George Bushes we should be demonizing. We need to honor the saints in our midst, not the fools, the small heroes, not the big louts. Arundhati Roy writes that "we have to support our small heroes. (Of these we have many. Many.) We have to fight specific wars in specific ways. Who knows, perhaps that's

what the 21st century has in store for us. The dismantling of the Big. Big bombs, big dams, big ideologies, big contradictions, big countries, big wars, big heroes, big mistakes. Perhaps it will be the Century of the Small. Perhaps right now, this very minute, there's a small god up in heaven readying herself for us."

The Sufi poet Hafiz wrote, "Clever men place the world into cages, but the wise woman who must duck under the moon throws keys to the rowdy prisoners." Let's throw keys to the rowdy prisoners. Sustainability is about freedom from tyranny, from empire, from corporate rule, the freedom to honor life. Let's create, in Janine Benyus' memorable phrase, "a world conducive to life."

Paul Hawken *is an author, entrepreneur, and activist. He is the author of* Growing a Business, The Ecology of Commerce, *and* Natural Capitalism. *This essay was adapted from a speech delivered at the Bioneers conference in October 2002.*

From *Utne Reader*, May/June 2003, pp. 50-54. © 2003 by Utne Reader.

An Emerging Culture

RUDOLF STEINER'S CONTINUING IMPACT IN THE WORLD

by Christopher Bamford and Eric Utne

Beginning at the end of the 19th century, a relatively unknown Austrian philosopher and teacher began to sow the seeds of what he hoped would blossom into a new culture. The seeds were his ideas, which he sowed through extensive writings, lectures, and countless private consultations. The seeds germinated and took root in the hearts and minds of his students, among whom were individuals who would later become some of the best known and most influential figures of the 20th century. Since the teacher's death in 1925, a quiet but steadily growing movement, unknown and unseen by most people, has been spreading over the world, bringing practical solutions to the problems of our global, technological civilization. The seeds are now coming to flower in the form of thousands of projects infused with human values. The teacher, called by some "the best kept secret of the 20th century," was Rudolf Steiner.

Steiner, a truly "Renaissance man," developed a way of thinking that he applied to different aspects of what it means to be human. Over a period of 40 years, he formulated and taught a path of inner development or spiritual research he called "anthroposophy." From what he learned, he gave practical indications for nearly every field of human endeavor. Art, architecture, drama, science, medicine, economics, religion, care of the dying, social organization—there is almost no field he did not touch.

"My meeting with Rudolf Steiner led me to occupy myself with him from that time forth and to remain always aware of his significance. We both felt the same obligation to lead man once again to true inner culture. I have rejoiced at the achievements his great personality and his profound humanity have brought about in the world."

Albert Schweitzer

Today, wherever there is a human need you'll find groups of people working out of Steiner's ideas. There are an estimated ten thousand initiatives worldwide—the movement is a hotbed of entrepreneurial activity, social and political activism, artistic expression, scientific research, and community building. In this report we limit our investigation to a tiny, representative sampling of these initiatives, primarily from North America.

Waldorf Schools

EDUCATION FOR THE HEAD, HANDS, AND HEART

Waldorf education is probably the most widespread and mature of Steiner's many plantings. There are more than 150 Waldorf schools in North America and over 900 worldwide, double the number just a decade ago, making it possibly the fastest growing educational movement in the world. Steiner's interest in education was lifelong. As a young man, he earned a living as a tutor, starting at 14 helping fellow students. Then, from the age of 23 to 29, he lived in Vienna with the family of Ladislaus and Pauline Specht, undertaking the education of their four sons, one of whom, Otto, was hydrocephalic. At the age of 10, Otto could hardly read or write. His parents were uncertain whether he could be educated at all. Steiner took responsibility for him. Believing that, despite appearances, the boy had great intellectual capacities, Steiner saw his task as slowly waking the boy up and bringing him into his body. To do this, he knew he first had to gain the child's love. On this basis, he was able to awaken his dormant faculties. He was so successful that Otto went on to become a doctor.

Waldorf students create their own "main lesson books" for each subject.

For Steiner, Otto was a learning experience. As he says in his *Autobiography:* "The educational methods I had to adopt gave

Lao Tsu (604-531 BC) Tao Te Ching, Chapter 42

The Tao begot one.
One begot two.
Two begot three.
And three begot
the ten thousand
things.

Dear Reader,

Over the last 30 years I've encountered Rudolf Steiner's ideas in a number of different venues: as an active parent of four Waldorf-educated boys; as a natural foods merchant distributing Biodynamic® foods (grown according to Steiner's indications); as a truth seeker, struggling unsuccessfully to understand Steiner's dense and, for me, impenetrable writings; as a former architecture student intrigued by Steiner's contributions to 20th-century art and architecture; and, more recently, as the seventh and then eighth grade class teacher at City of Lakes Waldorf School in Minneapolis.

Despite all this exposure to the manifestations of his philosophy, I didn't begin to fathom Steiner's own thinking until several years ago when I began reading his writings in earnest. His language suffered from translation, was often time- and culture-bound, and frequently filled with archaic and new-agey references. Yet, as I kept at it, his ideas soon became more accessible and increasingly meaningful to me. After I "graduated" with my class in June 2002, I decided to meet some actual people whose lives had been touched by Steiner's ideas. Last summer, my 17-year-old son Oliver and I traveled 2,500 miles around Europe, visiting centers of Steinerian activity. In Järna, Sweden, we participated in an international youth conference for some 200 Waldorf-educated 16- to 30-year-olds from every race and 40 countries. In Dornach, Switzerland, we met the leadership of the worldwide General Anthroposophic Society, founded by Steiner. In other places we met people who have been involved in various aspects of Steiner's work for two or three generations. Since returning, I've been taking similar people-meeting excursions to the East and West Coasts.

What I've found is fascinating and heartening to me, and I wanted to share it with you. So I went to see the folks at the Rudolf Steiner Foundation and asked them to underwrite the costs of researching, writing, and publishing a special section on the continuing legacy of Rudolf Steiner. They turned around and raised the funds from private donors. My co-author of this section is Christopher Bamford, who has written widely on a variety of topics, including the recently published *What Is Anthroposophy?* (Anthroposophic Press, Great Barrington, Massachusetts) and "An Endless Trace: The Passionate Pursuit of Wisdom in the West" (Codhill Press, New York).

As you read the section I think you'll agree that the people influenced by Steiner's ideas are at least as interesting as the ideas themselves. Like the rest of society, they are a diverse lot. Some are well-scrubbed and impressively accomplished, like the actresses Jennifer Aniston and Julianna Margulies, and American Express president and CEO Kenneth Chenault, all of whom are Waldorf educated. Others, like me, are rather wacky, basically inept, unreconstructed idealists and malcontents. But then, I never had a Waldorf education!

The people involved in Steiner's ideas that I find most compelling are working within the framework of communities, in Waldorf schools, Biodynamic® farms, anthroposophical medical clinics, Camphill Villages for the handicapped, early childhood and elder-care centers, and artistic collaboratives. They're not isolated and alienated, stuck in institutions inhospitable to their values. They're developing the social skills necessary to form real, viable communities. If they study anthroposophy, Steiner's nonreligious path to self-knowledge, they're struggling to learn what we all sign on for in this human life—they're learning how to love.

There are an estimated ten thousand initiatives around the world that trace their lineage to Steiner and his ideas. These initiatives add up to an insurgent movement today that just may be the seedbed of a new, more just and humane emerging culture—the alternative that so many of us have been searching for all our lives. I believe these people, the heirs to Rudolf Steiner's legacy, are building, in our midst, a truly viable template for a greener and kinder world.

—Eric Utne

---

me insight into the way that the human soul and spirit are connected with the body. It became my training in physiology and psychology. I came to realize that education and teaching must become an art, and must be based upon true knowledge of the human being."

As with everything Steiner did, his curriculum for Waldorf education began with a question. In 1919, in the chaos following the First World War, Emil Molt, director of the Waldorf Astoria Cigarette Company, asked Steiner to help with the creation of a school for his workers. Four months later, the first Independent Waldorf School opened in Stuttgart, Germany. From that spontaneous beginning arose the now worldwide Waldorf School Movement.

Waldorf Education: It's All in the Curriculum

Whenever he visited a Waldorf school, Rudolf Steiner's first question to the students was always, "Do you love your teacher?" Similarly, he would ask the teachers, "Do you love your students?" The class teacher accompanies the children from first grade through eighth grade, i.e., from childhood into the beginning of adolescence. Children and teacher grow together. Making and doing, creating beauty, and working with one's hands—knitting, crocheting, painting, drawing, and woodworking—are an integral part of the educational and developmental process. Besides teaching manual dexterity and training eye-hand coordination, the work with color, form, and different materials develops an aesthetic sense, which permeates all other activities. Coordinated physical movement, learning through the body, accompanies all stages of development. The practice of Eurythmy—Steiner's art of movement, which makes speech and music visible through action and gesture—allows the child to develop a sense of harmony and balance. Rhythm is an important component of all these activities. Rhythm (order or pattern in time) permeates the entire school day, as well as the school year, which unfolds around celebrating festivals drawn from different religions and cultures.

"I loved school. I hated being sick because I didn't want to miss anything. I felt teachers cared about me so much, it gave me confidence. Now I feel there's nothing I can't do."

Jessica Winer '80,
artist

The curriculum is based upon an understanding of the developing child. From birth through ages six or seven, children absorb the world through their senses and respond primarily through imitation. As they enter the primary school years, they are centered more in feeling and imagination. Then, as they continue their journey into the middle school, rational, abstract thinking begins to emerge. The curriculum respects this developmental process and gives it substance. Based on the idea that "ontogeny recapitulates phylogeny," that a developing child goes through the phases of human cultural evolution, children at different ages study what is appropriate to their development. Thus they learn reading by first "becoming" the letters, through physical gesture. In their "main lesson" books that are their textbooks, crayoned pictures of mountains and trees metamorphose into the letters M and T, and form drawings of circles and polygons become numbers.

Most Waldorf kids actually like school and develop a real love of learning.

Movement, music, and language (including foreign languages) begin in first grade. They hear fables and stories of the holy ones of different cultures. They learn to knit and crochet and play the recorder. Leaving the "paradise" of the first two grades, they encounter the sacred teachings of their culture. For example, in North America, the stories of the Old Testament are taught. In Japan, ancient Shinto stories are told. Farming, gardening, house building, measurement, and grammar now enter the curriculum. They memorize poems and begin to play stringed instruments.

With the fourth grade comes mythology, embroidery, zoology, geography, and geometric drawing. Mathematics and languages become more complex; art becomes more representational. In the fifth grade, history enters; they recite poems, begin botany, learn to knit with four needles, and start woodworking. And thus it continues, each grade providing more wonders.

Rather than pursuing several subjects at a time, the Waldorf curriculum unfolds in main lesson blocks of three or four weeks. The students create their own texts, or "main lesson books" for each subject. This enables students to live deeply into the subject. In this age of distraction, Waldorf children learn to be able to concentrate and focus.

Students learn the alphabet by first discovering the forms of the letters in nature

With high school, the mood changes in harmony with the tremendous developmental changes occurring at this time. Students no longer have a class teacher, but specialists in different fields who teach the various blocks and encourage dialog and discussion. Exact observation and reflection are prized. The aim is to engage students in the present and build on the confidence and ability to think for oneself that developed in the lower grades.

Waldorf Schools in North America

Waldorf education in America developed almost imperceptibly. The first school was founded in New York in 1928 and, over the next 20 years, only six more schools were founded. But something had germinated and slowly began to spread. Looking back, the growth was steady. The number of schools more or less doubled every decade. The reasons for this success are not hard to find. Waldorf schools appeals to parents seeking a truly holistic, child-centered, loving, artistic, practical, and wonder-filled education.

An Example:
The Green Meadow Waldorf School

The Green Meadow Waldorf School in Spring Valley, New York, founded in 1950, is one of the oldest Waldorf schools in North America. As you approach the wooded suburban enclave you realize that this is a different kind of school. The several buildings are clustered around a courtyard, forming a little campus, which in turn is surrounded by mature oaks and white ash. Gardens, large climbing logs and stones, and sculpture abound. Each building has its own character and form, yet the entire assemblage works as a whole. The colors are warm and natural, not bright. There's no graffiti. The roofs are shingled and gently sloped. Many of the walls are set at softer, more oblique angles. Even many of the windows have their rectangular shapes softened with another edge, making them five- or six-sided instead of just four-sided.

There is something peaceful in the air. The impression intensifies as you enter. Warmth pervades the space. Your senses begin to dance. Beauty, color, and natural flowing forms surround you. Children's paintings adorn the walls. Muffled sounds filter through the classroom walls and doors as you walk down a corridor. You can hear musical instruments, singing, children reciting a poem, the calm voice of a class teacher. And the smells! Bread baking in the kindergarten, fragrant plants and nontoxic paints. When you enter a classroom, the impression is confirmed—this is what a school ought to be. The children are happy, they are learning, they seem to love their teachers and each other.

"My parents... felt that the Waldorf school would be a far more open environment for African Americans.... I think the end result of Waldorf education is to raise our consciousness.... It taught me how to think for myself, to be responsible for my decisions. Second, it made me a good listener, sensitive to the needs of others. And third, it helped (me) establish meaningful beliefs."

Kenneth Chenault,
President & CEO,
American Express Corporation,
Waldorf alumnus

The Green Meadow School is home to a veritable United Nations of religious diversity. Of the 388 students (K–12) in Green Meadow, more than 60 are of Jewish descent, approximately 25 are the children of members of the nearby Jerrahi Islamic Mosque, and the rest come from Protestant, Catholic, Buddhist, agnostic, atheistic, and who-knows-what other religious traditions. Waldorf schools are sometimes assumed to be Eurocentric because of their European origins, yet the curriculum turns out to have universal appeal, adapting well in cultures as diverse as the *favelas* (slums) of Sao Paolo, Brazil, the black settlements of South Africa, rural Egypt and urban Israel, Eastern Europe, India, Southeast Asia, Australia, Japan, and the Pine Ridge Lakota Indian reservation in South Dakota.

Waldorf Graduates

Parents considering Waldorf want to know "What will become of my child?" According to Harm Paschen from the University of Bielefeld, Germany, studies of European Waldorf high school grads show that Waldorf graduates do very well indeed. Kids who go to Waldorf schools are as likely, or more likely, to attend college as students from public and other private schools. And after college, they are more likely to be employed than non-Waldorf grads. They are disproportionately well represented in teaching, the arts, business, medicine, and the social services professions. Similar research with North American grads is clearly needed.

On a recent college visit, Donna Badrig, associate director of undergraduate admissions for Columbia University, told one student, "We love Waldorf kids. We reject some students with 1600s on their SATs and accept others based on other factors, like the creative ability Waldorf students demonstrate." Similar enthusiasm for Waldorf grads was heard from admissions officers at Wesleyan University. City of Lakes Waldorf School (K–8) and Watershed High School (a new Waldorf charter school), both in Minneapolis, have seen their students go to such colleges at Sarah Lawrence, Juilliard, Wellesley, Hampshire, Wesleyan, and MIT, among others. But not all Waldorf grads go to college after high school. Many take a break from study to travel or do volunteer work before getting a job or going on to higher education.

Waldorf education is possibly the fastest growing educational movement in the world.

From our own observations, Waldorf students seem to share certain common characteristics. They are often independent and self-confident self-starters. They have genuine optimism for the future. They also tend to be highly ethical and are compassionately intelligent. They keep their sense of wonder about learning and the interdisciplinary sense that everything is connected. They seem to have a very healthy measure of what author Daniel Goleman calls "emotional intelligence," a much more reliable predictor of "success" in life, by any definition, than IQ or SAT scores. Generally speaking, they are both artistic and practical. They seem to know intuitively how to do many things.

Waldorf grad Paul Asaro, an architect, says: "I still draw upon the problem-solving skills that were nurtured… during my adolescent years." Other graduates stress independent thinking, imagination, and the relationships they developed and enjoyed with faculty and fellow students. "That's what's so wonderful about Waldorf education," says actress Julianna Margulies. "You're exposed to all these different ideas, but you're never given one view of it. You're encouraged to think as an individual." Rachel Blackmer, a veterinarian, writes: "Waldorf education is learning in its purest form. It is learning to think, to feel, and to act appropriately and with conscience." Mosemare Boyd, president and CEO, American Women Presidents, adds: "At Waldorf, we were taught to see things from the perspective of others. We saw that doing things together… was always more fun.… We learned to love learning."

Behind the Scenes

According to the Association of Waldorf Schools of North America (AWSNA), in the United States there are currently 56 full member Waldorf Schools, 15 sponsored Waldorf Schools (on their way to full membership), 69 developing Waldorf Schools, and 29 Waldorf Initiatives affiliated with AWSNA. Besides this there are a number of Waldorf-inspired or Waldorf method charter schools, as well as other Waldorf-related initiatives in the public schools.

>"A Steiner education teaches you to think differently from the herd. I've found that independent ideas can be very valuable in the investment world."

David Nadel '87,
managing director,
Bear Stearns

Trained, qualified Waldorf teachers are much sought after. In North America each year, schools hire a combined total of between 300 and 400 new teachers, yet the various teacher-training centers graduate less than half that number. Many of the teachers are parents making a mid-life career change, perhaps seeking new challenges or a way to contribute to society. Robert Amis, who sold a successful equipment leasing company and took early retirement at 46, found himself accepting an offer to become a class teacher at City of Lakes Waldorf School in Minneapolis. "It's the hardest work I've ever done," he says. "I feel like I'm in a crucible, much the same as my students; and we're all wondering what changes are being wrought."

Side by Side, a leadership development program of Sunbridge College, trains 17-to 23-year-old youth who then facilitate weeklong arts and environmental overnight camps for underserved children ages 8 to 12 in New York and Los Angeles.

There are five full teacher-training centers: Rudolf Steiner College in Sacramento, California; Waldorf Institute of Southern California in Northridge, California; Center for Anthroposophy/Antioch Graduate School in Keene, New Hampshire; Sunbridge College in Spring Valley, New York; and Rudolf Steiner Center in Toronto, Ontario. In addition, there are two sponsored centers, one in Eugene, Oregon, and one in Detroit; and five developing centers—in Duncan, British Columbia; Sausalito, California; Honolulu; Chicago; and Seattle. And the Rudolf Steiner Institute, a summer school for adults and children, presently located at Thomas College in Waterville, Maine, provides a strong introduction to Waldorf education.

Waldorf in the Public Schools

According to George Hoffeker, former principal of the Yuba River Charter School in Nevada City, California, "Waldorf methods are so exciting and enlivening for all children that they shouldn't be reserved just for those who can afford it." Mary Goral, a professor at St. Mary College in Milwaukee and director of its early childhood education program, echoes this sentiment. She says, "I truly believe that what is needed in public schools is something much more like Waldorf, something that engages the whole child—body, soul, and spirit."

The first move in this direction began in September 1991 when the Milwaukee Urban Waldorf School opened—with 350

students, more that 90 percent of them African American—as part of the Milwaukee Public School System. Robert Peterkin, then superintendent of schools, had seen the need for a healthy education to serve the special needs of children in educationally deprived areas. Public school leaders, Waldorf educators, public school teachers, and scholars all worked together to found a school that would bring the integrated artistic, intellectual, and developmental Waldorf curriculum into the heart of an American city. Under the direction of Ann Pratt, an experienced Waldorf teacher, the experiment pioneered the development of an intensive teacher-training program for public school teachers. The result: reading scores increased and attendance stabilized. The school became a safe, quiet, well-ordered, attractive place to learn. A visitor recounted a telling anecdote. Waiting to see the principal, the visitor found himself seated opposite a student who was also waiting. According to the visitor, the student was, "threateningly large and had clearly committed some infraction. But there he sat outside the principal's office, quiet and self-composed, knitting."

Some publicly funded Waldorf schools are currently in transition. The Milwaukee experiment is still regrouping since losing founding principal Dorothy St. Charles to promotion. St. Charles' departure, combined with the school's move to "the worst zip code in Milwaukee," led to the loss of half its certified Waldorf teachers. The school, under the leadership of new principal Cheryl Colbert, is working with Cardinal Strich College to develop a teacher-training program to fill the need for certified Waldorf teachers. And the Sacramento school district, which operates a Waldorf-method magnet school, and the Twin Ridges Elementary School District of North San Juan, California, which operates seven Waldorf-inspired charter schools, including the first charter school in the United States to use Waldorf methods—the Yuba River Charter School—are in the midst of a court battle. The plaintiff's suit asserts that Waldorf education is religious in nature and that the two school districts are therefore in violation of the U.S. and California constitutional separation of church and state. The district court dismissed the suit, but on appeal, the circuit court gave the case new life, sending it back to district court.

>"Society tells you that there is only one way to do things. Steiner students learn to create their own initiative and to be can-do thinkers."

Deborah Winer '79,
playwright

Opponents of Waldorf education, which is based on Steiner's insights into child development, equate the curriculum with anthroposophy, which they claim to be a religion. Waldorf advocates respond that Rudolf Steiner's anthroposophy is determinedly nonreligious and isn't taught in Waldorf schools anyway. The Waldorf curriculum stands on its own, they say, no matter what else Steiner taught or believed. "Anthroposophy is a founding philosophy, not a curriculum," says John Miller, a teacher at Watershed High School in Minneapolis. "Look at John Dewey, the educational reformer. Did anyone accuse his followers of teaching 'Deweyism'? No, because they just used a methodology he developed."

Critics also point to Steiner's early involvement in the Theosophical Society and to his more controversial views, such as his references to the lost continent of Atlantis. Several racist-sounding comments are often quoted to paint him as a racist. Waldorf's defenders say they reject racism out of hand. They say that Steiner was a person very much of his times, that his comments were made at the turn of the century, taken out of context, and are completely at odds with the vast preponderence of his statements having anything to do with race. They point out that many of Steiner's most reputable contemporaries shared beliefs with him that may appear today to be suspect or downright silly (Mahatma Gandhi was a member of the Theosophical Society, and Albert Einstein believed that Atlantis was a historical reality).

Despite the controversy, Waldorf-inspired charter schools are popping up all over the country. It is difficult to say just how many charter schools there are. Conservative estimates put the number at about 20 and growing. Though some fear a watering down of Steiner's principles, Donald Bufano, chairman of AWSNA, says, "Parents, and especially children at Waldorf or Waldorf-methods schools can enjoy the benefits of the education without commitment to its foundations just as one can enjoy Biodynamic® food or anthroposophic medicine whether or not they know how they work or where they come from."

Early Childhood Initiatives

The Waldorf approach to education is not limited to school-age kids. Recent students have pointed repeatedly to the critical importance of the nurturing children receive in early childhood, when infants and children are especially at risk. The combination of the breakdown of the family, the need for two working parents, and the growing number of single-parent families has left caregivers, whether at home or in daycare, uncertain how to care for children. Activities that were once natural and instinctive, like what to eat and how to bring up a baby, must now be learned consciously.

"Children," says Cynthia Aldinger, "are like sponges. They drink in everything and everyone around them." It is not only a question of the physical surroundings. What we say and do around a child, even how we think, is critical. A grassroots organization growing out of the Waldorf Early Childhood Association, Life Ways is devoted to the deinstitutionalization of child care. Founded in 1998, Life Ways provides courses and training in parenting and child care and is expanding to establish child care homes, centers, and parenting programs throughout North America.

A related effort is Sophia's Hearth in Keene, New Hampshire. Taking its name from the ancient goddess of wisdom, Sophia's Hearth works with "the art of becoming a family." As founder Susan Weber puts it, "Our work supports families in creating an atmosphere of loving warmth, joy, and respect for their infants and young children, while at the same time nurturing each parent."

The Caldwell Early Life Center at Rudolf Steiner College acts as a center for these and similar initiatives. Only two years old, but with a prestigious advisory board including naturalist Jane Goodall, well-known authors and researchers Jane Healy and Joseph Chilton Pearce, and education and child advocate Sally Bickford, it is halfway through raising the $2.5 million needed to complete a building to house its activities. These will cover the full range of early childhood needs, from working to reduce stress and isolation for families in ethnically and economically diverse neighborhoods to the creation of a demonstration daycare component.

Another Example: The Wolakota Waldorf School

In the early 1990s a group of Lakota Sioux educators began to look for a better education for their children and discovered Waldorf education. They found that it paralleled their own wisdom traditions in many ways. Their hope was to create not only a school but also eventually a model community. In 1993 they created the Wolakota Waldorf Society as a nonprofit organization.

The Wolakota School is located on 80 acres of the Pine Ridge Reservation, near Oglala Lakota College, in Shannon County, South Dakota, the poorest county in the United States. Pine Ridge, the site of the Wounded Knee massacre, has been home to many famous Native American leaders, including Black Elk, Chief Red Cloud, and Fool Crow. The school serves 24 Lakota children. Among Waldorf schools it is unique, depending entirely on donations. There are only two teachers, Susan Bunting and Chris Young, who do everything from cooking breakfast and lunch to transporting children. If funds and space can be found, Edwin Around Him, Sr., will be hired next year as the school's third teacher. This year Edwin teaches Lakota and operates the van, when it's working.

Sponsored by Rudolf Steiner Foundation and Utne Magazine

From *Utne Reader*, May/June 2003, pp. 1-14. © 2003 by Eric Utne and Christopher Bamford.

THE FUTURE OF EDUCATION

STUDENT OPTIONS

IRVING H. BUCHEN

Many people in the United States are unhappy with public education. Teachers complain about being battered and intimidated, educational administrators find themselves and their contributions unappreciated, school boards are increasingly criticized for micro-managing, parents are beset by a whole new set of alternative schooling choices, and students are being tested to death.

> Teachers once were evaluated on how they organized lesson plans, gained student interest, and involved the entire class in discussion.

In spite of stresses and strains on the educational system, there is more to celebrate than to lament, especially over the long term. In short, education has a future—indeed, a significant and interesting one. If we could leap ahead 25 years to view the current educational scene, we would see four factors driving educational change: decentralization and educational options; performance evaluation and success measurement; changes in leadership and leadership roles; and reconfiguration in learning spaces, places, and times.

SCHOOL CHOICES

Although competition arrived late in the history of education, it rapidly changed virtually everything. By offering a wide range of possibilities rather than a single focus, competition has given education a new lease on life.

Traditionally, education offered three choices: public, private, and parochial schooling. Public education dominated, and for good reason: It educated the poor and middle classes, pre-pared them for work or college, acculturated wave after wave of new immigrants, and provided significant employment for many professionals. Private and parochial schools continue to appeal to middle- and upper-middle-class families disenchanted with public education; homogeneous and traditional, their future is rooted in the attitudes of the past.

The variety of educational choices has dramatically increased. Home schools, for instance, enrolled an estimated 850,000 students in the United States in 1999, according to the National Center for Education Statistics, and support for this method of instruction continues to increase. Charter schools enrolled nearly 580,000 students, according to Center for Education Reform 2001 statistics. Run by different private groups in a variety of ways, charter schools receive public financial support from their home district.

Because high schools with large numbers of students can be unmanageable, school district administrators have restructured many into a series of schools within a school, each with a core of teachers serving between 100 and 150 students. Students and teachers in each smaller school know and relate to each other. Although restructuring does not alter class size, it reduces student-teacher ratio.

Private educational management companies have intensified the competitive environment of education. Often invited to take over failing schools, many of these companies are publicly owned, have stockholders, and are committed to making a profit. Although evidence for their success is mixed, they are a permanent fixture on the educational scene and add significantly to the range of available choices.

Private companies such as William Bennett's "K12" education program offer online curricula through electronic schools, so students can complete and graduate from a basic high-school program online. Electronic offerings also provide advanced placement, language, and special studies courses that normally attract few students. They are a boon to small rural districts and serve as a key underpinning for home schooling.

In short, education in 2025 will be totally decentralized, offering parents, students, adult learners, and citizens in general a dazzling menu of choices. Many people will opt for an amalgam of different educational sources that may be altered as desired. Whatever the selection, students and their parents—not schools—will drive educational choice.

MEASURING SUCCESS

Major shifts will occur in the ways educational success is measured; some of these shifts are discernible now. Teachers were once evaluated on how they organized lesson plans, gained student interest, and involved the entire class in discussion. Now the focus is student achievement, usually measured by class performance on high-stakes mandated tests. Data now dominates the current educational scene, and its importance will intensify in the future.

Because allocating funds is increasingly tied to student performance, school district comptrollers often divert substantial appropriations to designing, administering, and evaluating tests, compromising instruction as a result. Many teachers, therefore, are "teaching to the test"—which would not be bad if, as one superintendent wryly observed, there was a really good test to teach to. School officials assign teams of extra teachers, tutors, and specialists to schools with low scores or failing grades, sometimes stripping the curriculum down to only tested subjects. Some schools in competitive environments advertise their test scores to attract students, further accelerating the process of constant testing. Parents have been known to request test scores of schools within a district to decide where they should send their kids.

Part of the difficulty of attracting administrators is that a principal's salary is not much higher than the highest paid teacher in a district.

In Florida and other states, students in schools that fail basic skills tests twice consecutively are offered financial vouchers to use in whatever school they wish. Preliminary research shows that voucher programs help drive improved student performance. Vouchers also drive choice and decentralization and significantly drain enrollment from "mainstream" schools.

A number of state governments have taken over failing schools, placing them under receivership or turning them over to private management companies. Philadelphia's school district was turned over to a private management company, Edison Schools Inc., because of poor student performance. In New York City, private management companies operate some 30 schools. Perhaps the most embarrassing consequence of this is a cynical reversal of graduation requirements in many states and

schools that tie graduation to test scores. Many schools have postponed implementing requirements, lowered minimum scores, or revised graduation tests for students failing to achieve minimum scores but who were already scheduled to graduate, accepted to college, or had jobs.

THE PRINCIPAL'S CHANGING ROLE

According to the U.S. Department of Labor, the school administration profession faces a shortage of 40,000 principals by 2005. That has been intensified by the reduction of school superintendents' terms of office to an all-time low of two to three years. Part of the difficulty of attracting administrators is that a principal's salary is not much higher than the highest paid teachers in a district; and when longer hours and more days of work are taken into account, the difference is often minuscule. As an indication of education increasingly becoming subject to business market forces, there is the trend toward hiring MBAs rather than education MAs, and even changing the title of superintendent in CEO. In fact, New York City split the top job into academic and business components. Los Angeles followed suit with an additional twist: Signaling the extent to which superintendency is increasingly political, the head of the Los Angeles school district hired a former governor of Colorado (Roy Romer) as school superintendent. But like the decentralization of schools, leadership is no longer solely of one type. The variety of leaders mirrors school choice.

Recently, the National Association of Elementary School Principals (NAESP) published a 96-page document calling for principals to be instructional leaders and to lead the charge on behalf of student achievement. To many outside the field, that might seem an odd request. Haven't principals always done that? Actually, they seldom did because of bureaucratic, financial, and security tasks heaped on their plates.

NAESP called for appointing assistant principals to provide relief and free principals to become instructional leaders. Whether school boards with tight or reduced budgets are willing or able to increase administrative staff at a time when teaching staff is stretched has yet to be determined. But if they do, a whole new corps of principals will emerge who are far more visionary, aggressive, and knowledgeable about school reform and improvement. They will resemble their business counterparts more than principals of the past do.

DO WE REALLY NEED PRINCIPALS?

Although clearly there are principals who are effective leaders no matter how burdened they are, a significant new form of management is appearing. At Chicago's McCosh School, for example, the principal and her team of teacher-managers run the school. The principal still reports to the superintendent and the board, but once she has her marching orders and budget, she and her team take it from there. How effective has that arrangement been? McCosh has the best test scores in the district, and the morale of teachers, students, and parents is high.

This arrangement has an advantage over even the most exemplary performance of a number of assertive principals: There are no subject matter or competency gaps between administration and instruction. The typical principal struggles with the handicap of being outside the classroom, perhaps for many years, and leading teachers in all subjects without possessing the credibility of pedagogical competence. But a management team of certified teachers already possesses subject matter competence. Harvard University education professor Richard Elmore calls this *distributed leadership* and sees it as the future of site-based management. It creates a democratized structure in which the traditional vertical management structure has been leveled to horizontal collective action.

Perhaps the most dramatic and radical version of distributed leadership is where the responsibility for running the school is in the hands of teacher-leaders and learning teams consisting of teachers, tutors, technical advisers, counselors, parents, and students. There are no principals at all. The teacher-leader oversees the team following the principle of author Robert K. Greenleaf: *primus inter pares*—first among equals. Being first is not fixed but rotates based on situation needs.

What business leaders discovered is that educators read and hearken only to other educators writing about education—they know little or nothing about the business world, the effect of increasing competition, the difficulty of balancing quality control with productivity—in short, precisely what education is newly encountering.

But perhaps the most futuristic aspect of this new development, setting it apart from other developments and standing perhaps the best chance of becoming a significant part of education in 2025, is its attention to both *external* and *internal integration*. Externally distributed leadership unites school, parents, students, and the community. Internally, through its basic collaborative governance structure, distributed leadership aligns and combines administration, instruction, and evaluation.

PARENTS' NEW ROLES

Parents are taking on more assertive roles, moving well beyond the stereotype of running bake sales. For example, parents in South Pasadena, California, serve as teacher aides and tutors. Their major task, however, is to raise substantial amounts of money annually to supplement the budget. They have successfully built and stocked a computer lab, turned the library into a state-of-the-art electronic information and resource center, and created an extensive budget for teacher professional development.

In this and other ways, parents have become leaders involved in significant and often unique school reform. One of the most promising examples is a proposal by the Parents Center for Education Reform for students to lead teacher and parent conferences. Under this arrangement, students would set the agenda and facilitate discussion about their own performance. The fact that this initiative arose from a parent's group rather than from the public education mainstream dramatizes the extent to which parents have assumed a greater leadership role. The U.S. Department of Education officially recognizes and facilitates parental leadership through its Partnership for Family Involvement in Education.

The National Network of Partnership Schools based at Johns Hopkins University focuses on a comprehensive and aggressive plan of parent-teacher-student involvement and interaction. It features a program for teachers to generate homework assignments that require family participation. Teachers and parents use holidays and summer vacations to develop skills, anticipate academic problems, and develop solutions. All these and other efforts improve communication not only between schools and families, but also within families.

LINKING BUSINESS TO EDUCATION

Driven by a desire for a well-trained and motivated workforce as well as a sense of social responsibility, many CEOs have forged partnerships with schools. For example, Florida-based Paradigm Learning, which develops corporate board games, developed a high-school game called "Strive to Drive." The game takes students through all the steps of choosing, buying, financing, maintaining, and paying for a car; the game significantly and rapidly improved reading, math, and planning skills in the process. Tutor Inc., an online tutoring service developed a partnership with the Boys Choir of Harlem, buying laptop computers for choir members to stay on top of assignments while traveling and providing access to the company's computer tutors to keep them current and on target.

The most important leadership contribution of business executives is that they are forming direct relationships with educational administrators, including sharing and exchanging different ways of effective management. Thus, the Public Education and Business Coalition received a grant to train some 100 principals in the Denver area. What business leaders discovered is that educators read and hearken only to other educators writing about education—they know little or nothing about the business world, the effect of increasing competition, the difficulty of balancing quality control with productivity—in short, precisely what education is newly encountering.

The Pearl River School in Rockland, New York, uses a continuous improvement business model to set incremental goals for students, raising achievement every year since 1989. The number of students graduating from Pearl River with the academically rigorous state regents' diploma has jumped from 32% to 86%.

A few business CEOs are sharing libraries, research resources, and attendance at executive conferences with education CEOs. There is a strong likelihood that such business CEOs may become school superintendents in the future. If so, then education may increasingly be defined or perceived as a business.

Business leaders have created a number of organizations to support school reform, such as the Business Coalition for Educational Reform, the National Association for Partners in Education, the National Employer Leadership Council, and the School-to-Work Learning Center. Looking only to education for education leadership impoverishes the resources and sources of change.

NEW LEARNING SPACES

Seldom, if ever, do parents or citizens who already have raised and schooled their kids revisit schools. If they did, they would find many things have remained the same but some things have changed dramatically. Technological changes would top the list, but these are perhaps predictable compared with the reconfiguration of learning places, spaces, and times.

The size, holdings, and sheer physical variety of a fairly new high school are overwhelming. Built to accommodate a small town of thousands of students, a new school is surrounded by many practice and playing fields—perhaps even a football stadium—as well as extensive parking spaces for daily student use as well as for athletic events. Inside is a modern gymnasium equipped with seats for 2,000 students and a huge auditorium with seats for 3,000 and state-of-the-art theater equipment. The library, equally enormous but generally underused, is completely computerized with relatively few real books in sight.

When demographics (especially in the suburbs) indicate a significant increase in the school-age population, municipal planners quickly draw up plans to build new school-cities. Of course, expenses for building a new school are higher than they were for building the last school, not only because of increased costs of construction and materials, but also because some communities try to outdo others by constructing bigger and more splendid high schools. Yet research studies suggest that schools can be too big and impersonal.

EXTENDING THE SCHOOL DAY

Once again, economics rears its ugly head when discussion of extending the school day, lengthening the school year, or reducing class size begins. In the face of severe budget cuts, many communities are naturally unwilling to extend the school calendar or reduce class size. The obvious solution is technology.

Technology can reduce class size to one student. School days can be extended easily and lap-top computers mean education can continue during vacations and trips. A total tested electronic curriculum already exists. It has been used by high schools that

do not have enough students to take certain advanced or specialized courses, foreign languages, or advanced placement courses. Electronic instruction has bailed out many rural schools with too few students to permit face-to-face teaching at acceptable costs. Electronics already has helped many high schools reconfigure themselves into smaller schools—within schools—by providing them with their own electronic curriculum, including specialization in arts, sciences, business, and communications. Moreover, the availability of such electronic courses has spread as a number of states bind together in electronic consortia, making their curricula available virtually without cost. Accepting technology as a legitimate and equal teaching partner will make this happen.

STUDENT-LED LEARNING AND SCHOOLS

Every school district placing an ad for administrators or teachers claims to have student-centered schools. Usually that means allowing students to express their views at great length, but ultimately ignoring them. Student-led schools are something else. Allowing students to conduct teacher-parent conferences is an example of a genuine learning and mastering experience for all involved, especially for the student. But many student-led schools go far beyond that.

In large part, what drives student learning is just that—student learning. The learning focus is not on different subjects but on comprehensive projects, including community-based ones. Because that requires knowledge of many subjects, an academic progression develops not unlike the system of apprenticeship. Using dialogue, mentors steer students to an initial plan to test the project. The process is subject to an incredible number of revisions. Gradually, the dominant mentor moves to the periphery as the student moves toward the center. The gradual exchange of positions signals the beginning of mastery. Only then does student leadership appear, earned through sweat equity and the accumulation of a knowledge and research base. Initially, the mentor talks and the student listens; eventually, the student talks and the mentor listens.

Such arrangements do not occur only at the high-school level or only with exceptional students. At Rover Elementary School in Tempe, Arizona, former principal Sandra McClelland explored the future of education with various organizational theorists, not just by reading materials about education. The result is not just a student-centered but a student-driven school. Student leadership teams have replaced the student council to make basic structural and political decisions. A collaborative group of teachers, students, and administrators implements the school's vision and goals. Team learning is the dominant mode; older students mentor younger ones. There is a concerted search for financial supplements and greater independence from state funds; toward that end, teachers are given, are in control of, and are accountable for their classroom budget. Finally, a formal pedagogical partnership has been formed with Southwest Airlines: The school shares its effective and collaborative teaching strategies, Southwest its team management training. Clearly, Rover is a futures lab.

WHAT TO EXPECT FROM EDUCATION IN 2025

Here are some of the most likely essential features of education by 2025.

- Education will be intensely decentralized, offering a significant number of choices to teachers, parents, and students.
- Increasingly, school and learning will be related to time rather than to place, available everywhere that there is connectivity 24 hours a day all year.
- Space and place for learning will exist for the community and no longer be reserved for the young.
- Increasingly, learners will become autonomous, almost totally free agents; nevertheless, they must earn their independence through mastery of prescribed knowledge bases.
- Cost controls and supplemental financing will steadily take hold as municipalities divert federal, state, and local funds away from education to other social crises such as health care

and the aged. Education has at most only another 10 or 15 years as the favored focus of funding and attention.

- Increasingly, teachers will be at the center of administration, instruction, and evaluation: in some programs they may replace principals.
- Horizontal collaboration among teachers, students, and parents—rather than vertical hierarchies—will characterize school governance. A commonality of vision and purpose will be arrived at and implemented collectively.
- Parents will become indispensable to effective learning. Very busy parents may hire parent surrogates as substitutes.
- Initially, business practices will only benefit education; eventually, educational innovations will provide models for business.
- Increasingly, minorities will take over educating minorities, mostly through charter schools. They will accomplish more through chosen rather than *de facto* segregation, and, in the process, save a whole generation of urban kids.

Mr. Buchen is a business and education consultant. From "Education in America: The Next 25 Years," by Irving H. Buchen, The Futurist, *January–February 2003, pages 44–50.*

Index

Index

Test Your Knowledge Form

We encourage you to photocopy and use this page as a tool to assess how the articles in *Annual Editions* expand on the information in your textbook. By reflecting on the articles you will gain enhanced text information. You can also access this useful form on a product's book support Web site at *http://www.dushkin.com/online/*.

NAME:

DATE:

TITLE AND NUMBER OF ARTICLE:

BRIEFLY STATE THE MAIN IDEA OF THIS ARTICLE:

LIST THREE IMPORTANT FACTS THAT THE AUTHOR USES TO SUPPORT THE MAIN IDEA:

WHAT INFORMATION OR IDEAS DISCUSSED IN THIS ARTICLE ARE ALSO DISCUSSED IN YOUR TEXTBOOK OR OTHER READINGS THAT YOU HAVE DONE? LIST THE TEXTBOOK CHAPTERS AND PAGE NUMBERS:

LIST ANY EXAMPLES OF BIAS OR FAULTY REASONING THAT YOU FOUND IN THE ARTICLE:

LIST ANY NEW TERMS/CONCEPTS THAT WERE DISCUSSED IN THE ARTICLE, AND WRITE A SHORT DEFINITION:

We Want Your Advice

ANNUAL EDITIONS revisions depend on two major opinion sources: one is our Advisory Board, listed in the front of this volume, which works with us in scanning the thousands of articles published in the public press each year; the other is you—the person actually using the book. Please help us and the users of the next edition by completing the prepaid article rating form on this page and returning it to us. Thank you for your help!

ANNUAL EDITIONS: Education 04/05

ARTICLE RATING FORM

Here is an opportunity for you to have direct input into the next revision of this volume.
We would like you to rate each of the articles listed below, using the following scale:

1. **Excellent: should definitely be retained**
2. **Above average: should probably be retained**
3. **Below average: should probably be deleted**
4. **Poor: should definitely be deleted**

Your ratings will play a vital part in the next revision.
Please mail this prepaid form to us as soon as possible.
Thanks for your help!

RATING	ARTICLE
	1. When I Was Young
	2. Is America Raising Unhealthy Kids?
	3. The 'Re-Engineered' Child
	4. College Isn't for Everyone
	5. More Families Hide Assets to Qualify for Financial Aid
	6. The 35th Annual Phi Delta Kappan/Gallup Poll of the Public Attitudes Toward the Public Schools
	7. Reinventing America's Schools
	8. There Is Another Way: A Different Approach to Education Reform
	9. Kudzu, Rabbits, and School Reform
	10. Four-Day School Week?
	11. School Choice—Really
	12. Sweeten the Pot for Middle America
	13. Last Holdout Against Educational Freedom
	14. Classroom Crisis: It's About Time
	15. Needed: Homework Clubs for Young Adolescents Who Struggle With Learning
	16. A Nation Deceived
	17. April Foolishness: The 20th Anniversary of A Nation at Risk
	18. "Of Course It's True; I Saw It On The Internet!" Critical Thinking in the Internet Era
	19. Values: The Implicit Curriculum
	20. Defeating the "Hidden Curriculum": Teaching Political Participation in the Social Studies Classroom
	21. Implementing a Character Education Curriculum and Assessing Its Impact on Student Behavior
	22. The Missing Virtue: Lessons From Dodge Ball & Aristotle
	23. Flunking Statistics
	24. A Profile of Bullying
	25. Bullying—Not Just a Kid Thing
	26. A Positive Learning Environment Approach to Middle School Instruction
	27. The Rewards and Restrictions of Recess
	28. Home Front

RATING	ARTICLE
	29. Education Is Critical to Closing the Socioeconomic Gap
	30. "He May Mean Good, But He Do So Doggone Poor!"
	31. Twelve Ways to Have Students Analyze Culture
	32. Language Differences or Learning Difficulties
	33. The Evils of Public Schools
	34. Can Every Child Learn?
	35. Challenging the NICHD Reading Research Agenda
	36. Bridging the Summer Reading Gap
	37. A Fresh Look at Series Books
	38. Andy's Right to Privacy in Grading and the *Falvo Versus Owasso Public Schools* Case
	39. Tales of Suburban High
	40. What New Teachers Need to Learn
	41. The Teacher Shortage: Myth or Reality?
	42. Developing Novice Teachers as Change Agents: Student Teacher Placements "Against the Grain"
	43. Preparing Teachers for Public Schools: Just More Cannon Fodder?
	44. Dreams of a Livable Future
	45. An Emerging Culture
	46. The Future of Education: Student Options

(Continued on next page)

ABOUT YOU

Name _____   Date _____

Are you a teacher? ☐   A student? ☐
Your school's name
_____

Department
_____

Address _____ City _____ State _____ Zip _____

School telephone # _____

YOUR COMMENTS ARE IMPORTANT TO US!

Please fill in the following information:
For which course did you use this book?
_____

Did you use a text with this ANNUAL EDITION? ☐ yes ☐ no
What was the title of the text?
_____

What are your general reactions to the *Annual Editions* concept?
_____

Have you read any pertinent articles recently that you think should be included in the next edition? Explain.
_____

Are there any articles that you feel should be replaced in the next edition? Why?
_____

Are there any World Wide Web sites that you feel should be included in the next edition? Please annotate.
_____

May we contact you for editorial input? ☐ yes ☐ no
May we quote your comments? ☐ yes ☐ no